The

Russian Autocracy

Under

Alexander III

Peter A. Zaionchkovsky

THE RUSSIAN AUTOCRACY
UNDER ALEXANDER III

Edited and Translated by

DAVID R. JONES

Academic International Press

1976

THE RUSSIAN SERIES / Volume 22

Peter A. Zaionchkovsky, *The Russian Autocracy under Alexander III*. Translation of *Rossiiskoe samoderzhavie v kontse XIX stoletiia* (Moscow, 1970).

Library of Congress Catalog Card Number: 74–81634
ISBN: O-87569-O67-X

Composition by Susan D. Long
Title page by King & Queen Press

Printed in the United States of America

A list of Academic International Publications is found at the end of this volume.

ACADEMIC INTERNATIONAL PRESS
Box 555 Gulf Breeze FL 32561

CONTENTS

EDITOR'S INTRODUCTION

Peter Andreevich Zaionchkovsky, professor of history at the University of Moscow, has long been recognized as the foremost Soviet historian of late nineteenth-century Russia. Apart from his numerous articles and editions of documents, he is the author of a number of major studies including two on the peasant reforms of the 1860s, one on the military reforms, and three on the period 1878 to 1904. As it is high time that his work was made more widely available to students in the non-Russian world, I am pleased to have the opportunity to help make this possible.

The present volume, *Rossiiskoe samoderzhavie v kontse XIX stoletiia* (The Russian Autocracy at the End of the Nineteenth Century), appeared in 1970 and is especially significant. Not only are the author's own scholarly standards of a high order but the period dealt with—from 1882 to 1894—is one that has been too long ignored by the majority of both Russian and Western historians. Although many of the vital decisions affecting the course of future government policies were taken during these years, the general reader and student has remained without a reliable guide to the debates involved. Now Zaionchkovsky has filled this gap for the Russian reader and hopefully this translation will enable him similarly to serve the English-reading public.

The value of this volume does not lie simply in the fact that he has filled this void. In his research the author has pioneered the investigation of the massive materials in Soviet archives, and his studies at once outline their contents for other scholars and provide large extracts that will be useful to researchers who do not have access to the archives themselves. No future studies of Russian legal, educational or administrative history will be able to ignore this present volume and, however their interpretations may disagree, they will have to draw heavily upon it.

Alexander III's reign is usually considered to be a period of "reaction." During the years 1882 to 1894 the government, which had seen the earlier efforts towards liberalism literally explode in the bombs that killed Alexander II, turned to consolidation, retrenchment and, in the view of some conservatives of that day, to "the restoration" of the government's powers. Alexander III, the new emperor, was a man of apparent limited abilities who believed that the mission of the "autocracy" was to unite a heterogeneous empire by means of russification and the propagation of a single faith—Orthodoxy. Meanwhile some public figures and officials, such as Pobedonostsev, Tolstoy, and Katkov, were disillusioned and became "reactionaries" (although the first, at least, remained a personally honest adviser at a time when such men were, in any country, all too rare). Indeed, even many "liberals" were horrified by what appeared to be the consequences of a too hasty introduction of Western European institutions into what was, essentially, an underdeveloped country, and the tensions created led to many bitter and lengthy debates. Frequently it is forgotten that orderly government, even in an autocracy, demands the careful examination and discussion of all measures in what may be called the "legislative" system. While the autocrat's word was legally final, he usually made decisions only after the completion of this process.

In Russia three separate bodies were involved: the Committee of Ministers, the State Council and the Governing Senate. In practice, major legislation would be referred from the Committee of Ministers to the appropriate departments (meeting as the Combined Departments) of the State Council, where it was defended by the individual minister concerned or his representative. After a detailed debate there, the bill would be discussed by the State Council as a whole, in a General Session, and then passed on to the emperor for a final decision. Once passed, the Governing Senate was left the task of interpreting the practical application of the bill within the context of existing legislation and of acting as a supreme court of appeal.

Here Zaionchkovsky's analysis is particularly useful and his careful treatment of the autocracy's legislative discussions demonstrates how opposition could delay some measures and change others, regardless of absolutist constitutional principles. The complaints of the "reactionaries" about a "liberal party" were, therefore, not without some basis; an opposition of sorts, in the persons of the many "liberal bureaucrats" inherited from the preceding reign, did exist. As such men were particularly numerous in the State Council, the debates on the creation of the institution of land captain and the other "counter-reforms" reveal the ability of this "opposition" to make use of the system and its positions within it. And, although the opposition failed to block the creation of land captains, Zaionchkovsky's discussion makes it clear that there was no autocratic monolith. As is always the case, the political process reflected a number of conflicting views and interests and this volume does much to underline the diversity that existed in the government of the last of the great autocratic Russian tsars.

The editor has attempted to present a full and accurate English version of Professor Zaionchkovsky's original Russian edition. The majority of the footnotes of the original Russian editor have not been included as they would be of little use to the general reader. Those retained either add to the information found in the text or allow the reader to draw his own conclusions concerning the validity of Zaionchkovsky's judgements. Occasionally the author refers to other published works and these notes, in the majority of cases, have been retained as a means of acquainting the reader with the extent of the existing Russian literature on the subject. In any case, all notes are placed at the end of the book. Otherwise, only one portion of the Russian text has been omitted from this edition. This is Zaionchkovsky's seven-page review of previous Russian studies on this period which, it is felt, is of no substantial value to users of this English-language edition.

At the same time, the latter may well be discouraged from further study by the scarcity of studies in Western languages. Charles Lowe's *Alexander III of Russia* (London, 1895) remains the only real biography of this autocrat, and Alexander Kornilov's *Modern Russian History from the Age of Catherine the Great to the End of the Nineteenth Century* (2 vols., New York, 1916) has been the only major Russian study to be translated. The latest reissue of this work (New York, 1970) contains a bibliography, compiled by John S. Curtiss, and the enquiring student will find this useful. Equally important is David Shapiro's *A Select Bibliography of Works in English on Russian History, 1801-1917* (Oxford: Blackwell, 1962). This contains a full listing of the major articles and studies of the various aspects of Russian life available for this period, and supplements Dr. Curtiss's bibliography. Noteworthy are the biographies of two of the leading statesmen of this period: Martin Katz's *Mikhail N. Katkov: A Political Biography, 1881-1887* (The Hague, 1966) and Robert F. Byrnes' *Pobedonostsev: His Life and Thought* (Bloomington, 1968). Some of the most important documents for this period are translated in George Vernadsky *A Source Book for Russian History From Early Times to 1917* (3 vols., New Haven, 1972), Volume 3, pp. 669-690. The numerous relevant entries in *The Modern Encyclopedia of Russian and Soviet History* (MERSH), edited by Joseph L. Wieczynski (Academic International Press, 1976–), should be consulted as well. Otherwise, Western studies of the era of Alexander III have been even scantier than those in Russian.

The actual translation of Zaionchkovsky's study presents a number of stylistic difficulties. An attempt has been made to retain some of the tone of the original text and of the official bureaucratic documents so often cited. In this context special mention should be made of a number of Russian terms which may prove difficult for Western readers. The word *dvorianstvo,* for instance, literally means the "nobility," but here it is often translated as "gentry." This is due to the particular nature of the Russian nobility, into which, after Peter the Great, it was easier to gain entry than into similar classes in Western Europe (because

Peter made state service—both civil or military—the main prerequisite for such rank, rather than purely hereditary status). Although hereditary rights remained of importance to the nobility, the majority were usually closer to the English squires or gentry than they were to the great aristocratic figures usually conjured up by the word "nobleman." In this translation either "gentry" or "nobility" is used, depending on the context.

Similarly, the Russian word *soslovie,* or "estate," might also confuse a Western reader. In some contexts it might seem, in English, to refer to the land, rather than to the "class" of the gentry. *Soslovie* refers, of course, to an "estate" in the sense of the French "third estate," but in this translation it is sometimes replaced by "class" so as to make the sense of the passage absolutely clear.

Another problem concerns the use of the words "administrative" and "arbitrary" (*administrativnyi* and *proizvolnyi*). The former refers to the administrative system or, rather, to the executive arm of the government. When "arbitrary" is coupled with "administrative" reference is made to actions by the executive bureaucratic system that may be merely "arbitrary" but which also often are only quasi-legal or simply illegal. Because of this wide range of meaning the word "arbitrary" is usually retained in order to indicate the broad sense that Zaionchkovsky has in mind, but in some passages it has been translated simply as "illegal."

Mention should also be made of the word "*derevnia,*" which means "village" as well as "countryside." Although occasionally the Russian phrase "in the village" is maintained as a means of retaining the flavor of the text, it is usually rendered simply as "in the countryside," meaning rural areas.

All additions made by the author to the quotations he cites are marked, as in the Russian text, with parentheses. Substantial additions to the text inserted by the editor are identified by square brackets.

In dealing with proper names and the transliteration of Russian terms, the Library of Congress system has been used with a few minor modifications where these seemed to improve the style and appearance of the English text. Thus the diphthongs "ia" and "iu" are, at the beginning of names, transliterated "ya" and "yu". Where there are common English first names—or, in some cases, German proper names—these forms have been used rather than the Russian form. An exception has been made in one case: "Constantine" has been retained as "Konstantin" so as to facilitate reference in other standard works where the initial K. is often used (for example, "K.P. Pobedonostsev" rather than "C.P. Pobedonostsev"). Also, for the convenience of the modern reader the names of the Baltic provinces have been translated as "Lithuania," "Latvia" and "Estonia" rather than as "Kurland," "Livonia" and "Estland."

I must express my thanks to my wife, who has patiently corrected my long, hand-written manuscript, to Professor Blair Ross, who proofread the typescript, and to all those who have helped me in one way or another.

David R. Jones

Cambridge Station, Nova Scotia

FOREWORD

This book continues my earlier work[1] and examines the Russian autocracy's internal policies during the period of reaction from 1882 to 1894. It begins with Count Dmitry A. Tolstoy's appointment in 1882 as Minister of the Interior as this event clearly revealed the government's intention of openly pursuing a reactionary goal. Yet by 1895 its policies had been weakened by new social developments. The latter were initially apparent in a revival of public activity during the famine of 1891 and 1892, and later in the founding of the Marxist "Union of Struggle for the Liberation of the Working Class." At the same time industrial development increased in tempo and the immediate result was growing labor unrest. This, coinciding with a stronger student movement, naturally helped change government policies.

Here attention is concentrated on the activities of the highest administrative institutions and the government's apparatus in the provinces. The policies implemented in the fields of justice, education and censorship are analysed and the preparation and introduction of the government's counter-reforms examined. Financial and economic policies already have been the subject of detailed studies, and they are examined here only when they affect the government's general considerations. Labor policy is inseparably bound up with the history of the workers' movement and, as this has been specifically treated earlier, it is not covered in this work. The legislation has been analysed by I.I. Shelymagin[2] and a number of general studies are devoted to the history of the Russian working class.[3] Other questions have been the subjects of dissertations by my students.[4] These issues are examined here in less detail and reference is made to these studies when appropriate.

It must be stressed that reactionary policies could be implemented only because of the given conditions existing in the 1880s and early 1890s. Among these were the infirmity of the popular political movement, the absence of revolutionary parties, an insufficiently active liberal opposition, and the inertia of large numbers of the intelligentsia. But the concrete forms taken by the government's policies depended upon other factors. "There are innumerable interacting forces, an infinite series of parallelograms of forces," wrote Frederick Engels to Joseph Bloch[5] in 1890, "and from these intersections comes the one result—the historical event." Among these "infinite number of factors" the statesman plays no small part. A ruler's role, especially in an autocratic state, is very significant. For this reason the personal characteristics of the men then governing Russia are described in some detail.

I wish to thank A.I. Filatov and N.V. Zeifman, students in my history seminar at Moscow University, for their information concerning archival materials.

P.A. Zaionchkovsky

INTRODUCTION

PERSPECTIVES

After the murder of Alexander II on March 1, 1881, his son ascended the throne as Alexander III. The long period of domestic political reaction which followed is usually associated with his name, but it did not begin at once. In spite of his own reactionary views, Alexander III did not immediately introduce conservative measures and did not even announce the basic principles of his own politics. In the first weeks only the persecuted Jews felt—and "felt" literally—the effects of the change of sovereigns.[1] At the end of March, 1881, the new emperor secretly moved to the palace at Gatchina, where he practically lived as a prisoner, protected by a large guard of infantry and cavalry.

Contrary to the expectations of the terrorists, the murder of Alexander II sparked no anti-government demonstrations, either in St. Petersburg or elsewhere. The "Executive Committee" of the "People's Will" party lacked the strength to support its act with anything, be it a "second edition" of the Kazan demonstration of 1876 or a rising of either students or soldiers.[2] They were too weak to continue even the terrorist struggle. "The revolutionaries," wrote Vladimir I. Lenin, "exhausted themselves on March 1, while the working class had no broadly based movement or firm organization. As for the liberal public of this time, it proved still so politically undeveloped that, after the murder of Alexander II, its opposition was limited to mere petitions." Even the intelligentsia, and especially the young, were disillusioned with both the "People's Will" party and the doctrines of revolutionary populism. The act of regicide did provoke a public reaction, but it was the exact opposite of that expected by the terrorists.

All this allowed the new emperor to issue on April 29, 1881, the "Manifesto on the Inviolability of the Autocracy" that openly proclaimed a policy of reaction.[3] Yet this declaration of a new course did not mean its immediate realization. "The government of Alexander III," wrote Lenin, "even after the manifesto . . . still believed it was necessary to try to fool 'the public' and did not immediately show its claws." Only a year later, when on May 30, 1882 Count D.A. Tolstoy was appointed Minister of the Interior, did the regime clearly reveal its intentions. Thereafter the reaction grew stronger every year. It continued unabated until the middle 1890s when, under the influence of new social developments, it began to weaken.

Political reaction was possible because of the unique social conditions of that time. There was, first of all, no large popular movement:

the peasant disturbances were still local in character, and the workers' demonstrations remained small in scope in view of the industrial crisis and depression. Although the Morozov strike of 1885 and the limited increase in incidents of labor unrest that followed did frighten the government (compelling it to promulgate a law on the labor question on July 3, 1886), there remained insufficient cause for a change in the general direction of the government's course.[4] The revolutionary movement also was incapable of opposing the reaction. A major crisis had divided the revolutionary populists and led to the disintegration of their organizations. The Social Democrats, passing through their "pre-natal period" of development, naturally were unable to render any opposition to the administration. The liberal movement remained as weak as ever, an opposition that could have no real significance. Among the intelligentsia a decadent mood prevailed; the "theory of small deeds" and the idea of non-violent resistance to evil grew widespread.

The onset of the 1890s brought a new resurgence of public activity. It found its main expression in the work of the "Union of Struggle for the Liberation of the Working Class," which opened a new period for the Russian liberation movement.[5] While such developments could not compel the government immediately to change its policies, they nonetheless did dilute the political reaction.

Any account of the historical circumstances in which the Russian autocracy implemented its reactionary policies would be incomplete without mentioning the economic situation. The period was one of rapid industrial progress and despite domestic policies aimed at preserving some "feudal relics" (strengthening the role of the gentry and maintaining a "patriarchal" atmosphere in the countryside) the government's economic policies mainly promoted capitalism. They were typified by the customs legislation (that created a system of protective tariffs to encourage native industrial development) and the attempts to attract foreign capital into Russia. Consequently the regime's economic policies directly contradicted those it adopted in other spheres. Laws were implemented to preserve the existing remnants of feudalism, whereas both fiscal and defense interests necessitated policies leading to the growth of industry. Furthermore, even the measures taken by the authorities to preserve patriarchal relationships in rural areas failed in the face of economic realities, for the autocracy was helpless to check the processes of capitalist development.

In these historical conditions Russia's autocracy planned and implemented a program of political reaction during the 1880s and early 1890s.

SOURCES

The sources used in preparing this study can be divided into (1) documents and records of an official nature; (2) memoirs (both diaries and recollections); (3) correspondence; and (4) the work of journalists.

The basic sources belong, naturally, to the first category. This group can be divided into a number of subgroups, to the first of which belong documents of a general legislative nature. These include all materials relating to individual laws, beginning with the preparation of a draft and ending with the final statute as recorded in the *Complete Collection of Laws*.

At this time both the State Council—the highest body to discuss proposed legislation—and the Committee of Ministers (which was more conservative in composition) were of major importance. This latter body often prepared the more reactionary legislative proposals, such as "The Statute on Measures for the Protection of State Security and Public Tranquillity," "The Provisional Regulations for the Press" of 1882, "The Regulations on the Property Responsibility of Individual Village Communities for Forestry Offenses," among others.

The committee's journals are particularly useful for the general study of governmental politics. Apart from discussions of legislative proposals, they record the consideration given *zemstvo* petitions and the reports of various governors-general. These, along with the emperor's own "notations" or comments, are of great interest. Further, these minutes report the debates on increasing the authority of governors and other similar matters. Nonetheless, these journals are laconic in content and usually do not contain the details of disputes. When disagreements are occasionally mentioned, they are outlined only very generally. Worse still, at times it is obvious that the journals have been falsified. A clear example, established through the diary of Ivan A. Shestikov, concerns the committee's discussion of the forest offenses in Ufa province. Further, the protocols of actual meetings (used in compiling the journals) have been lost, although appendices to the journals do include proposals from ministers and other officials as well as the annual reports of the governors, which the committee examined.

The records of the State Council's proceedings are more complete. This body examined the draft laws proposed by ministers or department heads and their detailed justifications for each measure. Its archives also contain the comments of persons who had been given copies of the proposed laws, the remarks of appropriate ministers on these comments, and the journals or decisions both of meetings of the Combined Departments and the General Sessions of the State Council. Sometimes the protocols for debates of both bodies are contained in appendices and

these allow the course of discussions to be traced. Even so, such protocols are not always detailed. This is demonstrated by the differing
accounts of Konstantin P. Pobedonostsev's speech during the State
Council session of December 17, 1888, during debate of the draft law
on land captains. A comparison of Pobedonostsev's letter to Alexander
III, in which he described his speech, with the account in the protocols,
shows that the former reported the speech in greater detail. In his letter
Pobedonostsev dwelt on aspects of his speech that would have been distasteful to the emperor so as to prove groundless the suggestion that he
had kept silent.

Among the most important State Council materials are the files of
the Department of Laws dealing with the university statute (No. 53 for
1889), the "Statute on Land Captains, their Sessions and the Provincial
Office for Rural Affairs" (No. 44 for 1889), the "Statute on Provincial
and County Zemstvo Institutions" (No. 23 for 1890), and the new municipal statute (No. 38 for 1892). All these files contain protocols for
the meetings of the Combined Departments. Yet not all proposed laws
were examined by either the State Council or Committee of Ministers.
Sometimes they were adopted by the tsar on the basis of the report of a
minister or some other person. In an autocratic system any decision of
the head of state is considered to be law, regardless of the form in which
it is promulgated.

The second sub-section of official documents comprises the reports
of ministers and department heads. It includes both the regular yearly
reports of the operations of the ministries and those presented on specific matters. For this period the ministers' annual reports are lacking,
except for that of the Minister of Education for 1884. This is especially
noteworthy, as it contains Ivan D. Delianov's program for his future
activity. Among other significant documents in this group are carbon
copies (possibly meant for distribution) of the report of the Main Directorate of the Press for the decade 1882 to 1891. This contains a mass of
information illuminating the functions of the censor's department. Unfortunately the appendices, in which exiles are listed, have not survived.

The reports of the Minister of the Interior are also of great interest.
That of D.A. Tolstoy to Alexander III, dated December 18, 1886, is
particularly important, as it contains the program for counter-reform.
This minister's reports on the censor's department have been preserved
almost intact and contain proposals for the punishment of various newspapers and journals. Among his other reports, that dealing with the end
of the Kakhanov Commission deserves special mention.[6] Nonetheless
the archives of the chancellery of the Ministry of the Interior are very
incomplete and many of the minister's reports to the tsar are missing.

But in the case of the Minister of Education, it is fortunate that a number of carbon copies of his reports, preserved in Delianov's personal files, are available.

The annual reports of the various governors to the emperor belong to this subgroup. Two copies of each have survived. The copy received by the tsar, and containing his comments, is in the files of the Committee of Ministers, while a second, sent to the Ministry of the Interior, is filed in the archives of its Department of General Administration. These reports are vital for a study of the governors' activities in general, and allow the main characteristics of the activities of the local administration to be outlined. Here the relations of the crown authorities with the zemstvos and self-governing municipal councils are important. The reports of the most reactionary governors (such as Alexander K. Anastasiev, of Perm, and later Chernigov, and Alexander N. Mosolov, of Novgorod) are particularly interesting. They clearly illustrate the reactionary tendency of all the labors of the provincial authorities and reveal the governors' desire to "introduce order into the countryside," abolish the zemstvos, and so on.

Finally, this subgroup of official documents contains a special report of the Department of Police. Entitled *An Historical Survey of the Organization and Activities of the Department of Police, Presenting Materials For a Review of the Activities of the Ministry of the Interior for its Hundredth Anniversary*, and prepared for the ministry's official history, it is in the Police Department's archives. The *Survey* contains detailed information on the department's structure and work during the 1880s and 1890s. A number of sections attached to this *Survey* contain statistical data on the activities of the different branches of the department (the number of political prisoners, administrative exiles, and the like).

A third subgroup of official papers embraces the instructions or circulars of the Minister of the Interior to his subordinates, those of his ministry's separate departments and directorates (the Department of Police and the Main Directorate of the Press), and the circulars of the Minister of Education. The collection of circulars of the Minister of the Interior, published as a volume in 1896, and found in the files of the ministry's Department of General Administration, has many gaps. Those of the Department of Police, retained in its archives, and of the Press Directorate, are much fuller. The latter are exceptionally useful for the study of official censorship policies. Some are in the directorate's own files, while others are in the archives of the chancellery of the Governor-General of Moscow and the Moscow Censorship Committee.

A fourth subgroup of official documents includes the files of miscellaneous commissions and conferences, various types of governmental correspondence, and so forth.

Before going further, it should be noted that many of the most important documents in the four subgroups mentioned above have not survived. For example, the documents of the Pahlen-Plehve Commission [on the Jewish question], which met in the 1880s, have disappeared from all archival collections. The Pahlen Commission's work is reflected only in printed reports which contain general conclusions. For the later transactions of this commission, when it was headed by the Assistant Minister of the Interior, Viacheslav K. Plehve, there is not a single known source. A similar situation exists with regard to the Special Commission for the Compilation of a Projected System of Local Administration—the so-called Kakhanov Commission. Its files, preserved in the Central State Historical Archives, contain only printed materials (various kinds of reports, projects, and journals of the sessions). The collection contains some 119 files and is obviously incomplete.

That the surviving materials of the Ministry of the Interior are very incomplete is indicated clearly by the insignificant size of the files of the ministerial chancellery. There is almost nothing about the "Black Cabinet" and its extensive examination of private correspondence. Some data on its activities does exist in the files of the Department of Police, but only for two years (1883 and 1884), though these make up some 16 folio volumes. Many of the Ministry of the Interior's papers, and in particular those of the Department of Police, were deliberately destroyed. On the cover of the latter's file number II, which deals with the expulsion of the Jews from certain regions of Russia, was stamped: "To be destroyed." In this case the files cover the years 1910 to 1916 and it is clear that only the revolution prevented their destruction.

A quantity of other documents is found in the personal archives of individual officials (Alexander III, Plehve, Delianov, and others). In Alexander's papers, for instance, is Senator Nicholas A. Manasein's report on his inspection tour in 1882 of the provinces of Lithuania and Latvia. Other official materials—especially those dealing with legislation on the peasants and the famine of 1891—are retained in the Plehve archives, while Delianov's papers number many carbon copies of his reports to the tsar on certain questions of educational policy.

A second main grouping of sources is made up of memoir materials, including both diaries and recollections. For the study of domestic policy these materials are irreplaceable, as they make possible the investigation of the more obscure aspects of government politics. Moreover, these memoirs considerably supplement the official documentary sources and allow a more accurate assessment of various protocols, journals of sessions, and so on. It might even be said that this study would have been impossible without such unofficial sources, and a large number of them have been consulted. These are mainly the diaries and reminiscences of public officials of the period.

The diary kept by Alexander A. Polovtsov for almost a half-century (from the end of the 1850s until his death in 1908) is the most significant. It is an especially valuable source for the 1880s and early 1890s, when Polovtsov was state secretary and the real director of business in the State Council (and when his diary is most detailed and complete). An intelligent and observant man, he moved in the highest circles and recorded many interesting facts. These cast a great deal of light on government policy and offer numerous details of the life and customs of official society and the imperial family. But his notes on the proceedings of the State Council are of particular importance. Polovtsov frequently supplements the existing protocols of meetings and also reveals off-the-record opinions of council members that are unavailable in any other official or unofficial source. Further, the diaries record many intriguing stories about Grand Duke Michael Nikolaevich, the chairman of the council, some of its other members, ministers, and other persons. Because of his special position within the State Council (frequently he served as chairman), Polovtsov was in direct contact with the tsar and he recorded a number of their conversations (mainly dealing with matters examined by the council).

Polovtsov's diary thus affords an excellent commentary on the government's domestic policies without which our study would have been very difficult. But it must be remembered that Polovtsov observed events through the spectacles of a statesman loyal to the regime and so tended to vindicate its policies. It is also possible that he over-estimated his own role and that his descriptions of individuals reveal his own personal prejudices. Nonetheless, his diary remains extremely accurate as to factual information.[7]

After Polovtsov's, the most useful diary is that kept by Admiral I.A. Shestakov from the time of his appointment as director of the Naval Ministry in 1882 until his death in 1888. It has detailed entries on the meetings of the Committee of Ministers and on the proposed reforms. Shestakov also describes many prominent people, including Alexander III. But the admiral himself was no reactionary and actually was fairly critical of the counter-reforms then being prepared.

The diary of Eugene M. Feoktistov, head of the Main Directorate of the Press and previously editor of the *Journal of the Ministry of Education,* is also helpful. A man of great intelligence, Feoktistov went from being a student of T.N. Granovsky and friend of Ivan S. Turgenev to being the "playmate" of D.A. Tolstoy.[8] In his latter years he directed the censor's department and ruthlessly persecuted both Russian literature and the periodicals which published it. Yet in the privacy of his diary Feoktistov could be very frank and frequently gave uncomplimentary portraits of his chiefs and colleagues. Here are very unflattering remarks about Delianov, Ivan N. Durnovo, and Vladimir P. Meshchersky, and he was quite critical about both D.A. Tolstoy and the frivolous empress, Maria Fedorovna. While he did not actually disapprove of Alexander III, nonetheless Feoktistov did record facts showing the emperor in a less than favorable light. He also provides details of the arbitrary administrative practices of the governors and gives devastating descriptions of Governor Paul V. Nekliudov of Orel province and A.K. Anastasiev of Chernigov province, among others. All this makes Feoktistov's diary of great significance although unfortunately it is brief and fragmentary.

At this point mention should be made of Feoktistov's later memoirs. Published in 1929, they span a half-century and are of considerable value.[9] Here, notwithstanding his complete devotion to the autocracy, Feoktistov is extraordinarily honest, vivid and subtle in characterizing the powerful of his world (not even the emperor is spared). Though Feoktistov devoted little space to the particular period of this study (only one and a half chapters out of ten), his reminiscences remain a noteworthy source.

On several subjects the memoirs differ from the diaries both in interpretations of fact and in the opinions expressed about individuals. An example is Feoktistov's inconsistent descriptions of I.N. Durnovo, Minister of the Interior:

Diary	Reminiscences
Ivan Nikolaevich is sly and has a great reserve of cunning, but he is able to keep it masked by such frankness and cheerfulness that most people see him as a man who wears his heart on his sleeve. He, the pal of all, is really the friend of none.	Durnovo owed his success exclusively to his remarkably sympathetic and very generous personality. He was a "good" man in the true sense of the word, and he considered himself lucky when he was able to do someone a favor. He was always ready to listen to your troubles and was incapable of hiding his own opinions.

Another fascinating source is the unpublished diary of the conservative slavophile, General Alexander A. Kireev.[10] Consisting of some 3,000 pages and devoted to the years between the early 1860s and 1910, the diary notes were collected by Grand Duke Konstantin Nikolaevich. Kireev stood close to the highest figures in the Russian state and his notes contain many illuminating comments. Among his acquaintances were Michael N. Katkov, a number of ministers, and members of the imperial family, so that Kireev was frequently at the center of events.

Although a monarchist, he could still be highly critical of governmental policies and often disapproved privately of the actions of D.A. Tolstoy, Pobedonostsev, Delianov, and others. This makes his diary notably provocative, as is illustrated by his comments about the attitude of Alexander III and his circle toward the fiftieth anniversary of the death of the poet, Alexander Pushkin: "The Sovereign has no one to give him sound advice on matters of a public (and sometimes highly important) nature. Today all of Russia is mourning the unhappy anniversary of the death of the great Pushkin, but at Court there is a ball! And as if on purpose Alexander Pushkin,[11] (a general of the Suite), who is usually excluded from balls held in the concert chamber, was invited to this one! The cumulative effect of such trifles is considerable and certainly has a harmful influence on the Court's public standing. Surely if there had been *anybody* at Court who was capable of reminding the Emperor that it is 'not done' to dance on the anniversary of Pushkin's death, he would have postponed the ball; but there was *no one* to be found. All these *illiterates* (Vorontsov, Trubetskoy, Dolgorukov, Obolensky),[12] all of them are Russians, are they not? And yet not one of them thought of it!"

The diary of A.N. Mosolov, formerly the director of the Department of Spiritual Affairs for Foreign Confessions in the Ministry of the Interior, and later governor of Novgorod, covers the years 1866 to 1904. Episodic in nature, it consists of only two typewritten notebooks corrected by its author. He kept his diary irregularly: there are gaps not only of months but of years. In places the diary seems more a book of recollections, some events being recorded weeks or months after they had occurred. Mosolov's diary is particularly useful for examining the relations between the provincial administrative authorities and the zemstvos, and in particular for the light it sheds on what is known as the "Cherpovets affair" [the closing of the Cherpovets county zemstvo].[13] Mosolov also expressed his opinion on the situation in the provinces and the institution of land captains, and gives sketches of Peter A. Cherevin, Apollon K. Krivoshein, Durnovo, and many other people.

The diary kept by Grand Duke Konstantin Konstantinovich (from the age of nine until his death in 1915) is more regular. Basically it is a very personal document and devoted to descriptions of his own life and experiences. Unlike the majority of diaries it is not prone to self-justification; at times it is even self-critical, and the grand duke did not hesitate to record those very intimate experiences that most people prefer to leave unchronicled. Yet this record is of public value because of its sketches of members of the imperial family and accounts of conversations with Alexander III. A poet and, since the late 1880s, president of the Academy of Sciences, Konstantin Konstantinovich knew many writers, composers, and scholars. Entries for 1880 concern the novelist Fedor M. Dostoevsky, while those in other years touch upon the art and music critic Vladimir V. Stasov and the poet Apollon N. Maikov. He also speaks of the composer Peter I. Chaikovsky and the latter's death.[14] These elements make the diary a useful historical source.

The daily notebooks of Alexander III, with his own brief jottings, are mainly helpful for defining the emperor's character. These notes are devoted to describing his daily routine (the weather, his pastimes, the presence of guests, the time he went to sleep, and so forth). The sole exception to such dull notes is the entry concerning the death of the Minister of the Interior, Count D.A. Tolstoy. Otherwise these notebooks are similar to those kept by a social secretary.

The diaries of Alexandra V. Bogdanovich, published in an abbreviated form, should be mentioned even though the entries begin only at the end of the 1880s.[15] For descriptions of public figures (Pobedonostsev, Manasein, and Nicholas V. Muraviev) and of the activities of the higher judicial bodies (in particular the Special Office of the Governing Senate), Anatole F. Koni's fascinating recollections are of tremendous importance.[16] Writing in the early 1900s, Koni described the condition of the central judicial institutions with his usual talent and brilliance. He maintained that during the 1880s many of the highest judicial officials gradually had become corrupted. This was especially true of many senators as was revealed by the work of the Senate's Special Office. The trial of March 1, 1887, conducted by this body, is a particular case in point.[17] Alexander Kizevetter's reminiscences[18] aid in gauging the mood of the public in the 1880s, and the unreliable recollections of Prince V.P. Meshchersky should be consulted.[19] Otherwise, the diaries and recollections of Dmitry A. Miliutin[20] and Boris N. Chicherin,[21] among others, contain much worthwhile material.

The correspondence of the statesmen of this era provides the third major group of sources. These documents are useful for examining the "behind-the-scenes" aspects of events and are perhaps of greater importance than the memoir literature. As a rule letters are more candid and avoid the retrospective judgements typical of reminiscences and even of diaries. Pobedonostsev's correspondence, especially his letters to the emperor, are especially valuable for understanding the unofficial aspects of government politics. They bear witness to Pobedonostsev's role and demonstrate the extent of his influence upon Alexander III. Although published without commentary or notes, their appearance was an event of major significance.[22]

The correspondence of Meshchersky with the emperor, retained in the archives of Alexander III, is no less clearly of interest for this study.

The letters for the 1860s and 1870s provide an insight into the earlier relationship between the two men, while those of the 1880s and early 1890s demonstrate the personal influence exercised by the editor of the *Citizen* upon the emperor and his policies.

Apart from ordinary letters, Meshchersky wrote letters to the tsar in the form of diaries. In November, 1885, he forwarded a diary to Alexander, writing: "I am making so bold as to send You several drafts from my diary for the last two weeks. In them You will find some thoughts, some rumors and gossip, and some scandals. I wrote, or more correctly, simply jotted down what came to mind, rather than composed an essay. Forgive me if I have made a fool of myself, but if all this is worthy of Your attention, then it will have served its purpose."

Actually, Meshchersky used these diaries to outline his views on questions of domestic and foreign policy, as well as to pass on bits of tittle-tattle and to denounce others. In one, for instance, he wrote about Michael N. Ostrovsky, the Minister of State Domains: "I don't know any of our statesmen who has such a false conception of the Emperor's personality as Ostrovsky." It is certainly difficult to see this as anything but an outright denunciation!

The nature of Meshchersky's diaries may be further gauged by their contents for the last week of October, 1885. On October 22 he wrote "On graft in the Department of Justice;" on the 23rd, "On the profits of taverns;" on the 24th, "On Bulgaria" and "News from Oreanda;" on the 25th, "Thoughts on the orders issued concerning the Prince of Bulgaria;" on the 27th, "Rumors and talk;" on the 28th, "On autocracy;" on November 1, "Talk, gossip, and rumors;" and so on.[23] By using this diary form Meshchersky found a way to pass to the tsar disgustingly crude flattery in the guise of his innermost thoughts. "Today a ray of light brightened my dismal corner," he wrote in his diary. "I received a kind reply from the Sovereign. I thank Him from the bottom of my heart . . . ."

M.N. Katkov's wide correspondence with official and public figures is as informative as Meshchersky's or Pobedonostsev's. Among Katkov's correspondents, apart from D.A. Tolstoy, Delianov and Feoktistov, were officials such as Tertii I. Filippov, Alexis D. Pazukhin and Alexander I. Georgievsky. The Katkov archives include both the letters he received and copies of his letters to others. In this way an opportunity is provided for studying both sides of the correspondence. Among the copies are Katkov's letters to Alexander III.

Equally worthy of examination is the correspondence of D.A. Miliutin, who had retired to his Crimean estate of Simeiz. During 1882 to 1886 he received regular and detailed letters from Alexander V.

Golovnin, a member of the State Council. These give accounts of the political events taking place in the capital.

The few remaining letters from D.A. Tolstoy and Pobedonostsev to V.K. Plehve merit attention. They bear upon certain questions of domestic policy and are particularly helpful in examining the preparation of the counter-reforms. N.V. Muraviev's letters to Plehve are also useful, though mainly for the extraordinarily vivid portrait they give of their author as an unprincipled sycophant.

Feoktistov's correspondence is naturally indispensable for studying the censorship. In his files survive letters from D.A. Tolstoy, the State Controller (T.I. Filippov), and a great number from Pobedonostsev. These latter prove the role played by the Director-General of the Holy Synod in shaping the policies of censorship.

Finally, the manuscript of Nicholas Kh. Bunge, entitled "Notes from Beyond the Grave" and found in Alexander III's archives, requires careful attention. The notes consist of an unsigned and undated record, written by a clerk, but on the first page the tsar wrote "The notes of N.Kh. Bunge." The latter began with the explanation that "Although I have neither a diary nor a set of notes to leave, I consider it my duty to Your Imperial Majesty, my most August student, to express frankly my thoughts on the events that I have witnessed since 1880. In this way I may be able to continue to serve Your Majesty even after my own death."

Bunge reviewed the measures which the government had passed during Alexander III's reign. On the whole he assessed these favorably, although he viewed many of them critically. Bunge's views on socialism are especially intriguing. "It is necessary to see socialism," he wrote, "not as something that cannot be eradicated, but as something that we should introduce to a certain extent. It is as impossible to eliminate socialism as it is to eradicate microbes. Without the hope of happiness and the efforts to achieve it, life itself would become paralysed." Bunge considered one cause for the growth of socialist ideas to be the existing system of communal peasant landownership and these notes give a comprehensive picture of his generally conservative political views.

The fourth main group of source materials consists of the newspapers and periodicals of that day. Four publications are particularly worthy of study. Of the reactionary newspapers Katkov's *Moscow News,* which throughout its existence was for all practical purposes the government's official newspaper, and Meshchersky's *Citizen*, deserve attention.

The *Russian News* was the leading liberal newspaper to survive the censor's persecution during the first half of the 1880s. It served as a mouthpiece for the liberal professors of Moscow where it was published under the editorship of V.M. Sobolevsky. The other journal of impor- tance was the monthly *European Herald*, and its "Domestic Review," written by Konstantin K. Arseniev, is unusually informative.

The *Moscow News* and the *Citizen* had no hesitation in supporting every reactionary measure adopted by the government. The *Russian News* and the *European Herald*, on the other hand, criticized the gov- ernment's policies within the limits permitted by the censorship.

Together these materials provide the basic sources for a detailed study of the autocracy's internal policies during the 1880s and early 1890s.

CHAPTER I

ALEXANDER III AND HIS ADVISERS

THE TSAR AND TSARITSA

On March 1, 1881 the second son of Alexander II mounted the throne as Alexander III. This inaugurated a protracted period of reaction hidden, as D.A. Miliutin put it, "behind a mask of nationalism and orthodoxy."

Alexander III, born the second of five sons in 1845, had not been expected to become emperor. He was given, therefore, only the very simple education needed for coping successfully with the demands usually made upon a Russian grand duke. A grand duke, after all, was expected to end his career as the commander of a Guards division, or perhaps the Guards Corps, which usually brought command of the Petersburg military district as well.

According to his teachers and the evidence of his own diary, the future ruler displayed no great breadth of interest. The young Alexander, like his four brothers, was dull and obstinate, although industrious and tenacious. His teachers' reports mention his pranks, inattention, outright disobedience and other delinquencies, but note diligence as one of the young grand duke's better qualities. In a report for June, 1844 two of his tutors (N.V. Zinoviev and G.F. Gogel) comment that he kept at his writing lessons "very earnestly and diligently." By the time he was five, Alexander's instructors also mentioned his efforts at military drill: in September, 1850, for instance, his determination and seriousness while marching are mentioned five times. But he was still weak in more academic pursuits and never became completely literate, even in his own native Russian. At times he made serious mistakes, such as changing the word "*energiia*" to "*inergiia*" and writing the adverb "*ele*" (hardly) as "*eli*" (they ate).[1]

Neither his boyhood nor adult diaries give any indication of intellectual curiosity. Alexander recorded only the superficial details of his life and rarely mentioned any personal experiences or opinions. He mechanically listed everyday incidents like the weather, visitors, the routine schedule he followed, and even, though very demurely, included the events of his wedding night. Compared with these diary entries, Alexander's jottings in the notebooks he kept after mounting the throne are even briefer. These merely record the times he got up and went to bed, his success in hunting and fishing (with a precise description of each animal shot and each fish caught), and so on. Sometimes he entered the total distances travelled over several months. Thus in the notebook for 1889 he noted the following: "1887—from November 22 to December 20: 103 *versts;* 1888—from April 10 to May 29: 98 *versts;* from October 21 to December 30: 330 *versts;* 1889—from 9 March to May 23: 101 *versts,*" and so forth.[2]

Yet it is wrong to see Alexander III as simply stupid. He is described better as a limited and uneducated man who possessed little intelligence and was incapable of subtlety. He could recognize stupidity in people like his uncle, Grand Duke Nicholas Nikolaevich the Elder. During the Russo-Turkish War of 1877-1878 the latter commanded the Balkan theatre of operations, and Alexander, explaining the reasons for Russian failures to his wife, remarked: "Uncle Nizi (as he was called in the family circle) was always stupid—we need to find some kind of *genie* who can turn a stupid man into a wise one."

In 1865, after his elder brother's unexpected death, Alexander Alexandrovich became the heir to the throne.[3] As "tsarevich" he inherited his brother's fiancé, the young Danish princess, Dagmar. Although frivolous and not particularly intelligent,[4] she was strong-willed. In October, 1866 when Dagmar married the future Alexander III, she took the name of Maria Fedorovna and, with her own firm views, undoubtedly became an influence on her husband. It is likely that his hostility to Germany was partly due to her. The Danes had lost Schleswig-Holstein to Prussia and Austria in the 1864 war; this had not endeared Germany to the Danish princess and Maria Fedorovna retained this hatred for the rest of her life.

It was probably her influence that caused the tsarevich to take a view of the Franco-Prussian War of 1870 so completely different from that of the rest of the imperial family. His father, Alexander II, was an open Germanophile. Revering his uncle, William I, the king of Prussia, Alexander II tactlessly showered unprecedented honors upon him and his General Staff. In 1869, on the hundredth anniversary of the creation of the Military Order of St. George, Alexander II conferred the first class of this order upon the Prussian king. Then, during the Franco-Prussian conflict, the tsar was equally generous in awarding St. George crosses to Prussian officers and soldiers. "At the beginning of October (1870)," War Minister Miliutin later recalled, "Major-General Gern of the engineers was sent to the German army with a mass of St. George Crosses for both officers and soldiers."[5] This reflected Alexander II's lively interest in the German successes and, according to Miliutin, he was "almost as pleased as if they had been victories for his own Russian army." Grand Duke Alexander Alexandrovich, however, reacted to these events in the opposite manner. On August 24, 1870, he noted in his diary: "What terrible news . . . MacMahon is crushed, his army has surrendered, and Emperor Napoleon is a prisoner! This is terrible."

As the tsarevich could hardly have reached such conclusions on his own, it seems he had been influenced by his wife, with whom he was very deeply in love.[6] She also caused him, shortly after their wedding, to break off his friendship with Prince Vladimir Meshchersky. The empress had no particular love for Pobedonostsev either and, in the long run, this may help to explain the later coolness between her husband and his favorite teacher. On becoming heir to the throne, Alexander Alexandrovich had tried to complete his education under Pobedonostsev's tutelage. The latter remained Alexander's mentor for a long time, although he never had much success in improving his pupil's formal knowledge.

During the 1877-1878 war the tsarevich, along with a great many other members of the imperial family, served in the active army. He commanded an important detachment but, like the rest of his relatives, demonstrated no military talent.

Alexander's simple education explains the crudity of his political views. He had imbibed reactionary and conservative attitudes "with his mother's milk" and these were strengthened by his education. Pobedonostsev then completed the conditioning of the future autocrat's political beliefs, which remained confined in the straitjacket of Uvarov's old formula of "Orthodoxy, Autocracy, and Nationalism."[7] The use of the government to propagate the Orthodox faith, to introduce Russian as the sole language, to suppress anything that could possibly threaten the autocratic form of government, and to strengthen ties between the "first estate" (the nobility) and the throne—these were the practical goals Alexander set himself during his reign.

The tsar's idea of Christianity was simplistic. He interpreted the Gospels with a believer's crudity and considered that the Jews, as a people, were cursed by God for having "crucified the Savior." For this reason Alexander sincerely believed that "although their fate is indeed sad, it has been preordained in the Gospels"[8] and felt that his attitude to the Jews must conform to that ordained by Providence. This is the probable reason for Alexander III's anti-Semitism. "In the depth of my soul I am always happy when they beat the Jews," the emperor once told General Joseph V. Gurko, the governor-general of Warsaw.[9]

Such attitudes naturally played a major role in determining Alexander's policies, which were, domestically, openly reactionary (even though it proved impossible to pursue consistently those aiming at the preservation of remnants of feudalism). But in foreign affairs he could be guided by common sense. The emperor's open opposition to the prevailing reverence for Germany inevitably led to a *rapprochement* with France. While this policy was in line with Russian interests, sometimes he did blunder. The Balkan question is a case in point, for Northern Bulgaria's "voluntary" union with Eastern Rumelia, undertaken by Bulgaria in 1885 without the sanction of the Russian government, so enraged Alexander that Russia actually appealed to the sultan of Turkey and complained that the decisions of the Berlin Conference of 1878 were being broken![10]

Despite his own intentions, Alexander III found it impossible to act as a real head of the country's administration. Quite apart from gaps in his knowledge, his mind proved incapable of understanding and digesting the essence of many problems. The emperor experienced great difficulty in dealing with the reports or "memorials" from the State Council, which usually outlined two opinions on each question and left a final decision to him. The tsar had special summaries prepared from these memorials (which were themselves abstracts made from the minutes of the council sessions). On his appointment at the beginning of 1883 as state secretary, A.A. Polovtsov was told by Grand Duke Michael Nikolaevich, chairman of the council, "that one of my duties will be to write for the Emperor a very short abstract of the memorials sent to him. This is secret and the procedure has been introduced only by the present sovereign so as to ease the load that his many tasks placed upon him." Later the grand duke remarked that "he (the emperor) destroyed these papers after reading them."[11]

Otherwise Alexander III did no serious reading. He was especially pleased by the books of Boleslav Markevich,[12] but disliked—and evidently did not understand—the works of Leo Tolstoy. He was unacquainted with the writings of Turgenev and, naturally, those of the radical Nicholas G. Chernyshevsky. Once the tsar read in the testimony of a recently arrested prisoner that "when I was young my heroes were Lopukhov and Bazarov," and noted in the margin: "Who are they?" Evidently he was interested in discovering if the two persons named were still at liberty.[13]

Just as he had tried sincerely to understand military affairs as a child, Alexander, on becoming sovereign, attempted to broaden his understanding in other areas. Such attempts ended in failure. A.V. Golovnin, in a letter to D.A. Miliutin, wrote that Alexander "reads many files from the archives" and at first people believed that the young ruler would really be able to take part in administering the state. But his ignorance and, above all else, his stupidity and narrow-mindedness, soon proved insurmountable obstacles.[14] To make matters worse, Alexander did not even read newspapers. In February, 1888 General A.A.

Kireev noted in his diary: "He reads little, although this would be the only way to compensate for his lack of unofficial contact with the people. Nonetheless, the press remains a closed book to him." In 1891 Kireev, again in his diary, observed that "extracts" of the newspapers' reports were being drawn up and forwarded to the tsar. But, as these extracts were reviewed first by the head of the Main Directorate of the Press and the Minister of the Interior, they merely reinforced Alexander's simplistic and one-sided perceptions of reality.[15]

The emperor could be surprisingly crude. He frequently used epithets such as "brute" and "scoundrel" and at times was personally brutal. The fatal birching of N.K. Sigida, a political prisoner in the Kara penal camp, was carried out on the personal instructions of Alexander III. Feoktistov wrote that Durnovo, the Minister of the Interior, said he had sent the tsar a report about Sigida's insulting behavior to a gendarme officer. Alexander III simply commented: "Flog her." On receiving this Durnovo "immediately submitted a second report in which he pointed out that while it was true that women prisoners were not exempt from corporal punishment, the upper limit of this has been defined as one hundred blows. In view of the fact that the culprit in this case had received some education and that her nerves had been affected by her prolonged imprisonment, he would suggest that her penalty be lightened, so that she receive the minimum punishment. But on this report fresh instructions were returned to 'give her the hundred strokes.' "[16]

The ruler's personal mode of life was modest. He was conscientious, disliked dishonesty, and was a good "family man." Unlike his father, uncles and brothers, Alexander avoided what A.A. Kireev called "amorous entanglements." Although the tsar did drink, he preferred to do this quietly with his chief of security and old friend, General P.A. Cherevin, rather than in some sort of orgy.[17] But when drunk the sovereign had a very original way of entertaining himself. As Cherevin later described it, the emperor "lay on his back on the floor and waved his arms and legs about. He stopped behaving like a man and became a child, trying to get to his feet and then falling down. It was only when this happened that one knew that he was in his cups."[18] In the later 1880s, when Alexander III contracted a kidney disease, he was forbidden alcohol. The empress took great care to see that he obeyed the doctors, but she was not always successful. "In spite of this," reported Cherevin, "His Majesty still often ended the evening by lying on his back on the floor, waving his paws about and squealing with pleasure."

Alexander and Cherevin evolved very complicated procedures to outwit the empress. "He and I, that is the Emperor and myself," Cherevin recalled with a sly smile, "managed to get by; we ordered jackboots with special waders, in which we could carry a flat flask holding the equivalent of a bottle of cognac. When the Tsaritsa was beside us, we sat quietly and played like good children. But whenever she went off a little, we would exchange glances. And then—one, two, three! We'd pull out our flasks, take a swig and then it would be again as if nothing had happened. He (Alexander III) was greatly pleased with this amusement. It was like a game. We named it 'necessity is the mother of invention.' 'One, two, three. Necessity, Cherevin?'—'Invention, Your Majesty.' 'One, two, and three'—and we'd swig."

Such was the character of this Russian autocrat who, as noted previously, was not overly intelligent.[19] This latter judgement is confirmed by his contemporaries. E.F. Feoktistov, one of the leading government officials during Alexander's reign, was in general favorably disposed to the emperor. Nonetheless Feoktistov wrote: "In the future, when some or all of the various instructions and notes written by him have been published, and when people who have had direct contact with him have written their recollections, the general impression will be that he often showed his sound common sense. But, there will also be those who are struck by his straightforward, child-like naïveté and simple-mindedness."

This view is basically correct. "Simple-mindedness and childish naïveté" contributed more to his personality than did "common sense." Even Sergei Yu. Witte, who defended Alexander III and wrote in his memoirs of his love for this monarch, agreed that the tsar was a man "of comparatively little education. In fact, it must be frankly admitted that he had had a quite commonplace upbringing." All in all, Witte concluded, "Emperor Alexander III had very little wisdom of the mind, but a tremendous store of wisdom of the heart."

THE TSAREVICH

Like his father, Grand Duke Nicholas Alexandrovich, the future Nicholas II, possessed a limited intelligence and narrow education. His tutor, General Grigory G. Danilovich, kept a close watch on his upbringing, but was unable to force any kind of serious learning upon his student. According to Polovtsov, the tsarevich's education was "very shallow and unsatisfactory." When the heir was twenty-two years old, he recited from memory one of Pushkin's poems to his second cousin, Grand Duke Konstantin Konstantinovich. The latter, with some astonishment, recorded the event in his diary with the following words: "And I thought that he, with all his kindness, was capable of nothing but hunting." As for politics, Pobedonostsev was one of the tutors who had a great influence upon the young Nicholas.

Even as an adult (that is, when he was past twenty), the tsarevich behaved rather oddly. Apparently this was a result of his upbringing. His mother continued to consider him a child and for a long time would not let him go anywhere without her. Count Vladimir N. Lamsdorf, describing the tsarevich in his diary of 1892, wrote: "The heir, now twenty-four years old, makes a strange impression. He is half-boy and half-man, small of stature, thin, and undistinguished in appearance. All the same he is, they say, obstinate—and displays an astonishing amount of thoughtlessness and insensitivity."[20] Consequently a lack of will power, indifference, and obstinacy, must be counted among the future emperor's most important characteristics.

Beginning in the late 1880s the tsarevich served as a probationary junior officer in the Life Guards Hussars, and then in the Preobrazhensky Regiment. During this time he picked up the vices rather than the virtues of an officer's life. In the Life Guards Hussars, commanded by his uncle, Grand Duke Nicholas Nikolaevich the Younger, the tsarevich grew familiar with all the traditional charms of a Hussar's existence. He was thrown into the life of unrestrained drinking that marked an officer's life in this regiment. Another officer later described the shocking finish of some of their bouts: "They would frequently spend an entire day and evening drinking, until they began to hallucinate. For some this became almost habitual and the servants in the officers' mess grew accustomed to the gentlemen's strange behavior. Then the Grand Duke, who commanded the regiment, and some of the other Hussars of the company often began to believe that they were no longer humans, but wolves. They all stripped naked and ran out into the street. . . . There they would crouch on their hands and knees, raise their drunken heads to the sky and begin to howl loudly. The old club waiter knew just what to do. He would carry a big wash tub out onto the porch and fill it full of vodka or champagne. The officers would then rush on all fours to the tub and lap up the wine with their tongues as they yelped and bit one another."

The heir to the throne spent his youth in circumstances such as these. "No one could fail to notice that Nicholas Alexandrovich's body was being poisoned by alcohol, as his face was becoming yellow, his eyes glistened unhealthily, and bags were beginning to form beneath his eyes, as is customary with alcoholics."[21]

As a young officer Nicholas Alexandrovich naturally read little and entertained a very confused idea of the true state of world affairs. Apart from Pobedonostsev, Alexander III entrusted the development of the heir's political ideas to his friend, Prince Meshchersky. As editor of the *Citizen* the latter was an experienced warrior in the battle against sedition. He sent Nicholas a diary containing thoughts on various burning questions of the day. Feoktistov noted: "Each week Meshchersky forwards to the Tsarevich the diary that he writes for Him. In this diary he discusses the most important current questions. He has been given this task by the sovereign himself, who does not want the heir to get His information indiscriminately from newspapers that interpret events in a random fashion. [The Sovereign] prefers that such interpretations be provided by a completely reliable and loyal person." "In this way," Feoktistov observed, "Meshchersky educates the Tsarevich for the high mission which awaits Him in the future. He is being inspired with the proper ideas, and the Emperor, through whose hands each number of the diary passes, is pleased. The teacher gets good marks."[22]

Meshchersky seems to have been completely successful in properly preparing the tsarevich for the throne. As early as January 17, 1895, Nicholas, now emperor, held an audience for a deputation of zemstvo representatives. In answer to an address of the Tver zemstvo, which spoke of the necessity of "basic reforms," the young emperor declared that these were "senseless dreams" as his fundamental aim was to "preserve the autocratic principle." At this moment the student lived up to his teacher's fondest hopes.[23]

THE GRAND DUKES

With a very few exceptions, the grand dukes shared the emperor's intellectual gifts and expelled from their midst the few who proved exceptional.

Alexander III, on becoming emperor, immediately removed Grand Duke Konstantin Nikolaevich from the posts of chairman of the State Council and General-Admiral (which was, in practice, the same as naval minister). Konstantin Nikolaevich was an intelligent and broadly educated man. Notwithstanding his extravagant and somewhat unbalanced character, he was one of the greatest statesmen of the earlier reform era. His political views had made the grand duke the "ideological leader" of the liberal bureaucracy, and he was a firm supporter of a "bourgeois transformation" [that is, further reform]. This did not endear him to Alexander III, who practically accused his uncle of being involved in the murder of Alexander II, as many believed this act had been provoked by the policies of the liberals.

Konstantin Nikolaevich's younger brother, Grand Duke Michael Nikolaevich, followed him as chairman of the State Council. His personal qualities made him more palatable to Alexander III but, although he had served as viceroy of the Caucasus and chief of artillery, Grand Duke Michael was a very limited man. He was "a remarkably foolish chairman for the State Council," recalled Feoktistov, who added that the Empress

Eugenie [wife of Napoleon III], after a conversation with Michael when he was viceroy of the Caucasus, remarked: "This is not a man, but a horse."

One of the darker sides of Grand Duke Michael's character was his great cowardice. He always thought and acted as the emperor demanded (a not too difficult task for his own views were basically reactionary). Count Michael T. Loris-Melikov knew him well and, in a letter of October 20, 1886, he described the grand duke in the following terms: "An egotist, envious, and false in the full sense of that word, the Grand Duke is as frightened and timid as a rabbit, both on the battlefield and in time of peace. His fear has led to the embarrassing behavior typical of him since childhood . . . . All the Grand Duke's above-mentioned flaws are masked in public by his very handsome outward appearance and the gentle courtesy with which he addresses everyone. Being an ignoramus who does not trust in his own abilities, he willingly defers to those who surround him. Because of this he blindly fulfills his wife's wishes and carries out her instructions, as well as those . . . of his adjutants and the other people who have his ear."[24]

In this connection Polovtsov described the grand duke's lack of principles in the following manner: "One is prepared to stumble daily upon difficult moral issues, but certainly I had not expected to meet with such servility and contempt for moral duty." Earlier, during the war of 1877-1878, Grand Duke Michael, then commander-in-chief of the Caucasian front, had displayed his complete incompetence. At this time, according to Prince Nicholas I. Sviatopolk-Mirsky, he was fond of repeating a remark that became his special proverb: "I am now certain that in war time it is better to be a coachman than a commander-in-chief." But apparently he did not find the job of being commander-in-chief quite so difficult in peacetime.

Grand Duke Alexis Alexandrovich, a younger brother of Alexander III, was appointed General-Admiral. He was dissolute and spent less time on the fleet than he did on drinking bouts and various love affairs. Otherwise, he was addicted to gambling at cards and was constantly in need of money.[25] As Grand Admiral he was responsible for the disasters suffered by the fleet in the war with Japan of 1904-1905.[26]

Among the grand dukes holding high office mention must be made of the tsar's two other brothers, Vladimir and Sergei. Grand Duke Vladimir (1847-1909) was one of the more intelligent offspring of Alexander II. He became commander of the Guards Corps, replacing Nicholas Nikolaevich, or "Uncle Nizi," who had been renowned for his stupidity.[27] In spite of all his energy Vladimir Alexandrovich spent most of his time in fruitless frivolity and gluttony. Even his close friend,

A.A. Polovtsov, was anything but kind in his comments about the grand duke. "Vladimir," he observed, "is intelligent, attentive, kind, and has more education than the others.... Yet from childhood he has been inclined to be lazy, absent-minded, and a glutton."[28] His brother, Grand Duke Sergei, was a reactionary chauvinist of the worst type. In the 1880s he commanded the Life Guards Preobrazhensky Regiment and actively encouraged the depraved debauchery that flourished in it. In the early 1890s he was appointed governor-general of Moscow. There he was given every opportunity to put into practice his reactionary and chauvinistic ideas. All in all, Sergei Alexandrovich disgusted Polovtsov, who observed in his diary that "if the two elder brothers have contempt for humanity, the third enjoys the utter contempt of humanity."

It is no exaggeration to assert that the members of the imperial family were for the most part rather stupid individuals who divided their lives between the barracks and the restaurant. Only two of them— Grand Dukes Konstantin Konstantinovich and Nicholas Michaelovich —were in any way exceptional, but they took little part in affairs of state. Konstantin Konstantinovich, a poet and dramatist who wrote under the initials "K.R.," spent much time on his musical and literary interests. He completed a fairly good Russian translation of Shakespeare's *Hamlet* and mingled with writers like Dostoevsky, Ivan A. Goncharov, Ya.P. Polonsky, A.A. Fet, and V.V. Stasov, and was a friend of the composer Chaikovsky.[29] Konstantin recorded in his diary that Stasov once praised his verses. "It seems," the young grand duke wrote, "that he considers my brothers, the grand dukes, to be generally incapable of anything and is pleased when some one from our *milieu* can undertake some kind of work."[30] At the same time, however, Konstantin's political attitudes were simple and reactionary. Following the death of Alexander III, the grand duke favorably assessed the results of his reign and suggested that "he raised Russia to a very uncommon grandeur."

For his part, Grand Duke Nicholas Michaelovich grew seriously involved in archeology and history. Subsequently he wrote a number of monographs on early nineteenth-century Russian history.

POBEDONOSTSEV

The members of Alexander III's intimate circle with the greatest influence upon government policy were K.P. Pobedonostsev, Count D.A. Tolstoy, M.N. Katkov, and Prince V.P. Meshchersky. The views and aspirations of this "quartet" agreed utterly with those of the emperor and they were able to a large extent to influence his policies.

The first three composed a peculiar triumvirate. E.M. Feoktistov, who was close to them all, described their relations as follows: "The supposed accord of these three persons recalls the fable of the swan, the pike, and the crayfish. On basic principles they were more or less agreed, but that did not mean that they could act in unison. M.N. Katkov would get excited and fly into a rage, pointing out that it was not enough merely to refrain from dangerous experiments and curb the party seeking to change the whole political system of Russia. He believed it was necessary to be energetic rather than to sit by with folded hands. Katkov was irreconcilably the enemy of stagnation and his mind continually probed for a way to lead Russia onto a beneficial path of development. Count Tolstoy, however, was puzzled as to just where one should begin this work and how best to achieve the desired goals. He would have been glad enough to do something worthwhile, but he had a very fuzzy idea of just what this 'something' should be. As for Pobedonostsev, he remained true to form, merely sighed, lamented, and threw up his hands in despair . . . . It should thus come as no surprise to find that a chariot handled by three such drivers made very slow progress. Katkov and Tolstoy never saw each other. Pobedonostsev did meet Katkov, but after nearly every meeting he was full of complaints, so hot did he become under Michael Nikiforovich [Katkov's] merciless attacks."

Feoktistov's depiction of the characters of these three men and their interrelationships is accurate enough. It should be added that Tolstoy was personally close to Pobedonostsev, even though he held no contact with either Katkov or Meshchersky. The latter individual, the fourth member of the "quartet", held to the shadows and attempted to influence the tsar—his close friend in the past—by means of the letters and the diaries that he sent him.

During the 1880s Konstantin Petrovich Pobedonostsev was Alexander III's closest adviser. He was, in fact, the emperor's real mentor, particularly during the early years of the reign. Born the son of a professor in 1827, Pobedonostsev received a solid education at the Law School and began a civil service career in the Moscow Department of the Senate. During the five years from 1860 to 1865 he was a professor at Moscow University, holding the chair of civil law. A.F. Koni, who heard him lecture at this time, recalled that "a figure with a pinched, pale, clean-shaven face, and wearing thick, heavy tortoise-shell glasses, through which his intelligent eyes continuously peered, would approach the lectern . . . ." Then, Koni continued, "a lazy, quiet, monotonous voice would issue from his bloodless lips. We knew Pobedonostsev from his writings and his reputation as a famous lawyer, with experience in civil cases, but he did not excite us and seemed indifferent to his own subject."

In 1865 Pobedonostsev was appointed a consulting member of the Ministry of Justice, in 1868 he became a senator, and in 1872 he became member of the State Council. He was also busy with scholarly work, writing a four-volume study of civil law and a number of legal historical studies. By the 1860s Pobedonostsev was already close to the imperial family, being tutor in jurisprudence to the grand dukes and to the future Alexander III in particular. At the initiative of the tsarevich, with the support of Loris-Melikov, in 1880 Pobedonostsev was appointed Director-General of the Holy Synod. He was to hold this position for a quarter of a century.

As far as his political views were concerned, Pobedonostsev represented the extreme reactionaries. He supported an unlimited autocracy, championed the preservation of the nobility's privileges, and became a zealous enemy of Western European forms of public life. "Democracy is one of the falsest political principles. It is regrettable that since the French Revolution the *idea* has gained currency that every kind of authority comes from the *people* and has as its basis the popular will," Pobedonostsev wrote in 1896 (in his article "The Great Falsehood of Our Time"). "Out of this," he continued, "grew the theory of parliamentarianism which the misguided masses of the so-called intelligentsia until now have accepted." This theory had, unfortunately, turned some "ignorant Russian heads" and "continues to keep its hold on the minds of some stubborn, narrow fanatics, in spite of the fact that daily its falsity is more clearly revealed to the entire world."

In the early 1860s Pobedonostsev had thought differently. Then he was enthusiastic about the abolition of serfdom and, on March 9, 1861, in a letter to S.P. Engelhardt, a Smolensk landowner, he wrote: "At this time we still have evaluated insufficiently the full importance of this change, but—Good Lord!—what a great change it is. Just stop and think of what Russia will be like *without serfdom!* No longer will there be people who have to think of themselves as property. No one without rights! We are still incapable of comprehending the true significance of all this . . . ."

At this time Pobedonostsev helped prepare the judicial statute of 1864. Koni recalled that he was "particularly insistent on the high principle of public proceedings. He did not approve of the chancellery method of Themis, in which her business was conducted with her eyes blindfolded." Once, when he was lecturing on this theme to Koni and his fellow students, Pobedonostsev argued that when matters are "concealed from the light and examined in secret . . . what is true becomes false; and if the aim of justice is to reflect the truth, to redress and convict falsehood, and consists in the observance of the law, then it cannot fear the light and its entire activities should be conducted openly." If in later years Pobedonostsev was transformed from a liberal into a reactionary, he merely shared the destiny of his partners, Katkov and Tolstoy.

Pobedonostsev's personality was a strange mixture. He enjoyed a good, sharp, subtle intellect and a broad education; yet he was a narrow-minded, intolerant and fanatic obscurantist. He despised humanity and did not believe human nature had retained positive characteristics. Man was so bad that, in his view, the only possibility was to keep him firmly in hand and allow him no opportunity for discussion. As he could not endure diverse opinions, be they political or religious, Pobedonostsev felt a special hatred of the intelligentsia. He believed further that only autocracy promised Russia any chance of progress. Hence he opposed variety in thought and religion, as well as all trends promising authentic progress. "The Sovereign," Pobedonostsev wrote in 1896, "recognizes only one faith from among all others as the true faith, and supports and patronizes only a single church; all remaining churches and faiths are thus excluded. This means that the remaining churches generally are seen as false or only partially orthodox. In practice this is expressed in a number of ways, ranging from non-recognition and censure to outright prosecution."

These principles guided Pobedonostsev and, as Director-General of the Synod, he persecuted Old Believers, sectarians, and members of other religions. During his term in office the so-called "Multansky affair" occurred, when ten Udmurts were charged with a ritual murder. Describing Pobedonostsev as director-general, Koni wrote that he "ruthlessly attacked all elements of contemporary culture, including popular representation, the courts, the press, freedom of conscience, and described them all as 'frauds' and 'deceptions.' " Meanwhile, Koni continued, Pobedonostsev insisted that "the Church's parochial schools were not frauds and deceptions but the preceptors of the nation's spiritual upbringing and virtues." He similarly valued, Koni claimed, "his missionaries, who in the name of Christ invoked the secular sword and submitted fictitious lists of the converts they had brought to the bosom of a loving Mother Church."

The close relations between Pobedonostsev and Alexander III began when the latter was still tsarevich. During the late 1870s they grew still closer, a conclusion confirmed by the many letters sent by Pobedonostsev to the heir. Pobedonostsev began to lecture Alexander from the moment he mounted the throne, and he became not merely his closest political counsellor but, in practice, his mentor. According to Feoktistov, as early as the evening of March 1, 1881 Pobedonostsev was ensconced in the emperor's Anichkov Palace and imploring the new ruler to dismiss Count Loris-Melikov.[31] On March 6 the director-general sent Alexander III a long letter of advice on the future course of government policies. "If they begin," he wrote, "to sing to you their previous siren songs on the necessity of remaining calm, of continuing in the direction of liberalization, and of yielding to so-called public opinion, for the love of God, Your Majesty, do not listen and believe them. This would be a disaster for Russia and yourself. To me this is as clear as day." Once again he advised the tsar to dismiss Loris-Melikov from his position as Minister of the Interior and recommended that Count Nicholas P. Ignatiev be appointed in his place. "Do not keep Count Loris-Melikov," he wrote; "I do not trust him: he is a trickster and capable of playing a double game. If you place yourself in his hands, it will be the ruin of yourself and Russia."

Pobedonostsev was not satisfied with giving the tsar this political advice, but anxiously took it upon himself to go further and to recommend a number of other precautions. "When you go to bed," he wrote on March 11, "please make sure that you yourself bolt all the doors—not only of your bedroom, but of the adjoining rooms, right up to the front door." Before retiring the emperor was advised to check personally the condition of his bell pulls and to examine all the furniture in case terrorists were hiding under the sofas or armchairs. Further, on Pobedonostsev's recommendation, Nicholas M. Baranov was appointed as police chief of St. Petersburg. An adventurer and liar, Baranov's pessimistic outlooks served merely to increase the general mood of panic.

The meeting of the Committee of Ministers of March 8 discussed the so-called "constitution" proposed by Loris-Melikov and the director-general declared himself a resolute opponent of this project. Describing the session in his diary, the war minister, D.A. Miliutin, noted that all the speeches of Sergei G. Stroganov, Lev S. Makov, and Konstantin N. Posiet were colorless and insignificant in comparison with the long, Jesuitical oration delivered by Pobedonostsev. "It was," Miliutin continued, "not only an expression of opposition to the particular measure being discussed, but a complete and indiscriminate condemnation of all the reforms carried out during the previous reign: he dared label all Alexander II's great reforms as criminal errors!" This speech, which was delivered with "rhetorical enthusiasm," seemed to Miliutin "an echo of the vague theories of the Slavophiles." It denied "everything that went to make up European civilization. Many of us could not help shivering nervously at some of the phrases of this reactionary fanatic."

During the months of March and April, 1881, a struggle broke out between the various groups within the government. Pobedonostsev, as leader of the reactionaries, now revealed his great ability in matters of intrigue. In April he "made his peace" with Loris-Melikov, but behind the latter's back he prepared the manifesto of April 29 on the "inviolability of the autocracy." He was, in fact, both the initiator and the author of this proclamation. Further, as previously mentioned, the director-general recommended Ignatiev for the position of Minister of the Interior, but a year later he had him dismissed for proposing to call a *Zemskii Sobor* [Assembly of the Land].[32] Now Pobedonostsev played an important part in getting Count D.A. Tolstoy appointed in Ignatiev's place. Judging by his correspondence with Alexander III, the director-general took a very active part in negotiations on this matter. Later he helped gain the appointment of another reactionary, I.D. Delianov, as Minister of Education.

Pobedonostsev continued to exert great influence during the preparation of the university statute of 1884 and throughout the early 1880s launched and carried through various policies inspired by his own crude nationalism. Then, during the second half of the decade, his influence gradually began to wane. Both Pobedonostsev and others attest to this fact.[33] In July, 1889 the director-general, in a letter to Polovtsov (concerning the appointment of T.I. Filippov as State Controller), wrote: "Unfortunately I am helpless. They pay little attention to me—if they pay any attention at all." Polovtsov, himself a close friend of Pobedonostsev, noted in his diary on October 31, 1889: "At five o'clock Pobedonostsev called on me and complained bitterly that he has been deprived of all influence .... Pobedonostsev said he was determined in the future to keep aloof from everything except the affairs of the Synod. I charged him with being himself the cause of his own misfortunes, as he had got himself too mixed up in matters that did not concern him. In answer to this he contradicted what he had been previously saying, replying: 'Yes, but you evidently don't know how things stood before.' When I had not seen him [the tsar] for two weeks, he used to write me little notes, saying something like: 'I haven't seen you lately. Drop by, for I have many things to discuss with you,' and so on."

Although a number of the director-general's other contemporaries also testify to his loss of influence,[34] the cause of this decline remains to be explained. Basically it seems that although Pobedonostsev had arrogated to himself the job of mentor, he found difficulty in fulfilling the role. In other words, whereas he was able to criticize "all and sundry," the director-general had no positive program of his own.[35] As Count S.G. Stroganov once remarked, "he always knew exactly what should not be done, but never knew what should be done instead." Or, as Anatole N. Kulomzin put it, Pobedonostsev was "imperious by

nature . . . critical of everything, always upset with those who questioned him, and yet he would never suggest anything himself."

COUNT D.A. TOLSTOY

At the end of May, 1882 Alexander III dismissed Ignatiev as Minister of
the Interior and appointed Count Dmitry A. Tolstoy in his stead. Known
to his contemporaries as "the evil genius of Russia," Tolstoy was a very
intelligent and highly educated man. Having graduated from the Alexander Lycée, he became a historian and wrote a number of scholarly
studies.[36] Originally Count Tolstoy was a liberal who counted the poet
and member of the revolutionary Petrashevsky circle, Alexis N. Pleshcheev, and the liberal satirist, Michael E. Saltykov-Shchedrin, among his
closest friends. In his reminiscences Feoktistov recalled that "Tolstoy
and Pleshcheev were inseparable and that Pleshcheev dedicated his first
book of poems to his friend.[37] The ties existing between them were so
close that when Pleshcheev was imprisoned, all their mutual acquaintances assumed Tolstoy would suffer the same fate."

During the 1850s Tolstoy occupied the post of director of the chancellery of the Naval Ministry. He was an "ardent *Konstantinovets*," as
those who shared the political views of Grand Duke Konstantin Nikolaevich were known. (At this time the grand duke was gathering a circle
of the liberal-minded civil service opposition.) Yet during the drafting
of the peasant reforms Tolstoy, the young liberal, grew dissatisfied with
the substance of the plan and went over to the reactionaries. In 1860
he presented to Alexander II a report on the draft law submitted by the
Editorial Commission. Tolstoy proposed that the peasants be given a
farmstead and a third of the land then in their use as a grant, with the
remainder going to the landowners. Apparently this suggestion was
motivated by Tolstoy's own phenomenal stinginess and greed and, as
time went on, his acquisitive instincts grew in strength. During the
1860s he and his wife literally robbed his—or rather, her—serfs by ap-
propriating 441 and a half *desiatinas* of their land.[38]

B.N. Chicherin, who knew Tolstoy well, described him as "an intelligent man of firm character, but a bureaucrat to the core. Narrow and
stubborn, he saw nothing beyond his St. Petersburg world and abhorred
any independence of action or sign of freedom. Being devoid of any
moral sense, he was mendacious, greedy, evil, vindictive, crafty, and
prepared to do anything in order to achieve his personal ends. At the
same time, he carried his servility and obsequiousness to those extreme
limits which pleased the Tsar, but aroused loathing in all decent people."
Chicherin concluded this accurate portrait with the comment that Tolstoy had "been created in order to serve as the instrument of reaction."

By this time Tolstoy was a fervent reactionary. In the summer of 1865 he was named Director-General of the Holy Synod. Most people were surprised by this appointment for Tolstoy had displayed a supreme indifference to matters of faith.[39] But personal piety was not expected of a director-general, and even perfect atheists were appointed to the post. In any case other considerations held much more importance. One was the fact that Tolstoy was a fervent admirer of the religious reform of Peter the Great (who had envisaged the Church as simply another government department). According to Feoktistov, Tolstoy believed that "every bishop in the very depth of his soul cherishes the dream of becoming Pope; if you give them more independence the bishops will use every means at their disposal to attempt to subordinate the state to the Church."

His view of the role and significance of the Church accorded perfectly with the attitudes and interests of the autocracy. Then, after Dmitry V. Karakozov's attempt on the life of Alexander II in 1866,[40] Tolstoy was appointed Minister of Education as well as director-general. While holding these posts he managed to earn the hatred of every segment of the public—from the revolutionary intellectuals to the highest bureaucrats. In a letter to his secretary Loris-Melikov wrote that Tolstoy, "by his brutal, arrogant, and often clumsy methods, was able to unite against himself not only the teachers and students, but even his own family." Therefore the government, when it decided to adopt a more liberal course after the bomb explosion in the Winter Palace in February, 1880, made the dismissal of Tolstoy one of its first measures.[41] This action brought Loris-Melikov great popularity. "The dismissal of this Minister of Education," Nicholas K. Mikhailovsky wrote in the *Leaflet of the People's Will,* "is the real merit of the dictator." Tolstoy's dismissal had been difficult to obtain and the event was a major victory for Loris-Melikov. "After two months of work and effort," he wrote to his secretary, "I was at last successful in getting Count Tolstoy—that evil genius of Russia—replaced. This was greeted with general joy throughout the realm. Everyone remembers how, even in the Winter Palace, people embraced at the morning service and greeted each other with the words: 'Tolstoy is replaced—He is replaced indeed'."[42]

Tolstoy's reappointment in 1882, now as Minister of the Interior, revealed to everyone that the government seriously intended to pursue the reactionary goals announced in the manifesto of April 29, 1881. Yet the appointment evidently took Tolstoy himself by surprise. A.V. Golovnin told Miliutin that, according to one of Tolstoy's friends, when Alexander III offered him the post Tolstoy replied that he found it "difficult to accept, as the Sovereign did not know him." Alexander was surprised, and pointed out that he had read reports prepared by Tolstoy, where-upon the latter replied that this meant merely that the emperor knew him as a Minister of Education. Otherwise, Tolstoy said, "his opinions on matters of internal administration were unknown to His Majesty. The Emperor would scarcely wish to have as his Minister a man who was convinced that the reforms of the previous reign had been a mistake; who believed that earlier we had had a tranquil and prosperous popula-tion, ruled by the more educated (the serf-owning gentry); that then the various branches of the government did not get in each other's hair; and that local affairs had been managed by government agencies con-trolled by other agencies of the same authority. The Sovereign could not really want a man who believes that the population now consists of a ruined, beggarly, drunken, discontented peasantry and a ruined, dis-satisfied gentry; that the courts continually hamper the police; that six hundred talkative zemstvos are opposing the government; and that, in view of all this, the job of the Minister of the Interior would seem to be not to increase, but to paralyse all opposition to the government."

As might be expected, this declaration only impressed Alexander III and in no way weakened his determination concerning the appointment. But Tolstoy, just as when he had become Minister of Education, began his career in the Ministry of the Interior without a proper program.[43] Not until 1885 did he receive a plan of action from A.D. Pazukhin, one of the most active representatives of the gentry. This plan was actually a program for counter-reform. Making Pazukhin the director of his chancellery, Tolstoy, with his own characteristic stubborness and the help of Katkov, set out to implement policies of aristocratic reaction. His efforts were cut short only by his death. This caused the emperor great sorrow and, on April 25, 1889, he wrote in his notebook: "Poor Count Tolstoy is done for. It's a terrible loss! So sad!"

M.N. KATKOV

Michael Nikiforovich Katkov, the ideological inspiration and troubadour of Tolstoy's political reaction, was the son of poor parents. Although his father was a personal noble who served in the Moscow provincial administration, he had died young. Katkov's mother, according to his friend, Alexis V. Stankevich, was a matron in one of the Moscow prisons. Despite this handicap, Katkov received a good education and, finishing his studies in the philological faculty of Moscow University in 1838, he passed his Master's examinations in 1839. By this time he had entered the literary world, first as a translator and then as the author of his own works. He became a regular contributor of articles and reviews to the journals *Moscow Observer* and *Notes of the Fatherland.*

Even as a child he had shown an uncommon ability in scholarship. A.V. Stankevich, who studied with Katkov at the boarding school of Professor M.G. Pavlov, recalled that even then he was "a big, serious boy, who seemed older than the rest. Among his comrades he was not known for his gaiety or friendliness. . . . I remember him as being a rather thick-set lad of fifteen who almost always—even during the recreation periods—had a book in his hand."

In 1837, while still a student, Katkov joined the group or "circle" of Nicholas V. Stankevich (though only after the latter had already gone abroad). There he became friendly with Vasily P. Botkin, Vissarion G. Belinsky, and Michael A. Bakunin, among others.[44] It was during this period that Katkov became infatuated with German philosophy, firstly that of Schelling and later that of Hegel. He and Belinsky became close friends and the latter's many approving comments about Katkov belong to this period. For instance, in his letter of November 1, 1837 to M.A. Bakunin, Belinsky described Katkov as "a nice fellow" who "will go far because he already believes in being reconciled to life. A lucid mind and a pure heart—this is Katkov."

This friendship lasted for a few years, but in the early 1840s Belinsky began to realize that while Katkov's mind was really "lucid," his heart was far from being "pure." In a letter to V.P. Botkin, dated February 6, 1843, he described Katkov somewhat differently: "Here is a Khlesta-kov[45] in the German style. I now understand why, when I was caught up in my imaginary friendship with him, I was so strongly struck by his glassy green eyes. You were never sufficiently concerned with his brutal crimes against the truth, but—and honor and glory to you for this—you were still absolutely correct in your assessment of his nature. You saw into the very heart of the man. And it is not that he has changed; he has only become more truly himself. Now he is a heap of philosophical sh. . . . We must wage a struggle to obliterate and conquer him."

Apart from the baser qualities in Katkov's nature, Belinsky was repelled by his defense of the reactionary doctrines of Schelling and his hostility to the socialist ideas which captivated Belinsky. "Katkov," wrote A.V. Stankevich, "never had that quality which people call decency in a man. For some reason this was absent in his relations with others. He was arrogant and could stand having only those about him who bowed completely to his authority and allowed themselves to be used unquestionably as his tools and obedient servants."

After 1845 Katkov occupied himself with teaching, and for five years was an assistant lecturer in philosophy at Moscow University. Then, beginning in 1851, he spent a further five years as editor of the university newspaper, *Moscow News,* and after 1856 joined Professor P.M. Leontiev in editing the *Russian Herald*. During the next few years, when public opinion grew agitated in the wake of the Crimean War, Katkov was a moderate liberal. He wrote widely in favor of the British form of government and supported the abolition of serfdom as well as the projects for reforming the government. He was particularly enthusiastic about the proposed zemstvos and the new judicial system. In 1861, in an issue of the *Contemporary Chronicle* (which appeared as a supplement of the *Russian Herald*), Katkov argued for the British system and wrote: "I know it is impossible, but a citizen should be in such a position that he does not have to conceal his thoughts and say what he does not believe. Yet in England, more than anywhere else, this is precisely the situation." By such arguments he tried to stress the possibility of peaceful change. "The English teach a method of reform without revolution and we have nothing to lose by emulating them."

In 1863 the *Moscow News* was leased to Katkov, and Leontiev and Katkov began to move towards a more reactionary stance. This change of face took several years to complete, but its first symptoms coincided with the Polish uprising.[46] After 1866, when the government adopted a policy of open reaction, Katkov became its troubadour. He openly attacked the judicial statute, the zemstvos, and other recent reforms. The question arises as to what real change in views was reflected by this change in behavior. A.V. Stankevich gave one possible answer. He observed: "We have already spoken of Katkov's lack of real conviction and well-defined ideas. Since he did not have these to guide him in his activities, the question remains open as to his goals." And, Stankevich concluded, "the aim of his efforts was the satisfaction of his own pride and love of power." On the other hand, this change in behavior may well have resulted from a natural evolution in Katkov's views, especially as conservative principles can already be discerned in his attitudes as early as the 1840s.

Whatever the case, his articles in the *Moscow News* became particularly sharp and abusive. Speaking of these, one contemporary, Alexander V. Nikitenko, recalled that "the government on certain occasions found it necessary to chain up its watchdog (M.N. K[atkov]). At times it would turn him loose, and then not know how to control him." Actually, the government frequently tried to keep Katkov quiet—especially in the latter 1880s—but such attempts did not always meet with success.

Katkov's influence upon the government and its policies was not only a result of his journalism. The direct influence he could bring to bear on the ministers, and at times on the tsar himself, was also of major importance. Because he was particularly interested in education policy, the Minister of Education was always a primary object of attention.

Count Tolstoy, who assumed this position in 1866 and held no particular ideas as to what he should do, immediately became Katkov's captive. Tolstoy, Feoktistov says, "knew only that he must do something, but as to just what—this was his insoluble riddle."

Here Katkov could help and he prepared a program for Tolstoy. Indeed, Katkov not only told him what to do, he even recommended his own confident, A.I. Georgievsky, who soon became Tolstoy's right-hand man. As chairman of the Committee of Studies, Georgievsky was installed as Katkov's plenipotentiary within the ministry and it is no exaggeration to say that all education policies implemented during the latter 1860s and 1870s originated with the editor of the *Moscow News*. Georgievsky faithfully kept him informed about everything that occurred within the ministry and then received the appropriate instructions. The reform of the gymnasiums in the early 1870s, the preparation of a draft for a new university statute, and many other policies—all these were inspired by Katkov. Although he did manage to exert some influence on government policies in other fields, he was nowhere as successful as in the area of education.

Katkov reached the pinnacle of his glory during the reign of Alexander III. The editor of the *Moscow News* fully shared the political ideals of the emperor and his newspaper became recognized as a vehicle of government opinion. But as an official newspaper it proved somewhat peculiar and at times a minister, or sometimes even a complete policy, was sharply and boldly attacked in the name of Katkov's own ideal of autocracy. For Katkov envisaged the forces of reaction waging an offensive on every front and resolutely condemned everything connected with the reforms of the 1860s and 1870s. He greeted Alexander III's manifesto of April 29, 1881, which reaffirmed the principle of autocracy, with a burst of enthusiasm. "Now," he wrote in the *Moscow News* leading article for April 30, "we can breathe freely. It is an end to half-heartedness, an end to differences of opinion. . . . The nation's soul has been hungering for these regal words as for manna from Heaven. It holds our salvation! It has restored an autocratic and Russian Tsar to the Russian people!" Later Katkov helped obtain Tolstoy's appointment as Minister of the Interior. This gave him particular satisfaction and, in speaking of Tolstoy, he exclaimed: "His very name is in itself a manifesto and a program."

Throughout these years Katkov seemed omnipotent. The *Moscow News* was transformed into an independent government department that worked out proposals on various issues of internal policy. The editor wrote in February, 1884 in a letter to Alexander III: "*My newspaper was not simply a newspaper, for at times it played a role in the government's activity. Not only did it reflect events, many decisions were reached within it. It took part in events, and it will be left to history not only to bear witness as to what was done, but also to judge whether these decisions were correct or not."*

The *Moscow News'* editorial offices on Strestnoi Boulevard became a veritable Canossa[47] to which various statesmen attacked by Katkov would come, hats in hand. In the early 1880s he devoted his energy almost exclusively to the battle against the university statute of 1863. Together with Pobedonostsev, Katkov conducted a vendetta against Baron Alexander P. Nikolai, the Minister of Education. "I recently had the good fortune," he wrote Alexander III on February 7, 1882, "to be able personally to speak with full frankness to Your Majesty about the situation in the Ministry of Education and to give my opinion about the only sure way that now exists out of these difficulties (that is, the dismissal of Nikolai). Your Highness, by Your own wise and autocratic decision, save the children and youths of Your future reign!" Once Nikolai had been replaced by Katkov's friend, I.D. Delianov, matters moved more swiftly and in 1884 a new university statute was promulgated.

The editor of the *Moscow News* also exerted great influence in foreign affairs. During the 1880s he declared himself an ardent Germanophobe and called for a *rapprochement* with France. Meanwhile Katkov waged major campaigns against Finance Minister Bunge and Foreign Minister Nicholas K. Giers. Since he had his agents situated in all the highest government offices, the editor often could print information in his newspaper that was unavailable to other journalists.

In 1885 Katkov placed A.D. Pazukhin's article, "The Present Situation in Russia and the Question of Estates," in the *Russian Herald*. In the article Pazukhin suggested a detailed program of counter-reform. This aimed at destroying the reforms of the 1860s and 1870s and envisaged the creation of local institutions of a class nature, in which the gentry would play the major role. Thereupon Pazukhin became Katkov's apprentice in the fullest sense of the word. Evidently with the latter's help, he was appointed director of the chancellery of the Ministry of the Interior by Tolstoy. From that time on he played a leading role in the work of preparing new legislation. But Pazukhin's own guide, both ideologically and otherwise, was Katkov. He directed Pazukhin (sending him instructions by letter) while the latter kept his ideological chief fully informed on the progress made in preparing new measures. At times Pazukhin even sought Katkov's personal assistance. In a letter of July 7, 1886 he wrote Katkov: "Tomorrow K.P. Pobedonostsev leaves for the south and will stop in Moscow for two or three days. You will, in all likelihood, be seeing him. It would be useful if you could try to free him from the influence of Manasein (the Minister of Justice) who is more than ever becoming his master."

In reality Katkov was all-powerful. On December 10, 1886 Polovtsov, in his diary, thus described his influence: "Alongside the legal government of the state there has been established a kind of shadow government in the person of the editor of the *Moscow News*. He has a great number of accomplices at the highest administrative levels, including Delianov, Ostrovsky, Pobedonostsev, Vyshnegradsky and Pazukhin. This entire cabal gathers at Katkov's . . . and openly discusses the necessity of replacing such-and-such a minister with some other person, or of pursuing this policy with regard to that question. In short, they impudently issue their own commands, publish their censure or praise and, in the final analysis, achieve their aims."

Hence it is no exaggeration to maintain that Katkov was one of the foremost figures of the reign of Alexander III, even though he usually acted behind the scenes. Sometimes his articles—especially those on foreign policy—brought the emperor's wrath upon his head. Such outbursts were, however, of short duration and it was never long before the editor of the *Moscow News* again found his proper place in the heart of his sovereign. During this period Katkov received the rank of privy councillor, and his daughter was created a maid of honor to the empress.

But what were the moral qualities of this powerful figure? The following appraisal, given by the Moscow liberal, B.N. Chicherin, appears the most accurate: "He entered the field of journalism at a time when the bonds that constricted Russian thought had been loosed and journalists had gained a position of major importance. By his own talent and intelligence he won first place among his fellows; but then, instead of holding high the noble banner bequeathed by his predecessors, he cast aside both the restraints of morality and of literary decency. It was he who schooled Russian writers and the Russian public in the arts of brazen deception and foul language, as well as to a contempt for all humanity. He was an example of a corrupt journalist who, misusing his education and talents, achieved unprecedented success through insolence and flattery. He then turned success into an instrument for achieving his own selfish ends."

Here the evidence of State Secretary Polovtsov also merits attention. He wrote in his diary that, according to the ex-Minister of Finance, Alexander A. Abaza, "Katkov's heirs found in his papers evidence of the fact that [Lazar S.] Poliakov had been paying their father the yearly sum of 35,000 rubles. Supposing that this money represented the interest of some capital invested with Poliakov, the heirs asked that the capital be returned. Poliakov replied, however, that there was no such capital, but that he had been, in fact, paying Katkov 35,000 a year for his [Katkov's] articles in the *Moscow News*."[48]

In his youth Katkov's views were not distinguished by their firmness (it is possible that he sometimes simply followed the fashion) but this certainly was not the case after the 1860s. Then he firmly believed in what he was writing and sought to establish a single, reactionary school of thought in Russia. It is evident that for him this meant that the doctrines of Orthodoxy, Autocracy and Nationality were to be the only school of social thought. His predecessor in this was "Kuzma Prutkov,"[49] who had once proposed a scheme entitled "The Introduction of Conformity of Thought in Russia." Katkov's last words were: "I sought conformity." But in this he failed.

PRINCE MESHCHERSKY

Prince Vladimir Petrovich Meshchersky was the kind of man about whom "no one ever speaks a kind word." Lacking even the ordinary standards of human decency, meddlesome, insolent, and an unprincipled toady, Meshchersky was a petty informer and tattler, as well as a creature of perverted sexual tastes. At the same time he was still another troubadour of conservatism, editor of the newspaper, *Citizen*, and an extravagant novelist who wrote pulp novels about life in high society. Even Meshchersky's political compatriots spoke of him with a touch of distaste. Thus Feoktistov described him as "a brazen scoundrel and a man without conscience or principles, but one who declared himself to be an ardent and zealous patriot." Furthermore, "although he never uttered a caustic comment about devotion to either Church or Throne, all decent men were disgusted by his verbiage and no one could, or would, believe in his sincerity."

Alexander III and Meshchersky became friends in the early 1860s and were already very close when the former became tsarevich. Judging by Meshchersky's letters to Alexander, the friendship began in 1862 when the future emperor was seventeen years old. They were very intimate and Meshchersky wrote without ceremony, addressing Alexander in familiar terms. Feoktistov, in his recollections, says that the young grand duke was then paying court to Meshchersky's sister. Whatever the truth of this story, during the latter 1860s the tsarevich broke with his friend. This occurred, Feoktistov maintained, because Meshchersky proved to be an embezzler,[50] but the latter naturally had a different explanation. He claimed that someone had "slandered" him, turning Maria Fedorovna abruptly against him, so that she forbade her husband to see him again. Alexander's brothers, he said, also had a large share in "defaming" him (evidently Vladimir and Alexis, as Sergei and Paul were then still too young to have played any part in the business).

It is possible that this "slander" consisted of a charge of "embezzling." What is more important is that the heir to the throne did not completely finish with his former friend. In the early 1870s Meshchersky, in a letter marked "Read and Burn" requested—and received— 80,000 rubles for his private use to meet the costs of publishing a newspaper.[51] It is typical of Meshchersky's insolence that he told the tsarevich how the money should be obtained, so that no one could discover the purpose. "In order to avoid any talk, you should write the Court Treasurer: 'Give to me by such and such a date 80,000 rubles,' and say nothing else. You can call me in the next day and give me the money. In the event of questions about its expenditure, you should say: 'I needed it,' and nothing else."[52]

Despite this crude approach the money was apparently forthcoming, for in that same year (1872) publication of the Citizen began. Nonetheless, Meshchersky's insolence and importunate behavior had irritated Alexander. Meshchersky wrote to him, pleading: "You accuse me of being infinitely demanding in general, as well as of using every particular pretext for a request. Alas, I must admit that the charge is fair enough, because such demands are an inevitable product of my restless character." In another letter he wrote: "If you were not so terribly implacable, I would resolve to dare throw myself at your feet and, on my knees, say to you: Dredge up and forgive everything that makes the present so difficult and the future seem so gloomy and dreadful, so that from this I might draw the courage to beg you for a pardon . . . ." This new quarrel seems to have been rooted in more requests for money, but a complete rupture was still avoided. In the letter just quoted, Meshchersky announced plans to travel abroad and wrote: "In order not to compromise you, I will correspond via K(onstantin) Petr(ovich) Pob(edonostsev) . . . ."[53] In this way Meshchersky remained in touch with the tsarevich through the latter's tutor, and it is a fact that Meshchersky did not see Alexander once during the ten years from 1873 to 1883.[54]

When Alexander became tsar, he saw Meshchersky more frequently. During the summer of 1883 they evidently met in secret.[55] Meshchersky also wrote the emperor regularly and sometimes received letters in return—evidently through Pobedonostsev. Some time in the mid-1880s Meshchersky began to send the emperor not only letters but also his diaries, which were really letters written in a diary form. As previously mentioned, these lent him an opportunity of ingratiating himself with Alexander III. In one of the first of these notes, he wrote: "The Sovereign granted me the favor and joy of permitting me to write a diary with the purpose of having him read it."[56] In another entry we read: "It is difficult to express just how happy I am today. My meeting and conversation with my Sovereign have firmly convinced me that he values sincere words just as much as previously . . . ." Frequently the diary notes contain denunciations not only of Meshchersky's enemies but also of his closest compatriots.

He condemned Grand Duke Vladimir Alexandrovich and his wife for support of the Baltic Germans, informed on Pobedonostsev's improper conduct in establishing a trusteeship over the von Derviz estate, attacked Katkov (following his death) for contacts with the Jews, and made many similar accusations against others.

Relations between Alexander III and Meshchersky clearly remained close, if conspiratorial in nature. Until 1887 Pobedonostsev played the role of middleman, and it was through him that Alexander III sent his letters and announced his desire to see Meshchersky. But in that year Pobedonostsev's relations with Meshchersky were ruptured. On December 31, 1887, in a letter to Pobedonostsev marked "for you alone," Meschersky wrote: "During the last two months always there has been some good fellow to bring me a daily report of the merciless and evil opinions and the terrible words with which you have been branding me." This charge seems to have been justified. On October 21, 1887 Admiral I.A. Shestakov noted in his diary: "They are saying that Meshchersky has been given a subsidy of 120,000 after which he gave a dinner for Delianov and some others. The next day Pobedonostsev supposedly congratulated Delianov on having dined with a man who the previous day had been caught with a trumpet player of the Guards." Having recorded this, Shestakov remarked: "This astonished me, as I had considered Pobedonostsev to be Meshchersky's patron."

Alexander's intimacy with Meschersky became a scandal among the liberal public and in official circles. One observer, A.N. Kulomzin, wrote in his memoirs: "Russia's misfortunes consisted of, among other things, two circumstances in particular. The first was the [Emperor's] intimacy . . . with Prince V.P. Meshchersky, who had come to be a friend of the former heir.[57] In spite of his undoubted intelligence and literary talent, Prince Meshchersky was not the type of man whose objectivity suited him for the task of being a counsellor. Quite the contrary: who can forget the passion and sharpness with which he assaulted any person whom he suspected of liberalism or the extremely rash way in which he spread gossip as if it were fact, only to apologize when the stories were later proven to be false? Who can forget those banal eulogies that he would write when he hoped for some kind of favour from a minister . . . or his groundless assaults on other ministers, which would suddenly be broken off when the object of the attack humbly appeared before

him—having come to Canossa. Finally, who can forget the vague conclusions with which he would accompany his discussion of any point of
policy, but which never contained any concrete suggestion."

General A.A. Kireev, who belonged to conservative, Slavophile circles,
was particularly indignant over the emperor's patronage of the *Citizen*.
In 1887 he noted in his diary: "A gift of 100,000 rubles to Meshchersky for the publication of his paper! And this (instead of exiling M[esh-
chersky] to Siberia) at the very moment when we are putting all our
efforts into cutting expenses." Kireev further observed that "by an evil
irony of fate this sum was taken from the budget of institutions for
women's education (the Fourth Sec[tion]). Clearly this enemy of education for women has managed to harm its financial support."

Why did Alexander III become so close to Meshchersky? There is no
doubt that he must have been sickened by a number of the darker sides
of Meshchersky's nature, and in character the two men were very
different. It seems, though, that the emperor was greatly impressed by
the political convictions of the editor of the *Citizen*. And this, despite
the fact that many of Meshchersky's moral qualities would otherwise
have alienated the sovereign, brought them together.

Meshchersky's political beliefs were the quintessence of reaction.
Some impression of their nature may be gained by glancing at only two
of his pronouncements, taken from the diaries he sent to Alexander III.
The first is a hymn to the birch, regarding which Meshchersky wisely
observed: "There is nothing in Russia that the people recognize as the
unquestioned truth. Here is the basis for the use of the birch. Meanwhile
everyone is aligned resolutely against this necessity. The opponents are
not only the liberals, but include conservatives such as Tolstoy, Ostrovsky, and Co. Yet everywhere one goes, only a single cry is heard from
the people: Beat, beat! In answer to this, what do the authorities reply?
Anything, except the birch. What is the result of this contradiction?—A
terrible lack of discipline, the destruction of the father's authority within the family, drunkenness, crime, and so on . . . . I see only two
real governors—Tatishchev of Penza and Anastasiev of Chernigov. It is
as if they both had come to the same conclusion: there is nothing that
the people fear except the birch. Where there are blows there is order;
there one has far less drunkenness; there is found greater respect for
fathers; and there the prosperity is greater."[58]

The second extract appears to have been Meshchersky's program for
education. After the discovery of a student plot against the emperor's
life led by Alexander I. Ulianov and Peter Ya. Shevyrev, on March 1,
1887, Meshchersky turned his attention to this area of government
policy. In his diary he railed at Delianov for indecision, writing: "And it

would be so simple to have ended all this: stop the entrance of new students to 150 gymnasiums this year, leaving one school for every two provinces; in each of these establish a boarding school; with the savings from the 150 closed gymnasiums, progymnasiums and modern schools [Realschulen] establish professional and vocational schools; and then gradually limit the universities to an average of 500 to 800 students. This done, there would be a maximum of fifty students in each course in each faculty."

Prince Meshchersky had written to Alexander III earlier on this subject in his "Diary Fragments" for 1884 and 1885. At that time he had suggested a need for a sharp increase in tuition fees: "For tuition in a gymnasium or progymnasium a fee of not less than 200 rubles a year in the provinces and 300 rubles a year in Moscow and Petersburg (that is, an increase of from 10 to 15 times) should be charged and a certain percentage of the non-propertied classes should be admitted, on crown scholarships established on the basis of examination marks." He proposed a similar policy for university education, with the tuition fees to be raised to 200 rubles a year "and, in addition, a deposit to guarantee the keep (of the student) of not less than fifty rubles a month in the capitals and forty in other cities." Stipends were to be abolished but a "certain percentage" of "crown pensioners" might live in "crown" lodgings, apparently depending on the "crown" for everything (as in a barracks).

It is hardly necessary to comment on these proposals, although it might be observed that throughout the entire nineteenth century no other reactionary statesman or public figure in Russia recommended such stern measures. Meshchersky's advice, which would, in fact, have meant the end of any real "enlightenment,"[59] was echoed only by the satirist Saltykov-Shchedrin's heroes, who believed it was necessary to "bury science." This sketch of Meshchersky completes the present account of the close associates of Emperor Alexander III, himself both poorly educated and limited in ability.

CHAPTER II

GOVERNMENT POLICY

THE EARLY YEARS

The reign of Alexander III may be divided generally into two periods. The first opened with D.A. Tolstoy's appointment in May, 1882 and lasted until the end of 1885. During this time the government openly declared its reactionary intentions, but no actual program of reactionary reforms yet existed. Only the first steps were taken: the new university statute and the Provisional Regulations for the Press were approved. Apart from these measures, little was achieved.

Behind this inactivity lay the fear of the revolutionary terrorists. This fear gripped the government both during the coronation of 1883 and afterwards. Peasant discontent was also a factor. In 1883 and 1884 this increased and, although it was still very small in scale, the number of outbreaks more than doubled such instances during the years 1879 to 1881. As a result the government did not even dare to disband the Kakhanov Commission, which was detested as a liberal "talk shop" by everyone in the reactionary camp. Nonetheless, during these years the general contours of future reactionary developments—which held the aim of strengthening the role of the landed gentry—became apparent.

In May, 1883, at the time of his coronation, Alexander III greeted a group of peasant elders who were being presented to him with the order: "Listen to your Marshals." These words were underlined by the ceremony accompanying the declaration. Katkov, describing the event in the lead article of the *Moscow News* for May 22, stressed that "when the district elders entered the Court to congratulate His Majesty, these representatives of the peasantry were grouped by provinces. At the head of each group came the Marshal of the Nobility . . . . Turning to the peasants, His Majesty was then pleased to greet them with the most gracious words concerning the presence of the Marshals of the Nobility, who thus united in one being their own as well as the other estate."

A further and especially strong indication of the gentry's predominant role was contained in the manifesto marking the centennial in 1885 of the Charter of the Nobility. "We recognize as being beneficial for the realm," the manifesto read, "that the Russian nobility, in the present as in the past, should retain the foremost place in military leadership, in affairs of the local administrations and courts, in the disinterested care of the indigent, and in the spreading, by their own example, of the maxims of faith and loyalty and of sound principles in national education." Polovtsov, writing of this centennial celebration in his diary, noted that "throughout these festivities one hears about a sharp change in the government's policy . . . . This may be excellent, but one should not swing too far in the opposite direction."

In these ways the general shape of a program of aristocratic reaction was outlined during the first half of the 1880s. During this same period the emperor's closest circle of advisers—Pobedonostsev, Tolstoy, Katkov, and Meshchersky—waged a battle to exclude from the government "members of the differently-minded party." Their first objective was the rejection of the "liberal charter" or constitution proposed by Loris-Melikov. In this struggle the "quartet" was joined by Minister of State Domains M.N. Ostrovsky.

A typical bureaucrat and careerist, Ostrovsky originally had been close to Loris-Melikov. Michael S. Kakhanov claimed that Ostrovsky, at the moment when Loris-Melikov's more liberal policies were winning support, offered the latter his services. But later Ostrovsky became a supporter of Ignatiev, and then betrayed him as well. Minister of Justice Dmitry N. Nabokov described Ostrovsky in unflattering terms to D.A. Miliutin. He had, Nabokov said, "proved much more harmful than anyone could have imagined. He was an ambitious intriguer. Having won Katkov's friendship, he did his best to please him and interfered in other people's business even when this had nothing to do with the work of his own ministry."[1]

Here the "liberal party" under attack by the reactionaries should be defined. In general it included liberal bureaucrats who had adopted more or less moderate positions. "This party or, to be precise, coalition of ambitions," Katkov wrote in 1886, "suffered a defeat the day of April 29, 1881. Yet, judging by the declarations in its press . . . it does not consider itself entirely beaten. It has merely retreated, but has not abandoned the field, having, it believes, only lost some positions temporarily. And, having maintained other positions, it still can maintain watch over events and actively intervene in them." Katkov claimed that "formerly this party pinned its hopes on the Ministries of Education, Justice, and Finance, and even then only on the last two. Now these hopes center solely on the last one, for it controls the country's vital forces." Hence it would appear that the representatives of this "party" were A.P. Nikolai, D.N. Nabokov, and N.Khi Bunge, the Ministers of Education, Justice, and Finance respectively. The battle was carried on against them in this precise order and Baron Nikolai became the first victim of the reactionaries' onslaughts. These began in the last months of Ignatiev's term as Minister of the Interior and ultimately

I.D. Delianov, one of Tolstoy's closest aides, was appointed Minister of Education.

Delianov was a stupid man—a "clown."[2] Being lazy and lacking initiative, he remained obedient to the wishes of those in power. Katkov had good grounds for telling Feoktistov: "I know very well that Ivan Davidovich is a feeble fellow who has proved to be 'all thumbs' at his work. But I will keep a careful eye on him. As long as I am here he will not make a solitary step without seeking my advice." After his appointment as Minister of Education, Delianov presented to the State Council the draft of a new university statute that Tolstoy had prepared earlier. The reactionaries' belief that this was a most important reform is revealed by Katkov's letter to Pobedonostsev, dated November 27, 1883. "University reform," Katkov wrote, "should be the first basic measure of the present reign; after it others must unquestionably follow in the judicial department, in local administration, and so forth." Delianov, notwithstanding the opposition of the State Council, succeeded in getting this new university statute approved (although not quite in the form that Katkov wished).

Nabokov, the Minister of Justice, was the reactionaries' second target. Here most criticisms were levelled against the judicial statute of 1864, and particularly against the principles of an independent judiciary, public proceedings, and jury trials. Meshchersky, for instance, wrote in one of the diaries he prepared for Alexander III: "All Russia had discovered from the experience of twenty years of woe that trial by jury is a disgrace and an abomination; that public court proceedings are poisonous; that an irremovable judiciary is an absurdity; and so on. And meanwhile, what an absence of courage there is in the business of altering the judicial statute; what alleged *wise prudence* and, in this same matter, what *terror* there is of doing simply and firmly what is necessary to fulfill the desires of all Russia and to strengthen the autocracy in the opinion of the judicial department." Katkov and Pobedonostsev were even more active in their attacks upon the judicial statute. The Director-General of the Holy Synod, who otherwise advanced no positive program of his own, did, at the end of 1885, present to the emperor a special report on the necessity for judicial reform. At the top of his list of items to be changed were the independent judiciary and jury trials.

The Minister of Justice, D.N. Nabokov, made no attempt to conciliate Meshchersky, Pobedonostsev and Katkov. He assumed naively that Alexander III supported the existing judicial system. Miliutin recorded in his diary that the sovereign, according to Nabokov, "frequently expressed a firm wish to support and strengthen the existing basis of our judicial structure." Miliutin further maintained, again according to the minister himself, that "Nabokov has had very frank discussions with the Emperor on this matter and always found him to have healthy—and not at all retrograde—opinions. He in no way shares Katkov's hatred of the whole judicial department." But it seems that Nabokov was prone to interpret his own hopes as reality, for Alexander III and his minister actually had very different ideas on strengthening and supporting the "basis of the existing judicial structure." Nabokov tried in every possible way to preserve intact the existing judicial order and continued his efforts even in 1885 when, on the insistence of the reactionaries, efforts were made to liquidate the independence of judges by creating a Supreme Disciplinary Office.

But Nabokov was forced to maneuver continually. In the spring of 1884 Pobedonostsev wrote A.N. Shakhov, the president of the Moscow Judicial Bench: "I consider the reform of our judicial system an *urgent necessity*. Nabokov does not contradict me; only he is always preparing projects rather than carrying them out, and all the while promising that he will make an immediate start." Consequently, despite all his equivocation, Nabokov was dismissed at the end of 1885. "Dear Dmitry Nikolaevich," wrote Alexander III, "you are well aware of the deficiencies of our courts and of my desire to see them remedied. With regret I see that my wishes are not being fulfilled with enough dispatch and therefore I must request your resignation as Minister of Justice."

Senator N.A. Manasein, a protégé of Pobedonostsov, was appointed to replace Nabokov. Nonetheless, Meshchersky was dissatisfied and in his letter-diary earlier had informed the emperor of the rumors surrounding Nabokov's dismissal and the possible appointment of Manasein. "The latter," he wrote, "is an intelligent man, but of a boundlessly passionate and highly democratic turn of mind. His appointment would inevitably introduce a *hatred* of the role of the gentry into the judicial sphere." It might be added that Meshchersky's ideas about Manasein's democratic and anti-gentry attitudes were, to say the least, very exaggerated. Still, as long as he was Minister of Justice no real infringement of the judicial statute occurred and he never prepared any plan for judicial counter-reform. For this a new Minister of Justice proved necessary. Manasein's own behavior in complicated situations (brought about by such matters as the conviction of the Lutheran pastors and the discussion of the law on land captains) demonstrated that he would not always act against his conscience. Indeed, on certain occasions he displayed real civic courage.

The reactionaries now turned on the third of the "pillars of liberalism," the Minister of Finance, N.Kh. Bunge. Famed as an economist and a specialist in police law, Bunge had been professor and then rector at the University of Kiev. He was appointed minister when A.A. Abaza retired at the time of the manifesto of April 29, 1881. Viewed objectively, Bunge's economic thought and financial policies were progressive in nature. This fact strengthened the belief of the reactionary ideologues that he was a political sympathizer of Abaza and Loris-Melikov. The newspapers of Meshchersky and Katkov, along with the rest of the reactionary press, systematically heaped torrents of filthy abuse upon Bunge with complete impunity.

In this connection the diary of E.M. Feoktistov, the head of the Main Directorate of the Press, is particularly informative. On January 9, 1886, he wrote: "Last Saturday (January 4) Count Tolstoy passed on to me a letter he had received from Bunge, the Minister of Finance. It began very solemnly: 'While I am indifferent to everything that the press may say about me personally, I cannot, however, disregard that which affects the ministry entrusted to me.' Then a series of complaints about the press followed . . . . This is not Bunge's first attempt to protect himself from his critics. But the howls against him grow stronger daily and Count T(olstoy) is convinced that the criticism is fully justified. What can one do in such a case? 'I am,' said T(olstoy), 'raising this question for the Sovereign's decision; Bunge's letter gives me a good opportunity to talk about his financial measures in general. For some years I have been receiving reports of ruin from every side—and we are headed toward a *Pugachevshchina*.'[3] Yesterday, on returning from a meeting with the Sovereign, Tolstoy sent me the following note: 'With regard to the Minister of Finance's letter on the curbing of our press, there is no necessity for taking any kind of action and one need not answer him.' Here is another warning for Bunge."

All four representatives of reaction—Tolstoy, Katkov, Pobedonostsev, and Meshchersky—actively persecuted Bunge. Tolstoy denounced him as politically unreliable and informed the tsar that persons with seditious connections were working in the Ministry of Finance.[4] Katkov's lead article in the *Moscow News* on February 26, 1886 claimed that the party defeated on April 29, 1881 now had placed all hope on the Minister of Finance. Pobedonostsev, through Nicholas P. Smirnov, his deputy and Assistant Director-General of the Holy Synod, sharply criticized the state of the finances and accused Bunge of carrying out policies that contradicted the basic guidelines established by Alexander III.

Evidently the emperor was influenced by all this pressure and in the end he agreed to remove Bunge. "I am convinced," he told Meshchersky, "that I must part from Bunge," and the question was settled by the end of 1886. But Bunge was not retired. Instead he was appointed chairman of the Committee of Ministers, a post that was largely honorary inasmuch as a Minister of Finance played a greater role in politics than did a chairman of the ministerial committee. But, while Ivan A. Vyshnegradsky, who was recommended by Meshchersky, replaced Bunge as Minister of Finance, the latter's new appointment stunned Alexander III's closest advisers. As Katkov wrote to Pobedonostsev: "I have heard an unbelievable rumor from a source that is deserving of confidence: it is said that Bunge has been appointed the Chairman of the Committee of Ministers. This event is having a stupifying effect on the whole 'Christian world.' An incompetent minister, who has brought so much evil upon the land, is not simply dismissed—and given some ordinary honor; instead, he is raised still higher to that post from which there can be no further promotion. It is hard to know whether the appointment of an incompetent minister to the post of Chairman of the Committee of Ministers will prove to be good or bad." In the opinion of the editor of the *Moscow News*, such an appointment could have only unfortunate consequences. "A certain pseudo-liberal party," continued Katkov, "considers him to be their man . . . . This promotion can only raise the spirits of this party and rekindle its hopes . . . ."

Bunge's appointment was made without even Tolstoy, the all-powerful Minister of the Interior, having any inkling of what was in the wind.[5] According to Polovtsov, the decision was made on the recommendation of Michael Kh. Reutern (Bunge's predecessor as chairman). "On Saturday, December 20, Reutern arrived at Gatchina and asked to be relieved of his duties as Chairman," Polovtsov noted in his diary on December 29, 1886. "At the same time he recommended that Bunge take his place." In Polovtsov's opinion "one sensed in this appointment some initiative and a wish to demonstrate independence from Pobedonostsev's tutelage."[6]

Although all four of the tsar's closest advisers were opposed to Bunge and did not dream such an appointment was even possible, there was nothing extraordinary about it. Bunge was not really the liberal he seemed to be to the reactionaries, and no general contradiction existed between his political views and the domestic policies of Alexander III. Moreover, on one of the most important of these policies—that of nationalism—Bunge's views were basically identical to those of the emperor. The Minister of Finance accepted Alexander III's thesis of "Russia for the Russians" utterly and advocated that "the Russian state must be dominated by the *Russian state system* (that is, by a Russian state authority and Russian institutions, adapted, of course, to fit the conditions existing among the other nationalities and in the borderlands); by the *Russian nationality* (that is, freeing it from the predominance of foreigners); by the *Russian language* as the dominant one; and finally, by *respect for the faith* which is the creed of the Russian people and their state."[7] It was only natural that such opinions commanded the respect of Alexander III.

On other domestic issues Bunge did take a moderately liberal, or to be precise, a moderately conservative position. He criticized the law on land captains (for the disproportionate power it gave the gentry)[8] and the existing system of administration in the provinces. Further, he believed it advisable to add to the State Council "each year one or two members of the gentry who had played an intimate part in the work of the zemstvo institutions," and he was a resolute opponent of communal landownership,[9] and so on.

THE ERA OF COUNTER-REFORM

The second part of Alexander III's reign (the years 1886 to 1894) is characterized by the preparation of a detailed general plan of ultra-conservative reform and of concrete projects, many of which were implemented. In 1885 a long article, "The Present Situation in Russia and the Estate Question,"[10] appeared in Katkov's *Russian Herald*. It was written by A.D. Pazukhin (marshal of the nobility of Alatyr county in Simbirsk province) and outlined a program of reactionary reforms. In it Pazukhin maintained that "the present situation in Russia is one of turmoil and uncertainty. In recent times the life of the nation has been filled with events inflicted upon us by the domestic opposition. The rapid spread of anarchist teachings, the collapse of any kind of real authority, the development of mercenary instincts among the public, the decline of religion, morality and the family principle, are all facts that serve as symptoms of social disintegration, and they compel the healthy elements to give thought to the future of our society."

Having described the existing situation in these terms, the author turned to the principles by which the country could be returned to a healthy condition. In Pazukhin's opinion, the abolition of serfdom had been a great necessity and had been implemented in a very satisfactory manner. The basic virtue of the statute of February 19, 1861 was, he believed, that it had preserved the landed gentry's political significance and leadership in peasant life. The "rural arbitrators" had seemed ideal leaders for the peasants and defenders of their interests.[11] In this way the really retrograde aspects of the reforms (that is, the preservation of some of the feudal sides of Russian life) were represented by Pazukhin as being the most beneficial.

But what were the causes of the nation's deplorable condition? Pazukhin found this condition to be the consequence of the reforms implemented after the abolition of serfdom. It was a fact, he observed, that "at the base of all the reforms that followed . . . there lay the principle of equality or of the so-called merging of estates, not only with regard to their personal (civil) rights but also of all service (political) rights." Pazukhin saw the bourgeois principle of classlessness—the equality of estates—as the chief evil, and from this viewpoint subjected the "great reforms" to devastating criticism.

For the most part he concentrated on the zemstvo reform. Pazukhin thought that both the membership and the activities of the zemstvos were haphazard in nature. The electoral meetings "of private landowners are either a meeting of separate individuals or of groups of people of diverse social positions, ways of life, educational backgrounds, and levels of moral understanding." He was sickened by their ill-assorted member-ship which forced the gentry to rub shoulders with manufacturers, saloon-keepers and prosperous peasants (*kulaks*). This "classlessness," he believed, deprived the zemstvos of any purpose they might have had. The municipal statute was open to the same criticism. This statute, Pazukhin wrote, "pushed our old city estates of merchants and trades-men out of the administration of the city's economy and created instead classless city councils." Further, "the zemstvo and city reforms were the most important because they had disrupted the historical order of our life," and had brought a new order of life that had disorganized Russia.

Having dealt with the zemstvos and city government, Pazukhin next attacked the new judicial institutions. They, he said, were based "on a foreign model," and their most unacceptable aspect was the independ-ence given the judiciary. The new courts "adopted a belligerent posture and openly stood in opposition to authority, to order, and to the prin-ciple of class;" again he saw "classlessness" as a major flaw of the new courts. He believed that because of this principle the gentry were being ousted from their positions as justices of the peace. "It is not difficult to foresee," Pazukhin observed, "to what further depths the institution of justice [of the peace] will fall because of a full celebration of the principle of classlessness." Finally, Pazukhin concerned himself with the state of education. In this sphere the same dangerous principle was at work but the damage had been minimized by strengthening the role of the classical gymnasiums within the educational system.

In summary, Pazukhin concluded that "the reforms, built on a class-less base, have broken the direct bonds between the supreme authority and the social estates upon which our state system had been based, and have led to the gradual disintegration of these estates." The gentry had suffered most because this process alienated these educated leaders from the peasants. Nonetheless, "the course of history had tied these two estates (of gentry and peasantry) together with such strong moral bonds

that the reforms of the last reign are powerless to tear them asunder."
Further, Pazukhin maintained, "the landed gentry enjoy the full confidence and deep sympathy of the peasantry . . . . They (the gentry) in-
tercede for them with the authorities and defend them from the en-
croachments of the kulak and the extortioner." Hence Russia's salvation
lay in rebuilding institutions founded on the basis of social estates in
which the gentry could play a leading role. "If the greatest evil of the
reforms of the last reign is seen as the destruction of estate organizations," he wrote, "the task of the present must be to restore that which
was destroyed."

It is only fair to add that while he was fighting "to restore that which
was destroyed," Pazukhin did realize the impossibility of turning the
clock backwards. Therefore he recognized the necessity of preserving
the zemstvos and institutions of city government, but wanted them re-
organized on an estate basis. The leading role in both, as well as in all
aspects of provincial life, should be given, naturally, to the landed gentry.[12] This ultra-reactionary, yet demogogic ideal also demanded that
the gentry be accorded special rights and privileges. Hence Pazukhin's
program put into concrete form all that Alexander III's speech to the
peasant elders at the time of the coronation, and the manifesto cele-
brating the centennial of the Charter of the Nobility, had vaguely suggested. It was also the program most likely to please Tolstoy, and its
author was quickly appointed director of the chancellery of the Ministry
of the Interior. Although poorly educated, Pazukhin proved energetic
and intelligent by nature, and he quickly became Tolstoy's right-hand
man. Still, as Polovtsov observed, although Pazukhin was "intelligent,"
he was bitter and narrow. "Such people do not create."

The most important issues in the years 1886 to 1894 were those
arising from the introduction of several administrative reforms, including
the statute on land captains (which practically abolished the institution
of justice of the peace) and the zemstvo counter-reform. Apart from
these measures the reaction, in the persons of its chief ideologists (Pobedonostsev, Tolstoy, Katkov and Meshchersky), pressed for a general
revision of the judicial statute. In 1885 Pobedonostsev presented to
Alexander III a memorandum envisaging the abolition of jury trials and
of the independent judiciary. Yet neither Nabokov, nor his successor,
Manasein, prepared the necessary legislation. Although the latter narrowed appreciably the area in which the judicial statute (and particularly
jury trials) was applicable, the Ministry of Justice still offered no program for a basic reform of the courts. Further, during discussions of the
law on land captains, Manasein exerted himself to preserve the justices
of the peace. "Manasein's official firmness," A.F. Koni later recalled,

"varied considerably. The peacemaker (the emperor), who was blessing Russia with land captains could not forgive his temporary opposition to Tolstoy and in various ways continually made him aware of this distrust." This, ultimately, predetermined Manasein's dismissal.

The new Minister of Justice, N.V. Muraviev, was a man of intelligence and organizational ability. He had made his name at the trial of the murderers of Alexander II when he had risen to the rank of prosecutor. Later he became prosecutor for the Moscow Judicial Bench where he won favor by his shameless grovelling before "the strong of this world." Lacking principles, he was an immoral careerist and toady who even stooped to bootlicking. Sometimes Muraviev served Plehve as an errand boy, finding some estate or house for him, and as a reward he obtained his sinecure in St. Petersburg.[13] At times Muraviev went further than simply carrying out Plehve's personal commissions and even committed breaches of official trust. This is substantiated by his letter to Plehve of October 23, 1890 concerning the case of V.D. Gadzhello, a minor police constable of Moscow, who had been charged with brutality.[14] In his letter Muraviev confided: "The other day we had a deplorable occurrence about which I wish to inform you in the fullest confidence. My efforts to ensure that the case of Pol(ice) Con(stable) *Gadzhello* passed quietly, smoothly, and peacefully would have been crowned with complete success if it had not been for our own higher administration . . . . The trial took place in the chamber, *behind closed doors,* and everyone tried to smooth over the sharper edges of the outrage, apart from . . . the police themselves; their officials conducted themselves quite insolently and with incomprehensible frankness."[15] On becoming Minister of Justice Muraviev undertook the preparation of legislation for judicial counter-reform. But, because of "circumstances beyond his control," he failed to implement his program. The new social developments of the mid-1890s, as well as the growth of the labor movement, thwarted all his efforts.

In this second period the government's policies were also characterized by the principle of "Russia for the Russians." As proclaimed by Alexander III this ideal took practical form in policies of extreme chauvinism. Meanwhile, illegal and arbitrary administrative procedures became much more common and met with almost no opposition from the highest government bodies or from the autocrat of the Russian empire himself.[16] On the contrary, it seemed that the emperor actually approved of the arbitrary behavior of his own subordinates.[17]

THE COMMITTEE OF MINISTERS

Among the central institutions of government the Committee of Ministers played the most significant role during the reign of Alexander III,

just as it had during that of Nicholas I. More limited in membership than
the State Council, the committee included only ministers and those of
an equivalent rank, such as the chairmen of departments of the State
Council and some members of the imperial family. This made it more
obedient than the State Council, which had a larger and more varied
composition.

For this reason most draft laws that directly contradicted the provisions of existing legislation were examined by the Committee of Ministers rather than the State Council. During the early 1880s this procedure was followed with regard to the more reactionary laws (such as
the statute of August 14, 1881 "On Measures for the Protection of State
Security and Public Tranquillity," the "Provisional Regulations for the
Jews," and the "Provisional Regulations for the Press"). Then, during
the latter 1880s and early 1890s, such breaches of legal form grew less
frequent and the State Council examined the intended counter-reforms.
Nevertheless, the decisions of the Committee of Ministers became marked by increasing illegality.[18] Its conclusions about the responsibility of
various governors for acts of malfeasance often contradicted existing
legislation.[19] Frequently, and particularly during the late 1880s and
early 1890s, the Committee of Ministers, acting as the court of highest
appeal, violated the law and decreed severe punishments for sundry
deviations from the official religion.[20]

After the resignation of Peter A. Valuev[21] in the fall of 1881, the
aged M.Kh. Reutern was appointed chairman of the committee. He had
served as Minister of Finance for a long period in the 1860s, but his
work in the committee was brief and irregular. Apart from long periods
of illness, Reutern only held the post for five years. Then, as mentioned,
N.Kh. Bunge was appointed to the post.

THE STATE COUNCIL

At this time the State Council was a fairly large body with seventy-two
members, although no more than fifty actually took part in its sessions.
Members were nominated for life from among the various dignitaries of
the realm, former ministers, governors-general, senators and members of
the imperial family.[22] Ministers took part in the council's work even
though they were not actually members. Grand Duke Konstantin Nikolaevich, an intelligent and fairly energetic man who had become the
leader of the liberal bureaucracy, served as chairman, but he was replaced by his brother, Grand Duke Michael, in the summer of 1881.

In 1883 State Secretary A.A. Polovtsov, a man of great intelligence
and wide knowledge, began to play an important role in the council's
work. Although politically a conservative, the fact that he was a great

capitalist entrepreneur affected his views and caused him to favor some economic and social progress. It is no exaggeration to see Polovtsov's role in the work of the State Council as more important than that of its chairman, whom he served as a self-appointed tutor.

In the years between 1882 and 1894 the council's members included a number of former ministers (Count L.T. Loris-Melikov of Interior, A.A. Abaza of Finance, A.V. Golovnin and Baron A.P. Nikolai of Education) and other representatives of the liberal bureaucracy. Two of this group (Baron Nikolai and Abaza)[23] headed two of the council's three departments, and this meant that the reactionaries met a certain opposition from this body. The fact that members were appointed for life also encouraged a certain independence of conduct. For this reason Alexander III entertained no special liking for the council. He believed that the "attitude of the majority" of its members assured their "audacious opposition." Pobedonostsev evidenced a similarly negative attitude. According to him, "one should lock up this institution in a castle and toss the key into the Neva."[24]

The State Council discussed various legislative proposals and frequently amended them. Sometimes drafts were even rejected by a majority of the council's members, as in the case of the bill on land captains, which was basically a measure of counter-reform. Yet a vote rejecting a proposed measure possessed no real significance, for the emperor maintained that the council's approval was not essential for a new law. Despite this fact, the reactionary newspapers *Moscow News* and *Citizen* continually abused the State Council as a self-appointed parliament. Both Katkov and Meshchersky waxed especially indignant when a minister's proposed law was modified as the result of the council's deliberations. "Instead of legislative drafts being enthroned as law in all their purity," Katkov wrote in a lead article of 1884, "they are sometimes amended, with something being added here or cut out there. This is not done with the aim of improving the draft, but to win the support of a majority. As a result we sometimes end up with half-measures which cannot possibly be of any use, or which lead to further difficulties in the very problem they were supposed to resolve." He reiterated the same thought in his lead article of May 6, 1886. "Is it really necessary," Katkov asked, "that parliamentary games of majority and minority are played in our State Council? That members of the State Council, appointed by the will of the monarch, so as to serve him with their advice, should transform this high appointment into the role of members of a party, a group, or a coalition subordinated not to their own reason but to the commands of a leader?"

During Alexander III's reign officials who previously had not been members of the council were appointed to this body. Thus, in 1886

Professor I.A. Vyshnegradsky, the Minister of Finance,[25] became a council member. He was a world-famous professor of mechanical engineering who also had demonstrated outstanding abilities in finance (which he had frequently used for his own gain). As a businessman he enjoyed a very dubious reputation and the Department of Police had placed him under observation for reasons that had nothing to do with politics. Tolstoy told Polovtsov that the Department of Police had collected a special dossier on Vyshnegradsky, that on this basis a report had been drawn up about his activities and that both the chairman of the State Council and the emperor had seen this document—a story supported by other sources.

Other examples of such irregular appointments occurred in 1883 when Alexis V. Bobrinsky, the Moscow provincial marshal of the nobility, and Gregory P. Galagan, a public figure and county marshal of the nobility in Poltava province, became members of the State Council. Then, in the early 1890s, Alexander A. Tatishchev, the former governor of Penza who had recently become a senator, and A.K. Anastasiev, the former governor of Chernigov and illegitimate son of the well-known police official, Fedor F. Trepov, also were appointed. Both were Meshchersky's creatures and were distinguished by their love of the birch, the pleasures of which they had generously bestowed upon the peasantry in the provinces under their control.

Anastasiev's unprecedented promotion from governor to member of the State Council aroused great dissatisfaction in official circles. Feoktistov, the head of the Main Directorate of the Press, noted in his diary that "Senator Tatishchev and Governor Anastasiev of Chernigov have been appointed members of the State Council. About the first of these there cannot be any possible disagreement: he is a blockhead in the proper sense of the term . . . . But it would be a crime to equate the latter with Tatishchev; he is no fool, speaks smartly, and has learned his program from the *Citizen*." In describing Anastasiev, Foektistov added that "it would be unfair to berate him for his views on European civilization; civilization is something that is utterly beyond his comprehension." Indeed, Anastasiev, who had begun his brilliant career as a county police chief, was an uneducated man. Durnovo, the Minister of the Interior, shared Feoktistov's opinion. In a letter to the latter, Durnovo wrote: "During the several months he has sat in the State Council no one has heard his voice; whatever the topic under discussion, he is as dumb as a fish." And, Durnovo concluded, "again an insoluble question is posed: why was this *ci-devant* county policeman, this perfect ignoramus, ever planted there?"[26] In fact, the answer to this question is clearly rooted in Alexander III's desire to destroy any "party" within the council's membership. By appointing people such as Tatishchev and Anastasiev the emperor hoped to turn it into an obedient instrument that would simply rubberstamp the draft laws laid before it by the ministers.

THE SENATE

During the period under study the Governing Senate consisted of eight departments, two of which were courts of appeal. The First Department was administrative. It was responsible for publishing and interpreting the laws and for ensuring their implementation. This department supervised the local administrative offices and the judicial system while the Second Department, commonly known as "the Peasant Department," was the highest body of appeal for various peasant complaints about decisions of the Provincial Offices for Peasant Affairs. It was also charged with supervising the implementation of the emancipation statute of February 19, 1861 and other laws relating to the "situation in the village." At first, in 1883, a special section on peasant affairs had been formed in the First Department. But the range of problems and the volume of business necessitated the creation of the special peasant department, which began to function on January 25, 1884.

A third department, which had no number in its title, was the Department of Heraldry and was responsible for the protection of estate (class) rights. The Fourth and Fifth were the appeals departments for the courts of the pre-reform judicial system (which still existed in a number of the empire's border regions). Another department oversaw land surveying, while the last two formed the highest appellate bodies (criminal and civil) for the judicial institutions established by the judicial statute of November 20, 1864. In addition there existed the Special Office of the Senate, created in 1872 "for the trial of crimes against the state," but it practically ceased to function during the years 1882 to 1894 inasmuch as political cases were usually tried in military courts.

A review of the Senate's activity as the highest authority in supervising the implementation of laws must begin with the Solicitor-General, or Minister of Justice, and conclude with the chief justices and prosecutors of the Senate. It must be noted that the growth of arbitrary administrative behavior in the late 1880s and early 1890s encountered no consistent opposition from the Senate. This is explained by a number of circumstances, including a change in personnel both among the senators and the Senate's prosecutors. "Among the senators," remarked A.F. Koni in his memoirs, "there arrived governors who had flogged the 'Yids' and peasants for imagined mutinies, along with a whole string of unsuccessful Directors of the Department of Police who, having feathered their nests, were permitted to protect their precious skins as senators."

In 1891 Major General Valerian D. Martynov, the director of the Stables Administration, was made a senator. "All the senators are furious," Feoktistov noted in his diary, for "they all consider such an appointment to be an insult. Manasein is blamed. He was ordered to prepare the edict on Martynov and present it to the Emperor, and he only worried about one detail: was it not at least necessary first to appoint Martynov to the post of *Stallmeister, Hofmeister,* or something like that, so that the smell of the stables would not cling to the edict and still later to the Senate? He wrote of this to the Emperor, as he was not permitted to outline these considerations in a personal report, and received this answer: 'It is all the same to me whether it is proper or improper, as it is I who appoint senators and I consider that General Martynov is completely suitable for such a position.' " All in all, Feoktistov concluded, "it surely could have been worse. Caligula seated his horse in the Senate and now only the stable boy is sent. No matter what is said, it is progress."[27]

A change in the Senate's membership was not the only factor making it more "pliable." More important was a gradual evolutionary process that transformed the majority of these "men of justice" from disinterested servants of Themis into unprincipled opportunists, either because of expectations of "great and rich favors" or simply because of their own cowardice. Chief Justice Nicholas A. Nekliudov, who served as prosecutor for the Special Office during the trial of the affair of March 1, 1887, is one example of this evolution. Koni wrote of Nekliudov: "Although the latter long believed in the rule of law and had in his legislative and appellate decisions attempted to steer a middle course as a supposedly rough and ready peacemaker, he was nonetheless a nervous and impressionable man who could never forget the past brilliance of his youth. The author who had not been permitted to defend his dissertation (*Criminal Statistical Studies*), the publisher of [John Stuart] Mill and [G.H.] Lewes, the brilliant commentator on Burns, and the popular rural arbitrator then would never have thought that he would someday demand the death penalty. He was absolutely overwhelmed by the task given to him, especially when one of the defendants (in the March 1, 1887 case), the remarkably talented mathematics student, Ulianov, was the son of his beloved teacher in the Penza gymnasium. He suffered during the trial, but while in the courtroom nevertheless he succeeded in acting in accordance with the general mood of supposed horror expected of all loyal subjects."

It might be added that during the session of the Special Office in which the appeals of the accused were heard, Nekliudov continually demanded that the sentence be applied in full rigor. He maintained that any reduction was impossible even though it was well known that the mere planning of a terrorist act did not, from the legal point of view, make the full penalty mandatory. Meanwhile the hearing of the case of Ulianov, Shevyrev, Generalov and the others went so well that one senator, P.A. Dreier, received, according to Koni, 2,000 rubles "for medical treatment." This was apparently a payment "for five heads."

The Senate's highest official—the Solicitor-General, who was also Minister of Justice—played the major and decisive role in its activity. Whereas Nabokov almost never overstepped the existing laws (in the early 1880s when there was no particular need to do so), Manasein did so frequently,[28] although he too could display civic courage on certain occasions.[29] As for Muraviev, it cannot be said that he paid any attention whatsoever to legality, and he always did what the emperor and the others closest to him wanted. "Muraviev exerted a harmful influence," observed A.F. Koni, "and it was reflected in judicial decisions in a particularly tangible way. He would even send confidential circulars to local prosecutors concerning the necessity, 'in the view of the government,' of interpreting questions as to just what constituted an offense against the faith in ways that contradicted the Senate's earlier instructions." Efforts to ensure action according "to the view of the government" (that is, in opposition to the existing laws) grew more and more widespread during the second half of the 1880s and in the early 1890s. During these years there were virtually no senatorial "reviews" or investigations of the activities of local institutions and this further facilitated an increase in the illegal and arbitrary behavior of provincial administrations.

THE CHURCH ADMINISTRATION

During the 1880s and early 1890s the Director-General of the Holy Synod was an especially powerful figure. "It is difficult to describe just how musty the atmosphere has grown in the Church's administration," A.N. Lvov, the managing librarian and archivist of the Synod, wrote in his diary. "Everything centers on the desires and pleasures of Pobedonostsev. Everyone and everything lives and breathes for him." By this time the significance of the Synod itself had diminished to almost nothing, for the director-general and his assistants made every decision. Pobedonostsev's every sentence was acted upon. To this end special members were appointed to the Synod, which usually met only during the summer. "No matter who serves in the Synod in the winter," wrote Lvov, "no matter how much it (the Synod) opposes the government's illegal actions, or how often it postpones the Director-General's proposals as being illegal—it all comes to absolutely nothing. This is because in the summer, when the leading figures depart for their dioceses and their 'summer' replacements are called in, any proposal may pass easily." Naturally this roused great dissatisfaction among some of the higher clergy. Polovtsov, outlining in his diary a conversation with Metropolitan Platon of Kiev, noted the latter's complaints about the director-general. He "hotly condemns Pobedonostsev's short-sighted and despotic ways," recorded Polovtsov.

This era was also one of increasing laxity and corruption among the clergy. Isidor, the ninety-year-old metropolitan of Petersburg, was surrounded by rogues who held him tightly in their grasping claws. For many years he was close to one Matrena Egorov, a captain's widow, whom he considered to be a pious person and worker of miracles. Later Isidor grew closer still to a woman named Denker. "A certain Denker," commented A.V. Bogdanovich in her diary, "visits His Reverence every Tuesday and every time gets him to do extraordinary things. She meets with the priest Polkanov, a well-known good-for-nothing, . . . then arranges various matters with the Metropolitan and, receiving money for this, she divides it with him (Polkanov). She arranged for one priest, Drozdov, to become a member of the Consistory, and received for this 1500 rubles. This Denker was a beggar, who once received five rubles charity from the Metropolitan and who now travels by carriage." Similar situations existed in other dioceses. According to Lvov, Illarion A. Chistovich, the director of the Synod's examiners, investigated the Warsaw diocese and discovered there "a perfectly organized commerce in permits for reversions from the Orthodox Church to the Uniate or Catholic Churches."

Meanwhile various saints, of whom John of Kronstadt was typical, gained prominence in church affairs. The emergence of such figures originated in popular drives for the canonization of miracle workers such as Feodosia of Chernigov, Anna of Kashinsk, Serafim of Sarov, and others. Local bishops and governors displayed a touching anxiety in this work. Worth recalling is the remark of Anastasiev, governor of Chernigov, in his report on that province for 1889. "I consider it my devoted duty to report," he wrote, "that the reverent feeling of the faithful awaits the opening of the relics of the saintly Feodosia of Uglich. In the eyes of the people the sainted Feodosia is already their own saintly representative before the throne of the Almighty."

Among the Synod's other activities, Pobedonostsev's efforts to subordinate elementary education to the Church by founding parochial schools deserves mention. Otherwise the Synod demonstrated special zeal in its support of the government's nationalistic policies. Official policies favoring Russification found their main outlet in conversions to the Orthodox Church. The Orthodox Missionary Society, which undertook to carry the faith among the "heathens" and Mohammedans, frequently carried on its work with the help of the police. At the same time the persecution of Old Believers[30] and sectarians increased in strength and frequency while the diocesan bishops enlarged the role they played in the official life of the provinces.

THE IMPERIAL BUREAUCRACY

This review of the higher administrative institutions concludes with a glance at His Imperial Majesty's Own Chancellery. It contained a number of departments[31] and from the mid-1820s until the 1880s it had existed as a separate state within the state. Over the years the First Section of H.I.M. Own Chancellery had undergone fundamental changes. With the abolition of the other sections it became simply H.I.M. Own Chancellery and had within its purview all questions concerning careers in the civil service—dismissals, promotions, rewards and decorations awarded to all service ranks. This illustrates Alexander III's efforts to control personally all civil service appointments, regardless of the rank involved, and moreover provides further evidence of his clear distrust of his own ministers.

In 1892 a Highest Decorations Review Committee was formed as part of the Chancellery. Then in May, 1894 an edict followed that transformed this body into the Committee for Civil Service and Decorations. According to this edict the emperor recognized the "necessity to subordinate to Our direct guidance and administration all matters concerning the supervision of persons holding rank in the Empire's civil service. This will be accomplished by concentrating the administration of these persons in Our Own Chancellery." The edict centralised decisions concerning the appointments, dismissals and transfers of all civil servants, including collegiate registrars, and naturally upset the heads of the various departments.

Muraviev, the Minister of Justice, presented an illuminating report to the emperor on the subject of this edict. He had just received from H.I.M. Own Chancellery a copy of the "Edict of the Governing Senate on the Establishment of the Service Committee for Officials with Civil Rank," which Alexander III had signed on May 6. Dumbfounded, he immediately asked the emperor to delay publishing the law "pending the presentation by myself and the other ministers of memorandums on a measure as important as this." Touching the essential point, Muraviev pointed out that "in its present form the aforementioned edict is very vague: if put into practice it could be the cause of very serious misunderstandings and embarrassment. Furthermore, it might also extraordinarily complicate and retard the work of each department in the administration of the sphere of official activity allotted to it." This law, he continued, "could undermine a minister's necessary authority over persons in posts subordinated to him and hence exert a very undesirable and harmful effect upon the government's authority."[32]

Alexander III took no action on this report, returning it to its author covered with miscellaneous comments. At the top of page one the emperor wrote: "I am astonished by this odd report." At the end, opposite the sentence suggesting a suspension of the edict's publication until the ministers presented their memoranda, the tsar observed: "If I wished to receive *negative* comments, then of course I would turn to the ministers." The law was promulgated and in June, 1894 General Kireev noted: "We do everything in a somewhat haphazard manner, without considering any of the pro's and con's.... So an edict appears which restores the Inspector's Department for the civil service. The initiator (of the scheme) has turned out to be (N.I.) Neporozhnev—the head of the Office of Heraldry. Previously the ministers generally have acted in an arbitrary and unrestrained manner, but now we have gone to the other extreme. Now *all* nominations must be made by means of an Imperial order. It is obvious that the Sovereign cannot have the slightest notion about those who serve him in some remote outpost like Okhotsk. But, as it now turns out, it will be the Emperor who is responsible for the appointment of every idiot or swindler, whereas previously it was a minister or governor who had to answer!"

One other proposal concerning civil servants that was discussed but never adopted was a suggestion to replace the old Table of Ranks[33] with a new hierarchy of categories of official posts. On October 23, 1883 a Special Secret Conference was created to investigate the methods of promotion within the civil service. Chaired by Alexander S. Taneev, the director of H.I.M. Own Chancellery, it included M.S. Kakhanov, Edward V. Frish, A.A. Polovtsov and Konstantin K. Rennenkampf. The abolition of the existing system of ranks had been discussed frequently in the Secret Committee of December 6, 1826, in 1846, and in 1856, but despite decisions favoring such a step in principle, nothing practical had been done.

In its first session (on February 29, 1884) the new special conference recognized the usefulness of discarding the old civil ranks because "at present the correlation between a person's rank and the post he holds in the service is almost accidental in character; consequently rank has lost all useful significance." Guided by this consideration, the conference decided that it was necessary "to replace the presently existing system of civil ranks with a special new hierarchy of posts, so as to allow the rights and privileges now conferred upon rank to be attached to posts at the various levels of the civil service hierarchy." Alexander III approved this conclusion on April 2, 1884, whereupon the question was considered further in the sessions of the conference of May 3 and December 20, 1884, and January 3, January 18 and March 10, 1885. The final meeting proposed that the matter be discussed in the State Council. Alexander III agreed, but this plan was dropped because of the ministers' opposition.

Despite apparently progressive aspects, the real aim of this measure was the transformation of the gentry into an exclusive caste. The abolition of the Table of Ranks would have ended the chances of commoners gaining access to the noble "estate" through government service. This estate, in Polovtsov's mind, in the future would be replenished solely from among the great landowners.

In this connection it is worth examining the estate origins and property positions of the senior bureaucrats (those holding the highest posts in the state administration). The abolition of serfdom and impoverishment of the gentry had led to an increase of the non-gentry element within this group. On one hand this process was characterized by a growth in the number of civil servants who belonged to old—and frequently titled—noble families, but who were not landowners. On the other hand, there was simultaneously a noticeable increase in the number of newcomers (from the clergy, the merchants, and other strata of the population) to be found among the higher officials.

This process is illustrated by data on the property position of the higher officials, based on an analysis of the *List of Civil Servants in the First Three Ranks,* published February 1, 1888. At that date there were no civil servants of first rank (Chancellor and Actual Privy Councillors of the First Rank). Consequently this analysis concerns only officials of the second rank (Actual Privy Councillors), of whom there were, in February, 1888, some 83, and of the third rank (Privy Councillors) of whom there were 516. In the first of these groups (the second rank) there were:

a) Court ranks of the first class   10
b) Members of the State Council   30
c) Ministers and chief directors of departments   7
d) Senators   14
e) Higher ministerial and departmental officials   11
   (members of the ministerial councils,
   departmental directors, and so on.)
f) Envoys and ambassadors   5
g) Academicians, professors and directors of
   scientific institutions   6

Of these some 38 (45.7%) were not landowners.[34] Of the remaining 45, 26 (31%) possessed hereditary family estates, nine others did not own estates in their own right (as these belonged to their wives) and another nine had acquired land either by grant or purchase. Accordingly, it can be seen that almost 70 percent of the higher civil servants did not hold family estates.[35]

In terms of comparative size the land holdings of this group were as follows (in desiatinas):[36]

To 25	100-500	501-1000	1001-5000
1	4	8	18

5000-10,000	10,000-25,000	Above 25,000	Not Designated Entailed Other
3	8	2	2 —

If great landowners are defined as those holding 1000 or more desiatinas, among the higher officials of the second rank only 33 (39.7%) can be so designated.

The 516 officials of the third rank were distributed in the following manner:

a) Court ranks of the second class	46
b) Ministers and directors-in-chief	3
c) Members of the State Council	4
d) Senators	104
e) Assistant ministers	9
f) Envoys and ambassadors	12
g) Higher ministerial and departmental officials (members of ministerial councils, departmental directors, superintendents of educational districts, directors of judicial institutions, and so on)	236
h) Governors	19
i) Marshals of the nobility (provincial and county)	7
j) Academicians, professors, directors of scientific establishments and educational institutions	51
k) Others (honorary wardens of charitable institutions, medical chiefs of hospitals, justices of the peace, mayors of cities, and so on)	25

Of these, 288 (55%) owned no land, 155 (29.6%) possessed family estates, 26 had wives with family estates, and another 50 had acquired (by purchase or grant) estates. Thus the non-landowners among officials of the third rank were somewhat more numerous than in the second rank: 55.7 percent in the first case as opposed to 45.7 percent in the second. This is due mainly to the inclusion in this category of "academicians, professors, and the directors of scientific and educational institutions," who generally owned no land. But the percentage of officials with hereditary estates was virtually identical: 31.3 percent in the second rank and 29.6 percent in the third. Therefore it may be concluded that in both cases some 70 percent of the higher civil servants did not belong to the landed gentry.

Equally interesting are the figures on the extent of land ownership among the officials of the third rank (in desiatinas):[37]

To 25	To 100	101-500	501-1000	1001-5000	5001-10,000	10,001-25,000	From 25,000	Not Designated	
								Entailed	Other Ownership
7	3	30	36	87	23	14	14	7	7

Thus 152 officials (29.5%) can be counted as great landowners (owning over 1,000 desiatinas). This is 10.2 percent lower than among the bureaucrat-landowners of the second rank.

Having sketched this overall picture, it is worth looking at some of the individuals involved. Of the senior officials holding the highest posts in the imperial administration (ministers, Director-General of the Holy Synod, state controller, chairman of the Committee of Ministers, chairmen of the departments of the State Council), only Count D.A. Tolstoy, the Minister of the Interior, may be called a great landowner (owning over 10,000 desiatinas).[38] Manasein, the Minister of Justice, owned 800 desiatinas and belonged to the middle range of the landed gentry. Further, so did I. Stoiansky, the chairman of one of the departments of the State Council, who possessed 900 desiatinas. The remainder belonged either to the landless service gentry, or to other social estates: Pobedonostsev and Vyshnegradsky were of clerical origins, while Ostrovsky came from a merchant's family.

Of the higher administrators mentioned, the Director-General of the Holy Synod (Pobedonostsev), the chairman of the Committee of Ministers (Bunge), the Minister of Finance (Vyshnegradsky), and the State Controller (Dmitry M. Solsky) owned no land at all. Other ministers (Nabokov, Ostrovsky, and Giers), and the other State Council departmental chairman (Nikolai and Abaza), had obtained their estates solely

as grants. Yet property position and class origin held no relation whatsoever to the political views of these men. The priest's son, Pobedonostsev, and the merchant's son, Ostrovsky, were no less zealous in uphold-
ing the gentry's interest than was Count D.A. Tolstoy. It must be added
that among these leading officials who belonged to old and aristocratic
Russian families, many owned no land at all. Among the latter were
the prominent court dignitaries Prince Ivan M. Golitsyn and Prince
Boris F. Golitsyn; the ambassador to Spain, Prince Michael A. Gorcha-
kov; the Assistant Minister of the Interior, Prince Konstantin D. Gagarin;
the envoy to Austria-Hungary, Prince Alexis B. Lobanov-Rostovsky; and
Prince Sergei A. Dolgoruky, a member of the State Council (a full list
would be much longer). Moreover, among those of the third rank are
included the great railroad magnate, Samuel Solomonovich Poliakov,
and the merchant and manufacturer, Peter Ionovich Gubonin. Neither
held government positions but as wardens or superintendents of various
philanthropic and educational institutions they had gained official rank.

This data provides convincing evidence of the fundamental changes
that had occurred in the social composition of the civil service since the
abolition of serfdom in 1861. To illustrate at once the general growth
of the bureaucracy and the change in its position with regard to landownership, it is rewarding to note the data of 1854 for officials of the
first three ranks examined above. At that time there were, in all three
ranks combined, 217 persons (two of the First Rank, 35 of the Second,
and 180 of the Third). Thus, during the succeeding thirty-four years
the number had almost doubled, reaching 599 in 1888. As for land
ownership, in 1854 the two officials of the first rank—Count Karl G.
Nesselrode and Prince Alexander N. Golitsyn—were both great landowners with estates of over 10,000 desiatinas. The former had received
his land as a grant, while the latter's was hereditary.

Of the 35 officials of the second rank in 1854, 27 (77.3%) had
inherited land, four (11.35%) had acquired or been granted estates, and
the remaining four (11.35%) were landless. Of the 180 officials in the
third rank, 88 (48.9%) had their own hereditary estates, 11 (7.1%) had
wives who had inherited family estates, 24 (13.3%) had acquired or been
granted properties, and 57 (31.7%) possessed no landed property. Therefore it is obvious that the percentage of higher civil servants with landed
interests was considerably greater in 1854 than in 1888. It must be noted
further that among those officials of the third rank who owned family
estates in 1854, a large number held small holdings: of the 88 persons
in this group, 27 (30.68%) held estates of only two to 200 desiatinas.
In 1888, by contrast, the percentage of these persons had dropped
considerably.

OFFICIAL NATIONALISM

During the period 1882 to 1894 the government's policies toward the non-Russian nationalities were characterized by persecution and determined Russification. At this time nationalism among the Great Powers generally assumed particularly intolerant and militant forms, and this was the case in Russia. Pobedonostsev, and those who shared his views, were the ideologists of the nationality policies. In describing their attitudes, Polovtsov wrote that such thinkers "set up some imagined distinctiveness as the ideal of Russian political life. This (distinctiveness) finds its expression in the worship of the samovar, *kvass,* and bast sandals, combined with a contempt for everything that has grown out of the life of other peoples. It follows from this that everyone who does not bear the Great Russian stamp must be persecuted. The Germans, the Poles, the Finns, the Jews, and the Muslims—all are seen as one common problem and declared to be the irreconcilable enemies of Russia. A cruel and heartless hatred motivates the passing of a death sentence on anyone who differs in faith or in race and anyone who makes a pretence of superiority."[39] Alexander III shared and wholly supported such views. Russian chauvinism found expression in the persecution of other national cultures, the restriction and victimization of non-Russians, and the forcible Russification of those of different faiths through conversion to Orthodoxy. This last, of course, was the task of the Holy Synod.

Alexander L. Apukhtin, the superintendent of the Warsaw Educational District, was especially active in the cause of "Russifying the borderlands." In early 1883 he ordered all instruction at the University of Warsaw—even in the course in Polish literature—henceforth to be carried on in Russian. The students responded by organizing a campaign of obstruction.[40] Then, in April of that year, one Zhuikevich, a student of the university's faculty of law (who was himself a Russian) answered Apukhtin's actions by slapping his face. The emperor, however, took somewhat a different view of the superintendent's conduct. A few days after the slapping incident an imperial rescript to Apukhtin was published in the *Government Herald* which announced: "In recompense for your particularly zealous and unswervingly steadfast efforts in the branch of the administration entrusted to you, to carry out Our designs for a closer union of the Trans-Vistula District[41] with the other parts of the Empire, We are most pleased to confer upon you the Knighthood of the Imperial Order of Alexander Nevsky."

Russification of the secondary and elementary schools in the Kingdom of Poland had been introduced immediately after the Polish uprising of 1863. By 1881 the governor-general of Warsaw, Peter P. Albedinsky, reported "a weakening in the zeal of peasant communities for their

schools" in direct proportion to the extent that they had been transformed "into a weapon for the Russifying of the peasant class." For
this reason he recommended a number of measures to restore order in
the educational system of the Kingdom of Poland. Baron Nikolai, the
Minister of Education, wished to present for the emperor's approval a
draft decree that would define the share of participation by parish and
village communities in the appointment of teachers, introduce teaching
in the Polish language and alphabet into those schools where the majority
of students were of Polish nationality, and establish a legal basis for
religious teaching by Roman Catholic priests (upon a petition of parish
and village communities). Tolstoy and Delianov rejected this proposal
and a law dated March 5, 1885 preserved the existing state of affairs.
This meant that officials of the Ministry of Education retained their
powers of appointing teachers and that teaching in all subjects was to
be carried out in Russian "with the exception of the religious teaching
of the foreign confessions [non-Orthodox] and the native language of
the students, which also may be taught in that language. Cases of doubt
as to exactly which language should be recognized as the language for
teaching the aforesaid subjects are to be resolved by the superintendent
of the educational district, in agreement with the governor-general of
Warsaw."

As a result even the teaching of the Polish language might be carried
out in Russian. Worse still, even private schools had to teach in Russian
and students in government schools might not even converse among
themselves in Polish during their stay in the educational institution. As
A.S. Valk observed in his article, "The Domestic Policies of Tsardom
During the 1880s and Early 1890s," "Russian was introduced as the
language of instruction even in the schools for the deaf and dumb." The
governor-general of Warsaw, J.V. Gurko, in one of his reports to the
emperor characterized the existing attitude toward Polish children in
the public educational institutions of Poland as follows: "In the government schools of the Kingdom, the Polish children are not only treated
without love,[42] but even with outright hostility; for them the schools
are a reproach to their Polish ancestors, an insult to their national feeling, and places where their religion is scorned and their own native
tongue is ranked in importance below the foreign languages French and
German . . . . The educational authorities demand a better knowledge
of the Russian language and its grammatical rules from the Polish children than they do from the Russian ones."

While the Ministry of Education deserves first prize for its work in
Russifying the Poles, it was not the only department engaged in this
pursuit. J.V. Gurko, the governor-general just quoted, made his own

contribution by introducing Russian as the language of private business transactions on the railways, for posters, for various labels, and so on. In 1885 the Polish Bank was closed down and turned into the Warsaw branch of the State Bank. Such administrative measures sought to transform the Kingdom of Poland into the Trans-Vistula District and to force Poles to become Russians.[43]

In Finland the government introduced the same program of narrow nationalism. Until the mid-1880s earlier policies, based on the principle of autonomy, continued on the basis of simple inertia. Finnish military units were created and in 1886 the Finnish Diet received the right to initiate legislation, while the Representatives of the Land were to be convened every three years.[44] But by the end of the decade Russian policies had become more nationalistic and the Finnish public naturally became apprehensive.

On February 28, 1891, Alexander III addressed a rescript to the governor-general of Finland. It answered an address he had received from the land marshal of the Diet and speakers of the Estates. They had informed him of "the uneasy mood in the region" provoked by implementing measures that sought to "tighten the union of the Grand Duchy with the other parts of the Russian State." In his rescript the tsar noted the governor-general's "unseemly care for the well-being and internal development of Finland" and underlined that the "Finnish District" (but not Duchy) was "a property and a state belonging to the Russian Empire." At this time a number of measures were adopted that aimed at the destruction of Finnish autonomy. In 1890 the independent Finnish postal system was abolished and subordinated to the Main Administration of Posts and Telegraphs of the Russian Ministry of the Interior, while the acceptance of Russian currency became obligatory. Then, in 1892, changes were made in the Finnish Senate for the purpose of weakening its political significance, and a special conference was established to discuss the future of the Finnish constitution. Such measures were merely a beginning. The major effort to russify the grand duchy arrived only in the latter 1890s and is associated with Nicholas II and N.I. Bobrikov.

Policies of russification were applied in the other Baltic provinces of Latvia and Estonia. Here they meant the introduction of the Russian language and the replacing of local judicial, administrative, and law enforcement offices by the institutions common to the empire as a whole. Yet the situation was not quite the same as in Poland or Finland. In the Baltic area the Russian language replaced German rather than Latvian or Estonian.

Judicial and police reforms were implemented in these provinces at the end of the 1880s. Before this time both the courts and the police

had been entirely controlled by the German gentry and remained practically independent of crown authority. The introduction of the general
judicial, administrative and police laws of the empire, even with limitations, undoubtedly was a positive step inasmuch as this weakened the
dependence of the Latvians and Estonians upon the German gentry. The
government's policies in the Baltic provinces were forward-looking in
an objective sense even if still marked by chauvinistic overtones. The
latter were particularly blatant in relation to religious persecution and
the forced, or semiforced, conversions to Orthodoxy. The activity of
the provincial administrations of Sergei V. Shakhovsky, governor of
Estonia, and Michael A. Zinoviev, governor of Latvia, were marked by
the most unrestrained, illegal and arbitrary behavior. (Shakhovsky was
particularly notorious for such conduct.) The autocracy was clearly
placing every obstacle possible in the way of the efforts of various
nationalities to develop their own cultural identities.[45]

OFFICIAL ORTHODOXY

Russification by means of conversion to Orthodoxy was nothing new.
But never before did it reach the pitch recorded during the 1880s and
1890s. The intensification of such efforts began to become more common in the Baltic province of Estonia in 1883 when several hundred
peasants of Gapsal county petitioned "to be converted to the Orthodox
Church on the day of the holy coronation of Your Imperial Majesty."
Obviously this "movement" was organized by the authorities who had
used various promises and bribes.

Here the complaint of the president of the Evangelical Lutheran
General Consistory to Minister of the Interior Tolstoy, dated June 23,
1883, is illuminating. "The pastor of Leal Parish," he wrote "informs
the Estonian Evangelical Lutheran Consistory that, shortly after the
celebration of Holy Easter, rumours spread in the district of Leal that
several men from among his parishioners, induced by false promises of
various secular advantages—such as freedom from all taxes or obligations,
free land grants, and so on—had decided to adopt the Orthodox faith.
This movement has aroused considerable excitement and Adu Pebo, a
a tailor of Oidenorum, was pointed out as its leader."

The president went on to state that in Pebo's possession were found
numerous copies of Bishop Platon's pastoral letter to newly-converted
Estonians and Latvians and of the article "Ruhwa armastus." This latter
offered a closer union with the Russian people, and an acceptance of
their faith, "to the Estonian people as the only means of freeing themselves from their oppressive yoke."[46] Nonetheless they were cautioned
that any request for conversion to Orthodoxy should not mention the

circumstances compelling them to this step, but should declare "that love of the Sovereign Emperor and of the Russian people, as well as personal conviction, created this desire in you, after which the advantages for the Estonian people also became apparent." The pamphlet recommended that they accept Orthodoxy "on the day of the holy coronation."

In addition to the demagogic promises proffered by individual zealots, the Orthodox clergy was equally active. In the spring of 1887, for instance, one Toropil, a peasant of the village of Pedaspe, complained to the Evangelical Lutheran General Consistory that a priest, Karp Tizik, a deacon of the Orthodox Assembly of Reval, had come to the village and converted three of his children to Orthodoxy.[47] According to the Lutheran Consistory's report to the Ministry of the Interior, Father Tizik, on arriving in the village, had suggested that the inhabitants meet with him. The three Toropil children were curious and went to the house in which he was staying. After some time with the priest they "returned to their mother and told her that he had convinced them that they would do well to become Orthodox, and then they would no longer be burdened with studies. After this the priest placed something in their mouths, embraced them, and then let them go, saying they were now of the Orthodox faith." The evidence of another, nearly unintelligible report on this matter, submitted by the Orthodox Consistory of Riga, suggests that this is precisely what had occurred.[48]

The Director-General of the Holy Synod ignored all this. In his report of 1886 to Alexander III he discussed the massive conversions of Estonians and Latvians and expressed no doubts about their validity. Instead Pobedonostsev reported: "Regarding the motives behind this massive acceptance of Orthodoxy by Lutherans, Bishop Donat writes that no one can say that the foreigners had any hopes of gaining any material rewards in return for their conversion to Orthodoxy."

In 1885 it was calculated that over the span of two years 3,314 persons had joined the Orthodox churches of the province of Estonia while, during the course of Alexander's reign, some 37,416 Lutherans converted to Orthodoxy. As a rule these conversions were of a formal nature and usually both the converts and their children continued to practice their former rites. Earlier, in the 1840s, there had been a similar massive conversion of Latvians to Orthodoxy in Latvia province. Even Pobedonostsev admitted (in his memorandum of February 16, 1884 to the Minister of the Interior) that the cause "had been the diffusion of rumors among the Latvian peasantry that they would, by converting to Orthodoxy, earn from a Russian Orthodox Tsar relief from the severity of their lot. They expected to receive land allotments and to be freed

from the obligation of laboring for landowners and pastors." Hence the
same peasants who had been recorded as converts remained Lutheran
by tradition and naturally went to the pastors for religious rites. Besides,
the crime of "defection from the faith" was not prosecuted during the
1860s and 1870s.

In the mid-1880s such prosecutions were energetically renewed. Their
basis was suggested by an official letter of M.A. Zinoviev, the governor
of Latvia, to Donat, the bishop of Riga. In September, 1886 Zinoviev
wrote that study of this matter had convinced him that in the province
of Latvia there were many peasants "who, having been baptised in the
ritual of the Orthodox Church and therefore entered in Orthodox Church
registers, later were confirmed by Lutheran pastors, whereby these pastors also had entered them into their books." It was his wish, he continued, "to spare" the inhabitants of Latvia "from various unpleasant-
ries and misfortunes." Therefore he requested that the local priests
should "make known the unfortunate consequences to which those who
proved guilty of above-mentioned crimes ('defection from the faith' or
backsliding) would be exposed." For, Zinoviev pointed out, an Orthodox
citizen who had continued in the Lutheran ritual could hold no public
office. Furthermore, "those peasants who were baptised in the Orthodox rite, but married in Lutheran churches, will be subject to even
worse consequences, as their marriages will not be recognized as legal.
This same illegitimacy attaches to the children born of such unions . . . .
Orthodox parents who raised their children in the Lutheran faith are,
according to Article 190 of the Code of Punishment, subject to prison
terms of from eight (months) to one year and four months." He concluded by expressing his confidence that, following this advance warning,
such backsliders "will change their minds and act as the law demands."

This letter was read in the churches following services and quite
naturally aroused great anxiety among the "Orthodox" Latvian population.[49] Once it became public it provoked a strong reaction from Lutheran German circles. Baron F.A. Meiendorf, provincial marshal of the
nobility for Latvia, wrote Count Tolstoy that "this matter affects tens
of thousands of souls who, although they are recorded in registers of
the Orthodox Church, do not belong to it by their inner convictions,
and some decades ago returned to their own, ancestral Evangelical Lutheran Church."[50] In view of this, Meiendorf concluded, "there exists
only one way out of this disastrous situation: all those persons who have
transferred back to the Evangelical Lutheran Church should be removed
from the registers of the Orthodox Church." But the government had
no intention of accepting this solution.

Government persecution affected not only persons counted as Orthodox, but also the Lutheran pastors charged with "seducing from the

faith." After the mid-1880s a number of pastors were prosecuted for holding services for those Lutherans who had been entered in Orthodox registers. Up to 1895 some 178 criminal charges were brought against such pastors in Latvia alone.[51] Manasein had suggested the basis for these prosecutions in 1884, during his tour of inspection in Latvia. At that time, according to A.F. Koni, he ordered that actions against the pastors "be carried out not under Article 193 of the (Criminal) Code as was the practice in the province, but under Article 187–'proselytism' because the teaching of the law of God for the purpose of conversion was proselytizing. The difference was enormous. Under Article 193 . . . the penalty for the first offense was removal from office for six months to a year, and for the second, deprivation of spiritual orders and police supervision; but a man convicted of proselytism was deprived of all civil rights and exiled to Siberia for life. The first victim prosecuted under Article 187 was an aged pastor, Grimm, whom the Riga district court sentenced to loss of civil rights and then deported to Siberia.

These practices were not confined to the Baltic provinces. Russification of the peoples of Siberia, again by bringing them "into the bosom of the Orthodox Church," was prosecuted with unbelievable hypocrisy. The diffusion of Orthodoxy among the "heathens and Mohammedans" was the task of the All-Russian Orthodox Missionary Society. Founded in Moscow in 1870, the society's activities expanded greatly between the years 1881 and 1894. By 1891 it claimed 13,214 members and capital assets of over 1,300,000 rubles. Further, it had forty-three diocesan committees active in the provinces[53] and, by 1894, some 8,544 Mohammedans and 50,933 heathens reportedly had been converted to Orthodoxy. The Irkutsk mission was especially zealous and brought Orthodoxy to the Buriats by methods even more aggressive than those practiced in the Baltic region.

In 1891 this mission utilised the tsarevich's journey through Siberia as the occasion for a forced mass baptism of Buriats. These latter all received, "with the assent of the heir and Tsarevich," the name of Nicholas, the police openly having helped the mission organize the ceremony. The buffoon who served as county police inspector in Irkutsk province sent a circular to the local Buriat administration, tribal chiefs and family elders, ordering them to gather fixed numbers of Buriats, "a list of whose names shall be submitted." As a result complaints were forwarded to Alexander D. Goremykin, the governor-general of Eastern Siberia, and to Petersburg, which was visited by a special Buriat delegation. News of these disgraces eventually reached the press. Prince Meshchersky, in his "Diary" for February 11, 1892 (which he published in his ultra-reactionary *Citizen*), lamented: "Eastern Siberia—The reports from Irkutsk province are still distressing: they tell of the terrible violence used in converting Buddhists to Orthodoxy . . . . Fortunately, these terrible happenings came to the notice of the Governor-General of Irkutsk and an investigation has begun. But at the same time this event is doubly unfortunate: firstly, because of the forcible baptism of those who were rounded up in the forests, of those frightened persons who—and this includes even pregnant women—suffered the tortures inflicted upon them by the police in response to the demands of the local priesthood; and, secondly, because of the fact that these unspeakable deeds have been connected with a name dear to all Russians—that of the ruler's first-born."[54]

The *European Herald* also deplored these events but even in this case the Synod—in the person of Pobedonostsev—was able to rebuff the attacks. He labeled them the false slander of socialists. As he saw it, "these complaints, signed with the names of illiterate aliens but written in a literary style with biting phrases, were composed in the places of exile of the Socialist criminals. These persons, because of their own anti-religious convictions, for their own purposes continually engage in composing petitions to harm the Orthodox faith."

In Siberia the fate of those who "seduced" others from Orthodoxy was the same as in the Baltic provinces. Again harsh punishments were imposed for this offense and the records of the Committee of Ministers contain a number of files concerning the luring of baptised Tatars back to Islam. The ministers spent whole sessions reviewing decisions of the Ufa district criminal and civil court which had exiled people to hard labor for "seducing" baptised Tatars and Bashkirs to return to Islam. On Durnovo's suggestion the court's sentences were eased in three of these cases, for "in affairs of this kind it is not so important that the defendants be punished by severe penal measures as that any possible movement, seeking the abandonment of Christianity for Islam, be suppressed." The sentences were so "considerably" eased that the "seducers" and "seduced" were merely exiled permanently by administrative order "to a place not too distant" in Siberia and deprived of all their rights.[55]

PERSECUTION OF THE JEWS

The Jews were subjected to special persecution. In 1882 the "Provisional Regulations for the Jews" were issued. From one point of view these seemed designed to prevent anti-Jewish disorders but they also imposed many restrictions upon the Jews themselves. Perhaps the most important was the prohibition of Jewish residence outside of towns and villages, apart from existing agricultural colonies. These regulations were introduced as a "provisional" measure, pending "a proposed general review of all existing legislation that concerns the Jews."[56]

In the early 1880s no further special measures were adopted. There was no agreement on the Jewish question within the government and, as Bunge observed in his "Notes," since the Minister of the Interior was himself indifferent about this issue, the governors-general of Kiev and Vilna were left to take the most aggressive stands. Otherwise, as Polovtsov admitted in October, 1883, financial considerations forced the government to remain passive. Discussing the role played by the Rothschilds in the negotiation of foreign loans, he cynically observed: "Success with the Rothschilds is possible only on condition that something is done about the Jewish question. This 'something' should consist of an announcement of several regulations, approved by the Emperor, that aim at improving the conditions of Jewish life and which subsequently would not hamper further legislative action." It is noteworthy that the Ministers of Finance remained firm opponents of anti-Jewish legislation throughout this period. They maintained this view regardless of their personal convictions as is illustrated by the positions taken by both Bunge and Vyshnegradsky.

Despite these suggestions, no "regulations approved by the Emperor" were issued concerning the Jews. But at the beginning of 1883 a "Supreme Commission for the Review of the Laws in Force in the Empire Affecting the Jews" was created under the chairmanship of Count Konstantin I. Pahlen. Despite its title, the commission's membership was hardly authoritative: not a single minister or even assistant minister was included, so that this commission seems in some ways to have been a declaration of intent. Nonetheless, it continued its work until the summer of 1888, by which time the members still had not reached agreement. The commission's majority (seven members, headed by the chairman) did suggest some very progressive general principles. Their decision, adopted by only a single vote, concluded that the "most important of these principles may be formulated as the following points: a) The main task of legislation concerning the Jews consists *of assimilating the Jews as far as possible into the Christian population;*[57] b) There should be no new legislation drawn up in either the form of a 'Law' or a 'Regulation' that would in principle contradict the efforts of the government to break down Jewish distinctiveness; c) The system of repressive and exclusive measures should be replaced by a system that aims at (the Jews') gradual liberation and equality in law." The fourth and last point of the commission's recommendation stressed that "the greatest caution and measure" should be observed in solving the Jewish question.[58]

In 1885 the Committee of Ministers asked the Pahlen Commission to discuss "the overcrowding of secondary educational institutions by Jews" and the minority of the commission agreed to the establishment of a fixed allowable percentage of Jewish students. But the chairman and the majority considered that "restrictions on the entry of Jewish children . . . should affect exclusively those who belonged to the lower strata as, in the opinion of the superintendents of the educational districts, it is precisely this category of students that really causes harm within the educational institutions." Evidently this was a case of a class and not a nationalist prejudice.

At the end of 1886 Alexander III approved a proposal of the Committee of Ministers based on a report of the governor of Kharkov. This proposal allowed the Minister of Education to adopt at his discretion local measures limiting the entry of Jews into his ministry's secondary and higher educational institutions. Then in June, 1887 Delianov presented his own report to the Committee of Ministers (entitled "On Limiting Jewish Entry into the Secondary Educational Institutions of the Ministry of Education"). This document envisaged allowing only Jewish children whose parents were "hereditary and personal nobles, Honored Citizens, Commercial and Manufacturing Councillors, professors, artists, persons with completion certificates for a course in an institution of higher learning, and Merchants of the First Guild, to enter the gymnasiums and progymnasiums."

The Committee of Ministers rejected Delianov's proposal and observed that the question of preserving higher and secondary institutions "from an influx of Jews long ago attracted the attention of the government and in the past was settled through the individual decisions of individual ministries. Because of this a special discretionary authority had been granted to the Ministries of War, State Domains, Justice, and Communications, and the entry of persons of Jewish origins into the secondary and higher educational institutions subordinated to these ministries already has been limited to certain percentages. According to the declarations of State Secretary Ostrovsky and Adjutant-General Posiet, the further application of such measures presents no difficulty." It was further pointed out that the Minister of Education had similar powers and noted that, since most Jewish children belonged to the lower elements of the populace, the exclusion of this category would make the percentage of Jews in secondary educational institutions even lower than proposed by Delianov.[59]

Notwithstanding the ministerial committee's decision of June 16, a few weeks later Delianov issued a circular on this same question. Dated July 10, 1887, this document evidently had the tsar's sanction and it established the percentage of Jews permitted in secondary educational institutions within the Pale of Settlement at ten percent, outside the Pale at five percent, and in the capitals at three percent. These percentages were to be effective from the beginning of the 1887-1888 school year[60] as were the similar regulations which applied to the higher educational institutions.[61]

As for Pahlen's Supreme Commission, the conclusions approved by the majority were found unacceptable. Then, as Bunge put it, "in view of Pahlen's departure," V.K. Plehve, Assistant Minister of the Interior, was appointed chairman. According to Simon S. Dubnow, author of the article "Fouror judofobicus" [sic!] , during the last years of Alexander III's reign Plehve drew up a plan of legislation on the Jewish question. The Ministry of the Interior then circulated this program to the governors, who were requested to submit their comments.[62] Plehve supposedly proposed some forty points. These envisaged the creation of separate Jewish areas or ghettos in large cities, a strengthening of the "Provisional Regulations for the Jews" of 1882, a restriction of their commercial activities, and a reduction of the privileges allowed several categories of Jews (merchants of the first and second guilds, honored citizens, persons with a higher education, and so forth).

Apparently this program was intended for the State Council. A.A. Polovtsov's diary supports this supposition. On October 22, 1890 he recorded that Nicholas S. Abaza said that, "owing to the insistence of Vyshnegradsky, the Minister of the Interior has put off presenting in the Council new restrictive measures against the Jews." Again this intervention by a Minister of Finance was motivated by a very real danger that the publication of new restrictive laws would seriously harm the possibilities of obtaining foreign funds. Public protests—both within Russia and abroad—against the persecution of the Jews probably also had some effect. On December 10, 1890 a meeting of two thousand people in London addressed a petition deploring the position of Russia's Jews to Alexander III. The latter, of course, never replied.

That summer the philosopher Vladimir S. Soloviev had organized a similar petition of protest against the badgering of Jews carried on in the Russian press. Signed by the leading representatives of the Russian intelligentsia, including Leo N. Tolstoy, Vladimir G. Korolenko, Vladimir I. Gere, Paul N. Miliukov, Alexis N. Veselovsky, Sergei A. Muromtsev, and others, the protest read: "The anti-Jewish feeling being spread by the Russian press is a hitherto unprecedented violation of the most basic demands of justice and humanity." But, thanks to the intrigues of Dmitry I. Ilovaisky and others of his ilk, this protest never saw the light of day.

During the 1890s, after the death of Count D.A. Tolstoy, the persecution of the Jews increased in tempo. While Tolstoy himself had been more or less indifferent about the Jewish question, Durnovo, his successor, was an active anti-Semite and naturally received the full support of the emperor. Moreover, Grand Duke Sergei Alexandrovich played no small role in fueling the anti-Jewish campaign. "Durnovo, the Minister of the Interior," confided Polovtsov to his diary, "told me that the Emperor had given him instructions to expell the Jews from Moscow, explaining, 'My brother Sergei does not want to go to Moscow unless it is cleared of Jews.' "[63] Then, on March 28, 1891, Grand Duke Sergei was appointed governor-general of Moscow. Exactly one month later a law entitled "The Prohibition of the Settlement of Jewish Artisans, Distillers and Brewers, General Craftsmen, and Workmen, in Moscow and Moscow Province" was approved on the basis of a memorandum from the Minister of the Interior.[64] This latter official, in agreement with Grand Duke Sergei, proposed by this law gradually to evict these categories of Jews. Then, at the end of 1892, again on a report of Durnovo, a second law— "The Restriction of Discharged Jewish Enlisted Men, and Members of their Families, who Enlisted in Cities Outside the Province and Served under the Former Recruit Statute, from Residence in Moscow and Moscow Province"—was promulgated. As a result of these two laws, some 20,000 Jews were expelled from Moscow.

The eviction of Jews to the Pale of Settlement was not restricted to Moscow. On January 14, 1893 Durnovo issued a circular to the governors cancelling the provisions of the Ministry of the Interior's instruction of April 3, 1880[65] (which had suspended "pending special orders" the expulsion of Jews "who did not have the right of residence outside of the Pale of Settlement" from the provinces of the interior). Durnovo's new circular of 1893 evicted these Jews and allowed them a period of not more than four months to effect their departure. "The aforementioned four-month period," the circular read, "may be extended, but not longer than November 1 of this year."[66]

The Ministry of the Interior adopted several other measures against the Jews which were both illegal and, at times, even brutal. At the beginning of the 1890s, for example, circulars of the ministry prohibited temporary visits by Jews to the health resorts of the Black and Baltic sea coasts. The alleged legal basis for these orders was a law of May 3, 1882 which banned Jewish residence in rural localities.[67] The archives of the Department of Police contain many files on this matter. Labeled "On Granting Permission to Jews to Visit Watering Places for Treatment," they contain both the requests of individual Jews for permission to vacation at the health resorts and the petitions of summer home (dacha) owners who wished to rent to Jewish tenants. Nonetheless, in 1892 the governor of Taurida barred Jews from visiting Alushta and other points on the Crimean coast, and the governors of Riga and Kherson issued similar instructions for their areas.[68] Taken together, these

orders reveal clearly the wide scope of official anti-Semitism as it existed
in the early 1890s.

ECONOMIC POLICIES

Although it is not proposed to investigate the government's economic
policies in great detail, a brief outline of their basic trends is still necessary. Here the goals differed fundamentally from those desired in other
domestic fields where the government sought to preserve and to strength-
en the remnants of feudalism. For the economic policies were basically
bourgeois in character and designed to promote Russia's further progress
along the road to capitalism.

How is this contradiction to be explained? In general it resulted from
the fact that economic development entails the adoption of particular
measures. This meant that Alexander III, his closest advisors, and his
successive ministers of finance really could not have acted very differently. Fiscal interests demanded an increase in revenues to satisfy the
budget, and this in turn demanded industrial and commercial development as well as protective tariff policies. Similarly, a growth of state
spending brought efforts to increase income, a considerable portion of
which came from direct taxes. The old feudal methods of taxation did
not give—and could not have given—effective results in the new economic
conditions which existed in Russia. Hence the state debt mounted from
year to year and the transition to a new, modern system of taxation was
imperative. Finally, any increase in Russian defense capability necessitated the development of both a railway system and several other industries. In aggregate, these circumstances determined the government's
economic pursuits despite the fact that they sometimes conflicted utterly with the general trend of policy in other aspects of Russian life.

The nature of the government's other policies naturally had some influence on those in the financial field. This created some tension between the economic and the financial measures. Several of the latter
aimed at helping the impoverished gentry and thus obviously were out
of tune with both the other economic policies and the economic transformation occurring in Russia.

During the political crises of the early 1880s, Loris-Melikov and
Abaza, the Minister of Finance, planned numerous economic reforms.
These were implemented at the end of 1881 by Count Ignatiev and
Bunge. On December 28, 1881 a law made the redemption of land allot-
ments obligatory for the peasants but at the same time lowered the
amount of the required payments. Then, in 1883 Minister of Finance
Bunge proposed in the State Council the gradual abolition of the poll
tax, beginning in 1884.[69] To compensate for possible losses in revenue,

Bunge requested the introduction of new taxes on various forms of profits and in this way tried to shift part of the tax burden to the wealthier classes. This latter impost, even in the limited form suggested, failed to pass and Bunge's plan to tax great merchant and industrial enterprises in proportion to the size of their profits was rejected by the State Council in early 1884.[70] Yet the Minister of Finance did succeed in gaining the State Council's assent for a law to tax properties that were acquired gratis (that is, by inheritance, a grant, or some similar manner). On May 20, 1885, again at the request of the Minister of Finance, Alexander III approved another law that established a five percent impost on incomes derived from interest on securities and bank deposits.[71] In this way definite steps were taken toward the reconstruction of the tax system on new and bourgeois principles.[72]

Meanwhile indirect taxes (the excise duties on spirits, tobacco, and sugar) increased substantially. From 1881 to 1886 the alcohol revenues grew from 225,365,000 to 236,977,000 rubles, that is, by five percent. The proceeds from the excise on sugar, tobacco, and oil mounted from 16,463,000 to 35,262,000 rubles (or by more than 100 percent). These increases should have compensated easily for any revenue lost by lowering the redemption payments considering that, in addition, import duties were raised significantly during this same period (in 1883, 1884, and 1885).[73] As a result, the income from tariffs between 1881 and 1886 grew by more than thirty percent (from 85,763,000 to 112,447,000 rubles), and provided greater revenues while promoting the further development of native industry.

At the same time the government took steps to provide economic support for the landed gentry. The creation of the Nobles Bank in 1885 to mark the centennial of the Charter of the Nobility was the most important of such measures. The purpose of this bank was to extend credit to the landed gentry. Noblemen could obtain loans on very favorable terms, putting up their estates as security for periods of up to forty-eight years and eight months. Bunge opposed this measure and argued, according to Meshchersky, "that the gentry is a dying class." The creation of the Nobles Bank naturally meant diverting a large part of the state's wealth to the unproductive purposes of aiding this group; as a rule estate owners wasted or squandered their loans on drink rather than using them for "the improvement of the farm."

A second measure for the support of the gentry was clearly charitable. This was a law of May 15, 1883, approved by Alexander III on the day of his coronation. According to this statute landlords who had not converted their peasants into proprietors by January, 1883 were to receive redemption sums of 88.5 percent of the capitalization of the *obrok* rather than the 80 percent stipulated by the statute of February 19, 1861.[74] Yet the government's economic policies during the early 1880s—when Bunge was minister—were, despite such inconsistencies, basically progressive in character.

By the end of 1886 the intrigues of Pobedonostsev, Katkov and other reactionaries culminated in Bunge's dismissal and I.A. Vyshnegradsky was appointed in his place. Although famed internationally as a scholar, the latter's reputation as a great banking figure was somewhat more dubious.[75]

A memorandum Vyshnegradsky presented to Alexander III, outlining the tasks facing a finance minister, offers insight into his views. "In the immediate future the activity of the financial administration," wrote Vyshnegradsky, "should be directed mainly toward eliminating the deficits burdening our budgets." In his opinion, this should be achieved without cutting back expenditures, which "must be treated with the greatest prudence," or increasing direct taxes, which "would burden the population, diminish their productive capacity and, therefore, their tax potential." Rather, Vyshnegradsky believed, the government should create alcohol and tobacco monopolies and properly reorganize the railway rates. He estimated the revenues of an alcohol monopoly at no less than sixty million rubles, while a tobacco monopoly should raise the government's income by another forty million rubles. The efficient reorganization of railway rates would, he hoped, further increase revenues considerably. "With the aid of the three measures[76] outlined above," Vyshnegradsky predicted, "state revenues might grow by as much as 120 million rubles. This increase in revenues would re-establish a balanced budget and even provide some surplus above expenditures." Together with these measures, Vyshnegradsky considered it necessary "to embark resolutely upon a policy of establishing protectionist measures to encourage home industries" and he proposed "a systematic revision of our entire import duties in a protectionist sense."

This report demonstrates that with the exception of the creation of the monopolies, all measures recommended by Vyshnegradsky were essentially continuations of Bunge's policies. In practice the new minister increased indirect taxes on alcohol, tobacco, sugar, and oil. Between the years 1887 and 1892 the income from the alcohol tax grew by eleven million (or from 257,624,000 to 269,000,000 rubles). In this same period revenues from the tobacco, sugar, and oil taxes rose by eighty percent (or from 47,255,000 to 75,274,000 rubles).

The second half of the 1880s and early 1890s witnessed a continuous expansion in import duties. In 1887 protective tariffs were introduced on pig iron, iron, steel, needles, and other metal products. These imposts brought a sharp decrease in imports and in 1889 and 1890 further high duties were imposed on manufactured goods (with a rate of twenty percent being levied on most items). Then, after 1891, a new tariff rate was introduced. In his proposal to the State Council for a "General Revision of Import Tariffs," Vyshnegradsky stressed that this policy was necessary "in order to bring the separate parts . . . and the sum total of our tariffs into line with the contemporary conditions of our industry, and to give suitable and equal protection to all its branches."

The new duties both promoted industrial growth and increased the revenues drawn from the tariff system. Even though imports decreased, the income from duties climbed from 107,427,000 rubles in 1887 to 130,552,000 rubles in 1892. On several items import duties had increased eight to ten times over those existing at the end of the 1860s. Duty on a *pud*[77] of pig iron, for instance, had risen from about five kopeks to 45 to 52 kopeks, and that on machinery jumped from thirty kopeks to two rubles and 54 kopeks. The attendent fall in imports of manufactured goods was accompanied by a substantial rise in the influx of foreign capital, which created an additional impulse for industrial development. Over the twelve years 1881 to 1892 the amount of foreign capital invested in joint stock companies increased by 130 million rubles, whereas during the previous twenty years it had risen only by 88 million rubles.

Vyshnegradsky's expectations for the alcohol and tobacco monopolies proved unjustified. As a consequence he was compelled to seek further income by increasing indirect taxes and continuing to pressure the peasantry for their arrears in redemption payments and poll taxes, even though the latter were now abolished. Such back payments were collected in the most determined manner, being literally "extorted" from defaulters without considering the impact on the peasants' economic situation. The same desire for greater revenues prompted Vyshnegradsky to convert Russia's foreign loans to a sum of two billion rubles with the rate of interest lowered from five to four percent. This brought some saving in interest payments, while the amounts raised grew from 131,793,000 rubles in 1887 to 165,777,000 rubles in 1892.

The Russian government extended its control over railway finances, regulated rates and finally converted the railroads into a public rail system. These developments, combined with the bankruptcy of several lines, helped to improve the finances of the remaining railways and to raise their profits. In 1887 the railroads enjoyed revenues amounting to 53,400,000 rubles, rising by 1892 to reach some 111,100,000 rubles, an increase in revenue of over 100 percent. Meanwhile the railway network was enlarged significantly: in 1881 there were 21,228 versts of track and in 1891 some 31,219 versts, an expansion of 47 percent.

These measures allowed the government to erase the budgetary deficits and created the necessary reserves for the future adoption of the gold standard. Yet Vyshnegradsky, no less than Bunge, needed to make some effort to support the regime's policies favoring the gentry. In 1889 the Finance Committee recognized "the need to aid the gentry" and decided to lower to four and one-half percent the rate of interest paid by the gentry on loans from the Nobles Bank. The gentry was also granted other supplementary exemptions.[78]

In 1892 Sergei Yu. Witte replaced the ailing Vyshnegradsky as Minister of Finance. Witte was extremely intelligent and talented. He stood head and shoulders above his colleagues and later inspired the political policies which, in the early 1900s, promoted the transformation of the autocracy into a constitutional, bourgeois monarchy. At this time, however, Witte's views on Russian economic development remained quite incomplete (thus he still supported the preservation of the peasant commune).

For all his great abilities, Witte's moral principles remained questionable. He did not hesitate to profit from the friendship and support of Meshchersky or, later, in the twilight of his career, from that of Rasputin. Polovtsov remarked on Witte's intelligence but recognized that "his sense of honor and integrity did not inspire any confidence whatsoever." While in office Witte had no qualms about associating with various reactionaries and rogues. The thief, A.K. Krivoshein, whom Witte helped to get appointed Minister of Communications, is but one example. Evidently it was Meshchersky who helped Witte become friendly with Vyshnegradsky and obtain his support. In 1889 the latter's influence gained Witte his appointment as director of the railway department in the Ministry of Finance.[79] Then, in early 1892, again with the help of his friend Vyshnegradsky, Witte was appointed Minister of Communications. Yet Witte did not accord "his friend this same loyalty." Even when he was still a mere departmental director Witte had begun to intrigue against Vyshnegradsky. Later, although the latter was not yet incapacitated, Witte hurried to inform Alexander III of the poor health of his Minister of Finance. Subsequently, when Vyshnegradsky really became ill, Witte immediately assumed his place as head of the ministry. Once there, Witte's policies were no different from Vyshnegradsky's. He simply continued the work of the latter, particularly with respect to the protection of home industries.

It may be concluded that the government's economic policies remained essentially unchanged under all three ministers of finance. While the details might vary, the basic aim of all these policies was to increase budgetary income by raising indirect taxes and supporting Russian domestic industry. Such efforts naturally brought results. Protectionist policies promoted a rapid expansion of industry, and particularly of heavy industry. Between 1886 and 1892 metallurgical production doubled. Or, seen from another perspective, in 1880 home production satisfied 43 percent of Russia's demand for metals, and in 1892 some 79.6 percent. Hence the government's financial policies contributed to the powerful economic upsurge evident during the latter 1890s while Vyshnegradsky's reforms, which had aimed at enhancing the state's revenues, made possible the realization of Witte's own reform—the placing of Russia on the gold standard.

CHAPTER III

THE MINISTRY OF THE INTERIOR UNDER TOLSTOY AND DURNOVO

TOLSTOY AND HIS ASSISTANTS

"In the merry month of May," as P.A. Valuev sarcastically put it, Count I.P. Ignatiev was "banished from the court" and Count D.A. Tolstoy became Minister of the Interior. It was originally intended to give this post to M.N. Ostrovsky. On May 15, 1882, before Ignatiev's dismissal had become final, Alexander III wrote Pobedonostsev: "I think that at present there is only one man who can replace Ignatiev. This is Ostrovsky. In this case I intend to separate the Department of State Police and the entire Gendarme section from the Ministry of the Interior. I assume that Ostrovsky would agree to accept the ministry under these conditions."[1]

The question of splitting the ministry was, however, immediately shelved, and Tolstoy was advanced as a candidate. There is no evidence about precisely who suggested him, but Pobedonostsev seems to have been involved. This supposition is supported by the director-general's conversations with Tolstoy, which suggest that he was favorably disposed towards this candidate. On May 28, 1882, in a letter to the emperor, Pobedonostsev wrote: "This morning I carried out Your Imperial Majesty's instructions: Tolstoy was here and I had a talk with him. I explained that it was Your Majesty's firm intention to divide the administration of the Ministry of the Interior from the management of the State Police. On these terms Count Tolstoy is ready to obey Your will, and ready to do so, may I observe, with good will and ardor." In concluding, Pobedonostsev commended this candidate as "a highly educated man who is acquainted intimately with many of the major problems."[2] Although Tolstoy originally agreed to accept the new post without control of the Department of State Police, he soon agreed to serve as both minister and chief of the gendarmes.[3]

The appointment of Tolstoy—a man whose name was a synonym for reaction—upset liberals but delighted the reactionaries. "The appointment of Count Tolstoy," Katkov proclaimed in the lead article of his *Moscow News* for June 3, 1882, "is significant and important because everyone must see in it the expression of a living, autocratic will. The name of Count Tolstoy is in itself a manifesto and a program. (His appointment) more clearly defines government policies than any number of enactments could have done."

Professor A.A. Kizevetter described the reactions of the provincial intelligentsia somewhat differently, recalling: "I was a student in the sixth class of the Orenburg gymnasium. It was a warm May evening. City Boulevard, which ran along the steep bank of the river Ural, was crowded with strollers. Along the boulevard news spread that a telegram had just arrived announcing the appointment of Tolstoy as Minister of the Interior . . . . People on the street immediately broke up into small groups. Everywhere I saw frowning faces, and from all sides heard one and the same sentence: 'Tolstoy—it will be a reactionary government . . . .' I watched as the elderly, gray-haired men shook their heads and set out for home."

Konstantin F. Golovin, himself a civil servant and reactionary journalist, later noted: "Here was, first and foremost, a man with an iron will . . . . With this undoubted virtue (which is, however, not enough for a contemporary statesman) he combined two major defects. He distrusted almost everyone on principle and he lacked that inner enthusiasm which inspires and nurtures fruitful ideas. An armor of biased distrust protected him from outside influences . . . . Dmitry Andrevich had no 'system' whatsoever outside the area of schools. A hatred of elected offices and an assumption, or so it would seem, that a uniform would guarantee the fitness and loyalty of officials—these ideas exhausted the content of his miserable 'system.' " And Tolstoy, despite his firm political views, did indeed lack a positive program. He knew well enough what he felt should be done, but had no idea of how to do it. He hated the Kakhanov Commission, for instance, and longed to disperse it. Yet he did not manage to do this until 1885.

It should be remembered that the fear of terrorists still persisted. As observed above, during his first years in the ministry Tolstoy was terrified of dying at the hands of the revolutionaries. On December 18, 1883 he openly mentioned this to Pobedonostsev. "Now these scoundrels plan to kill me," he claimed. "Of course, my immediate subordinates are taking every precaution. But it is impossible to guarantee success when dealing with such brigands and it seems to me that we ought to consider now who should succeed me, just in case my luck does not hold."[4] In addition to these fears, a growth in peasant disorders further complicated the situation. In any case, it was only in 1885 that the ministry grew more active and work began on plans for the reorganization of local institutions as part of a larger program of counter-reform.

The minister's closest aides were his assistant ministers. These were I.N. Durnovo, V.K. Plehve (after 1889) and, in the Department of Police, General Peter V. Orzhevsky. The first of these gentlemen, Ivan Nikolaevich Durnovo, was closest to Tolstoy and subsequently his successor. A poorly educated man, Durnovo lacked any convictions or firm views whatsoever. E.M. Feoktistov, if one may judge from his memoirs, thought very highly of him and valued his "human qualities." Nevertheless, this same Feoktistov gave a very unflattering description of Ivan Nikolaevich as a figure of authority. "He displayed no brilliant ability as a statesman," Feoktistov wrote, "and his education was mediocre. I doubt that he had chanced to read a serious book, and he had no independent views or ideas." Another official, K.F. Golovin, remarked that Durnovo brought to the ministry "the habits and methods of a hospitable marshal (of the nobility) who is prepared to promise everyone the world and to keep his word about nothing." Cunning and always ready to manoeuvre, he was the "life of a party" and charmed everyone, especially women, with his tact and apparent benevolence.

In contrast to Durnovo, V.K. Plehve [who became an assistant minister in 1884], was extremely able and industrious. Educated as a lawyer and a jurist by profession, in 1881 Plehve was prosecutor of the St. Petersburg Judicial Bench. Yet he was the antithesis of that glorious pleiad of Russian jurists of whom A.F. Koni is representative. Plehve had tied his career to that of Count Konstantin I. Pahlen, a Minister of Justice who had tried whenever possible to minimize the impact of the judicial statute of 1864, and who had appointed to judicial posts unprincipled careerists who followed his orders without question.

In 1881, after the murder of Alexander II, Loris-Melikov obtained Plehve's appointment as director of the Department of Police. "The professional and moral qualities of Mr. Plehve," Loris-Melikov wrote Alexander III when suggesting Plehve's appointment, "serve as a sufficient guarantee that he will bring that same energy and understanding to his new activities as have always distinguished his service in the judicial department." In fact, on becoming director of the Department of State Police Plehve displayed great energy and became one of the initiators of the law of August 14, 1881—"The Statute on Measures for the Protection of State Security and Public Tranquillity." Further, a system of police spies organized by Lieutenant Colonel Georgy P. Sudeikin and usually known as the "Degaevshchina,"[5] was connected with and possibly inspired by the new director. Intelligent, energetic, and possessed of a good business sense, Plehve's horse-like capacity for work was invariably highly valued by his colleagues. He was, withal, a man of great ambition and like most bureaucrats he lacked firm views and convictions. Even Alexander III, who was not particularly noted for his insight, once noted on a report of Tolstoy (who had commented favorably on Plehve's "excellent beliefs"): "Yes, he has excellent beliefs . . . when you are there. But when you are not there, his beliefs will be different."

The third assistant minister, the gendarme commander, General P.V. Orzhevsky, was, as Feoktistov said, "undoubtedly an intelligent man of firm character, but extremely ambitious, bitter and envious." Seen against the amoral background of other gendarmes, he was far from their worst representative. But along with the qualities so accurately listed by Feoktistov, Orzhevsky was an intriguer who tried to intimidate Tolstoy with the terrorist threat and in this way keep the minister under his control. I.A. Shestakov, the director of the Naval Ministry, confided to his diary that "Orzhevsky is dismissed, they say, owing to the implacable hostility of (Peter A.) Gresser (the city governor of St. Petersburg) . . . . Orzhevsky simply maintains that Tolstoy will not dare to part with him because he pays him 2,000 rubles a month, (from the 60,000 supplied to the secret police) to ensure his (Tolstoy's) personal protection."[6] Orzhevsky, along with Durnovo and Plehve, assisted Tolstoy through most of his term of office and helped launch the new program of political reaction.

THE STATUTE OF AUGUST 14, 1881

The law of August 14, 1881—the "Statute on Measures for the Protection of State Security and Public Tranquillity"—did much to define the manner in which the Ministry of the Interior functioned during the reign of Alexander III. Because the law's effectiveness was limited to three-year periods, the Minister of the Interior regularly had to request the Committee of Ministers to extend its life "as a temporary measure for yet another three years." These requests were unhesitatingly granted, but some changes were made in particular articles of the law.

The most essential ammendment concerned Article 32. On June 21, 1883 the Committee of Ministers considered Tolstoy's complaint that the Senate was misinterpreting this article. In the opinion of the latter, this article permitted persons labelled as politically suspect to be exiled by an administrative order, but those simply labelled as "harmful" should be dealt with under the provisions of the regular criminal code.[7] Tolstoy argued that "instigators of student meetings, as well as of disorders and strikes among factory workers, should be included . . . in the category of persons harmful to state security and public tranquillity along with people who belong to illegal (political) organizations." He frankly admitted that action against these categories of persons, whose activities certainly disrupted the "tranquillity of the state," was very difficult. "Thus," he pointed out, "the act of inciting peasants to seize a landlord's property by assuring them that it is possible to change the existing system of landholding can be cited before the courts only in extreme cases." The Committee of Ministers acceded to the minister's request for a reformulation of Article 32 to allow the administrative exile of persons "recognized as harmful to state security and public tranquillity."[8] The new version of Article 32 naturally increased the chances for arbitrary administrative actions. The definition of persons "harmful to the state order and public tranquillity" became so broad that local authorities might place anyone they found objectionable in this category.

According to Article 34 of the law of August 14, 1881, a decision on administrative exile was to be made by a "special board" created for this purpose. This body consisted of five people: the chairman (an Assistant Minister of the Interior) and four officials (two each from the Ministries of the Interior and Justice). The Minister of the Interior then approved all their decisions. The actual restraints imposed upon an administrative exile were defined on March 12, 1883 by the Statute on Police Surveillance. This deprived exiles of the rights of entering the civil service, of teaching, and of taking part in any public activity. The local authorities held the right to examine their correspondence and exiles might leave their residences and travel within provincial borders only with permission of governors, and within county borders only with that of the county police chief. Trips beyond the province of their exile could be approved only by the Minister of the Interior.

Prior to 1889 the "State of Strengthened Security Measures" (provided for by Article 8 of the statute of August 14, 1881) had been declared in ten provinces (St. Petersburg, Moscow, Kharkov, Kiev, Chernigov, Volynia, Poltava, Kherson, and Bessarabia), in five counties of Tavrichesk province, and in certain cities and counties (Saratov, Kerch, Sevastopol, the St. Petersburg and Odessa city governorships, the Kronstadt and Nikolaev military governorships, and a number of larger centers in the Don Cossack region). Elsewhere in the empire, Articles 28 to 31[9] of the statute remained in effect. In 1889 the "State of Strengthened Security Measures" was lifted in Chernigov and Poltava, in the five counties of Tavrichesk, and in the cities of Saratov, Kerch, and Sevastopol; and in 1890 in the provinces of Kherson and Bessarabia. Thus, by 1895 this article was in effect in six provinces, in the cities of Taganrog and Nakhichevan, in the St. Petersburg and Odessa city governorships, the Nikolaev and Kronstadt military governorships, and in several large villages (*stanitsas*) of the Don Cossack region. In 1894 Syrdarinsk region and several counties of the Fergana region (Tashkent, Chimkent and Auliet) were declared in a "State of Strengthened Security Measures," and after 1883 Nizhny Novgorod and the surrounding counties were placed under this article every year during the fair. Each year the Committee of Ministers reviewed the Minister of the Interior's requests for continuing the term of "strengthened security measures" in the different localities and unhesitatingly approved them. Sometimes local administrators—the governors-general—asked the ministers to declare "strengthened security measures" in a particular area of the country, but these applications were sometimes unsuccessful.[10]

Once a "State of Strengthened Security Measures" was declared in an area, the governor or governor-general was given wider administrative authority. Occasionally they used the provisions of this article to conceal their own illegal actions, and in these instances they were censured by the Minister of the Interior. In the summer of 1888 the governor-general of Odessa, to cite one example', used [Article 8 of] the statute of August 14, 1881 as a basis for issuing regulations for the Odessa city hospital and shifting the cost of maintaining both the hospital and the medical inspector to the city's municipal council. The Minister of the Interior reported on this matter to the emperor, pointing out that "the governor-general's aforesaid decree not only abolished existing law, but simultaneously established a regulation that contradicts the Municipal Statute." The minister requested an "Imperial" order countermanding the decree of the governor-general.

But Alexander III regarded this issue somewhat differently. "The governor-general's decree is, of course, incorrect," he noted on Tolstoy's report, "but there was nothing else left for him to do. The city council would listen to no one and 'gave itself too many airs.' " So he ordered the governor-general's decree to "remain in effect for the time being." Meanwhile the Minister of the Interior was to present to the Committee of Ministers "a proposal for giving governors-general, governors, and city governors in areas where a 'State of Strengthened Security Measures' has been declared, general instructions regarding the limits of their right to issue decrees."

The Committee of Ministers discussed this question in February and March, 1889. It concluded that decrees issued on the basis of the "Statute on Measures for the Protection of State Security and Public Tranquillity" should deal "exclusively with matters related to preventing and suppressing breaches of the public order and state security." Nonetheless, the ruler's generous attitude to violations of his own laws hardly discouraged illegal and arbitrary behaviour.

THE DEPARTMENT OF POLICE

The Department of State Police was created at the end of 1880 by uniting the Third Section of H.I.M. Own Chancellery and the old Department of Police within the Ministry of the Interior. This new department was organized along the lines suggested by Count Loris-Melikov's memorandum to the tsar of November 10 of that year and consisted of three branches (administrative, legislative, and secret). At the same time a special judicial section was formed in the Ministry of the Interior to replace the judicial department of the defunct Third Section. This body's main function was the supervision of cases dealing with "crimes against the state." At the end of 1881 the judicial section was attached to the Department of Police and in February, 1883 separated again, once and for all. That same year the Department of State Police was renamed simply the Department of Police.

By the beginning of 1883 the Department of Police contained five branches. The First (administrative) managed the department's personnel and handled such matters as appointments, decorations, dismissals, the arraignment of members of the department and officials of the Ministry of the Interior, the preparation of budget estimates, the payment of allowances, and so on.[11] The Second Office (legislative) was responsible for "organizing police institutions in all localities of the empire" (that is, for regulations and instructions, and for the staffing and supervising of correct procedures "in local police posts"). It also dealt with questions concerning monastic institutions, religious associations, and measures "for the prevention and suppression of open seduction, lewd conduct, drunkenness, and begging." This branch regulated inns and taverns, drew up legislation and regulations concerning passports, supervised the passport system, kept a general watch over all foreigners within the country, and was responsible for drafting measures "to regulate relations between workers and factory owners, manufacturers and employers." Finally, the Second Office monitored all articles "appearing in the press that concerned any subject connected with the conduct of the department." In this way this branch's sphere of activity was extremely extensive and included, along with the supervision of monasteries, inns, and public houses, the preparation of legislation aimed at guaranteeing peaceful relations between the factory owners and their workers.

The Third Office's functions concerned "matters of the higher police and handled the departmental director's special correspondence." To be more exact, this branch supervised political prisoners in the Petropavlovsk fortress and checked the loyalty of persons who opened schools and workshops, wished to publish newspapers or magazines, desired to enter the civil service, or had applied for passports to travel abroad. It collected secret information on any event "that attracts the government's attention" and carried on correspondence "concerning denunciations by private citizens, acts of a generally criminal nature and other matters." Lastly, it was responsible for tracking down criminals.

Meanwhile the Fourth or Judicial Office prepared agendas for the "special board" on administrative exiles set up in accord with Article 34 of the statute of August 14, 1881, supervised the investigation of "crimes against the state," and dealt with "cases of political unreliability."

According to data of the Department of Police, during the years 1881 to 1894 inclusive, the special board examined some 4,295 cases and agreed to the administrative exile of 5,397 persons. A register in the *Historical Survey of the Organization and Activities of the Department of Police* provides more detailed information from which it is clear that those administratively exiled as politically suspect made up about fifty percent of the general total. In addition, the 532 participants in factory and agrarian disorders presumably should be regarded as political criminals, raising the number of people in this category to 3,082.

Finally, the Fifth (Executive) Office was charged with "executing verdicts reached in cases of 'crimes against the state' and in investigations of political unreliability," the implementation of various police laws (such as that of August 14, 1881, the Statute on Police Surveillance, and so on). This branch kept a "reference table" with alphabetical lists of everyone who was politically unreliable or worked in the antigovernment press, complete with photographs of those who had "drawn the attention of the police."[12] According to the *Historical Survey* "the most important task originally allotted to the Fifth Office was to investigate and report on people subject to public surveillance by the police, and to establish the period of the aforementioned surveillance."

Apart from these five branches, the Department of Police contained a secretarial section which handled the personal correspondence of the departmental director. Here the general journal of the department was kept, along with its archives. There was also an executive section which proposed members of the police for pensions, handled the appointment and dismissal of senior police officials as well as questions of decorations and promotions. To some extent this executive section obviously duplicated the work of the First Office.

Having outlined the structure of the Department of Police,[13] the personnel of both this agency and the Detached Corps of Gendarmes deserve attention. In the beginning the department's staff supposedly consisted of 52 people but, according to the *Historical Survey*, the real composition was somewhat larger. In 1881, apart from the regular staff, 28 persons were listed as attached to the department and 45 civilians were also in its employ. Thus, in 1881 the full complement of the Department of Police, apart from messengers and watchmen, numbered 125 persons. By 1895, if it is assumed that the number of regular officials had not increased, the total had risen to 161 persons (with 55 attached and 54 civilians).[14]

REGISTER OF CASES DECIDED UNDER ARTICLE 34 OF THE LAW OF AUGUST 14, 1881

1881-1894 (Inclusive)

Year	Number			Politically Suspicious		Factory Disorders		Agrarian Disorders		Sectarians		Depraved Conduct	
Year	Sessions	Cases	Persons	Cases	Persons	Cases	Persons	Cases	Persons	Cases	Persons	Cases	Persons
1881	11	615	615	467	467	18	18	31	31	4	4	95	95
1882	20	1840	1841	743	743	51	52	101	101	10	10	935	935
1883	8	338	394	271	273	2	10	13	38	3	3	49	70
1884	8	436	486	287	313	—	—	11	21	4	7	134	145
1885	5	89	121	50	57	1	2	8	28	4	4	26	30
1886	6	136	184	58	69	4	4	3	3	9	36	62	72
1887	6	121	196	62	81	1	19	12	19	7	34	39	43
1888	5	98	170	56	102	—	—	12	21	7	9	23	38
1889	4	52	160	30	37	3	37	4	7	4	28	11	51
1890	6	111	247	35	109	2	3	19	43	17	34	41	58
1891	7	112	200	41	86	1	1	7	11	28	59	35	43
1892	4	112	221	14	17	—	—	12	31	22	80	64	93
1893	4	109	187	25	26	—	—	7	28	18	42	59	91
1894	5	126	375	29	170	—	—	3	9	24	51	70	150
Total		4295	5397		2550*		146		386		401		1914

*In addition, 355 persons from the Kingdom of Poland were administratively exiled to Siberia, under the terms of the law of October 5, 1884, prior to 1894. Of these, 163 were exiled for being politically suspect, 88 for being representatives of emigre groups, 35 for religious propaganda, and 68 for depraved conduct. Thus, considering the first two categories as being political, the percentage of political exiles was 70.7 (or 251 persons).

In 1880 the Detached Corps of Gendarmes included 521 officers and 6,187 other ranks. After this date the force expanded slightly. On January 1, 1895 it contained 693 officers, 28 civilian officials, and 8,522 other ranks (6,930 of whom were sergeant majors and non-commissioned officers). This increase was mainly due to the inclusion of the railway administration's growing gendarme force.[15] Similarly, the numbers of officers and non-commissioned officers in provincial gendarme administrations displayed a slight growth after 1880. At that time these branches contained 328 officers and 2,290 non-commissioned officers, but by 1895 the figures had risen to 364 officers and civilian officials, and 2,474 sergeant majors and non-commissioned officers.

During the 1880s new gendarme institutions sprang up in the form of "Sections for the Defense of Order and Public Security" or, as they became commonly known, the *Okhrana* (defense) sections, or *Okhrankas*. A "Section for the Defense of Order and Public Security" first appeared in the Petersburg city governorship after Karakozov's attempt on the life of Alexander II in 1866. But until 1880 it dragged out a miserable existence and played no independent role in events. Then, on December 3, 1883 the tsar, on the recommendation of Count Tolstoy, approved the measure "On the Organization of a Secret Police within the Empire." According to the second paragraph of this law, "a special investigative section, modelled on the Section for the Defense of Order and Public Security that exists in the capital, may be created on the instructions of the Assistant Minister directing the State Police within the establishment of gendarme administrations, or of general police administrations, for the closest possible on-the-spot conduct of investigations." This allowed the organization of a network of Okhrana detachments; however, despite this provision, prior to 1900 such detachments existed only in St. Petersburg, Moscow, and Warsaw.[16]

Okhrana sections were not subordinate to the local gendarme command and acted with complete independence. Furthermore, their activity was not always confined to their own official administrative region within the empire. The Moscow Okhrana, for example, pursued its activities far beyond the borders of both the city of Moscow and Moscow province. Later, in 1896, the Moscow Okhrana even operated in St. Petersburg and arrested the printers of "The Peoples' Will Group." Although in Moscow the Okhrana was attached to the city police chief's office, and in Petersburg to the city governor's police office, such formal arrangements were unimportant and the sections were essentially autonomous.

Some idea of the Okhrankas' range of activities may be gained from a set of instructions entitled "The Administrative Authority of the St.

Petersburg City Governor for the Detachment for the Defense of Order and Public Security in the Capital," which Tolstoy approved on May 28, 1887. The first paragraph states that the section was created "to carry out secret and other investigations and inquiries into state crimes with the aim of preventing and suppressing the latter." The section's responsibilities were laid down as being: (a) to prevent strikes in plants and factories, and to investigate their causes; (b) to take measures to prevent and to investigate the causes of all prohibited demonstrations, meetings, and public gatherings; and (c) to maintain surveillance "on the basis of a special directive of the City Governor" over persons arriving in the capital as well as over the capital's educational institutions, clubs, societies and such similar organizations. The Okhrana was also "to adopt secret measures to prevent and investigate any disorders, meetings, and demonstrations occurring in educational institutions," and so forth. These instructions reveal that the responsibilities of the St. Petersburg Okhrana section[17] were similar to those assigned to the provincial gendarme administrations. But there was one major difference: an Okhranka's activities generally were conducted by secret agents, whereas those of the gendarmes—whether provincial or railway—were basically official investigations aimed at bringing criminals to trial and seldom involved the use of agents.

Officially the Okhrana sections had small staffs. As of August 5, 1883, the St. Petersburg section supposedly comprised only twelve persons.[18] That of the Moscow section was even smaller and in 1889 consisted of six persons in all.[19] But apart from these official establishments there also existed a large, unofficial, staff, known as the "Okhrana's external service." This was made up of secret agents (called "filers") and special, secret collaborators, or provocateurs. Of the Moscow section's annual budget of 50,000 rubles, 30,000 (60%) were allotted to surveillance, investigations, and the maintaining of agents.[20] Hence it is clear that these sections were almost exclusively concerned with the activities of secret agents.

Here it is worth looking at the general volume of work undertaken by the Department of Police. Its activities grew from year to year, as is witnessed by statistics on the flow of departmental documents. In 1881 the department received 30,900 documents. In 1885 the number had risen to 36,400, in 1890 to 49,205, and in 1894 to 56,766. Meanwhile, the output of documents showed a similar, if smaller, expansion from 25,644 in 1881 to 28,503 in 1890, and 38,880 in 1894. Another indication of the scope of the department's operations is given by its budgets. These show a considerable increase in the sums received for secret expenses during the early years of Alexander III's reign. By 1883 just under a million rubles were received[21] for these purposes and this figure remained stable until 1894.[22]

From 1881 to 1894 the Department of Police conducted 3,111 investigations into alleged state crimes. Of these, 1,882 were discontinued. During this period 13,219 offenses as defined by Articles 246 and 248 of the Criminal Code (speaking disrespectfully about the imperial family) were investigated and 6,267 of these were dropped. The percentages of discontinued investigations were very high, being 60.4 in the first case and 47.7 in the second. A fuller view is given by the following table:[23]

| Investigations of State Crimes | | | | Investigations under Articles 246 and 248 | | |
Year	Cases	Persons	Discon-tinued	Cases	Persons	Discon-tinued
1881	294	—*	222	875	—*	422
1882	416	—	304	1,253	—	740
1883	312	—	196	938	—	475
1884	254	—	120	1,110	—	623
1885	355	—	229	817	—	432
1886	256	—	159	791	—	431
1887	178	—	102	963	—	518
1888	140	353	74	888	832	277
1889	140	485	61	916	853	382
1890	129	490	39	916	853	301
1891	141	319	65	1,021	915	332
1892	151	753	83	881	810	275
1893	165	368	104	883	736	303
1894	180	815	124	938	726	806

*Prior to 1888 no precise register of charges was maintained.

Data on the number of political prisoners or persons administratively exiled in the period from 1882 to 1894 is unavailable. The *Historical Survey of the Organization and Activity of the Department of Police* provides these figures only for January 1, 1901. Such figures are generally acceptable for the earlier period inasmuch as the difference between them and those for 1895 would have been small.[24] "By January 1, 1901," the *Survey* states, "there were 4,113 persons serving court sentences or under administrative sentences for state crimes, political unreliability, depraved conduct, and other offenses. Of these, 180 were exiled to hard labor, 73 exiled to restricted areas, 16 exiled for life, 3,838 placed under open surveillance by administrative order, and 6 imprisoned by administrative sentence.[25] Assuming some sixty percent of those administratively exiled (and placed under open police surveillance) belonged to the political category, and using "political" broadly to include participants in peasant disorders and worker strikes, by January 1, 1901 roughly 2,577 people were imprisoned or exiled for political offenses.

POPULAR DISCONTENT

During the 1880s and 1890s the Ministry of the Interior began to realize the threat posed by the labor movement. Heretofore this matter had received no serious attention. But massive strikes in St. Petersburg at the end of the 1870s, the labor unrest that accompanied the Morozov strike in the mid-1880s and, most important, the development of the strike movement in the 1890s, slowly forced a change in attitude. As early as the end of 1881 a Provisional Commission on Factory Matters existed in St. Petersburg. Chaired by the city's chief of police, it included representatives of various ministries as well as other persons. In 1886, after the Morozov strike, Provincial Offices on Factory Affairs were established. Each such office included the governor, the vice-governor, the prosecutor of the district court, the chief of the provincial gendarme administration, the senior factory inspector, the district mining engineer, and four representatives of the manufacturers and factory owners. This office examined violations of the regulations then applicable to industrial enterprises and workshops, and was responsible for the "relationships between factory owners and workers."

In its *Historical Survey* the Department of Police described the growing labor movement in the following manner: "Along with the aforementioned criminal association (that is, the People's Will), after 1880 Social Democratic ideas were spread by various means among the workers. These had as their final goal the preparation of a social revolution in Russia and change of the state system. At first there were isolated

attempts at propaganda in the more populous workers' centres, such as
St. Petersburg, Moscow, Odessa, and Kiev. Later, after the early 1890s,
the development of this movement grew particularly noticeable." In this
way the labor question came to the notice of the Department of Police
in general and the Okhrana sections in particular. Their concern found
expression in the ideas of "police socialism" which began to appear at
the end of the 1890s.

The peasant movement worried the Ministry of the Interior less than
did that of the workers. Although Count Tolstoy tried to frighten his
colleagues with the threat of a "new Pugachevshchina," usually he did
this to gain support for a new reactionary measure. The government,
moreover, treated the peasants more roughly than it did the workers and
never felt the need to develop a form of police socialism for the countryside. Instead, peasant disorders were simply repressed by ever more brutal methods. At the beginning of 1885 the Minister of the Interior obtained from the Committee of Ministers permission for the governors to
order the mass floggings of peasants in cases of alleged "extraordinary
circumstances." The resulting circular of May 31, 1885 warned: "It is
necessary to use all due caution when resorting to this measure. It is not
to be ordered before the governor has visited the place of the disorder
and personally investigated the disturbance."[26] Despite this caution, the
decision of the ministers contravened existing law. Corporal punishment
had been abolished by the statute of April 17, 1863 except in cases of
persons exiled to hard labor, soldiers in penal detachments, and peasants.
And only the peasants' own volost courts might impose this sentence on
a peasant. Hence the ministerial committee's decision basically under-
mined the effectiveness of the provision of the law of 1863.

As the floggings were frequently carried out by military units summoned to suppress the disorders, the Minister of War was stirred to protest. Apparently he was motivated by the dissatisfaction this measure
aroused within the army. As a result, the Minister of the Interior issued
a circular on March 10, 1886 which pointed out that "the use of soldiers
as the instruments of corporal punishment is not consistent with the dignity of the military profession." This punishment therefore was to be
carried out "only by specially appointed members of the police, under
the protection of the troops."

It is noteworthy that the governors made fairly extensive use of the
right that had been granted them. It was by no means used "exclusively
in those cases that brooked no delay." For, quite simply, no such cases
arose during this period. Yet flogging was the most common method
used by many governors in dealing with the peasants. Among these were
Governors A.K. Anastasiev of Chernigov (later a member of the State

Council),[27] Evgeny O. Yankovsky of Poltava,[28] A.A. Tatishchev of Penza, P.V. Nekliudov of Orel, and N.M. Baranov of Nizhny Novgorod. Such methods apparently enjoyed the full approval of the Ministry of the Interior. I.N. Durnovo, writing from his estate in Chernigov province, noted: "One must admit . . . that a wise and energetic governor can now do much good. Anastasiev's administration has brought such order to peasant affairs that the countryside is now much quieter."

ILLEGALITY IN THE PROVINCES

Political reaction assumed not only the form of legislative measures aimed at preserving survivals of the past, but was reflected in a growth of administrative illegality throughout the system of government. These arbitrary actions were sometimes legalized, as in the case of the governors' use of corporal punishment. On many occasions, however, the higher authorities simply ignored such conduct and naturally this encouraged repetition. Illegality grew particularly common in the provinces where the majority of governors-general and governors attempted to extend their rights in all directions without a moment's consideration for the existing law. In some cases, especially in the early 1880s, the Minister of the Interior restrained their attempts, but in others the breach of legality was ignored and the governors were encouraged.

In the early years of Alexander's reign Prince Vladimir A. Dolgorukov, the governor-general of Moscow, twice petitioned the Ministry of the Interior for the right to banish to more distant localities persons exiled from the city, but who lived nearby and still illegally visited the capital. By the existing law these people should have been tried before a justice of the peace. But, in Dolgorukov's opinion, the justices who heard these cases were not sufficiently severe. For this reason the governor-general asked for the right to deal with these offenders by administrative order. Interestingly enough, even though he did not consider it necessary to address his petitions to the Committee of Ministers, the body competent to decide such questions, his requests were turned down. General Orzhevsky told the governor-general that "the application of such unusual measures . . . to those exiles who violate the laws to which they are subjected by freely visiting Moscow would, in the opinion of the Honorable Minister, be unjustified either by the substance of the violation—for which the guilty persons should be brought to trial—or by any real necessity for the adoption of such exceptional measures." Yet only a few years later Dolgorukov's successor, Grand Duke Sergei Alexandrovich, was permitted to expel the Jews.

In some cases the illegal conduct of governors reached Herculean proportions. Anastasiev, governor of Chernigov, provides several of the best examples of such conduct and the accompanying petty tyranny. These are described by V.M. Khizhniakov in his memoirs, *The Reminiscences of a Zemstvo Member* (in the 1880s mayor of Chernigov and then chairman of the Provincial Zemstvo Board). According to him, Anastasiev resolved to do his chief—Assistant Minister of the Interior Durnovo—a good turn. The latter owned land in Chernigov province and wanted to sell the wood from one of his forest lots on the banks of the river Desna. To help him Anastasiev pushed a resolution through the Forest Preservation Committee permitting Durnovo to cut his trees on the grounds that they were infected by silk worms.[29] Then Anastasiev called in the leading men of the lumber industry and proposed that they buy the wood for 90,000 rubles.[30] They all refused to pay this sum, but Anastasiev succeeded in obtaining 75,000. Then, Khizhniakov reports: "Anastasiev wasted little thought about where he might obtain the remaining 15,000 rubles. Without hesitating he summoned the city rabbi, explained the situation, and sternly ordered that he collect within a week the remainder of the stipulated sum from the Jews. The rabbi was horrified and begged that the poor Jews be shown mercy. But he was sent off with the threat 'that were the instructions not carried out, the Jews would be sorry . . . .' And within a week the 15,000 rubles were collected."[31]

In December, 1891 the Committee of Ministers discussed calling Lieutenant-General, Prince A.D. Nakashidze, the governor of Elizavetpol, to account for sundry abuses of authority. These included willfully arresting and imprisoning "(a) four inhabitants of the village of Lakia in Areshsky county of Elizavetpol province who, in connection with the murder of the Lakia village elder, had been released during the court proceedings because the investigation had not produced sufficient evidence against them, and (b) thirty-nine inhabitants of various counties in this province by administrative order for terms of up to a year or longer."

Such actions, the committee observed, "were not permitted by either the general laws or any special authority." Earlier the prosecutor of the Tiflis Judicial Bench had presented a report to the Governing Senate bringing criminal charges against Nakashidze. The senate supported these charges and proposed that representatives of the judicial administration be appointed, at the Minister of Justice's discretion, to conduct a preliminary investigation. It further proposed Prince Nakashidze's removal from his post. Meanwhile Nakashidze, in answer to the senate's demand for explanations, replied that "a governor enjoys the legal right within the borders of the province to subject to detention or place in custody people he has some reason to believe are harmful, dangerous, or suspect of a crime." This right, he maintained, "required no special authority."

On receiving the Senate's decision, the Minister of Justice raised Nakashidze's case in the Committee of Ministers. This body's conclusions contradicted those of the Senate and the ministers decided "to request Your Most Imperial Majesty's permission to disregard the directions of the Governing Senate in this present case, and to refuse to permit any announcement of the Governing Senate's rebuke to Lieutenant-General, Prince Nakashidze, the Governor of Elizavetpol, for the impropriety of his orders." Alexander III agreed, commented that the procedural rules for investigating "illegal actions committed by a governor in the course of his official duties" were unsatisfactory, and demanded a change in the appropriate legislation. Thus Nakashidze avoided even a proper dressing-down, and got off with a simple reprimand.

The behavior of P.V. Nekliudov, governor of Orel, recalls the tyranny that usually is possible only in a medieval eastern despotism. On June 7, 1894 the Committee of Ministers discussed a report on "The Irregular Actions of Governor Nekliudov of Orel," which recounted the following events: One Pushchin, a landowner of Orel county, demanded that peasants of the village of Oboleshev work on a dam without pay. The dam was being built on the peasants' land for his mill. Originally the land captain had ordered the peasants to proceed with construction of the dam, but then he had postponed his decision pending a ruling on this question in an appeals court. While the land captain was negotiating with the peasants, the latter overturned several carts carrying straw for the dam to the mill pond. "For this act the land captain sentenced one woman from each household to three days arrest."[32] The peasants then refused to give up the women whereupon the village elder was unable to carry out the land captain's orders. "Meanwhile," according to the minutes of the Committee of Ministers, "Pushchin informed the governor of Orel of these events. On August 4, 1892 he (the governor) summoned the county police chief and the land captain and, despite the latter's declaration that he did not intend to implement his decision on building the dam until the case had been settled by a court order, and that the women could be arrested with outside help, ordered the county police chief to enforce both decisions."

Under these orders the police chief, accompanied by police officers, village constables and three hundred deputies, arrived in Oboleshev the next day. He announced to the peasants that the governor had ordered him to arrest the women. Many of the latter, "afraid of being arrested, had gone into the river Tson and stood up to their waists in the water holding infants in their arms." The police chief was equally unsuccessful in carrying out the second order. Construction could not proceed on the dam because the peasants would not allow straw and brushwood to be taken to the site. Thinking a resort to force impossible, the police chief reported to the governor that he intended "to seize the peasants' animals as a countermeasure." At the same time he informed the district court prosecutor of these events.

On receiving news of the "animal countermeasure," the governor ordered a company of soldiers to Oboleshev and instructed the land captain to draw up a list of the peasant women (or "*babs*") subject to arrest, and to make preparations for a mass birching. The journal of the Committee of Ministers gives full details of what followed: "On the next morning, April 7, the governor went to Oboleshev. Stopping at Pushchin's estate, he examined the lists of peasant women liable to arrest and of peasants who had resisted the land captain and the police. In this he was helped mainly by Pushchin, who marked opposite the name of each peasant the number of blows to be received. After breakfast at Pushchin's he (the governor) went to the village of Oboleshev where the peasants had been assembled and surrounded by the soldiers. When he appeared they all fell to their knees and begged for mercy. Without paying attention to their pleas, or to the peasants' offers voluntarily to heed the demands of the authorities, the governor read the names of fourteen persons from the list drawn up at Pushchin's house. He ordered four of these arrested and the rest to be punished by birching carried out in his presence, despite the warnings of a doctor who accompanied the expedition. Of those punished, five had played no part whatsoever in the insubordination of August 4, as they were already under arrest on the land captain's orders. When the punishments were finished, the governor ordered the women arrested for three days and the dam was built in his presence. Then he pointed out to the peasants that he was an old friend of Pushchin and told them that in the event of a new disturbance the punishment would be twice as severe. The next day, on the orders of Actual State Councillor Nekliudov, one peasant who had fled from Oboleshev on the previous day was punished in the town of Orel with seventy-five blows of the birch."[33]

The journal also noted that Pushchin's civil suit was dropped before a decision was rendered in either the Orel district court or the Governing Senate. But the Kharkov court dismissed his charges "because of the prosecution's failure to prove a case against several peasants of the village of Oboleshev for opposing the authorities, as their actions had consisted only of a passive refusal to meet the landowner's illegal demands." Hence Nekliudov's behavior was deprived of any legal basis.

The Senate, guided by the emperor's resolution in the case of Nakashidze, decided, "without going into the matter of the preliminary evidence, that a severe reprimand—to be included in his service record—is to be given to Actual State Councillor Nekliudov, the Governor of Orel." The Committee of Ministers then discussed this issue. It noted the governor's illegal actions but, maintaining there was no "criminal intent," suggested that they "resulted from his incorrect understanding of the limits of the authority granted to a provincial executive and that, further, though his actions were in themselves criminal, they had been performed while he was in such an excited state that evidently he was unable to control himself." Because of the governor's "easily excitable" nature, the committee approved the verdict of the Governing Senate and its decision received "His Majesty's" approval. Yet Alexander III, although he agreed to punishment, evidently did so only with "a heavy heart."[34]

Such cases illustrate the increasingly arbitrary behavior of the "provincial authorities," as governors were called in bureaucratic parlance. But they are also evidence of the tolerant attitude shown such behavior by the central government and the Autocrat of All the Russians himself. In November, 1894 one zemstvo man described this phenomenon in a letter to Vladimir I. Lamansky. "The weakening of the law courts' authority," he wrote, "has allowed an unpunished growth of every sort of excess and infringement of the law by the authorities. Individual, and particularly glaring examples—such as the circulars and orders of Anastasiev, Baranov, [V.V.] Val, and Nekliudov, the massive scourgings that accompanied the cholera and agrarian disorders—are behind these unfortunate legal actions against the authorities." Even General A.A. Kireev, who because of his own reactionary and Slavophile views generally approved the government's policies during the 1880s and early 1890s, sadly observed that "the administration takes unprecedented liberties. Absurd floggings are regarded as energy: Nekliudov has whipped a Knight of St. George, [N.M.] Klingenberg a whole parish, and [N.N.] Trubetskoy a lawyer."[35]

MINISTRY OF THE INTERIOR OPERATIONS

The governors' illegal and arbitrary administrative practices reflected similar tendencies within the Ministry of the Interior itself. There too the law was often shown scant respect.

At the end of 1888 Count Tolstoy, as Minister of the Interior, requested permission from the Committee of Ministers to evict twenty peasant families from the village of Gorozhanov in Kovrov county of Vladimir province. They had, he charged, systematically refused to pay taxes and, in particular, their redemption payments.[36] Hence the governor of Vladimir, supported by Finance Minister Vyshnegradsky, proposed the expulsion of the peasants from their land. In Tolstoy's opinion these peasants, "because their stubborn attitude remains unshaken despite the measures adopted heretofore, offer an example of unpunished defiance to the law and are therefore a very dangerous element in the region." The Minister of the Interior proposed, "in the event of further stubborn- ness," to seize their land allotments and farmsteads as a means "of compensation for their defaulted redemption payments," and to remove the guilty peasants "by administrative order (that is, to exile them) to Eastern Siberia." The first part of this suggestion—the seizure of the land allotments and farmsteads—was completely legal, but the second was illegal in the extreme.

The Committee of Ministers discussed Tolstoy's request on January 17 and May 20, 1889. In the end the ministers agreed to exile the peasants in question to Kansk county in Tomsk province,[37] despite the fact that earlier, in December, 1886, they had labelled a similar decision an unprecedented breach of the law! At that time they had dealt with another proposal by Tolstoy, who was supported by the Ministers of State Domains and Justice. This requested "the issuance of legislation, in the form of a provisional measure for the province of Ufa, to deal with crimes committed by armed bands in crown and private forests. In these cases the entire wealth of any village commune in which a 'corpus delecti' (?) was found concealed would be held as surety for the punctual payment of fines for similar offenses."

This proposal would have permitted the provincial administration to punish an entire village commune, regardless of the guilt of its in- dividual members. Manasein, the Minister of Justice, objected that the courts would not uphold such a law because it contradicted "a basic principle of our criminal law. It is fundamental to the latter that penal- ties levied against property as a result of criminal acts can be charged only against the person recognized by a court verdict as guilty of these acts." Nonetheless, despite its illegality, Manasein considered that this measure might be implemented by administrative methods. By these he had in mind the exceptional rights and powers conferred on adminis- trative authorities by the law of August 14, 1881 (the "Measures for the Protection of State Security and Public Tranquillity").

After discussion the Committee of Ministers charged Tolstoy with preparing such a regulation on basis of the statute of August 14, 1881. The drafting of this illegal measure evidently proved difficult and re- quired almost half a year. On April 19, 1889 it was finally presented to the committee. On that occasion, according to the minutes, "Privy Councillor Plehve, the Assistant Minister of the Interior, told the com- mittee that because of the observations of the Minister of Justice on several articles of the draft regulation, the Ministry of the Interior realized the impossibility of presenting this regulation in its present form . . . ." Plehve's strange announcement was placed in the committee's minutes to conceal the rejection of the law as proposed by the Minister of the Interior. The diary of I.A. Shestakov makes this obvious. On April 19 he noted: "Again Tolstoy has suffered a defeat in the ministerial committee. He suggested that in Ufa province the communes as a whole should have to pay fines for forest offenses committed by individual members. Baron Nikolai observed that this question should be discussed in the State Council for it entailed a change in the existing law. I supported him, saying that the fact that this proposal violated an existing principle of legality (for the innocent rather than the guilty might be punished) made it all the more a proper subject for the State Council, and that an extreme measure, such as the one proposed, was permissible only in an enemy country during wartime."

Thus it was that Tolstoy's proposal failed to gain passage. But the Minister of the Interior had not reconciled himself to failure and a half year later another draft appeared. Entitled "Provisional Regulations for the Responsibility of Village Communes in Ufa Province in Cases of Willful Forest Offenses in Crown and Private Forests," it was now presented by a new minister—I.N. Durnovo. Once again, to the honor of the Committee of Ministers, the measure was rejected, and the Minister of the Interior was told to take it to the State Council for adoption by the normal legislative process. Not only therefore had the Ministry of the Interior condoned the illegal and arbitrary conduct of provincial authorities, frequently it had taken the initiative in such behavior.

The latter years of Alexander's reign revealed one other trait that deserves mention. This was the ministry's constant efforts to depict the existing situation as one of manifest prosperity and of "the peace and harmony of God's paradise."[38] To some extent these tendencies were reinforced by the personal qualities of the new minister. Durnovo, in contrast to Tolstoy, his predecessor and the pillar of reaction, held no systematic views. He merely desired to please the emperor and his intimates. V.N. Lamsdorf, describing Durnovo in his diary, commented that "the stupidity and careerism of Mr. Durnovo surpass anything one could have imagined . . . . Durnovo is merely a bureaucrat who seeks to please his superiors and is completely incapable of giving any sound advice."

It is impossible to blame Durnovo for the famine of the years 1891 and 1892, as this was primarily caused by drought and worsened by other factors (such as the plundering of the peasantry during the abolition of serfdom and all the autocracy's policies since that event). Nevertheless,

Durnovo's actions helped increase the scale of the disaster, for he long tried to deny the very existence of the famine. "In 1891 apparently," A.N. Kulozmin later wrote, "I.N. Durnovo, then the Minister of the Interior, refused to recognize the beginnings of what was obviously a disaster for Russia. He sent [A.G.] Vishniakov, the director of the Department of the Economy in the Ministry of Interior, to inspect the unfortunate provinces. (Vishniakov) reported that there was a crop failure, but not a famine." When it became impossible to conceal the extent of the disaster, Durnovo blamed Vishniakov and the latter was dismissed.

It is only fair to admit that Durnovo was not alone in treating the famine lightly. Until at least February, 1892, Alexander III did not take the disaster seriously. On October 14, 1891, Prince Vladimir M. Golitsyn, the mayor of Moscow, observed in his diary that "Russia is undoubtedly passing through a difficult and dangerous moment of her life . . . . And her master hunts in Danie and will leave in a few days for more hunting in the Crimea." N.K. Giers, according to his protege Lamsdorf, agreed: " . . The Minister (Giers) told me in complete confidence that he is terrified about the attitude taken by the Emperor and the inner circle of the imperial family toward the disaster. His Majesty does not want to believe that there is any famine. After a lunch with the family at Anichkov Palace (Giers') description of it was almost hysterical: there they consider that much of the relief work is really being used to demoralise the people. Some take it upon themselves to set out for the provinces to help out in this business and he (the Emperor) suspects that they are doing this only because the press is squandering praise upon them. It seems this point of view is shared by the whole family and my Minister sadly observed that the Tsarevich was listening to this conversation and smiling his approval."

Meanwhile, as early as the autumn of 1891 Count Vorontsov-Dashkov, Minister of the Imperial Court and one of the people closest to the emperor, had informed him of the terrible situation in the countryside. On August 27 he wrote Alexander III from his estate in Tambov province and, after telling him of the extent of the disastrous famine, Vorontsov-Dashkov suggested that they should found a committee for famine relief headed by the empress or the heir to the throne. He concluded: "If Your Majesty would announce that in view of the general calamities of this year there will be no balls or great dinners held at Your Highness's court, and that instead the money usually spent on these events would be donated by You as the first 'contribution' to the funds of the Relief Committee, this undoubtedly would make a very consoling impression upon the people. Forgive me, Your Majesty, for this letter, but believe me, the contrast between the starvation existing in the peasant's dark *izba* (hut) and the Petersburg dandies' luxurious suppers in the illuminated *a giorno* halls of the Winter Palace, makes one somewhat ashamed and depressed." Comment on this, of course, is quite superfluous.

Yet the Minister of the Interior continued to play down the extent of the disaster. His efforts were expressed in numerous circulars.[40] "Never since the days of Nicholas I," recalled V.N. Lamansky, one of the active workers in the zemstvos, "had official lies reached such proportions and gained such significance as they did in the recent past (that is, the first half of the 1890s). All the known facts clearly testify to their importance as a major cause of that famine which, after 1891, had such unfortunate results. So long as loud talk of the famine did not spread, the Ministers (Durnovo and Ostrovsky) decided not to tell the Emperor of the true state of affairs."

Later, at the end of December, 1891, Durnovo did present a plan entitled "The Adoption of Several Measures Concerning the Nation's Food Supplies" in the State Council. This presented his evaluation of the crop failure of 1891 and raised the question of providing some relief for those suffering from famine.[41] In 1892, according to the records of the Committee of Ministers, the government loaned 26,582,868 puds of grain to the starving and to organized public works projects in a number of provinces. All in all, this aid proved insufficient and the bureaucratic methods by which these measures were implemented frequently diminished their results.

Leo Tolstoy's letter "Why are the Russian Peasants Starving?", published in the London *Daily Telegraph* on January 4, 1892, described this situation. Speaking of the parasitic ruling classes, Tolstoy revealed their complete inability to combat the famine. "The privileged classes," he wrote ironically, "have grown fat and chubby thanks to the labor of the people's calloused hands and cannot move a hand or foot without the people's help. Now they bustle about and want to feed the people." Meanwhile the government placed every possible obstacle in the path of such persons. Even so, the general public played a tremendous role in the struggle against this "disaster of all the Russias."

PEASANT POLICIES

The government's peasant policies were of major concern to the Ministry of the Interior. Such policies had two major purposes. The first was to find some means of satisfying the peasants' land hunger (while not, of course, infringing upon the property of the landowning class) while simultaneously reducing their tax burden. Both aims had been formulated in some detail by Loris-Melikov's earlier program and, with the exception of the question of peasant migration, to some extent settled during the first years of reaction (when N.P. Ignatiev was in office) by the formation of the Peasants Land Bank, a lowering of the redemption payments, the introduction of compulsory land redemption, and the abolition of the poll tax. The second major purpose was the preservation of patriarchal and feudal aspects of village life and a strengthening of the gentry's role as "guardians" of the peasantry. These two goals determined the basic trend of agrarian legislation during Alexander's reign but, as far as the first was concerned, only the question of migration received any attention. In any case, the agrarian policies have been examined sufficiently elsewhere and need only be outlined here.

By 1880 there still existed no legislation promoting the migration of peasants to free land. During the period of crisis (1878 to 1882), when a tense atmosphere existed in the countryside (caused by widespread rumors of a "black repartition" and the government's fear of a possible union of the People's Will with a spontaneous peasant movement), Loris-Melikov's reports frequently raised this issue. No legislation was enacted, but in 1881 a draft law on the migration of the more needy peasants to free land was drawn up by A.N. Kulomzin and Alexis S. Ermolov in the Ministry of State Domains. This envisaged helping those peasants who owned "soul allotments" which were no larger than one third the size of the higher or standard allotment, or those peasants who had received no land at all. The draft would permit their migration to free crown lands in seven provinces (Kherson, Taurida, Ekaterinoslav, Samara, Saratov, Ufa, and Orenburg), but only allow the departure of not more than fifty percent of the eligible "souls" from each village commune.

As discussion of this bill was never concluded, N.P. Ignatiev brought to the Committee of Ministers a draft for "Provisional Regulations" on this matter. These provided the peasants with considerably fewer opportunities for migration than did the proposals suggested by Kulozmin and Ermolov. The "Provisional Regulations," approved on July 10, 1881, granted the right of migration only with the approval of the Ministers of the Interior and State Domains. This permission would be given only to persons whose "economic situation makes this necessary." Meanwhile the Kulozmin-Ermolov project was transferred for further discussion to a commission headed by the chairman of the statistics committee of the Ministry of the Interior, Peter P. Semenov (later Semenov-Tian-Shansky). The commission urged the vital need to organize migration on an extensive scale because of the exceptional demand for such a measure in the central black earth provinces. Accordingly it proposed, in effect, the migration of anyone who wished.

This recommendation was then transferred for discussion by so-called "informed persons," chiefly marshals of the nobility and chairmen of zemstvo boards) chosen by the Minister of the Interior. A majority of these "informed persons" agreed to the principle of full freedom of migration. At the same time they recommended that only minimal privileges and grants be allowed the migrants. Naturally such a decision would have been merely declaratory in nature, but as things turned out neither this decision nor the draft of the Semenov Commission had any practical results.

In 1884, before the government's reactionary policies had been fully defined, Count Tolstoy sent a memorandum to Alexander III outlining his views on the migration issue. He suggested that no general law be promulgated because the government possessed insufficient unused land. The pressure for migration, he believed, was felt in only twelve provinces (Tula, Orel, Voronezh, Kursk, Riazan, Penza, Tambov, Kharkov, Poltava, Chernigov, Simbirsk, and Kazan) and migration from other provinces should be prohibited. In the twelve provinces indicated the migration question should be left in the hands of the provincial administration, which would have the right "firmly to prevent emigration in each particular case if it believed that the move was being undertaken with insufficient forethought, without the necessary means, and without clearly selected aims." In other words, the provincial administration was to resolve this question at its own discretion, a procedure which could only limit the scale of the migratory movement. The minister further believed that migration should be open only to the most needy peasants and he concluded with some very general comments about "wide privileges," as well as grants, which should be given migrants.

Tolstoy's memorandum or, more precisely, proposal, was discussed in April, 1884 by a ministerial conference, attended by Alexander III. This meeting approved his suggestions, with the exception of the section on privileges (which were considerably reduced) and accepted them as the basis for further work by a commission (under V.K. Plehve, Assistant Minister of the Interior) which was to draw up a detailed draft law on the matter.

This law was prepared in the usual bureaucratic manner. The draft was completed, then passed back and forth among the ministers and department heads for their comments, and modified in the light of their replies. Normally the process took about five years. It might be noted that the Ministers of Finance, both Bunge and Vyshnegradsky, stressed in their comments the need of drafting the law on migration in such a way as to prevent any comparison with the emancipation statute of February 19, 1861. They wished to prevent its being interpreted as a means of providing supplementary land allotments to peasants who earlier received an insufficient amount.

By the spring of 1889 the Plehve Commission had completed its draft law and Tolstoy presented it in the State Council. The procedure for permitting migration was, according to the draft, to be identical to that introduced by the "Provisional Regulations" of 1881: permission would be granted if the Ministers of the Interior and State Domains determined that peasants were forced to migrate "because of their economic situation." Thus a migration on a massive scale was again precluded. Otherwise, land would be set aside for the migrants with the proviso that grants in European Russia would be temporary while those in Siberia and the steppe regions would be permanent allotments. The draft further envisaged grants of various privileges to the migrant as well as loans to encourage initial purchases.

On May 8, 1889 the Combined Departments (of Laws and the State Economy) discussed Tolstoy's plan. Recognizing the need for such a law, the departments observed that "all efforts by the government to stop and regulate this agrarian movement by administrative means have been in vain. Their helplessness compels the Minister of the Interior to use other means in the struggle against the aforesaid evil and to attempt to regulate the migratory movement by means of recognizing the legality of the settlement of those migrants who move with the permission of the authorities." Nonetheless the Combined Departments argued "that it is the government's responsibility to bring the migration rapidly under control rather than to stimulate it by giving various kinds of assistance to the migrants." According to the session's minutes this consideration "ought to be taken as the starting point in any plan dealing with the matter mentioned." Therefore a number of changes were made in the proposed law to limit still further the scale of migration. The departments narrowed the privileges granted migrants, excluded an article on preferential railway fares, considerably reduced the proposed budget for organizing migrations, and so forth. On June 8 the General Session of the State Council approved the decisions of the Combined Departments, and on July 13, 1889 Alexander III promulgated the bill as law.

Clearly the purpose of this statute was not the organization of migratory movement but its greatest possible limitation. One might think the government would have found it advantageous to organize a large scale movement of peasants to land that was not then in use. Such a policy could have led to assimilation of new and unused lands and promoted an improvement in the economic position of the peasantry that would, in turn, have increased its ability to pay higher taxes. The political consequences could have been even more profitable for the government and, above all, in the interests of the gentry. Such migration would have weakened peasant land hunger and hence diminished the tensions between peasants and landlords.

But a mixture of motives caused the government to act differently. In the first place, the authorities were afraid of any broad agrarian movement—even of one that was officially sponsored. As it was, the government organized a limited migration solely because it feared it. Further, the allotment of lands in new regions to peasants, and especially to those very peasants who had received insufficient allotments in 1861, would, in the opinion of the authorities, give the peasantry the idea that somehow the tsar had the responsibility to give all the land to the peasants. In this way, they feared, migration might promote a further spread of rumors of a "black repartition." Here Polovtsov's letter to Alexander III, written as a covering note for the State Council's memorandum on its review of the migration question, is illuminating. "Peasant migration," Polovtsov wrote, "is almost always a result of a false and harmful notion created by the statute of February 19, 1861. Then the principle was enunciated that each peasant, simply because of the fact of his existence, had an unconditional right to own a certain amount of land as an allotment. If at that time everyone agreed that it was impossible to act differently, by now this event long ago should have been buried in the pages of history. But, in fact, the peasants preserve the memory of this declaration and consider that each growing peasant family enjoys the right to a corresponding increase in the area of land it owns. If the orders of the government . . . reinforce this false idea and these disturbing hopes among the peasant population, some day they may find their expression in a massive criminal movement." In Polovtsov's opinion the State Council's decision, "including the amendments to the original draft, which itself had met with considerable opposition," was drawn up with such considerations in mind.

State Secretary Polovtsov was not the only person with such worries. Similar arguments apparently were put forward by several other prominent authorities and even after more than a hundred years the fear of a *Pugachevshchina* was astonishingly strong. There were, besides, other reasons why the government hesitated to organize a large scale migration. One was the worry that such a migration would produce a shortage or at least a restriction of the rural labor supply harmful to the interests of the landowning gentry. Further, the organization of a massive migratory movement necessitated the solution of a number of other important problems. Among the most important were the questions of the fate of the commune and the ownership of land allotments. During the period of reaction the preservation of this outdated institution, among others, was a basic government rural policy.

A number of government measures were designed to preserve the remnants of feudalism and serfdom in the villages. The law on measures to limit the partitioning of family allotments was a first step in this direction. Calls for restricting the peasant's right to subdivide his family allotment had become widespread among the landowning gentry in the early 1870s. The economic development that followed the reforms remained burdened by many old constraints and naturally was characterized by the impoverishment of a considerable group of the peasantry. The landed gentry were unable to comprehend the true causes of this phenomenon and concluded that it resulted from a splintering of the peasant family. They particularly worried about the political consequences a ruined peasantry might entail. An impoverished peasant class presented a greater threat to social stability than did a prosperous one and therefore they concluded that it was necessary to preserve a strong patriarchal family system, based on the conservative principle of the family head.

Under pressure from the provincial administrations and the landed gentry (although opinions on this question were far from unanimous), as well as from their own minister, officials of the Ministry of the Interior turned their attention to this topic. Although their examination of the economic processes at work in the countryside was conducted through the spectacles of one of Gogol's heroes in *Dead Souls*, the ministry nevertheless drafted a law to restrict the subdivision of family allotments. This bill, brought before the State Council in early 1884, roused a number of serious objections from members of that body. Finance Minister Bunge observed that such partitioning of land did not necessarily destroy the economic strength of a farm but that, on the contrary, sometimes the economic situation of divided family holdings improved with the course of time. Bunge accordingly recommended that detailed data be collected on the matter.

The Combined Departments agreed on the need for supplementary statistical data. Consequently serious discussion of the draft began only at the end of 1885. Once again there were numerous criticisms. "None of those present favored the draft," wrote Polovtsov, "and it was subjected to many attacks." In the end the Combined Departments generally approved the draft, but only with a number of substantive improvements. The most important limited the law's effectiveness to areas with communal land usage. Permission for partitioning the allotment would be given by the family head and then discussed by the village assembly. Here two thirds of the votes were needed for the division of a family's land.[42] On March 3, 1886 the State Council's General Session accepted this amended draft and on March 18 the statute was confirmed by Alexander III.

A second agricultural measure concerned the hiring of agricultural laborers and was enacted in 1886. Throughout the 1870s the question of the terms of such hire had been discussed at various levels of government. Commissions chaired by N.P. Ignatiev and Count P.A. Valuev had examined the problem and in 1876 it had been discussed in the State Council. The draft presented at that time envisaged the granting of considerable rights to the employers and the introduction of labor registers. Although approved in principle, some serious disagreements arose over details and the draft was returned for further work. A number of council members (including Pobedonostsev) opposed allowing employers to demand the forcible return of laborers who had left work without permission. They maintained that "to use compulsion to keep workers with their employers—to subject them to a condition of personal dependence—would be the same as serfdom."

In 1880 the bill was reintroduced in the council, then shelved because the time was felt to be inopportune for promulgating a law on hired labor. "At the present difficult moment," the council thought, "when criminals are attempting to overthrow the existing government and social system, it must be feared that the new law, in the event of approval, will serve as an occasion and means of strengthening criminal actions of the aforementioned kind, and might even assure them greater success than they have achieved hitherto." Yet, in this period of growing reaction, the gentry again pressed for a law on hired agricultural labor. A report by P.A. Krivsky, marshal of the nobility for Saratov province, offered a detailed outline for a future law. He envisaged the introduction of contractual registers allowing an employer to make deductions from his laborers' wages for carelessness at work, damage to agricultural property, and so on. Krivsky wanted employers to be given the right of firing a laborer, without any hearing, for rudeness, impudence, or carelessness, and he suggested the creation of officials to be called "section captains." These figures were to have both judicial and administrative authority and would protect the interests of the landowners.

At the end of 1885 the State Council considered a legislative proposal entitled "Statute on the Hiring of Persons for Agricultural Labor and for Services Connected with Agriculture." Drawn up by two ministers—Tolstoy of Interior and Ostrovsky of State Domains—the draft envisaged the employment of workers by individual contract, the violation of which would lead to prosecution. Moreover, a laborer who left work without authorization could be returned to his employer without any judicial interference. Other violations of the terms of employment, and rudeness and insolence to the employer and members of his family, were to be heard by a court without delay, while the laborer's presence at the hearing was not to be considered necessary. Finally, an employer who hired away the workers of another employer would be liable to severe penalties.

Discussions of this draft continued from the beginning of February to the beginning of May, 1885, and produced some serious criticisms. Boris P. Mansurov attacked the proposed law as ensuring only the landlord's position. In his opinion, Ostovsky's proposals endeavored "to protect in every way the interests of one side—the employers." Pobedonostsev, from another point of view, criticised the draft as "leftist." He opposed the grant to justices of the peace of the right "to apply rather strict penal punishments—and these in the sphere of labor, where agreement is demanded for successful results." For this reason he recommended a considerable lightening "of the penalties projected for both parties, and particularly for the employers." The director-general further insisted that this law should not apply to day labor and piecework, a proviso which would place great limits upon its effectiveness.

These arguments resulted in a number of changes in the draft statute. For one thing, the punishment to which employers were liable for violating the conditions of employment (inadequate living conditions, food, or medical aid) was deleted and, for another, the punishment levied against laborers for rudeness and insolence was strengthened. The most significant amendment or so-called "correction" greatly diminished the law's effectiveness by limiting its application solely to workers engaged on definite terms and not to those hired for piecework. Together these changes reduced the law's impact to a minimum.

The fate of the commune, especially after the reforms of the 1860s, stood at the center of Russian social thought and caused great concern in government circles. The proponents of its preservation included representatives of the reactionary ruling faction as well as populist revolutionaries. Both these groups, among others, saw in the commune a means of averting the prolitarianization of the peasantry.

The commune's opponents included both liberals and some of the more far-sighted members of the conservative gentry. These latter realized that the commune was an economic anachronism and saw a prosperous peasantry as a pillar for the autocracy. Supporters of this view had served earlier as ministers to Alexander II (P.A. Valuev, Alexander E. Timashev, and N.Kh. Reutern). During his son's reign, opponents of the commune included Bunge, the Minister of Finance (who was, on the whole, a conservative), Count Illarion I. Vorontsov-Dashkov, the Minister of the Court, and State Secretary Polovtsov (although he was not a member of the liberal bureaucracy). "Your Majesty," Polovtsov told Alexander III, "if during Your reign You destroyed the Table of Ranks and communal landholding, it would indeed be a great day and You would leave a completely different Russia behind You." He scornfully described the communal system of farming as "herds picking the land clean."

Even such a strong proponent of reaction as Katkov understood the commune's evils, although he would not actually attack it. Speaking of the repartition of communal lands, he wrote: "Is it not of the utmost importance that measures be taken to prevent these repartitions? They prevent peasants from fertilizing and improving the cultivation of their strips of land, for that strip will only be taken from the peasant in the first repartition and all his work will have been in vain. Hence these repartitions are the cause of the sad depression of peasant agriculture and the insignificant output of the peasants' land . . . . Should we not find a way to eliminate the evil that is causing such harm to the communal lands, while at the same time preserving the principle of communal land ownership?"

Clearly, Katkov was perfectly aware of the evils inherent in the communal form of land tenure. But the elimination of that evil and the simultaneous preservation of the commune itself was obviously impossible. It was natural that in high government circles opinions about the commune were somewhat ambivalent. From one point of view it seemed that this institution preserved "patriarchal" relations in the countryside and prevented the creation of a class of landless peasants. Yet, on examining the matter from another angle, it was also argued that the commune explained the low productivity of village agriculture because the peasants had no interest in land that did not belong to them personally. These contradictions explain the confused attitudes existing on this issue among the statesmen of that day.

The famine of 1891-1892 compelled the government to turn its attention to the commune. Some officials maintained that the crop failure was caused by the low quality of the cultivation practiced by the peasantry as well as the drought. The anonymous author of one book, *The Bad Harvest and the Danger of a National Disaster* (which appeared in 1892) argued this view and pointed out that "first and foremost among these (causes) are the conditions on which the peasants hold the land. Of these the chief problem is the practice of repeated repartitions. Carried out at irregular time periods by a decision of a village meeting, they allow the peasant no certainty about how long he will have the use of the share of land allotted to him."43

Polovtsov expressed similar views. "If there is any means by which he [the peasant] could fully possess, as owner, the land he holds," the state secretary told the emperor during a discussion of the causes of the famine, "he would cultivate it differently and obtain different results." And, he claimed, his views were shared by Bunge. At the end of October, 1891 Polovtsov had a conversation with Count Vladimir A. Bobrinsky and in his diary recorded that "an explanation of greater depth than climatic conditions lies behind the crop failure. The results of communal land tenure are catching up with and endangering us. One great Petersburg figure shares my views. This is Bunge, but he does not have the courage to espouse them openly." Meanwhile many governors reported continuing unofficial repartitions which led to "decreases or increases" in some land allotments. Consequently many peasants were being effectively deprived of land.

It is obvious that the communal form of land cultivation had failed to halt the disintegration of the peasant class. In fact, repartition of the land even served as an instrument for depriving some peasants of land while supposedly fulfilling the opposite purpose. Thus conditions seemed ripe for considering the abolition of the communal system of land tenure. Nonetheless, a really radical reform of the commune did not appear absolutely necessary. As a result attempts were made to restrict this institution's powers by half-measures. A crisis such as the 1905-1907 revolution was needed before the government would go beyond these efforts.

A draft law to regulate the repartition of communally held lands was prepared by the Ministry of the Interior at the end of 1892. This made a decision by two thirds of a village assembly necessary for any communal repartition. This same village meeting must have determined previously the term for which the proposed repartition was to be valid and this could not be less than twelve years. Further, the assembly's decision was to be subject to review by the land captain as well as confirmation by the county session of land captains. Unofficial repartitions were to be strictly prohibited.

The State Council approved these proposals with the addition, at Witte's suggestion, of one other item: if a peasant had improved his allotment, at the time of a repartition he must either be permitted to retain this land or receive compensation for the improvement he had made.[44] In this way the commune was preserved, although its right to redistribute land was restricted. A definite step was taken in the direction of giving some peasants security of tenure for their allotments or, if one prefers, towards a form of farmstead land tenure. But it was a very timid step.

A second government measure aimed at preventing an increase in the numbers of landless peasants by attempting to prohibit the free sale of allotment land that had been acquired as outright property. This issue had been raised as early as the 1870s when various zemstvos had suggested that the necessity might arise of banning sales of peasant allotments to avoid creating a landless peasantry. In the early 1880s similar suggestions were received from zemstvos in Simbirsk, Riazan, Yaroslav,

Kursk, and elsewhere. In 1881 the conference of "informed persons," formed to discuss the migration question, looked into this problem. A majority favored the abolition of Article 165 of the Statute on Redemption (which permitted the settlement of redemption payments before the scheduled term and, therefore, the land's further sale).

In the early 1880s the Ministry of the Interior began to draft legislation on the inalienability of allotment lands. But Tolstoy was in no hurry. He presented his proposed "Provisional Regulations" only in January, 1888 and then to the Committee of Ministers, not the State Council. Even there, however, his plan won no special support from the ministers and it was not even officially discussed by the committee. But in the middle of that year Alexander III ordered the creation of a special commission, under V.K. Plehve's chairmanship, to deal with this issue. This body concluded that allotment lands must be recognized as inalienable and that this principle be extended to cover land acquired through the Peasants Land Bank and by migration.

On the basis of these conclusions Durnovo, in May, 1890, brought a new proposal to the Committee of Ministers. He pointed out that "the passing of peasant land to other hands is continually increasing, and increasing to such an extent that in the future we are threatened with a considerable population of landless peasants. It is clear that this state of affairs is largely a result of the application of Article 165 of the Law on Redemption (on redemption before schedule). In the minds of those who drew it up, this article was to have served as a way for the more zealous cultivators to escape from the severe conditions created by communal guarantees and continual repartitions which deprived them of the possibility of making any improvements in their farming. In fact it has only served as a means of helping clever buyers find a way to acquire peasant land."

In this connection Durnovo suggested that the government should review all legislation concerning the peasantry and, pending this review, introduce "Provisional Regulations of Restriction." The Committee of Ministers agreed in principle but considered it necessary for this question to be discussed "in the legislative process" (that is, by the State Council). Consequently, at the beginning of 1891 Durnovo's proposal was transferred to the State Council.

Here this topic was not examined until 1893. Polovtsov recounts that the discussion of Durnovo's proposal was deferred at his initiative. "I received permission," he noted in his diary after a conversation with the emperor on March 14, 1892, "to withhold any presentation of the Minister of the Interior's proposal to limit the right of selling peasant land from the State Council. I argued that it would be awkward to touch this question in a year of famine." When the draft was finally discussed, it aroused great excitement in both the Combined Departments and the General Session. A number of council members, headed by Bunge, firmly opposed Durnovo's proposals. In his comments, which were distributed to all the members of the State Council, Bunge resolutely attacked the suggested measures and at the end of an extensive document pointed out that "any limitation upon the right of selling, of giving away, and of mortgaging property, and similarly upon private ownership and hereditary usage, is one of the greatest restraints in general and civil law. The sole result of a limitation on the peasants' ability to dispose of their land will be that the peasants will feel the government has an obligation to divide among them the lands not only of the state but also of the private landowners. By finally undermining in the peasants' minds their clear ideas of their rights of private ownership, the government will merely succeed in making the peasantry lose respect for the ownership of estates, and they will demand that they be divided."

Other council members supported Bunge but, notwithstanding numerous objections, a majority of the State Council approved Durnovo's presentation and, on December 14, 1893 Alexander III confirmed the council's decision. Among Durnovo's ardent supporters were Pobedonostsev, Ostrovsky, and Witte.[45] On State Secretary N.V. Muraviev's report of the council's decision, the emperor commented: "This is comforting and reassuring." The new statute absolutely prohibited the mortgaging of allotment land and permitted its sale only with the agreement of a peasant's fellow villagers. Land might still be redeemed ahead of schedule, but only with the permission of two thirds of the village meeting and the later approval of the county session of land captains.

During Alexander III's reign the Ministry of the Interior prepared, and the State Council examined, five draft laws dealing with agrarian questions. Except for the first (the law on migration), these laws set out to block the natural course of economic development and aimed at preserving remnants of the feudal past. Hence they made no real impression on the countryside and their practical results were negligible. The organization of the massive migration and resettlement of peasants, for example, would seem to have been the way to weaken their land hunger. But the law of 1889 restricted this movement as much as possible and placed obstacles in the path of those who wished to settle new land. Nevertheless, the evidence shows that in practice this law was unable to stem the torrent of colonization, which continued despite a multitude of legal prohibitions and regulations. Of the migrants who made their way to Siberia in the early 1890s, 60-85 percent were there "independently" (that is, without official permission or aid).

Reality would later compel the government to make concessions and to weaken the barriers it expected would hold back the migrants.

The law restricting family land partitions was equally ineffective. Notwithstanding the restrictions it established, the number of such partitions increased from year to year and over a nine-year period a total of 96,083 partitions of family land followed in eighteen provinces, 50,979 of which occurred "independently." The law on the hiring of agricultural laborers was equally ineffective. It did not deal with day or piece workers, and since these constituted the majority of agricultural workers, it could never have had great importance. Besides, the relations between employers and laborers was largely determined by existing conditions of supply and demand, regardless of legislative enactments.

The law of June 8, 1893 restricting communal land repartitions also yielded few positive results. Redistributions of communal land holdings continued and, no matter the law, increased in number. The data from zemstvo statistics and the local committees on the needs of agricultural industry offer convincing evidence of this fact. As for the law restricting the peasant's disposal of his allotment, its sole result was to curtail the advance redemption of land by approximately ninety percent. The law did not arrest the trend of allotment lands becoming concentrated in the hands of the capitalist element in the village. Consequently it must be concluded that the agricultural legislation adopted during the period of reaction exerted no serious impact on rural economic development.

THE MINISTRY AND THE ZEMSTVOS

The nature of the government's general policies naturally determined its attitude to the zemstvos. This attitude was reflected fully in the pages of the reactionary press. In the *Moscow News* Katkov frequently tried to demonstrate the worthlessness of these institutions and the need for their complete reorganization. In his lead article (of October 18, 1884) on the "restoration of government," Katkov called for a general political reaction. Attacking the advocates of liberal reform, he wrote: "The system of 'elimination of government' demanded that it (the government) be passive and recognize itself as worthless. The administration and its branches throughout the country are declared to be no concern of the government. The Land (*zemlia*) advances against the state, but by 'Land' actually is meant not the 'land' which is tilled... but the institutions of 1864, known as zemstvos. They form a cumbersome apparatus that during their twenty years of existence merely made themselves felt by the real land, by the people, in terms of their ruinous burden."

Meshchersky's article, "The Abolition of the Zemstvos," published in the *Citizen* in early 1885, screamed: "The bankruptcy of the zemstvos has reached a culminating point: the last ruble has been exacted from each zemstvo taxpayer, the zemstvo treasuries are emptied, the taxpayers are ruined, and nowhere in zemstvo economic life is there a sign of better organization. Everywhere resound groans and complaints of excessive, unneeded and therefore totally unproductive requisitions. In addition there is a repeated conviction that wherever zemstvos exist . . . nothing exists. Among the zemstvos there is found no moral authority, no state institution of any kind and no patriotic public environment. The zemstvos display neither a proper economic administration nor the concept of prudent use of resources. Finally, the zemstvos provide no practical instruction for life and living . . . . It is clear to everyone in Russia that the zemstvos long have lacked real force and are responsible for their own abolishment."

Alexander III considered the zemstvos to be enemies and believed that it was their nature always to oppose the provincial administrations. When the governor of Olonets reported in 1887 that the zemstvos "kept strictly within the law and in their activities worked hand in hand with the administration," the emperor observed in the margin: "A comforting exception."

The government's hostility to the zemstvos was obvious in the reception accorded zemstvo petitions. With very few exceptions these were simply rejected. Between December, 1883 and December, 1884 the Committee of Ministers examined thirty zemstvo petitions and turned down twenty-eight. The reasons behind the rejections are obscure. In October, 1884 a petition of the Novgorod zemstvo requested permission to call a conference of the zemstvo representatives from the northern provinces to discuss measures to counter epidemics. This was rejected, but at the same time approval was granted for an inter-provincial meeting to discuss actions against agricultural pests and animal parasites. In 1885 a petition of the Vologda provincial zemstvo for permission to organize a cattle and dairying exhibition was also disapproved. An analysis of the petitions rejected by the Committee of Ministers suggests the underlying cause can only have been the government's desire to limit in every way the zemstvos' activities. Evidence of this same tendency is found in a study of the reports of governors. Complaints concerning increasing zemstvo budgets and their "reckless" expenditure of resources emerge as a basic theme.

"Turning to the activity of the zemstvo assembly during the past year," the governor of Novgorod wrote in his report for 1883, "I consider it my duty to remark on the repeated efforts of the assembly to extend its activities beyond the limits prescribed by law. Thus, many county assemblies have alloted from zemstvo funds monies for projects not pertaining to local uses and necessities." The governor of Perm, in his report for 1884, made a similar observation: "With regard to the activities of the zemstvo institutions, it is impossible to ignore one important feature. Each year the zemstvo estimates increase and the assessments set by the zemstvo assemblies bear no relation at all to the material resources of the taxpayers or to the level of the grain harvest . . . . Although a large part of the assessments undoubtedly are demanded by the needs of the local population, it must be observed that this rapid increase in taxes, and the continuing need for care in their expenditure, places a heavy burden on the capacity of the tax-paying population." Finally, the governor of Poltava also complained similarly in his report for 1884. He noted the existence of "a justifiably censorous attitude towards the indifference of the zemstvo institutions to the needs of the public, the aggravating taxes, and the absence of thrift."

At the beginning of 1883 Katkov attacked the activities of the provincial zemstvo assemblies in the *Moscow News.* "In the majority of cases," he claimed, "they scarcely listen to budget reports. The estimates set out are quickly approved so as to gain time for the next item, business matters linked to positions on the board. The arguments that occur solely concern personal salaries, which are argued hotly and concluded satisfactorily, with almost all the salaries suggested for the boards or commissions being approved as if no one were present to witness this extravagance." Nonetheless, the apparent willfulness of the zemstvos and their seeming frivolity in expending public funds is really evidence of the government's attempt to curtail their activities, an attempt that was fully supported by the provincial administrations.

The governors joined the reactionary press in arguing for a change of the zemstvo statute of January 1, 1864. This request, in one form or another, is found in many of their reports. That of the governor of Perm for 1885 outlined a program of zemstvo counter-reform directed at limiting the economic activities of these institutions. In this governor's opinion it was imperative to limit the growth of the zemstvo budgets and to "pay strict attention to the current state of the population's tax capacity." He recommended that governors be granted the right to veto "all zemstvo budget items, including the optional ones, if they were believed to be unnecessary, inopportune, or incompatible with the ability of the people to bear taxation." Finally, the governor considered that the time period allowed for disallowing "zemstvo resolutions, estimates, and expenditures" by the provincial authorities should be increased.

The governor of Penza wrote in much the same vein, recommending the subordination of the zemstvos' economic activities to the governor's control and the inclusion of the largest zemstvo taxpayers (that is, the major landowners) as members of the zemstvo assembly. The governor of Chernigov wanted the activities of zemstvo institutions placed under the active control of the government and a large number of the most trustworthy gentry introduced into these institutions as members. He suggested this because the landowning gentry represented the conservative milieu "in which it will be possible to establish a proper and firm basis for the functioning of public life." Furthermore, he believed in the need of changing the existing system of elections and wanted "the right of each assembly to elect deputies from among the electors of other assemblies" abolished. In the end, of course, it was Pazukhin, in his article "The Present Situation in Russia and the Estate Question", who outlined the most complete program for zemstvo counter-reform.

After 1882 the zemstvos showed no signs of open opposition to the government but they continued to be considered an objectionable influence. In his report of 1886 the governor of Viatka informed Alexander III "of the harmful tendency of the zemstvos" and the emperor commented: "It is the same almost everywhere." The governor of Poltava, speaking of the zemstvos in his report for 1884, wrote: "The zemstvo deputies use every device to attempt to escape the limitations the law imposes, and raise and debate in the zemstvo assemblies matters outside their purview."

Similar opinions are found in the reports of other governors. Meanwhile, thanks to the impact of the growing reaction and a change in public mood, the membership of the zemstvo assemblies altered considerably. At the beginning of 1887 A.N. Mosolov, the governor of Novgorod, commented on the recent zemstvo elections. "Under the influence of the government's general policies," he observed thoughtfully, "the public's views have been appreciably sobered. The results of the last zemstvo elections serve as visible evidence of this fact. All persons whose oppositional tendencies or dubious moral qualities might have provoked disorders in zemstvo affairs have lost their seats to persons of more guarded tendencies and these already are making efforts to establish an orderly and honest administration."

Precisely because of such "orderly and honest administrations" there were, throughout the period 1882-1894, only two serious clashes between the zemstvos and the authorities. These occurred in Oster county of Chernigov province and in Cherepovets county of Novgorod province. In the first instance conflict erupted shortly after the appointment of the notorious A.K. Anastasiev as governor of Chernigov. In his report for 1887 he reviewed the state of his province and called the emperor's attention to the situation in Oster county. There, because of the weakness of the landed gentry, all intellectual influences belonged to "self-made men." They had captured the zemstvo and were behind its abuses. "A battle with this underground of intrigue and insinuation," the governor complained, "is impossible in the present state of affairs. The population is deceived and lost in the mass of conjectures and contradictions that greet it at every step. It is therefore clear just how harmful for the people are the activities of these bigwigs with their liberal games, and the extent to which their actions corrupt the moral foundations of the life of the people."

In Anastasiev's opinion Oster county was no exception and the zemstvos in the other counties were equally deplorable. Even the provincial zemstvo board seemed to him a seditious institution that "deliberately employs the most unreliable persons, and so on."[46] Yet Anastasiev's conflict with the zemstvos was not really a result of peculiarities in the Chernigov institutions so much as the antipathy of this zealous administrator for public institutions composed of "self-made men." In the event, a collision with the Oster zemstvo was avoided by the zemstvo itself—it held immediate reelections.

A more acute conflict broke out in the province of Novgorod. The governor, A.N. Mosolov, was a past director of the Department of Spiritual Affairs for Foreign Confessions whom Tolstoy had dismissed. Even so, like Anastasiev he was notable for his impatience with the zemstvos. In his report for 1884 Mosolov reviewed the provincial zemstvos and devoted much space to the activities of the Cherepovets zemstvo. "A striking exception," he wrote, "is the Cherepovets county zemstvo which is controlled by a small group long predominant there. For well over a decade the county zemstvo assembly and board systematically squabbled with almost every government institution: the governor, the police, the judicial investigators and the Ministry of Justice, the clergy, the public school inspectors, and the education district." According to the governor, the leaders of this zemstvo had attempted to avoid supervision of their activities and to gain exclusive influence on the population. "This influence," Mosolov claimed, "having had time to make itself felt by the confusion apparent in all branches of the zemstvos' own economic jurisdiction, now has introduced turmoil and disorder into every aspect of the county administration."[47]

Following Mosolov's charges, in December, 1885 the Minister of the Interior dispatched a special commission to investigate. This group included representatives of the Interior, Justice, and Education Ministries, and their report resulted in the administrative exile of four members of the Cherepovets zemstvo on instructions of the Minister of the Interior.[48] As for the zemstvo, the commission concluded that it should be debarred provisionally from taking part in school administration and that the zemstvo's library and book stores should be closed down. It further urged the creation of a provisional administration, attached to the county board, "for the detailed review of the accounts of past years and for an analysis of the propriety of the zemstvo's taxation policies and other questions."[49]

The governor of Novgorod nonetheless complained that the commission's verdict did not accord "with the facts that the commission had collected on the zemstvo's activities in this county." He suggested that it would be "more in accord with the government's dignity completely to terminate, for the moment, any activity by zemstvo institutions in Cherepovets county and to establish some form of government trusteeship over the zemstvo's property and business." To this end he recommended the creation of a special executive institution to conduct the zemstvo's business (combining zemstvo assembly and board functions). This body would "function throughout its term, under the direct supervision and guidance of the governor in the usual manner of the administrative subordination of county institutions." In Mosolov's opinion this institution would "correspond to the county zemstvo assembly" and should contain "the marshal of the nobility, the inspector of taxation, the mayor, the county police chief, three members of the former zemstvo" on the invitation of the governor, and "a special person, appointed by the governor." This group would undertake "the immediate management of the zemstvo's business." Executive management (with the responsibilities of the former zemstvo board) would fall to a provisional executive commission of three deputies and the "special person" mentioned above.

The Minister of the Interior supported Governor Mosolov's proposal in the Committee of Ministers. On this question Shestakov, the director of the Naval Ministry, claimed that Tolstoy was pursuing aims far beyond the immediate issue and was really "seeking to secure a weighty precedent on the general question of the zemstvos." In other words, the minister was seeking a weapon for future use in a battle to destroy zemstvo independence.

The committee discussed the fate of the Cherepovets zemstvo during the two sessions of March 21 and May 31, 1888. As Mosolov recalled in his memoirs, furious arguments arose and "a stormy debate continued for two hours on the matter of the Cherepovets zemstvo. The jurists and philosophers were filled with indignation. Tolstoy did not attend but sent his deputy, Plehve, who with Pobedonostsev and Delianov supported me. The Chairman, Bunge, questioned me in a very crafty manner, but I stayed very calm and gave straight-forward answers. Stoianovsky,

Abaza, and Baron Nikolai gave me especially difficult moments, but I did not let them confuse me. I was not present at the later session, but it was also very stormy and no decision was reached."

Hence discussions did not go smoothly, even in the Committee of Ministers. In the end, however, the ministers agreed with Tolstoy's and Mosolov's general proposal, although some changes were made in it. As a result the committee awarded the Minister of the Interior the right to "establish for Cherepovets county, for a term of no longer than three years, a Provisional Commission composed of persons chosen in agreement with the Ministers of Finance, and Education, and the State Controller." This commission was charged with the duties of the zemstvo board and "the representation of the local zemstvo in county institutions." During this commission's term of power, the zemstvo board was to remain inactive and the zemstvo assembly was not to be convoked. The Minister of the Interior could also request the ministerial committee to recall the commission before its term was finished and to restore the elected zemstvo.

For the first time in the twenty-five years of existence of these institutions a county zemstvo had been suspended for three years. This was the only major clash between government and zemstvos during Alexander III's reign. Despite this fact the government remained extremely irritated by the zemstvos' economic independence and uncontrolled—from the authorities' point of view—expenditure of zemstvo funds on local needs. Further, as increases in zemstvo expenditures held the promise of broadening zemstvo activities, such increases naturally roused the opposition of the government and primarily of the governors. The dissatisfaction caused these officials by growing zemstvo budgets was usually veiled as anxiety for the taxpayer. The governor of Perm, to cite one example, in his report for 1884 remarked on the continual growth of zemstvo estimates[50] and commented: "Although a great part of the assessments undoubtedly are demanded for the needs and well-being of the local population, one must still observe that this rapid increase in taxes, quite apart from the need for thrift in their use, places a heavy burden on the tax capacity of the population. The latter is being exhausted and this in turn not only greatly weakens the zemstvo's own efforts to improve the well-being of the local inhabitants, but also completely paralyses every government measure that seeks to maintain an equilibrium in the population's capacity to bear taxation."[51]

The new zemstvo statute of June 12, 1890 significantly strengthened the governors' control over zemstvo activities. This law envisaged the establishment of comprehensive control over zemstvo financial matters. This power was entrusted to the governors and the Provincial Offices for Zemstvo and Municipal Affairs, and in practice the local authorities readily availed themselves of their new rights. During the year November, 1891 to November, 1892 the provincial offices annulled 116 decisions of provincial and county zemstvos in eleven provinces concerning the spending of zemstvo funds. The officials of Vladimir and Ufa provinces proved to be the most zealous: in the former, 51 decisions were cancelled, and in the latter, 32. Both the governors and the Provincial Offices for Zemstvo and Municipal Affairs gladly used any formal error as an excuse to annul a zemstvo assembly's decision.

A few examples illustrate this tendency. The Vladimir provincial office rejected a Suzdal county zemstvo assembly's decision which had incorrectly made a single allotment of fifty rubles to the Gavrilov Posadsky Public Library from "the sums allotted under Article 10-L 'a' of the estimates" (that is, from reserve sums earmarked for unexpected expenses and to cover arrears in income). Again, the Ufa Provincial Office for Zemstvo and Municipal Affairs cancelled a decision of the Birsk county zemstvo assembly to carry over to the next year a sum previously allocated in the estimates, but not expended, for repairs to the local hospital. Similarly, the Vladimir authorities rejected the Yuriev county zemstvo assembly's decision "to repay lawyer Paskevich from surplus funds remaining from the budget the amount of 105 rubles, 18 kopecks, which he has spent from his own pocket in the course of zemstvo business." Finally, in 1891 the governor of Tver objected to nine items in the provincial zemstvo's estimates. In his confidential letter to the Minister of the Interior on this matter, he wrote: "All aforementioned allocations were made by the assembly without any objections being raised (evidently unanimously) because of its frivolous attitude to expenditures in general . . . . The frivolity displayed by the assembly in decisions on money questions is especially favored by the liberal party. It adopts a haughty attitude to such matters, but pursues its own political ends and sometimes makes use of the expanding estimates in order to ensure the implementation of some of its own ideas."

Any rational examination of the rejected decisions clearly reveals only one thing: the desire of the government and its officials to subordinate the whole zemstvo system to their control. Indeed, throughout the years 1882 to 1894 both the government and its local agencies continually sought to destroy the zemstvos' independence and repress their initiative.

CHAPTER IV

THE KAKHANOV COMMISSION

FIRST PROPOSALS

An examination of the work of the "Kakhanov Commission" is vital for any understanding of the first period of government activity (during the first half of the 1880s). Although the commission's labors and conclusions produced no practical results, the first drafts of the later counter-reforms were written by this group. The materials of the commission are, further, of great interest for tracing the stands of the liberal and reactionary segments of the bureaucracy, and very useful for evaluating attitudes toward administrative reform at the provincial and county levels.

As early as September 4, 1881 Count N.P. Ignatiev, then the Minister of the Interior, reported to Alexander III on the need of a program for reforming provincial institutions. The commission's practical work on this matter began in the second half of November of that year. Over three months (November–January) it drew up a detailed outline of future work. In April, 1882 the Committee of Ministers approved this plan. From the very outset the administration interfered as much as possible in the commission's investigations and hindered its examination of several essential problems. On January 23, 1882 Senator A.A. Polovtsov noted in his diary the following conversation with Michael S. Kakhanov: "I called on Kakhanov. He told me that during yesterday's session (Dmitry V.) Gotovtsev, Ignatiev's deputy, declared that the Commission should not take up the question of the police, as this would be separately examined and discussed in the State Council . . . . Further, Gotovtsev also warned that the rights of the zemstvos were not to be extended to the detriment of the authority of the Ministry (of the Interior)."

Count Tolstoy, who succeeded Ignatiev, was hostile to the commission from the first. In November, 1883 Tolstoy explained to Polovtsov his reasons for not dismissing the Kakhanov Commission at the time of his appointment. "I did not wish," Tolstoy said, "to finish it because I had no wish to open myself to the charge that I had prevented a great work from being accomplished. But now, as soon as they present the final results of their labors to me, I intend to ensure that their efforts are brought to nought." It seems that this was not Tolstoy's only reason. When he came to power he was simply afraid to close down the commission because he was still uncertain of the circumstances in which he was working.

During the first stage of its work, Senators Semen A. Mordvinov, A.A. Polovtsov, and Ivan I. Shamshin (all of whom had conducted inspections of a number of provinces between 1879-1881), and representatives of various ministries and departments, were added to the commission's membership. Then in April, 1882, once the commission's agenda was approved, a consultative committee under the chairmanship of M.S. Kakhanov was created from among the commission's members.[1] This body was to draw up the first drafts for reforms in the local administrative system. Apart from those mentioned above, several other senators, both of the General Session as well as of the senate's First Department (Mark N. Liuboshchinsky, E.V. Frisch, and Alexander D. Shumakher), were added to the conference's members, along with I.N. Durnovo, the Assistant Minister of the Interior, a couple of that ministry's leading officials (Fedor L. Barykov and P.P. Semenov) and some other people. The conference meetings that examined the drafts usually were attended by only eight to ten persons.[2] This body finished compiling and discussing its program in November, 1883.

After November, 1884 the membership of the Kakhanov Commission was considerably supplemented by representatives of various government departments and "experts" from the provinces. These latter were for the most part governors and marshals of the nobility.[3] "Fifteen experts," wrote one liberal, Ivan I. Petrunkevich, when describing these representatives of "provincial public opinion" in his memoirs, "from among those governors and landlords who had never reconciled themselves to the emancipation of the peasants or the zemstvos, shouted that the landowners could not exist in the countryside without the peasants and that the zemstvos were playing at revolution. One could scarcely imagine experts less likely to inspire public confidence." The leader of this "cohort" of gentry experts was Pazukhin.

The commission's actual examination of the draft for local administrative reform as drawn up by the conference began in October 1884 and was finished on April 6, 1885, thus concluding the factual side of the commission's history. The draft itself comprised seven sections: 1) the village association; 2) the volost administration; 3) the municipal administration; 4) the police; 5) the county administration; 6) the provincial administration; and 7) a system of supervision and review of disagreements. These sections, and the order in which they were placed, in themselves cast light upon the thought behind the conference's draft. In examining the existing organization of the village association the conference had concluded that it should include as members everyone living or owning property in the village[4] and thus include not only peasants, but persons of all classes or estates. All the business of the village association would be handled by a village meeting, composed of householders and males who had reached the age of twenty-five to thirty. This meeting would elect the village elder, who would have to implement its instructions. In this scheme the elder's function remained fundamentally the same as before (under the statute of February 19, 1861).

Alongside the village association the conference proposed the preservation of the peasant land commune as a judicial institution. Where communal landholding did not exist, it suggested the creation of "land associations composed of peasants who have received land allotments through consolidation and hold them on the basis of a hereditary right of participation." This association of peasants (who earlier had belonged to a single owner or to one land commune) was to hold meetings to manage its own local affairs. From this it is obvious that the conference envisaged the creation of a village association that would include all estates but, at the same time, wished to preserve a strictly estate [class] institution in the form of a peasant land association. Hence the existing village society would be retained in the form of the land associations whose powers were to be limited to hearing disputes concerning their land.

The second section of the draft dealt with the volost organization. The existing volost, in the opinion of the conference, "was to be abolished as a unit of peasant administration." Instead it suggested "the formation for general administrative purposes of a lower unit, directly subordinated to the county administration, that would retain the former name of volost." In composition this volost was conceived as a territorial-administrative entity which included not only the village associations but also those settlements, villages and towns that were without institutions of public administration. In this way the entire population living within its territory would be subordinated to the newly created administrative unit. (Involved was a volost that included people of all estates, but not the "classless volost" zemstvo with elective administration of which the zemstvo men dreamed). The new volost, as opposed to the existing institution of the same name, was to be purely an administrative unit and hold no police functions. The volost administration was to be concentrated in one person (the *volostel*). He was to be elected for a period of six years[5] by the county zemstvo assembly from among the inhabitants of the region possessing a secondary education.[6] On election the volostel was to be confirmed in his post by an Office of Provincial Administration. The conference believed that the peasants' volost court should be preserved in roughly its existing form. "Over the peasants of each village association (but not over all its members)," read the proposed law, "their own village court, as recognized in law, has exclusive jurisdiction for civil cases; with only a few alterations, the present (formally peasant) court should be preserved in the volost." But clearly neither village nor volost courts would have jurisdiction over non-peasant members of either the village association or the volost.

The institutions of municipal public administration were not to be changed in outward form. The conference concluded, with qualification, that "the organization of municipal administrations . . . is to be maintained on the existing basis, as established by the municipal statute of 1870." The functions of these institutions would be left much as before, although the composition of both electors and deputies was to be fundamentally amended. According to the law of 1870, electors of the town council were drawn from the taxpayers alone. These were formed, according to the amounts paid, into three electoral bodies or curias,[7] each of which elected an identical number of council deputies.[8] In the conference's proposals, participation in elections would be permitted to "a) property owners; b) owners of industrial and commercial establishments; and c) people who rented in their own names apartments for a yearly payment of a fixed amount." Each of these three groups would elect an equal number of council deputies.

The conference wanted to organize the police along the following lines: the county, for police purposes, was to be divided into *stany*, with an inspector in charge of each. Each *stan* was to be subdivided into "hundreds," with each hundred headed by a *sotnik* [hundredman] who would be the lowest ranked police official. Each village association was to be subdivided for police purposes into "tens" and a person chosen from the "ten" to act as constable in the community. This meant that the old institutions of village constable and the old collegiate county police administrations (with their "estate assessors") were to be abolished. All police authority in the county would now be centered in the hands of a county police chief, or *ispravnik*. Members of the conference disagreed about who should head the police administration at the provincial level. The majority thought "the governor should be recognized as the chief police official," while others recommended that the police be headed by a special official, the "Chief of the Provincial Police" (who evidently was not to be subordinated to the governor), and wished to "combine in this post the direct supervision of the police and the responsibilities of Director of the Provincial Gendarme Administration."

The proposals for county administration wanted "the immediate conduct of county administrative business to be headed by an institution comprising people appointed by the government and . . . of persons elected by the zemstvos." In this manner zemstvo institutions would be brought into the general administrative system, although the functions of the zemstvos themselves were to remain unchanged. These institutions would manage, "within the limits defined by law and in specific relationship with public and crown institutions," public education, public health, the supply of provisions, highways, and so on. Many of the collegiate county institutions (the General Office of Police Administration, the County Office for Peasant Affairs, the County Office on Army Affairs, the Administrative Committee, and the Education Council) were to be abolished. In their place a new institution, the Financial Administration, was to be established and serve, apparently, as a Fiscal Board in miniature.

The highest county authority was a proposed Office of County Administration. It would have three persons: a chairman, appointed by the Minister of the Interior from among three candidates elected by the county zemstvo assembly;[9] the county police chief; and the chairman of the zemstvo board.[10] For the examination of special questions, leading members of individual branches of the administration (both crown and zemstvo) were entitled to participate in meetings of this office. Thus zemstvo representatives would participate in county administration on an equal footing with those of the crown. Otherwise, the significance and role of the county marshal of the nobility remained almost the same as before: he would be honorary superintendent of various philanthropic establishments and retain "the right to inform the proper authorities of any irregularities observed in any part of the administration."

In the conference's opinion some very fundamental changes were needed in the system of zemstvo elections. It proposed that three electoral curias be created for the election of deputies. The first would consist of the county proprietors (and not just landowners), the second of city electors and the third of the peasants. Property qualifications were to be established for the first and second curias, but they were to be lower than the existing ones. The second curia would elect deputies in the city council and the third in village meetings by direct suffrage. The conference recommended that the schedule of deputies per county be revised and that this revision be governed in a large measure by the principle of equality, which would have made the zemstvos more democratic.[11] The conference was unable to agree on who should be chairman of the zemstvo assembly, but a majority maintained this post should be held by the chairman of the Office of County Administration. Another innovation of principle touched on the right of convening inter-county and inter-provincial congresses: in the former permission of the Office of Provincial Administration, and in the latter, of the Ministry of the Interior, would be required.[12]

Persons elected by the zemstvos and appointed by the government would be included in the institutions of provincial as well as of county administration. "With the purpose of uniting the work of the separate provincial institutions of both crown and zemstvos," argued the conference, "and also with the aim of simplifying the provincial administration . . ., in each province an Office of Provincial Administration is to be formed. These offices are to have a mixed membership, and be subordinated to the Governing Senate." The Office was responsible for the "supervision of all administrative business in the province and the examination of the most important issues of each branch, with the right of making a decision on these or submitting them . . . to the central government for its decision."

The governor was to be the director-in-chief of the province and chairman of the Office of Provincial Administration.[13] Members of this office would be the provincial marshal of the nobility, the vice-governor, the prosecutor of the judicial district, and the chairman, with one other member, of the provincial zemstvo board.[14] Crown institutions at the provincial level were envisaged as: a) an office for financial administration; b) the administration of excise taxes; c) state domains; d) posts and telegraphs; e) ways of communication; f) directorate of public education; g) public health; h) provincial engineer; and i) inspector of prisons. The elective zemstvo institutions involved would be the provincial assembly and its board. Hence a number of the existing institutions were to be abolished. These included the Provincial Directorate, the Provincial Offices for Peasant Affairs, City Affairs and Army Affairs, and the Provincial Statistical Committee, among others. The zemstvos' functions were somewhat enlarged and they were commissioned with allocating taxes and the collection of statistical information.

An analysis of the conference's project for local administrative reforms indicates that there would have been considerable movement toward abolishing the remaining survivals of the feudal past and a decisive step taken in the direction of transforming Russia into a bourgeois monarchy. The semi-feudal village and volost structure would have been replaced by a classless village association and volost. Further, the zemstvos would be integrated into the general system of the local county and provincial administration, their functions somewhat (although insignificantly) expanded, and their electoral system basically improved. Meanwhile the county and provincial administrative organs were to be reorganized in a more orderly fashion and, most important of all, the police-like character of local administrative institutions would have been altered. The head of the county would no longer be a police official, the ispravnik, but an Office of County Administration, half of whose members would be representatives from crown institutions and the rest from the zemstvos. The highest provincial administrative and police institution—the Provincial Directorate—would be replaced by an inter-departmental Office of Provincial Administration, subordinated to the senate rather than the Ministry of the Interior.

Tolstoy's comments on these proposals are typical of the reactions of the commission's opponents. As the Minister of the Interior wrote: "The absence in the draft of any proper guide for determining the true significance of all these legislative measures does not prevent us from drawing conclusions about the general sense of the project. We see that these conclusions are not accidental, but develop several general guiding principles which can be summed up in the following three propositions:
1) *The wide development of the principle of elections in zemstvo assemblies to fill posts in the local administrations.*
2) *The removal of any estate representatives from participation in the affairs of this administration.*
3) *The weakening of the orderly activity of the majority of local administrative institutions connected with an extraordinary increase in the functions of one (institution) which is formally charged with the supervision of their activities.*"[15]

THE COMMISSION'S DEBATES

As mentioned above, the conference's draft was forwarded to the Special Commission, which discussed it from October, 1884 to April, 1885. The commission made a number of amendments in the original draft which considerably changed it for the worse.

During discussions on the structure of the village association serious disagreements broke out within the commission. Two issues were involved. The first was the propriety of creating the village association and the peasant land association as separate institutions within the village. While thirteen members of the commission approved the conference's draft, eight voted against it, arguing that "the separate administration of the commune and the village association would be a complete innovation both in law and in life." The second issue provoking disputes was the composition of the village association. Half the commission (ten members) believed it unwise to establish classless associations. The remaining ten members favored the conference's proposal, but in the debates a majority actually spoke against the inclusion of persons not belonging to the peasant estate. Thus "the village association, composed of all classes," as proposed by the conference "was, in its essentials, rejected by the Special Commission."[16]

Serious disagreements also surrounded the proposed volost organization. The commission generally agreed that the existing volost structure did not meet the demands of the moment and that some sort of intermediate link (the "section" or *uchastok*) should exist between the county and the village. But opinions were basically divided as to what form this "section" should take. Ten members wanted a section that would be the executive organ of the general county administration –that is, the volost headed by a volostel.[17] Four other commission members (representatives of the landed gentry) thought the section should be an institution especially charged with supervising the peasant administration. "The foremost responsibility" of this organ should be, in their opinion, "not the implementing of zemstvo or governmental directives, but the supervision of those special institutions that deal with eighty percent of the Russian population. The complete supervision of the peasant administration should be concentrated in the hands of this institution and it should be predominantly, if not exclusively, concerned with the needs of the peasants."

These four believed that the section should be headed by a "section captain." This official, they maintained, "would acquire roughly the same importance that the rural arbitrator had once enjoyed" and his assistants should be the volost elders. As these four members were led by Pazukhin, it is not surprising that their proposed section captain was the prototype for the future land captain. In this regard one of these members, Sergei S. Bekhteev, the Elets county marshal of the nobility, proposed that both administrative and judicial functions should be concentrated in the section captain's hands so that he would assume the responsibilities of the justice of the peace.[18] This proposal was, however, rejected by the majority of the commission (twenty-three members) although there was general agreement on the need of the post of section captain. In other words, "the commission came to the unanimous conclusion that the section (captain) should have a dual significance. He was to be the executive official for implementing general, administrative directives of the government and zemstvo institutions, (and be placed in subordination to both the county administration and the provincial authorities), and be the official who supervised the peasant administration. For this purpose he was to be given the appropriate powers from among those which previously had belonged to the rural arbitrators." Yet no definite decision was reached on the means of choosing the person to head the section. Eleven members insisted that he be elected by the county zemstvo assembly, in accord with the conference's proposal on the method of electing volostels. Yet the majority (twenty-one) considered it expedient to have the section head appointed by the government.

Finally, the vote was also split on the question of whether the peasant volost should be preserved or abolished. Nineteen members of the commission found it impossible to agree with the conference's decision to destroy this institution (although they recognized its inadequacies and the necessity of correcting them). Nevertheless, fifteen members insisted that the peasant volost itself should be abandoned.

All in all the results of the commission's examination of the proposals of the conference on volost organization led to some very basic amendments. Or more correctly, the draft was completely rejected. Further, the proposed creation of a section, headed by a director whose functions were reminiscent of the rural arbitrator's, was evidence of the efforts being made to buttress gentry authority in the countryside. As for the volost's peasant court, the commission felt that its preservation was necessary, although with some changes in its organization.

The commission's reactionary attitudes were the result of the inclusion in its membership of members of the provincial administrations and, more important, of "experts" from among the landowning gentry. These latter were the authors of the above recommendations. Writing his letter-diary to the emperor, Meshchersky, in October, 1884 (when the commission had just begun to examine the conference's proposals), observed: "Saw one of the newly-arrived *Kakhanovtsy* [a member of the commission]. I learned from him that the disputes between the provincial and the St. Petersburg members are continually growing and becoming more clearly defined. It is now apparent that they cannot come to any agreement, for they are split from top to bottom . . . . The Kakhanov draft proposes a volost that will combine persons of every estate, and will balance the authority of the government with that of the public. But the newly-arrived members say, on the basis of practical experience, that there is no kind of classlessness in Russia and so all this is nonsense. As for a balance of authority, they say that there is no balance at present because of the weak authority of the government. One should not now be thinking of equality, but of strengthening the government's power everywhere. This is especially true in the county, as the closer the force of govern(ment) power is to the people, the clearer it will be for them. No college or office will do, as the people love an individual who has authority and hate any kind of college."

In the matter of municipal administration a considerable portion of the conference's proposal once again was rejected by the commission. The members rejected the idea that the various groups of electors should be granted equality of representation within the government. This was considered inexpedient as "the alloting of the number of deputies per category of electors should be in direct proportion to each group's ability to bear taxes that will benefit the city." The conference's suggestion that apartment tenants should be granted the vote was upheld only by the insignificant majority of two votes.

The special commission agreed with the conference that the isolation of the zemstvos from the rest of the administrative structure should be ended. It was thought expedient to consider the zemstvos as "institutions that do not fulfill their legal responsibilities independently from the figures and authorities of the government, but in close cooperation with them." The question of the range of zemstvo activities, as resolved by the conference, aroused no essential disagreement within the commission, but some new proposals were advanced on the nature of representation within the zemstvos themselves. As a result, a special sub-commission was created to discuss this matter. In this body, as in the commission itself, a minority maintained that the existing property principle, the basis of zemstvo government (apart from the peasants' curia), should be replaced by an estate principle. Otherwise, the sub-commission insisted that large landowners be included as members of the zemstvo assembly "as indispensible members not requiring special election." Although this decision won the support of the commission's majority, the sub-commission's objections to lowering the property qualifications were disregarded by a majority of the parent body. Yet a majority did reject the conference's proposal that provincial deputies be paid travel expenses for trips to provincial zemstvo assembly sessions (a provision that was particularly important for peasant deputies).

Hence the special commission not only rejected the most important proposals of the conference, but made a number of counter-proposals. It should further be noted that while many of the latter were advanced by a minority in this commission, they nonetheless contained the basic features of the future counter-reforms.

With regard to the conference's plans for organizing the police administration, the commission approved many of its suggestions. The ideas of transforming sotniks into proper police officials and of abolishing the collegiate county police administration were considered useful, but the commission voted to preserve the institution of village constable. At the same time, the question of combining the general police with the gendarmes was left unresolved as this measure would have provoked a great deal of passionate disagreement.

On the whole, the proposed reforms for the county administration, which stressed the need to combine the separate branches into a new

Office of County Administration, won approval. A majority of the commission felt, however, that it should be headed by the marshal of the nobility rather than someone elected by the county zemstvo assembly. Debates within the commission about the means of filling this office evidently provoked Meshchersky's article "By Election or By Appointment," which appeared in the *Citizen* on January 31, 1885. "At this difficult and desperate moment in the life of the Russian people, who already have been ruined by the exercise of the elective principle in the zemstvos . . . ," wrote Meshchersky, "these respected dignitaries—who have been invested with both authority and confidence by the government and who are paid by the government—amuse themselves by discussing under which authority and care the Russian people should be placed—whether it should be under some elective principle or under the Russian government!"

Finally, the commission unanimously concluded "that in the provinces an office, directly subordinated to the Governing Senate, must be created to unify the entire provincial administration."

An analysis of the commission's decisions makes it obvious that the conference's basic suggestions—the creation of a classless volost and the extension of the zemstvos' rights—were considered unacceptable. Further, one group of commission members made propositions that were directly opposed to those of the conference. These aimed at reinforcing the role of the landed gentry in both the peasant administration and the zemstvos. Nonetheless, in the matter of organizing the county and provincial administrations, the conference's plans were generally approved.

THE DEMISE OF THE COMMISSION

Even in this amended form the draft aroused the same distaste in the Minister of the Interior as had the existence of the Special Commission itself. At the beginning of 1885 he presented a report on the commission's activities to Alexander III. "It seems to me," Tolstoy concluded, "that the Kakhanov Commission's work has been fruitless. All these questions should be raised by the Min(istry) of the Interior and they are too important to be given over for discussion to such an enormous commission. Is it not time that we gave some thought to the question of how its activities are to be terminated?"[19] As a result the commission was given two months in which to complete its work. Thus in April, 1885 the Special Commission was disbanded, after having been at work for not much more than three years.

Count Tolstoy, discussing the commission's activities in one of his reports to the emperor, argued: "From the very beginning of its work

the commission itself adopted an incorrect attitude towards fulfilling
the tasks entrusted to it by Your Highness . . . . This is reflected in a
highly unsatisfactory manner in the general results of the commission's
labors. It took as its task the review of all the legislation presently in
effect concerning local administration and the simultaneous reform of
the latter on the basis of certain fundamental principles. As a result, the
commission came to conclusions that are obviously theoretical, frequently one-sided, and for the most part promise to be of little practical
use." Similarly Meshchersky, speaking of Alexander III's decision to
disband the commission (in one of the diaries intended for the emperor),
wrote: "One must say that this order came not *a second too soon*. It is
difficult to estimate the extent of the harm caused within Russia by
this ill-fated commission. It has provoked anxiety and raised troubled
questions of a ticklish political nature among the landowners. The anxiety is only now beginning to subside . . . . But there is no cloud
without a silver lining. The Kakhanov Commission's existence and debates undoubtedly gave the government an indication of what it can
expect from the so-called leading men, both from among its own dignitaries as well as from the liberal public."

CHAPTER V

JUDICIAL REFORMS

THE REACTIONARY PROGRAM

The judicial statute of November 20, 1864 had been the most progressive of all the great reforms. During the 1880s the men in power, including the emperor himself, therefore attempted to restrict this statute's effectiveness and in various ways amend it. Above all the reactionaries detested the principles of judicial independence—the irremovable judiciary, public court proceedings and the existence of jury trials.

Alexander III and his reactionary clique saw the existing judicial regulations as the root of all evil and wished to be rid of them.[1] Once, when a newspaper article referred to the "abnormal" activities of the courts, the emperor wrote Tolstoy: "We must pay strict attention to their activities and attempt to direct them in the proper direction, so that a healthier atmosphere will be created in them." "Here is still another example of the outrages found in our courts," the tsar observed in another note to Tolstoy. "It seems to me that in this case those guilty of conducting matters in this way could have been severely reprimanded. The government should not let such disgraceful illegalities get by. To do so is criminal." These extracts, despite their awkward style, testify to Alexander III's fierce hatred of the existing courts and their structure. It is equally noteworthy that the tsar "poured out" his complaints not to the Minister of Justice, but to the Minister of the Interior, who headed the administrative and police authorities of the empire.

Prince V.P. Meshchersky, the emperor's closest adviser, held the same view of the judicial statute. The *Citizen* overflowed with variegated curses directed at the court system. Meshchersky's greatest rage was roused by jury trials and the independence of the judiciary. "The government," he wrote in 1882, "by permitting juries and establishing an independent judiciary, inviolable verdicts and public proceedings, has abandoned the historical, sacred, strong, and healthy prerogatives of the Tsar's power, spread disorder and licentiousness and, by its own actions, divided society." Meshchersky held strong ideas about the proper content of future judicial reforms. These he outlined in the lead article of the *Citizen* on New Years Day, 1884. Although briefly stated, his program was of cardinal importance and asked: "Should we not for the moment immediately end trial by jury and entrust the responsibility for trials to the crown courts? Should we not abolish the articles of the judicial regulations dealing with the independence of members of the judicial system? Should we not, for the time being, entirely abolish public proceedings in criminal cases?" Fourthly, Meshchersky suggested, a "simultaneous" revision of the existing judicial statutes must be launched. His program, in effect, sought the abolition of all basic principles of the judicial statute of 1864.

Although once its proponent, Katkov also attacked the statute. Now he argued that the principle of an independent judiciary was inapplicable in Russia. In a lead article in *Moscow News* Katkov attempted to prove that in France, "where the government is only a party and does not represent the whole nation," and where supreme power passed from one dynasty to another, jury trials were perfectly natural. But, Katkov asked, "what sense can the absurd dogma of a judiciary, independent of state authority, have in Russia? Here, thank God, we have no pretenders and no state law exists other than that presently in effect." The editor of the *Moscow News* held similar views on the jury system and suggested that this trial method might be of positive benefit only where the jury's decisions had to be unanimous, as in England.

It was Pobedonostsev who outlined in his memorandum of October 30, 1885 the fullest program of judicial reorganization.[2] "Experience has yielded sufficient proof," he wrote in the preamble, "that the present judicial system and its institutions are incompatible with the needs of our people, the conditions of their existence and the general system of state institutions existing in Russia." Subsequently the Director-General of the Holy Synod pointed out the need for correcting such defects "while as much as possible retaining those aspects which are essential improvements" in the new courts as compared with the old ones. In his opinion this reform could not be carried out summarily, but would have to be implemented gradually, "according to a preconceived plan."

In the first part of his memorandum Pobedonostsev spoke of the need to "integrate the judicial authorities into the overall system of state institutions." He argued against the thesis that the courts in some way should be independent of the administration. "In the Russian state," he maintained, "there can be no separate authorities independent of the central authority of the state." Defining what in his view were the four most important questions, the director-general concentrated on the issues of an independent judiciary, public court proceedings, the status of lawyers, and trial by jury. "The establishment in principle of absolutely *irremovable* judicial personnel," he wrote, "is a strange anomaly in Russia and there is nothing to justify it." As for public court sessions, he proposed "as quickly as possible to put an end to the mood of demoralization spread among the public by the *publicity* given court sessions." To this end Pobedonostsev demanded court presidents be granted the "unconditional" right of closing the courtroom doors and he wanted to establish a category of cases that would always be heard in closed sessions.[3]

This memorandum called for resolute measures to be taken "to curb and limit the arbitrary behavior of attorneys." As for jury trials, Pobedonostsev claimed that "the use of juries in criminal trials has proven to be absolutely false for Russia and completely incompatible with the conditions of our existence and the structure of our courts .... We must rid ourselves of this institution if we are to restore respect for the courts in Russia." Realizing that an immediate abolition of jury trials would be difficult, he therefore suggested that various case categories be gradually withdrawn from eligibility for trial by jury. As a schedule for general judicial reform Pobedonostsev saw the abolition of the independence of the courts (by including them in the general system of state institutions) and the removability of judges as the first step. Secondly, public court proceedings should be abandoned and controversial legal procedures (as a move against "the arbitrary behavior of attorneys") restricted. Finally, trial by jury eventually should be terminated. Hence the Director-General of the Holy Synod, who had once helped draft the judicial statutes of 1864, now advocated a resurrection of the basic principles of pre-reform judicial procedures.

Pobedonostsev's memorandum raised other issues, including the reorganization of the justices of the peace system. In his opinion, the election of these officials "put them in a weak position. Their appointments were subject to all the vagaries of the electoral process .... Because of this the *Justice* was open to the threats and flattery of the electorate and was caught in the interplay of local interests and electoral parties. It is obviously impossible to expect from such a Justice either independence or firmness, let alone the knowledge and experience necessary for the conduct of his business." Further, he stressed the unfortunate results caused by the severe constraints the judicial regulations placed on executive authorities. The latter were finding themselves incapable of the quick action needed to deal with problems that had become the responsibility of judicial institutions, which "reached their verdict by slow and measured steps." While at first glance it might seem there were some grounds for Pobedonostsev's complaints, in fact the "constraints placed by the judiciary upon executive action" undoubtedly had reduced the chances of arbitrary administrative behavior.

Pobedonostsev held that the role of the chancellery in the court system (completely abolished by the judicial statute) should be restored.

The elimination of the chancellery had been a "great blunder," for the Chancellery Court had been an "important school" for the training of "distinguished judicial figures." Whether or not Pobedonostsev intended such a result, this measure also would have tended to reduce the place and significance of the regular courts. The preparation of cases outside the courts would signify a return to the pre-reform method of doing things (when a Chancellery Court drew up a summary of the basic materials and evidence of a case that served as the basis for the court's decision). Finally, Pobedonostsev raised two other points. He proposed the distinctions between types of appeals (cassate and appellate) be abolished and insisted on the need for reviewing the jurisdictions of the different judicial institutions, especially that of the justices of the peace.

The thoughts expressed by Pobedonostsev[4] were fully shared by the tsar. But despite these attitudes, neither the judicial institutions nor the methods of judicial procedure suffered fundamental amendment. Why was this? Clearly the given conditions then existing in Russia definitely favored a reorganization of the courts, and counter-reforms were undertaken in the field of local administration (the zemstvo and city legislation). What prevented similar reforms in the courts? The apparent answer is that legal reform, which would have affected a wide section of society and the middle classes in particular, had opponents within the government. Among these were a good number of officials of the Ministry of Justice, the foremost of whom was the minister, D.N. Nabokov.

NABOKOV'S POLICIES AS MINISTER

Nabokov adopted only one measure aimed at changing the judicial system. At the end of 1883 his proposal—"The Issuance of Orders and Modification of Several Articles in the Judicial System's Regulations Concerning the Supervisory and Disciplinary Responsibilities of Officials of the Judicial Department"—was discussed in the State Council. This proposal attacked the secure tenure of magistrates. At that time, Nabokov argued, "in disciplinary matters a judge can be given only a 'warning.' Such warnings, as is indicated by the sense of this word, do not constitute a punishment. In effect they merely express an opinion that in the future he should avoid such negligence. Thus one may say that a judge, despite his improper activity or clear negligence in carrying out his responsibilities, as long as this was not premeditated or done for personal profit, cannot be subjected to any punishment."

For this reason Nabokov felt that penalties for breaches of conduct should be increased to permit judges to be dismissed or transferred to other judicial positions. He recommended a revision of Article 295 of the judicial regulations to read: "When a judge is *brought to trial* or subjected to any punishment or penalty under the criminal law for a crime or misdemeanor not connected with his official duties, even if this does not entail the loss of his service rights, the *Minister of Justice may propose that the Higher Disciplinary Court discuss these circumstances with regard to the application of one of the measures indicated in subparagraphs 7 and 8 of Article 262* (that is, dismissal or transferral to another judicial position)."[5]

Breaches of discipline that might result in dismissal or transfer would, Nabokov suggested, be examined by a specially established Higher Disciplinary Court rather than in the General Session of the Senate's Final Appeals Departments. He considered the creation of a special court necessary because the discussion of disciplinary matters in the Final Appeals (Cassation) Departments' General Session would involve a great number of people[6] and therefore cause "no little difficulty and serve to slow up considerably the proceedings in matters of this nature."

The transfer of such cases to the Combined Office of the First Office and Final Appeals Departments for a ruling would be awkward "as, with its small number of members (seven senators, counting the senator-president) this represented the opposite extreme, and in the decision of a matter as important as a dismissal a greater number of judges would doubtlessly serve to guarantee a more thorough and wide-ranging discussion of the case." In Nabokov's opinion the new Higher Disciplinary Court should consist of the Combined Office of the First and Final Appeals Departments of the senate, supplemented by the senators-president of the Final Appeals Departments, and by four senators of these departments who would be appointed annually by "the Highest authority." Judges would then be dismissed for breaches of conduct by a decision of a higher judicial body of thirteen senators rather than by an administrative order.

Nabokov made this proposal because of pressure put on him by the reactionaries, and particularly by Katkov. On May 12, 1884, the day the proposal was first discussed in the State Council, Polovtsov noted in his diary: "Today Nabokov presented . . . his draft disciplinary statute or, more correctly, his reply to Katkov's orders that magistrates' security of tenure be destroyed." In any case, on May 12 and 15, 1884 the Combined Session of the State Council's Departments of Civil Laws and Spiritual Affairs examined the minister's proposal. "While being convinced," read the minutes of the meeting, "by the arguments contained in the presentation with regard to the inconveniences of the existing order, in which the most important disciplinary cases involving persons in the judiciary are examined by a large college composed of more than fifty persons, and recognizing the possibility of forming for the

consideration of the aforementioned cases a special disciplinary office . . .
the Departments doubt the necessity of a proposal that aims at increasing the penalties for judges and make several changes in the existing
order of disciplinary courts."

The measures presented by Nabokov would, in the opinion of the
Departments, encroach on the independence of the courts. "It is therefore evident," says the journal, "that the adoption of the aforesaid proposals would affect one of the basic principles on which we have founded
the edifice of the new courts. Special caution is therefore demanded, and
one cannot begin implementing such proposals without being fully convinced of their necessity. The proposal under discussion does not contain arguments sufficient to resolve doubts about the necessity of the
aforementioned amendments, which are of the most fundamental nature."

Obviously the members of the State Council received Nabokov's proposals with anything but delight. Furthermore, the Departments fundamentally changed the ministers' new version of Article 295. Whereas
Nabokov, as indicated above, wanted to transfer to the Higher Disciplinary Court only cases where a judge "is *brought to trial* or subjected to
some kind of punishment or penalty under the criminal law," the Combined Departments thought differently. Their amended version of the
article read: "When a judge, for the commission of a crime or misdemeanor that is not connected with his official duties, is subjected under
criminal law to a penalty or punishment, even if this does not entail the
loss of his rights in the service, or when he is subjected by legal or disciplinary bodies to a penalty for cases of judicial dereliction of duty, which
by their importance and frequency reveal the accused's clear neglect of
his responsibilities even if they do not entail his removal from office,
then these circumstances are to be presented by the Minister of Justice
to the Higher Disciplinary Office."[7] In this version the functions of the
Higher Disciplinary Office would be somewhat more circumscribed than
in Nabokov's.

This decision displeased the reactionaries. Apparently Alexander III,
under the influence of Pobedonostsev or Katkov, ordered a review of the
decision of the Combined Departments, and on March 11 and 18, 1885
they reconsidered their earlier conclusions.[8] As a result the Departments
redefined the Higher Disciplinary Office's sphere of jurisdiction and
considerably expanded the range of cases subject to the Office's discussion. "Should the Minister of Justice," read the new decision on this
question, "discover a) that a judge has committed a dereliction of
his duty that, although it does not entail his removal from his post
by a court, gives evidence, by its significance or recurrence, of the

unsuitability of the person accused to hold the position of judge, or of his clear neglect of his responsibilities; or b) that a judge has allowed himself, outside of his official life, to commit public actions that, although these did not result in his being brought to trial as a criminal, are still incompatible with the dignity of judicial office; or, c) that a judge, because of activities in the locality where he holds his appointment, has placed himself in such a position that there is reason to doubt his further calm and impartial fulfillment of his responsibilities, and he has nonetheless refused to accept a proposed transfer to an equivalent position in another locality, the Minister of Justice is to present these circumstances to the Higher Disciplinary Office for its consideration."

This conclusion, as compared to that reached earlier, allowed a certain extension of the rights of the Higher Disciplinary Office. However, the Combined Departments had not satisfied the reactionaries. On May 6, the day before this question was to be discussed in the General Session of the State Council, Katkov saw Count Peter A. Shuvalov and declared "that on reading the minutes (of the Combined Departments' sessions) that dealt with the Disciplinary Office, which had been sent to him in Moscow, he found Nabokov's proposal had made matters worse, not better." Katkov therefore travelled to see the tsar at Gatchina. While the exact results of this visit are unknown, it was followed by a stormy discussion of Nabokov's proposal in the meeting of the General Session of the State Council.

Polovtsov says that shortly before the meeting Ostrovsky, who was closest to Katkov's way of thinking, announced that he intended to make a motion concerning the draft under discussion. It would contain two parts. The first would raise the question of the Higher Disciplinary Office's examination "of acts that are morally offensive, even if they do not merit punishment under the criminal law." In this category of "morally offensive" actions he wanted to include everything that might offend the authorities. Secondly, Ostrovsky raised a major point about the membership of the Disciplinary Office. Unlike Nabokov, he suggested that this body should be formed not from Senators, "but from persons who were absolute outsiders as far as the judicial department was concerned." This would completely destroy the principle of the judiciary's security of tenure which was, of course, Katkov's aim. "Nabokov and Ostrovsky," Polovtsov says in his diary, "were invited to explain the matter to the Chairman. The discussion produced a very stormy scene in the Chairman's office. Ostrovsky's ideas were categorically rejected by Nabokov, who refused to accept anything that would be so insulting to the Senate and to the whole bar. 'This is all the idea of the editor of the *Moscow News,* who is always heaping filth upon both the judicial department and the State Council,' Nabokov shouted. 'You insult me,' answered Ostrovsky. The argument became so hot that Ostrovsky told the Grand Duke (Michael Nikolaevich): 'You are insulting His Highness, the Emperor, by intending to limit His right to choose people for this Office.'

The accusation that their opponents were attempting to encroach on the inviolability of the autocratic principle—such was the cry of Katkov and his friends who well knew how to upset their rather dull sovereign. Nonetheless, the arguments continued during the Council's sessions and on May 20, 1885 Alexander III approved the decision of the General Session of the State Council. He did so in spite of the efforts made by Ostrovsky, after the meeting, to convince him that the creation of this type of Higher Disciplinary Office would somehow infringe the autocratic prerogative were it to be granted the power to dismiss persons appointed by "His Majesty's authority."[9]

To what degree did this law eliminate the judiciary's security of tenure? On the whole this principle was left intact. It is true that the new law allowed the dismissal or transferral of persons in tenured posts both in instances of their trial and sentencing under the criminal law and as the result of a disciplinary action. But in the latter case the decision was made by a judicial board, composed of thirteen persons, rather than by a single individual. Further, during Alexander III's reign the activities of the Higher Disciplinary Office never enjoyed real significance. An analysis of the journals of this office for the nine-year period of 1886 to 1894 inclusive shows that during this time only two men were dismissed from their posts for reprehensible activities.

In A.F. Koni's opinion the law of May 20, 1885 did not affect the security of judges. "This concession of Nabokov's," wrote Koni, "gave what satisfaction could be given. To the great disappointment of those who had led the campaign against the judiciary, all their unreasonable and blind hopes had come to nought. This law purchased the essentials of the judges' continued security of tenure." As for Nabokov's role as a defender of the judicial statute of 1864, Koni concluded that "it will be clearer to a future historian of Russian judicial affairs than to contemporaries how difficult was the task which fell to the third minister to serve under the judicial statute and just how severe were the spiritual trials through which he had to live. And then he (Nabokov) will be given his just due." For the basic principles of the judicial statute were not altered seriously during the first half of the 1880s, despite the violent attacks of the reactionaries.

MANASEIN'S FIRST CONCESSIONS

Manasein was next appointed Minister of Justice. Like Nabokov, he was no proponent of abolishing the judicial statute. But the new minister was more pliable and conservative and, while he did not infringe upon the existing judicial practices as a whole, he did suggest changes in some details of the system.

On May 3, 1886 the Minister of Justice proposed in the State Council changes in Articles 620 through 622, and 624, of the Criminal Code. These articles dealt with the public conduct of judicial proceedings.[10] Manasein wanted several limitations of this principle added to Article 620 which, in the second point of the existing edition already listed certain cases that were to be heard behind closed doors. By Manasein's proposal two new points would be added: a first and a third.[11] "On the instructions of the presiding judge," read the first point, "entry to court sessions may be forbidden to: (1) minors; (2) grade school, high-school and university students, and those attending other higher educational institutions; and (3) persons of the female sex when this is demanded by the nature of the case." This article meant that a presiding judge might close the court to anyone under the legal age of twenty-one years and to all students, including those in universities.

Manasein's third point would expand still further the existing opportunities for barring the public from court sessions. According to his draft: "In addition to the cases mentioned in the previous Article 620, Point 2, the court's doors may be closed to the public during any judicial proceeding, either at the time of a particular part of the proceedings or for the whole of the trial: (1) when a public investigation of an aspect of the case at trial violates the demands of morality or insults religious sentiments; and (2) when banning the public from the court room appears to be necessary to guarantee a calm examination of the case and the rendering of an impartial verdict." This point would allow a presiding judge to close the court during any trial.

Article 621 also was to be amended. The existing version indicated that the court was to be closed as "an exceptional measure" and "only when it is clearly necessary," but Manasein's form omitted this qualification. Of even greater significance was his proposal to add a new section to this article. "Should the Minister of Justice discover," he suggested, "from the report of a local presiding judge, a dispatch from a member of the staff supervising the prosecution of cases, or from any information sent to him, that the public examination of a case may lead people astray and excite them, or if it is assumed that this examination will not be compatible with the maintenance of public order, the dignity of state authorities, or with the rendering of an impartial verdict, he may order that the court be closed for the entire hearing of the case, or only for a particular part of the trial, by means of a directive with which the presiding judge of the local court in question must comply."

Further, although only the practical application of Article 622 was to be changed, Article 624 was to be basically amended. In the existing version, even when cases were heard in a closed session, "the doors of the courtroom are to be opened" after legal arguments. The new version would open the court only when the verdict was announced.

All in all, Manasein's proposals would increase the opportunities available to both the Minister of Justice and presiding judges to close the courts to the public. On November 1 and 29, 1886 these revisions were discussed in the Combined Departments of Civil Laws and Spiritual Affairs and provoked a lively debate. Pobedonostsev was the most active. Describing the meeting in his diary for November 29, Polovtsov commented: "Manasein was silent, but Pobedonostsev defended the draft as if it were his own creation, pointing out the virtues of closed trials over public ones." In fact the arguments mainly centered on the question of who was to have the right to prohibit a public court session under Article 621—the Minister of Justice or the Senate. Half of the members present (five out of ten), headed by Pobedonostsev and Manasein, maintained that "to grant the Minister of Justice the right to close court sessions was a measure of the utmost necessity." The remaining five, led by N.I. Stoianovsky and M.N. Liuboshchinsky, resolutely opposed this proposition. According to the meeting's minutes, this group, "despite their readiness to meet the Minister of Justice half way in this matter, cannot agree that an order closing court sessions should be given on the individual authority of the Minister of Justice . . . . The courts operate only under the orders of His Imperial Majesty and a local court cannot be subordinated in any of its functions to any other authority than that of the highest instance in the system of local courts as authorized by His Majesty's autocratic authority." Following this line of reasoning, these members proposed "to allow the Minister of Justice . . . to suggest the closing of a court to the joint meeting of the First and Final Appeals Departments of the Governing Senate."

At Pobedonostsev's insistence, the Combined Departments expanded the kinds of cases heard in closed courts as listed in the second section of Article 620. This now included hearings dealing with "neglect of the faith, or with the Jews or Schismatics." Then, during the debate, further editorial amendments were made to the individual articles as proposed. Article 621, which dealt with the court's own decision to close its sessions to the public, was given a more guarded form. It now read that the closing of court sessions "as an exceptional measure is permitted . . . only when necessary." But on the whole the Combined Departments' discussion of Manasein's presentation revealed two points of view. One insisted that a decision on the closing of court sessions was to be taken by the Minister of Justice. The other believed this question should be resolved by a joint meeting of the First and Final Appeals Departments of the Senate.

When the General Session of the State Council considered this question on January 19, 1887, the debates became even stormier. "In the General Session of the State Council," Polovtsov wrote, "there was a hot debate over Manasein's proposals for limiting public court proceedings. Stoianovsky spoke without talent, but he hotly and sincerely defended the existing judicial statute . . . (Dmitry G.) Derviz insisted that on the basis of our laws Russia was now governed on a firm legal foundation, but that the proposed measure would introduce a principle of uncontrolled personal responsibility that is presently lacking in our legislation. Count Pahlen, who had himself been Minister of Justice for a decade, maintained that the acceptance of the proposed measure would make the Minister of Justice the unwitting protector of every immoral act performed by those who can always find a way of petitioning for the closing of the court that is to try them . . . . Against all this Pobedonostsev spoke very convincingly about the deficiences of the new courts. These defects were outlined with that simplicity, clarity, and conviction that distinguishes his speech. Yet his conclusions did not follow from his exposition. Manasein only repeated 'Non possumus' and glanced at Pobedonostsev, who forbade him to make any kind of concession."

In the end twenty members, headed by Grand Duke Vladimir Alexandrovich, Pobedonostsev, Ostrovsky, Vyshnegradsky, Durnovo, Plehve, and Manasein, supported the latter's proposals. On the other hand, thirty-one members (including Grand Duke Michael Nikolaevich, Egor A. Peretts, Kakhanov, Pahlen, and Shestakov) dissented. They wanted the closing of a court during particular aspects of a judicial hearing resolved by a joint sitting of the First and Final Appeals Departments of the senate. Otherwise, the General Session approved the rest of the Combined Departments' resolutions.

Following the meeting of the General Session both sides made a number of determined efforts in the hope of persuading Alexander III to approve their view of this issue. But the emperor apparently had been convinced already by Pobedonostsev and Manasein. When Grand Duke Michael Nikolaevich—however strange it may seem—actually took the initiative and suggested the creation of a special conference for an all-sided discussion of the issue, the tsar replied, according to Polovtsov, "that this was superfluous as his mind was firmly made up."

Polovtsov himself attempted to influence Alexander III. He wrote the emperor and proposed a compromise solution. The minority's opinion should be approved, but with the proviso that each time the Minister of Justice resolved to close a trial to the public, the decision should be approved by His Majesty. "As I reported to Your Majesty," wrote Polovtsov, "the Minister of Justice testified before the State Council that there would not be more than one or two such cases a year. It is evident that You, Your Majesty, . . . could not be troubled by these two cases. The Minister of Justice would also be that much the less bothered by these requests. Those appeals that feared the light of day would be silenced, so as to avoid being brought to Your attention. At the same time, when there were serious reasons of state for closing a court session —and only then—would the matter be brought to You. The periodical press, the provinces, and chatterboxes of every sort would then see that this remained an exceptional measure and not, as they are now saying, one aimed at the complete destruction of public trials."[12] But this idea was also rejected by the tsar. Alexander III made his final decision on this matter on February 12 and approved the "minority's opinion."

THE REFORM OF TRIAL BY JURY

In 1887 and 1899 laws were passed limiting jury trials. On February 25, 1887, immediately after Alexander III approved Manasein's law "On Limiting Public Judicial Sessions," the Minister of Justice brought another proposal into the State Council. This was entitled "On Amending the Regulations for the Compilation of Juror Lists." "From the first practical experiences with the judicial system as reformed by Alexander II's statute," Manasein declared, "the trial of cases by juries has shown that among the people sitting on juries there are often elements who are far from the best that society has to offer, and they are certainly not the ones the law had hoped to see involved in the process of criminal justice."

The participation of such elements, Manasein claimed, was directly reflected in the substance of the verdicts. As early as 1884 the Ministry of Justice had turned its attention to this subject and established a special commission of "senior members of the judicial department" to study this problem. This group had solicited opinions from the provinces and, on the basis of these, concluded that the unsatisfactory composition of juries could be explained by the following two circumstances: "(1) the legal rules used for determining the categories of persons for jury duty were imperfect and, (2) the legislation on the structure and conduct of work in the institutions supervising the general registration of persons liable for jury duty, and on selecting from among them the persons needed for a particular period of judicial sessions, was inadequate."[13]

In Manasein's opinion, the quality of jurors could be improved only by raising the qualification demanded in terms of income (from capital investment, employment in a profession or trade, or from the wages of labor). He recommended the setting of the following qualifications: for the capital cities not less than 1,000 rubles; in towns with a population of more than 100,000, 600 rubles; and in other places not less than 400 rubles.[14] For peasant jurors, Manasein believed that the required terms of service in elective posts or as zemstvo deputies should be lengthened. He also wanted a few minor amendments. These proposals were examined by the Combined Departments of Civil Laws and Religious Affairs on March 16, 1887, and by the General Session of the State Council on April 13. Then, on April 28, Alexander III approved them.

On the whole Manasein's suggestions were accepted and the methods of drawing up jury rolls changed. Now jurors had to read as well as speak Russian. Further, the qualifications for the "middle class" elements among the jurors (persons drawing "salaries or income from their own capital, profession, trade, or business") were doubled and, in some cases, more than doubled. For persons in the capital cities it was now increased from 500 to 1,000 rubles; for those in cities of not less than 100,000 persons,[15] from 200 to 600 rubles; and in other localities from 200 to 400 rubles. Meanwhile the qualifications for landowners were considerably lowered. The previous figure of one hundred desiatins (270 acres) was replaced by one of from ten to twenty desiatins (27-54 acres). But greater limitations were introduced for peasants. A three-year term was demanded of volost and village elders as well as from judges of volost courts (from whom earlier no specific term had been demanded).

The demand for a reading knowledge of Russian considerably lessened the chances for middle class members of the non-Russian population to serve as jurors, while increases in income qualifications exerted the same effect as far as the urban elements were concerned. The lower property qualifications for landowners, on the other hand, increased the possibility that prosperous peasants (kulaks)—politically a very conservative stratum—would be included in the lists of jurors.

In early 1889 Manasein presented another proposal ("On Amending the Order of Jurisdiction in the Cases of Several Crimes that are Tried by Jury in Local Courts") to the State Council. Juries, he claimed, had been returning many verdicts of not guilty in cases of crimes against the administrative order. "The figures on this for a recent nine-year period (1877 to 1885 inclusive)," wrote the Minister of Justice, "comprise from 42 percent to 61 percent of all verdicts in these cases, and the average is 56 percent." In contrast, he continued, "in the Warsaw Judicial District, where there are no jury trials, in cases of the type mentioned only 27 percent on the verdicts returned were not guilty." Manasein therefore wanted crimes against the administrative order withdrawn from the jurisdiction of jury trials. Among these he included cases of breaches of trust, as well as those "in which a proper decision depends upon the judge having special knowledge or experience of the service," those concerning "criminal acts for which the highest legal punishment is combined with the loss of only certain special rights and privileges" and, finally, cases related to crimes by minors. Crimes against the administrative order and cases of breaches of official trust were to be transferred to the jurisdiction of a special session of the District Court (with participation of jurors selected according to estate) and the other cases mentioned heard in the regular courts, but without juries.

The Combined Departments of Civil Laws and Religious Affairs approved the proposed measures with the observation that it would be better to replace the Special Session of the District Board, and its estate jurors, with the Judicial Bench. This latter body, they believed, would be more qualified and unprejudiced. Further, they stressed that cases involving minors should involve the discussion of all relevant aspects. At the same time the Departments examined Pobedonostsev's proposal that cases of bigamy should be exempted from jury trials, but resolved that it was better to retain the existing system in which such cases were first heard in a church court. On May 30 the General Session of the State Council approved all these decisions, except for that on cases of bigamy. The General Session favored the removal of these cases from the jurisdiction of juries to that of the Judicial Bench, with the participation of estate jurors. On July 7 Alexander III approved these decisions.

This law excluded a large number of cases from the jurisdiction of juries.[16] It is therefore clear that in the second half of the 1880s serious steps were taken to limit the range of such trials and simultaneously to raise the qualifications demanded of jurors. Nonetheless, despite these measures, the institution of trial by jury itself was retained.

FINAL EFFORTS AT JUDICIAL REFORM

The law of July 14, 1889 which created the institution of the land captain abolished that of justice of the peace and thus represented another serious attack on the judicial statute of 1864.[17] In the country-side the justice was replaced by the land captain (who united both judicial and administrative powers) and in the towns by a city magistrate appointed by the government.

This attack was directed against the Minister of Justice as well as the judicial statute. Later, on September 18, 1895, Polovtsov, who knew Manasein well, described him and his defeat in the following manner: "In the depth of his soul he was an ardent adherent of the judicial reforms but, on his appointment, the necessity of destroying the statute was explained to him. He began to move between these two positions and, as always occurs in such cases, earned the dislike of both camps. Count Tolstoy became his violent enemy and was able to smash him completely (in the battle over the land captains). He [Tolstoy] dictated to the Emperor the decision abolishing the justices of the peace and this was then revealed in the State Council without the Minister of Justice having been given even the slightest warning, so that it took him completely by surprise. After having received such a slap in the face, Manasein should have immediately resigned his office."[18]

The measures adopted to limit the judicial statute during the 1880s—during the ministries of Nabokov and Manasein—were piecemeal in nature. Although the basic principles of the statute (an independent judiciary, public trials and trial by jury) had been considerably restricted in their application, they had not been completely destroyed. But in 1894 an unprincipled careerist, N.V. Muraviev, was appointed as Minister of Justice. He immediately set out to revise completely the judicial statute. For this purpose a "Commission for the Review of Legislation on the Judicial Department," under the chairmanship of the Minister of Justice, was set up in the spring of 1894. It had a large membership of twenty-three persons. Among them were State Secretary V.K. Plehve, Deputy Ministers Peter M. Butovsky (of Justice) and Ivan L. Goremykin (of Interior), Senators S.I. Lukianov, Nicholas S. Tagantsev, N.N. Schreiber, and A.F. Koni, the director of the Zemstvo Section of the Ministry of the Interior, Alexander S. Stishinsky, the director of the Department of General Administration in the Ministry of the Interior, Nicholas Dolgovo-Saburov, and others.

This commission set to work on April 30, 1894. At that time four sub-commissions were created. One, chaired by Goremykin, dealt with local judicial regulations, and a second headed by Schreiber dealt with general judicial procedures. Lukianov headed a third group studying the judicial procedures relative to civil cases and a fourth, under Tagantsev, investigated procedures applicable to criminal cases. In all over fifty persons participated in the commission's work, including Ivan G. Shcheglovitov, the prosecutor of the St. Petersburg Judicial District, and the barristers Vladimir D. Spasovich and Fedor N. Plevako.

Muraviev's memorandum of April 6, 1894 is of particular interest for an understanding of his attitude toward this review of the existing statute. In opening he touched upon the judicial reforms of Alexander II. Although he saw them as being timely and useful, he maintained that they had never been co-ordinated with the system of state administration. They were, Muraviev said, "as uncomfortable as ready-made clothes." He also stressed their abstract and theoretical nature and complained that they displayed a liberal bias. Further, Muraviev was critical of the way in which these laws had been amended—that is, by the rephrasing of individual articles. This had unfortunate results and meant that the judicial institutions "are mutually incompatible and get in each other's way." "Not one single principle or institution has remained intact; all have been amended, shaken up, or hedged in with limitations and exceptions."

The task at hand, Muraviev argued, was to supply the existing judicial edifice with "a foundation, and to reconstruct it, making use of all the material available." Hence a reform of the judicial regulations should be sought through "a full, complete, and simultaneous review carried out in accord with a general plan and one guiding principle." In this process the following basic questions needed re-examination: "(1) irremovability of judges; (2) trial by jury; (3) the judicial-administrative institutions; (4) the Senate and appeals; (5) the investigative sections; (6) the procurator's authority; (7) lawyers; (8) civil courts and 'formalism' (the shame of the courts); (9) judicial system salaries; (10) raising the moral and intellectual levels of judicial personnel; and (11) simplifying, speeding, and reducing of costs of trials." Clearly, the independence of the judiciary and trial by jury headed Muraviev's list.

The commission's work is reflected in its report, "Basic Principles for the Proposed Unification of the Judicial System," which provides a full outline of the nature of the reforms envisaged. It is divided into three sections: (1) "General Principles;" (2) "Composition of the Judicial Establishment, Service Privileges of Judges and Officials of the Procuratorial Supervisory Branch;" and (3) "Responsibilities and Relationships of Judicial Institutions."

The first section yields the best insight into the proposed reform. The first paragraph of the "Basic Principles" indicated that "District Justices, County Members of the Provincial Court, Provincial Courts, Judicial Benches and the Judicial Departments of the Senate are recognized as judicial authorities."[19] The authority of district justices and county members was to be vested in individuals, but that for the remaining judicial institutions or establishments, in collegiate bodies. Further on, it envisaged that the conduct of investigations would be "the responsibility of the District Justices and County Members, or of a member of the Provincial Court."[20]

Paragraphs five and six dealt with trial by jury. The fifth dealt with cases where people were charged in the county or provincial courts with crimes entailing a loss of all civil rights or of all special rights. In these, the report maintained, jurors would be summoned to determine the guilt or innocence of the persons charged. Yet the sixth paragraph indicated that "for decisions in those criminal cases . . . which must be removed from the jurisdiction of trial by jury, estate jurors are to be combined with the membership of the Provincial Court and the Judicial Bench." Meanwhile the seventh paragraph of the "Basic Principles" concerned the procedure for appointing judges, stating that "all persons in responsible posts within the judicial system, with the exception of honorary justices of the peace, will hold office at the government's pleasure."

A number of conclusions can be drawn from these "Basic Principles." In the first place, the principle of the irremovability of judges—so hated by the bureaucracy—was to be done away with completely. The creation of the provincial court, in the place of the district court, would make the judicial institutions more dependent on the administration. Then, although jury trials would be preserved, clearly these proposals would have limited considerably their activity by removing particular categories of cases from their jurisdiction. The office of judicial investigator was to be abolished, although investigating magistrates would be entrusted with the conduct of investigations in exceptional cases.

The question as to whether or not the land captains would retain judicial powers remained unclear. Apparently trials in the county were to be transferred to the district justices and land captains would be retained merely as administrative officials. But one member of this commission, A.F. Koni, suggests the contrary in his memoirs. "In spite of the fact that Goremykin objected to land captains having any judicial power at all," Koni wrote, "and that (P.V.) Nekliudov, the representative of the Minister of the Interior, openly declared to the commission that he (the Minister) would willingly surrender all judicial functions for these sons of caprice, Muraviev categorically announced that he would not even permit this question to be discussed, as this would contradict the celebrated 'views of the government'."

Otherwise Muraviev's project would have destroyed the basis of the judicial statute of 1864 by significantly weakening bourgeois principles in judicial procedure while strengthening the feudal ones. But, as A.F. Koni makes clear in his memoirs, the social unrest that began in 1892 and 1893, accompanied by the growth of a broad labor movement and its union with the Social Democrats, prevented the government from realizing these goals.

CHAPTER VI

PRESS AND ADMINISTRATION

THE PROVISIONAL REGULATIONS

During Alexander's reign the censorship grew much more repressive, especially with respect to the periodical press. This persecution aimed at eliminating even the most moderate dissent and sought to establish in Russia that conformity of political thought of which Katkov had always dreamed. The latter believed that since his views were, in the final analysis, the truth, all others must be treason.[1]

The first moves facilitating the government's persecution of journalists were the "Provisional Regulations for the Press," drafted while Ignatiev was Minister of the Interior.[2] His retirement did not terminate this project for in August, 1882 Tolstoy presented it, under his own signature and with a few corrections, to the Committee of Ministers. On August 17 and 24 the Committee discussed these "Provisional Regulations," and on August 27 Alexander III approved them.

The regulations comprised three points. The first stated that "the editorial staff of a periodical appearing more often than once a week, which has received its third reprimand, are obliged when they renew (publication) after the period of suspension, . . . to present their issues to the Censors' Committee no later than eleven o'clock in the evening before the day it is to appear." The censors received the right, "if they decide that the distribution of such a periodical will cause significant harm, to prevent its appearance without benefit of legal proceedings against the guilty parties." This placed a newspaper that had received three reprimands in an intolerable position. Firstly, in practice such a newspaper would have to be printed by ten o'clock in the evening, allowing other papers the possibility of including in their issues news stories that had arrived much later. Secondly, since a paper could now be suspended by a purely administrative decision without intervention by judicial authorities, the chances of arbitrary decisions by the censors were greatly increased.

The second point obliged the editors of newspapers and journals that appeared without preliminary censorship to name the author of any article when asked by the Ministry of the Interior. Finally, the third point announced the creation of a special board (the Supreme Commission of the Press), comprising the Ministers of Internal Affairs, Education, and Justice, the Director-General of the Holy Synod, and the departmental heads concerned with the questions raised for discussion. This body was to decide on a journal's complete suppression "for an indefinite period during which its editors and printers were, as a consequence, prohibited from being the editors and printers of any other kind of periodical publication."[3] Thus the "Conference of Four Ministers" (as the Supreme Commission became known) received an extraordinarily far-reaching mandate. By preventing the editors and printers of a prohibited periodical from taking part in any further journalistic activities, the "Provisional Regulations" allowed personal rights to be limited by administrative action. Previously this could have happened solely as the result of a judicial decision.

It is obvious that the "Provisional Regulations" of August 27 greatly strengthened what the official terminology referred to as "administrative influence on the press." In practice a system of the most flagrant type of arbitrary administrative control was created. K.K. Arseniev, analysing these regulations in 1882, observed that "they kill ideas when they are only embryonic, distort, limit or completely prevent their expression, lower the general level of the press . . . and only strengthen the influence of opinions that flourish in the dark and rely upon silence."

E.M. FEOKTISTOV

On January 1, 1883 E.M. Feoktistov was appointed director of the Main Directorate of the Press.[4] In the 1850s Feoktistov had taught and had contributed to the liberal journal *Russian Herald.* Later he edited the newspaper *Russian Speech* and was close to the Moscow circle of Westernizers that included I.S. Turgenev and V.P. Botkin. In the early 1860s Feoktistov grew friendly with A.V. Golovnin's and D.A. Miliutin's group of liberal bureaucrats, joined the Ministry of Education, and played an important role in drafting a new law on book publishing. Meanwhile he contributed to the moderate liberal publication, *Russian Veteran,* the newspaper of the Ministry of War (or more correctly, of D.A. Miliutin, the minister himself).

During the 1860s Feoktistov followed the example of his friend Katkov and moved to the right. By the early 1870s he had earned the trust of D.A. Tolstoy, edited the Ministry of Education's journal, and was gaining powerful friends such as Count I.I. Vorontsov-Dashkov, M.N. Ostrovsky, and Pobedonostsev.[5] Hence the public saw his appointment as head of the Main Directorate of the Press as a signal of stronger censorship.[6] In fact this event did mark the beginning of a new stage, for the restrictions imposed by the censor, and the actual repression, both grew in force.

Pobedonostsev's hand was evident in all of this. "This pale, emaciated, and sick fanatic, this enemy of every progressive movement," wrote the

journalist and historian Michael I. Semevsky, "begins each day by reading all the now-very-colorless Russian newspapers. In their articles he
perceives various spectres and, wailing, he arrives at the Ministry of the
Interior, having marked many of the articles" for its attention. Once
Feoktistov was appointed, Pobedonostsev could appeal directly to him.
On the very day that Feoktistov assumed his new post, the director-
general sent him a memorandum. Discussing the newspaper *Russian
Courier*, Pobedonostsev wrote that "the *Courier* already has sufficiently
shown its colors. Why stand on ceremony with this abomination? I think
that it should be closed immediately."[7] A week or so later he pointed
out a report in the newspaper *Voice* that the *Moscow Telegraph* would
publish a new "philosophical work" by Leo Tolstoy.[8] "The tendency
of the philosophical works of this half-witted Count Tolstoy is well
known. Therefore it would not be superfluous for you to pay attention
to the above-mentioned announcement."

Many of these notes—like the one concerning L.N. Tolstoy—carry a
scornful and abusive tone. Almost all of Pobedonostsev's seventy-nine
letters or notes (preserved in Feoktistov's archives) concern some aspect
of the press. The director-general kept a close eye on the journalists and
Feoktistov himself recalled: "I was always amazed that he found enough
time to read not only the most widely circulated but even the most
insignificant newspapers, and to follow not only their leading articles or
correspondence, but also (and I am not exaggerating) the advertisements.
He noticed even little articles that did not really merit attention, continually sent me evidence of the lack of discipline in our press, and
complained that the measures taken against it were not sufficiently
energetic."

Katkov also influenced Feoktistov. Indeed, the head of the Main
Directorate of the Press served the editor of the *Moscow News* as an
obliging assistant. He kept Katkov informed of events in government
circles and of discussions in the State Council and Committee of Ministers, and obtained official documents for him. Feoktistov further reported what people said privately, and so on. "I am very sorry that you
were not in Moscow," Feoktistov wrote Katkov in 1884. "I deliberately
called to see you and give you some news." In that same year he made
profuse apologies to Katkov for being unable to provide the documents
concerning a proposal on grain elevators[9] then being debated in the
State Council.[10]

M.E. Saltykov-Shchedrin was absolutely correct in calling Feoktistov
"Katkov's slave." Yet it is a mistake to blame the persecution of Russian letters solely on Pobedonostsev, Katkov, and other domineering
persons. Feoktistov himself was a man of very fixed ideas and the

policies he implemented in no way contradicted his own estimate of his task. Meanwhile, the Minister of the Interior made no attempt to hamper this labor. "Personally," Feoktistov admitted in his memoirs, "I can have no complaints about Count Tolstoy. He gave me a completely free hand, approved every measure I considered necessary and always agreed with me. He was obviously satisfied that he had found a man who would act firmly and consistently." In some cases, in fact, Feoktistov had to exert pressure on the minister in order "to wring from him agreement for resolute measures."

RESTRICTED TOPICS

The government's battle with literature, and especially with the periodical press, was carried out in two ways. Firstly, the range of subjects open to writers was restricted while, secondly, individual journals were directly badgered.

The first method took the form of instructions that banned discussion by the press of many topics concerning the most important aspects of Russian life. These subjects included the activities of government institutions and the courts, of the zemstvo and city administrations, the peasantry, and educational developments. Circulars excluding the discussion of specific subjects began to appear immediately after Alexander III's manifesto on the inviolability of the autocracy. On May 28, 1881 an important circular of the Main Directorate of the Press ordered editors "to refrain from publishing any articles containing information about zemstvo or municipal council resolutions, decisions or addresses, or the reports of the above-mentioned institutions, without first obtaining permission from the appropriate authorities."[11] This effectively barred the press from publishing any information on the activities of the zemstvo and town public administrations. Further, in 1885, in connection with the forthcoming elections for mayor of St. Petersburg, instructions interdicted "the printing of articles about the people offered as candidates, as this can only aggravate relations between the electors and uselessly excite the public."

Restrictions concerning news of the government's activities were especially severe. On August 14, 1882 a circular informed editors that "articles attacking government institutions may lead to the sternest administrative and punitive measures being applied to the offending publication." Then, in March, 1884, the Main Directorate of the Press informed editors and printers that they had the right "to report in the press information about only those government measures that already have been published by the appropriate department in an official journal." Another circular (of April, 1885) instructed that "government documents of every kind must, on the basis of the decrees in force, appear first in an official government journal."

Apart from such general instructions, numerous circulars were issued to deal with particular questions. By these the press was forbidden to carry news concerning individual court cases or discuss the persons guilty of certain crimes (particularly the murderer of G.P. Sudeikin on March 1, 1887),[12] and so on. Finally, the criticism of leading statesman, as well as of particular government actions, was severely limited. In April, 1885 a circular of the main directorate observed that "comments on certain individuals have been appearing in publications subject to censorship, and especially in the satirical and humorous journals. But their public activities are not subjected to a calm and serious discussion, and improper, sharp, and even abusive expressions accompany mention of the names of the persons discussed." For this reason instructions were given proscribing the printing of "insulting expressions and comments about individuals, particularly when names are mentioned."

A ban on discussion of the agrarian question drove all examination of the most pressing contemporary issue from the pages of periodicals. As early as 1882 two circulars had dealt with public discussion of agrarian problems. The first barred the press from carrying any tendentious or seditious news about discord between peasants and landowners. The second circular categorically prohibited "the appearance in the press of any news about land repartition, equalization of landholdings, rumors and so forth, as well as of any articles concerning the utility or justice of change in the status of the peasant and the land." In July, 1883 Feoktistov issued another circular. This forbade consideration in the press of the question of peasant migration "as, at present, increased talk in the press about the migratory movement is reflected in the mood of the village population in a very harmful way."

The net result of this policy was that any real reporting about agrarian problems was impossible. This issue might not be discussed even from the historical point of view: all celebration of the twenty-fifth anniversary of the abolition of serfdom was prohibited and mention of this date in the newspapers or journals categorically forbidden. On September 18, 1885 a circular stressed that violation of this prohibition "will not be tolerated and the guilty publication . . . will be subjected to punitive measures." Some newspapers did attempt to mark this anniversary but, as Vladimir A. Rozenberg recalled in his memoirs, "on the night of February 19 (1886) the newspaper editors received an ultimatum: not one single article or one single word was to be printed about the peasant reforms . . . . They complied with this demand. Several papers appeared with articles on jute bags or other such burning issues of the day, and the *Russian News* did not appear at all .... (George) Kennan, who was visiting Moscow at this time, asked: 'Why is there no *Russian News* today?' They told him: 'Today the newspaper is honoring the twenty-fifth anniversary of the emancipation of the peasants with its silence'."[13]

Articles on the labor question were similarly proscribed. When, in the early 1890s, strikes began to multiply, the main directorate issued a confidential circular on this subject. The circular noted that some periodicals recently had "engaged in controversy over conditions in our factories and plants, and in doing so have touched on the workers' relations with the proprietors." The circular categorically ordered a complete ban on the publication of "such articles because their biased point of view or false information may cause real harm."

The reporting of developments in educational institutions, particularly in the universities, was also interdicted. In 1882 four circulars dealt with this matter. On March 19 the printing of "false or tendentious news about the internal life of both secular and religious educational institutions" was forbidden. Naturally, this "false and tendentious news" meant stories in the press about student unrest. Further, since no newspaper would have greatly valued deliberate falsehoods, inaccurate reporting would not have appeared, regardless of the circular's instructions. In October, 1882 the Main Directorate of the Press categorically proscribed the publication of all accounts of the "disorders" at the University of Kazan until "the official reports on this matter" were released. During December, 1882 another circular banned the publication of materials covering the trial of Semenov, a student of Kazan University who had insulted the superintendent of the education district. Several days later a new circular appeared. It ordered that no information about this case, "or about any similar case that might arise," was to appear in the press. Clearly, all press comment about public events at educational institutions, especially of the universities, was quite impossible.

The volume of these circulars was tremendous—only the most important have been cited. The main directorate issued hundreds of these circulars. They showered upon the heads of editors and printers, limiting and then utterly barring discussion of one important topic or event after another. At the same time these circulars served as the basis for the government's reprisals against the newspapers and journals it considered objectionable.[14]

THE PRESS

The periodical press (newspapers and literary monthlies) formed the sole expression of public opinion and the mouthpiece of social thought.

Despite all obstacles created by censorship, the journals continued to discuss the questions agitating Russian society, albeit in a veiled form. Here, for example, the question of a parliament was raised. During Loris-Melikov's dictatorship, when the rigors of censorship had weakened to some extent, the press frequently contained open references to a constitution. The newspaper *Country,* in connection with the murder of Alexander II, on March 3, 1881 wrote that "the basic outline of domestic political programs must be suggested by the representatives of the Russian land and, therefore, the responsibility is theirs. The tsar of Russia henceforth must serve only as the sacred symbol—having the sympathy of all—of our national unity and power, and of the further prosperity of Russia."

The government, in an atmosphere of growing reaction, naturally set out to deal immediately with the press and to suppress all dissenting thought. Feoktistov openly stated this in the main directorate's report for the decade 1882 to 1891. "The sad position," he wrote, "to which our press had been brought by the end of the 1870s was primarily a result of the freedom allowed it and the indulgent attitude shown it by the authorities. It had become necessary to restrict this freedom and, furthermore, for the government to adopt a sterner position. With this aim, on August 27, 1882 His Highness approved new regulations for the periodical press with the purpose of narrowing considerably its freedom and simultaneously increasing the powers of the censor."

Although an account of Russian journalism is a subject for a special work, the characteristics of those publications with greatest public appeal must be briefly outlined. Dominating public opinion and voicing the public's progressive mood was the democratic journal, *Notes of the Fatherland,* edited by M.E. Saltykov-Shchedrin. "During the 1880s," A.A. Kizevetter later wrote, "Saltykov's popularity reached its peak. His social satires were read with rapture. Each issue of the journal containing his latest 'Letter to Aunty' became in itself a great event." Saltykov's satires—his "Letters to Aunty" and "Contemporary Idylls"—exerted a tremendous public impact. The radical populist N.K. Mikhailovsky also wrote a great deal for this magazine and contributed most of the literary reviews and notices on new books. Among the other contributors were Sergei N. Krivenko, Niko Ya. Nikoladze, and Alexander I. Ertel, as well as other progressive writers and publicists. The reactionaries were fully aware of the ideological proclivities of *Notes of the Fatherland.* One of them, Boleslav Markevich, wrote Katkov on September 26, 1881 that the journal "directly and without restraint incites its readers to sedition and recognizes Zheliabov and Co. as heroes.[15] Whole issues of this journal contain article after article of this kind." Although somewhat exaggerated, this evaluation of the journal's tone is generally accurate and *Notes of the Fatherland* stood as the most influential voice of democratic thought.

Another publication of democratic leanings was *The Cause*, edited by Nicholas V. Shelgunov and Konstantin M. Staniukovich. It published the articles of the revolutionary Peter N. Tkachev, although under various pseudonyms. *The Cause* was really a continuation of the journal *Russian Word*, which had been closed down in the mid-1860s. Then during the latter 1880s, after Staniukovich had been arrested and exiled, the journal lost its democratic character. When Ivan S. Durnovo took over publication the magazine became a mouthpiece for the reactionaries. This left as the most influential journal apart from *Notes of the Fatherland* the thick literary monthly, *European Herald*. Edited by Michael M. Stasiulevich, its greatest claim to social significance lay in its "Domestic Review" written by the talented publicist and great scholar, K.K. Arseniev.

In the opinion of the Ministry of the Interior the general tone of the *European Herald* was "inspired by a systematic and implacable hostility toward every measure taken by the government to strengthen the fundamental basis of our state system, to establish the rule of law in the country, and to sober men's minds from the effects of false and harmful teachings." A report to Alexander III, written on the occasion of issuing a reprimand to this journal in 1889, observed that "the *European Herald* continually refers to the present as 'the time of the counterreforms' and opposes all the reforms and most important directives issued by the (present) administration."

The *Russian Thought* also held a certain importance, especially in the latter half of the 1880s. Although Vukol M. Lavrov directed this journal after 1880, Victor A. Goltsev, who joined the staff in 1884, became the real editor. Under his direction articles were published by N.K. Mikhailovsky, Vasily P. Vorontsov, and a number of other liberal populists. As for the liberal newspapers, the most influential was the *Russian News*. V.M. Sobolevsky edited it during this period and he attracted as contributors such democratic writers and public figures as M.E. Saltykov-Shchedrin, Gleb I. Uspensky, Peter L. Lavrov, Peter G. Zaichnevsky, and N.K. Mikhailovsky, among others. As Saltykov-Shchedrin explained to Sobolevsky: "I would like this collaboration precisely because I consider the *R(ussian) N(ews)* to be the only decent representative of the existing press, and I regret only that it is a newspaper and not a magazine."[16]

But this paper enjoyed no sympathy in the censorship department. According to one contemporary, Feoktistov once remarked: "It is a nasty newspaper, nasty when it speaks, and nasty when it keeps quiet."[17] Similarly I.N. Durnovo, describing the *Russian News* in a report to the emperor, noted that this paper "undoubtedly belongs among the ranks of the most harmful journals because of its passive opposition to the government. It shows great caution and does not venture to censure its (the government's) directives openly; but its pages never contain anything that can be construed as showing sympathy for its (the government's) actions."

Apart from the *Russian News,* several other papers belonged to the liberal camp. These were the *Russian Courier,* edited by V.N. Seleznev; the *Moscow Telegraph,* edited and published by I.I. Rodzevich; *Country,* edited and published by Leonid A. Polonsky; and *Order,* published by the *European Herald* and also edited by M.M. Stasiulevich. Still, the most widely read of the liberal papers was *Voice,* edited from 1863 to 1871 by Andrei A. Kraevsky, who after 1871 shared this task with the historian, Vasily A. Bilbasov. This paper took a moderate position and expressed the views of the liberal bureaucracy, which made it very informative. In the early 1880s *The Voice* listed a circulation of about 25,000. The paper *Country,* meanwhile, took a more radical position. It began publication in 1880, during the period of Loris-Melikov's dictatorship. Edited, as noted above, by L.A. Polonsky, its political ideal was a constitutional monarchy.

All these newspapers published, in one form or another, articles opposing the government and subjected various aspects of the administration to criticism. They all favored broadening the jurisdiction of the zemstvos, supported further modernisation, raised the question of popular representation, and published materials on peasant misery, the insufficiency of their land allotments, their heavy taxes, and so on.

The *Moscow News,* edited by Katkov, led the reactionary camp. He, with his paper, enjoyed an exceptional position, and represented an unique type of official spokesman. This uniqueness lay in the fact that although the *Moscow News* supported the government's policies in every way, it also sharply criticised particular details of policies and individuals in positions of authority. It is no exaggeration to say that any other editor responsible for publishing similar criticisms (with the exception, of course, of the *Citizen*) would have been exiled within twenty-four hours "to a place not too distant" from St. Petersburg and had his paper immediately closed down.

In the pages of the *Moscow News* Katkov literally persecuted ministers and other officials. Among his victims were Nikolai, Bunge, Giers, Nabokov, and A.A. Abaza. Moreover, on foreign policy the *Moscow News* took a different stand from that of the Ministry of Foreign

Affairs. Indeed, Katkov sometimes felt himself to be the real leader in this field. In 1886, for example, he sent his own man, General Evgenii V. Bogdanovich (who was an utter rogue) to hold unofficial conversations with the French government. The only connection between this envoy and the Minister of Foreign Affairs was that Bogdanovich was also a member of the Senate. Yet it must be admitted that Katkov's program in foreign affairs, which proclaimed the necessity of an alliance with France, reflected Russia's national interests to a greater degree than did the traditional, pro-German policies.

Katkov did not feel himself bound by any regulations or laws that existed for the rest of the press. In July, 1884 he angrily wrote Feoktistov, who evidently had reprimanded the *Moscow News* for not having published a "governmental communication." "I presume," Katkov wrote, "that the government does not regard itself as a blind machine that is guided by formalities. To be precise, the government cannot look upon decent men and rogues in the same light. And I have the weakness of not regarding myself as a rogue." Apparently Katkov saw only himself and possibly Meshchersky as decent men. He considered all the remaining gentlemen of the press to be scoundrels of various categories. Following Katkov's death, however, the *Moscow News* lost its exceptional position, suffered the censor's wrath and during this period received two reprimands.

Meshchersky's *Citizen* was a second official newspaper and, following Katkov's death in 1887, it took the place of the *Moscow News* in the reactionary camp. Although the editor of the *Citizen* was considerably inferior in both intelligence and education to Katkov, the journal stood firmly behind the government's reactionary policies and the emperor himself often listened to its views. As already noted, Meshchersky even received frequent subsidies from Alexander III. Thus Polovtsov recorded in his diary that in 1887 Meshchersky asked the emperor for 300,000 rubles. When Durnovo told the tsar that this claim was excessive, the latter replied: "We want to have conservative papers for a twenty-five kopeck piece. Just look at what Bismarck spends on the press." Yet the *Citizen*, despite the emperor's favor, never presumed to the liberties taken by the *Moscow News*. Nonetheless it was punished much more frequently than was Katkov's journal,[18] although all penalties imposed on both papers were mere formalities.

Among the reactionary newspapers also must be included the *New Times*. Its editor, Alexis S. Suvorin, had evolved from a liberal into a reactionary. Yet neither this newspaper nor its editor possessed a really distinctive political point of view and Suvorin's moral qualities were no higher than Meshchersky's. Saltykov-Shchedrin had good reason to describe Suvorin as a loathsome scoundrel.

At this time a new kind of journalism appeared: the so-called yellow or gutter press. This pandered to the baser tastes of the lesser bourgeois elements of the urban population (the *meshchanstvo*). Various entertaining reports—often imaginary—were published, detailing the chronicles of crimes, tales on sexual themes, and so on. A typical example is the *Moscow Leaflet* of N.I. Pastukhov, a man lacking any idea of integrity.[19]

PRESS HARASSMENT

After 1881 the persecution of the press increased in intensity. The number of administrative penalties imposed on newspapers and journals in each year is shown in the following table:

1881—20	1886— 5	1891—13
1882—26	1887— 8	1892— 9
1883—13	1888—15	1893— 7
1884—19	1889—13	1894— 5
1885—13	1890— 8	

The total number of penalties for the fourteen-year period was 174. In the first seven years there were 104, with 70 for the other seven. While the number of penalties imposed evidently was diminishing gradually, this by no means indicated a softening of the censors' grip. It is, rather, evidence that during the earlier years many of the journals considered most "harmful" by the government had been forced to close and the rest compelled to "toe the line."

It should be added that a simple total of the penalties imposed discloses merely a part of the picture. The severest penalties were the outright closure of a periodical or its liability to preliminary censorship. The first penalty, imposed by order of the conference of the four ministers, destroyed seven publications,[20] while eight others were shut by the censors (mainly by subjecting them to preliminary censorship).[21] Thus the total of terminated publications was fifteen.[22] The incidence of closures brought about by these two methods can be seen in the following table:

	Banned	Preliminary Censorship		Banned	Preliminary Censorship
1882	0	1	1888	0	0
1883	1	2	1889	1	2
1884	1	1	1890	0	0
1885	3	1	1891	0	0
1886	1	0	1892	0	0
1887	0	1	1893	0	0

It is further evident that the majority of newspapers and journals were banned or forced to cease publication during the first five years, prior to 1887, when the press suffered most heavily.

The government's hostility to the press was expressed in its attempts to prevent the appearance of new journals as well as in the penalties inflicted on the existing ones. Feoktistov, summing these up in his report on the main directorate's activities for the decade 1882 to 1891, remarked: "The change in the censors' attitude to the periodical press is revealed by the fact that, compared with the previous period, during the present decade permission for new periodical publications was granted with greater circumspection, and then only to persons about whose loyalty it was possible to be more or less assured. The data . . . clearly shows that the percentage of new publications has diminished with each year. Thus in 1882 the number of periodicals, as compared with the previous year, had increased by 7.9 percent. Thereafter the percentage of new newspapers and journals permitted, in comparison with the previous year, continually decreased, and in 1891 it did not exceed 5.5 percent." Here is evidence that despite a natural tendency favoring the growth of the number of newspapers and journals, the Main Directorate of the Press succeeded in artifically fostering a decrease.

An analysis of the above information demonstrates that the main repressive efforts coincided with Feoktistov's rise to power.[23] In 1883 three liberal newspapers (*Moscow Telegraph, Voice,* and *Country*) were forced to cease publication, and the *Russian Courier* followed them in 1884. The case of the *Moscow Telegraph* is revealing. Attacks on it began as early as 1881, the year of its first appearance, when its retail sales were banned for a fixed period. Then, in 1882, a torrent of penalties fell upon it. The *Telegraph* received four reprimands, its retail sales were again prohibited, and its publication was temporarily suspended. The Minister of the Interior hoped that the prohibition of sales would lead to the newspaper's closure. On December 15, 1882 Tolstoy wrote Pobedonostsev that "a ban on the *Telegraph's* retail sales is almost the same as its destruction." Nonetheless the paper survived. On January 13, 1883, Tolstoy, in a report to the emperor, acknowledged that the *Moscow Telegraph* "continued on its harmful course."[24]

Pobedonostsev was particularly insistent that this newspaper be speedily closed down. "It is high time that the *Moscow Telegraph* was taken in hand," he wrote Feoktistov on March 12, 1883. "Count Tolstoy said this would be done in the first week (of this month). Now the second week has practically passed." The next day Feoktistov informed Pobedonostsev that he was "at present compiling a report on the *Moscow Telegraph.* The day after tomorrow it will be sent to Count Tolstoy, who on this basis will raise the issue of the aforesaid newspaper." Several days later Tolstoy presented a report to Alexander III wherein he stated that the *Moscow Telegraph* "belongs among the most harmful publications," and stressed that "this publication . . . presents the existing state of affairs in the most detestable light." As a result, on March 19, 1883 the *Moscow Telegraph* was terminated by a decision of the committee of the four ministers.

In his official report Feoktistov, in describing the *Moscow Telegraph*, noted that "our press, apart from a very few exceptions, is at present generally not distinguished by its loyalty and it endeavors only to create difficulties for the government from the troubled circumstances of recent times. Two publications especially call attention to themselves by their harmful course and the impudence of their tone. Both of these—the *Moscow Telegraph* and the *Russian Courier*—are published in Moscow."

Although the *Telegraph* was finished, the *Russian Courier*, edited by V.N. Seleznev, continued to worry the authorities (and especially Katkov, with whom it continually polemicized). Pobedonostsev, as noted above, told Feoktistov on the latter's first day in office that this paper must be destroyed. Meanwhile the *Russian Courier* published articles on the zemstvo and city administrations, the situation of the peasants, and in every way defended the reforms of the 1860s. "For two years Mr. Katkov has with a persistence and zeal that deserve a better aim," wrote the *Courier* in its lead article of July 10, 1883, "busied himself in the *Moscow News* with condemning the reforms carried out in the last reign . . . . The most malicious of his attacks have been directed at the new courts and, after these, zemstvo and city self-government."

In 1882 the *Russian Courier* was suspended for three months, and in 1883 it received a reprimand. The cause for this reprimand was, according to the censor, "the harmful trend in its judgements of the existing state system and its false interpretation of the facts of peasant life; this trend is calculated to disturb people's minds." At the beginning of 1884 the *Courier* received a second reprimand for articles on the national question. "The principle of nationalism," it told its readers on December 24, 1883, "is in essence nothing less than the principle of the *equality and brotherhood of peoples*." The issue of December 28 returned to this subject and maintained that "for the sake of the future happiness of the Russian people, we, in Russia, are the supporters of the sincere, consistent and reasonably considered introduction of the principle of nationalism into the life of the people of the Russian state." When Alexander III learned of these opinions from a report on the matter, he solemnly commented: "It is disgusting to read such articles. And to think they were written by Russians." In any case, the *Russian Courier* received a second reprimand. After this it grew more cautious and the attempt to force its immediate closure failed.

In 1883 the newspaper *Voice* became the target of reprisals. Throughout its existence it had been plagued by various penalties, receiving forty-six after 1865, twelve of which were received in 1882-1883. This journal, thanks to its wide connections in government circles, was exceptionally well-informed and thus caused the authorities considerable annoyance, in spite of the very moderately liberal position it adopted.

Tolstoy and Pobedonostsev were especially impatient with the *Voice*. Feoktistov maintained that Tolstoy could not even remain calm when speaking about it, "as it always seemed to him that the *Voice* served as spokesman for some extraordinarily strong party, so that if a blow were struck against it, a mutiny would be almost certain to follow."[25] In consequence, the Minister of the Interior was very nervous about trying to destroy this paper. According to Feoktistov, it seemed that Tolstoy was afraid to act boldly against the *Voice* lest "his enemies claim that he was being guided by his personal interests,"[26] and the initiative for the paper's repression came from Feoktistov, not his superior.

The *Voice* received its third reprimand in February, 1883. The report to the emperor on this matter claimed that the paper "frequently exposes itself to punitive measures by continuing to adhere to its harmful course. Its comments on the existing state order, as well as its selection and false interpretation of facts, reveal an obvious intention to create turmoil in men's minds." Alexander III, on reading this report, commented with his characteristic coarseness: "It serves those cattle right!" Nonetheless the emperor entertained a very vague and confused idea of the state of the press and the people involved in editing the different periodicals. Only eight years after *Voice* was shut down did Alexander learn that the historian Bilbasov had been its editor. In his diary Feoktistov tells how the emperor, on a report concerning the banning of Bilbasov's book on Catherine II in 1891, jotted the following: "Unfortunately I did not know that Bilbasov was the same cow who, along with Kraevsky, edited the *Voice*."

Apart from a third reprimand, the *Voice* was suspended for six months and then subjected to preliminary censorship in accord with the Provisional Regulations of August 27, 1882. This placed the newspaper in an intolerable position. At the end of August, when the term of suspension ran out, the Main Directorate of the Press informed the *Voice's* editors that "each issue of the paper, independent of those copies forwarded to the Censorship Committee, must be presented to the censor, in four copies, not later than 11:00 p.m. of the day it is to appear." This meant further publication was impossible and as it was not resumed in

August, 1884, after the suspension, the *Voice's* existence was declared officially terminated.

Katkov, realizing that preliminary censorship would destroy the *Voice*, tried to buy the paper and transform it into a subsidiary of the *Moscow News*. "With all its vileness," he wrote to Feoktistov, "the *Voice*, thanks to its intrigues, has gained great influence. It would certainly be good to get hold of this power and use it in other ways." Evidently Tolstoy agreed to such a combination. In August, 1883 he wrote to Feoktistov: "I fully share your view that if new loyal editors are found for this paper (*Voice*), we should be lenient with it and not insist on the strict censorship measures."

The newspaper *Country* also ceased publication in 1883. It received a third reprimand at the beginning of the year and was suspended for four months. "The newspaper *Country*," wrote Tolstoy in his report to Alexander III, "in spite of two reprimands and a suspension of its retail sales . . . has stubbornly continued its harmful practices. These consist of systematic attempts to condemn unconditionally every action and directive of the government and to portray the general conditions of our society in the most dismal light." According to Tolstoy, this harmful attitude was expressed particularly clearly in the paper's lead article for New Year's Day, 1883. This, he claimed, "spoke with inadmissible impudence of an absence of 'sincerity' and 'any kind of rational framework of ideas' in government circles." As a result of the punitive measures imposed by the censor, the publication of *Country* was not resumed.

In this way Feoktistov made short work of the three most influential liberal newspapers during his first year as director of the Main Directorate of the Press. The censor's persecution had reached ruinous proportions. The police intercepted one letter that described the state of the periodical press at the end of 1883 as follows: "The censorship is also growing more fierce. Not long ago Feoktistov wrote Yuriev,[27] warning him to be as cautious as possible for he 'would not be spared.' *Notes of the Fatherland* is on the brink of ruin, and they are growing very bitter about Shchedrin . . . . All the newspapers and journals are trembling."[28] The historian, M.I. Semevsky, gave a similar estimate of Feoktistov's feverish activities in 1883. "And here, in the short space of six weeks," he wrote in his private notebook, "the newspapers *Country, Voice,* and *Moscow Telegraph* all have been banned. Literary journals, such as *Notes of the Fatherland* and the *Observer*, have been threatened. The *European Herald* has also been endangered indirectly. In brief, a gloomy cloud hangs over Russian literature, recalling the days of 1848 and 1849."

During 1884 it was the turn of *Notes of the Fatherland*. Feoktistov himself was especially active in attacking this journal.[29] He claimed that Tolstoy, just as in the case of the *Voice*, showed himself to be indecisive "once again mainly because he was afraid of stirring up public discontent."[30] In any case, on January 18, 1884 the council of the main directorate resolved to give the journal a second reprimand and Tolstoy's report to the emperor justified the decision. The Minister of the Interior explained: "Considering the fact that *Notes of the Fatherland* displays harmful tendencies, mocks and attempts to portray the existing social, civil, and economic structures of our and other European states in a hostile light; that, apart from this, the editors of the journal do not conceal their own sympathies for extreme socialist doctrines; and that, among other things, in the issue of this journal for January of the current year there is an article signed by (N.Ya.) Nikoladze and entitled 'Gambetta and Louis Blanc,' that praises one of the French Communards, Rochfort, I agree with the conclusion of the Council of the Main Directorate of the Press that it is necessary to give a second reprimand to the journal *Notes of the Fatherland*." Alexander III naturally approved Tolstoy's report.

The motives behind this reprimand were such that in actuality the journal's fate had been decided. "Judging by the strength of their feelings," Saltykov-Shchedrin wrote his friend Borovikovsky, "it is probable that a third reprimand will be received after this one, even if we were to distribute only blank pages. There is obviously a calculated plan at work here. Perhaps they will end the journal once and for all. But however that may be, I am writing you, so to speak, on the eve of a disaster." In an attempt to preserve the journal in some form, Shchedrin, in the summer of 1883, had written N.K. Mikhailovsky and asked: "Do you or do you not have some kind of combination in view with regard to *Not(es) of the Fath(erland)* which Kraevsky[31] could accept? I myself could only stay on if some sort of miracle occurred—if by some miracle Feoktistov were replaced or Katkov publicly disgraced."

Apart from Feoktistov, Katkov, and Pobedonostsev, V.K. Plehve, the director of the Department of Police, played a great and perhaps more significant role in the final persecution of *Notes of the Fatherland*. In August he had presented Tolstoy with an extensive report that dealt, in large part, with *Notes of the Fatherland*. Plehve gave details about ties between the populist revolutionary movement and journalists and maintained that "the journalists certainly wasted no time in helping to prepare the way for the outbursts of the young. A number of works by the advanced populist *literati*, who popularized West European socialism or pointed out the impoverished position of the people by means of

fabrications, and sometimes only by skilfully selecting or falsely interpreting aspects of the peoples' existence, appeared in the press . . . .
From the first these works served as a weapon of propaganda by en-
deavoring to create in the people a feeling of dissatisfaction with their
situation and to acquaint them with the basic teachings that socialist
fanatics see as the means for eliminating all social evils." The director of
police particularly mentioned the destructive influence upon the young
of the works and example of the poet Nicholas A. Nekrasov. As for the
existing state of affairs and the tasks of the Main Directorate of Press
Affairs, Plehve observed that the censor's department was "scarcely
strong enough to suppress the hostility of the press to the existing order
until the composition of the literary circle that guides the journals and
newspapers is changed. At present this circle is made up almost exclusively of people whose entire literary activity has been a continual
protest against the legal order. . . . *Notes of the Fatherland* is edited
by Saltykov (-Shchedrin) with the active participation of Gregory Eli-
seev and Mikhailovsky, and several exiles and persons under surveillance
are contributors . . . . All accounts lead to the conclusion that at this
historical moment the government finds itself in a struggle not with a
small group of monsters who can be rounded up by means of strengthened police activities, but with an enemy of great vigor and strength. As
this enemy is not only flesh and blood but is the world of certain kinds
of ideas and beliefs, the battle against it must take on a special character." On receiving this report Count Tolstoy wrote Plehve: "Thank you
very much . . . for compiling the report on relations between a certain
group of our journalists and the revolutionary party . . . . I have forwarded it to the Emperor."

Among the contributors to *Notes of the Fatherland* were many persons who had been arrested or exiled from the capital. In January, 1883
N.K. Mikhailovsky was exiled from St. Petersburg and in early 1884
S.N. Krivenko, A.I. Ertel, and Michael A. Protopopov were arrested.
These events allowed *Notes of the Fatherland* to be charged with open
sedition. Feoktistov admits in his memoirs that the Department of Police
took the initiative in closing the journal. "One day," he wrote, "Count
Tolstoy invited me to a conference with Orzhevsky and Plehve. They
claimed that the editorial office of *Notes of the Fatherland* was a den of
inveterate nihilists and that there existed strong evidence against several
of the journal's contributors. One of these already had been administratively exiled from St. Petersburg and it was necessary that the rest
of them now be routed." This meeting apparently took place at the
beginning of April or, possibly, at the end of March. In any case,
Professor Nicholas A. Liubimov informed Katkov as early as April 5

that the fate of *Notes of the Fatherland* was decided and a report on this matter prepared.

The draft "Government Report" on the banning of this journal was prepared by Feoktistov in concert with Plehve and Pobedonostsev, and a letter of Feoktistov to Plehve makes it clear that Pobedonostsev edited the document.[32] On April 19 the emperor approved this decision of the conference of four ministers and on April 20 the "Government Report" was published. This argued that "several organs of our periodical press bear a heavy responsibility for the events that have saddened the public in recent years . . . . Apart from making the guilty parties legally accountable, the government cannot permit the further existence of a paper that allows its pages to be used further to disseminate harmful ideas, and has as its closest collaborators persons who are members of secret societies." In this manner the government disposed of the leading democratic journal of that time.

The banning of *Notes of the Fatherland* evoked widespread public reaction. "Tolstoy has inflicted yet one more blow on the Russian public," wrote Saltykov-Shchedrin's friend N.A. Belogolov in the uncensored liberal paper, *Common Cause* (which was published in Geneva). "This blow," he said, "has been prepared for a long time and we were forewarned more than once. *Notes of the Fatherland* has been closed once and for all. It was closed without any kind of '*formes de proces*' and without any indication or reference to those particular crimes committed by it, but simply for its harmful tendencies . . . . In this journal the spirit of the great ideals of the 1860s still breathed. In it lived and developed that love of the people and the homeland which inspires Russian men with a hatred of oppressors." N.K. Mikhailovsky, writing in the illegal *Peoples' Will*, lamented that "this was practically the only member of the Russian press in which, through the smoke and soot of censorship, there shone some spark of understanding about the tasks of Russian life in all their magnitude. For this it had to be destroyed—and destroyed it was."

In 1884 the newspaper *East* was, on Pobedonostsev's insistence, also harassed by the censor. Edited by N.I. Durnovo, this remarkably harmless periodical (from the government's point of view) consistently adopted a position of extreme chauvinism. The *East*, however, had criticized Pobedonostsev's department. In 1882 it received a first and second reprimand for its "harmful tendency." Then, in 1884, it received a third reprimand and was temporarily suspended because of the stubborn opposition "expressed in its extremely sharp attacks on our church administration in general and on several individuals in the upper ecclesiastical hierarchy." Once it became subject to preliminary censorship, the paper was forced to cease publication.

In January, 1885 the Moscow newspaper *Light*[33] was banned by a decision of the conference of four ministers. In practice this paper had been edited by I.A. Rodzevich, the former printer and editor of the *Moscow Telegraph,* and it had been very critical of the government. "From its very first issue," the official report on this matter stated, "the newspaper *Light* has adopted a tone which our press has outgrown in recent times. It hurried to define its program clearly and in detail. For the most part this consisted of portraying the contemporary situation in the most gloomy and distasteful light. 'Our society,' the paper says, 'beginning with its ruling circles, is so lost and confused in its ideas, so impoverished materially and morally, so tired of the falsehoods and arbitrary behavior that surround it, so crushed by the daily little struggles, that it no longer worries over profound questions concerning essential vital truths and is beginning to lose the ability to separate good from evil. Giving these tasks up as hopeless, we now live only from day day, if only we can live'."

The reason for this attitude was, the report stressed, the paper's "shaky editorial board." The emperor readily approved the Supreme Commission's decision about *Light.* He simply commented: "I agree completely."

In December of 1885 the Supreme Commission of the Press resolved to terminate the publication of two more newspapers—*Health* in St. Petersburg, and *Droeba* [*The Times*] of Tiflis. Durnovo claimed in his report that *Health* had completely altered its principles following the arrival of a new editor, the politically unreliable P.N. Podmigailov. "From the very first," he charged, "Podmigailov did not hesitate to urge the need to increase peasant land allotments as the only way of helping them in their desperate situation." *Droeba,* published by a Prince Machabeli, was charged with separatist strivings. The same report stated that "the articles presented by him (the editor) to the censor are imbued with separatist tendencies. He does not even consider it necessary to express these by hints or in an allegorical form, but outlines them with striking frankness."

Finally, in February, 1885, the liberal newspaper *Echo* was eliminated. Published by V.P. Maksheev, A.V. Starchevsky and F.V. Troziner, *Echo* already had endured two punishments: a ban on its retail sales and on its printing of private advertisements.

During the three-year period 1883-1885 nine periodicals (of the total of fourteen for the whole period) were either closed or forced to cease publication because of persecution by the censor. By 1885 the government had emerged victorious in its struggle with the press. Nonetheless, in 1886 the conference of the four ministers decided the fate of the liberal Kievan newspaper, *Dawn.* Until 1885 it had been published and edited by P.A. Andreevsky. According to Tolstoy's official report, Andreevsky was merely the nominal editor—for all practical purposes it was directed by various politically unreliable persons. A short time before, M.I. Kulisher, the former editor of the Odessa paper *Truth,* (banned in 1880) had taken charge. The minutes of the Supreme Commission maintained that *Dawn* was subject to suppression because "its editors had shown that they were abusing the government's good faith."

A year later (in 1887) the illustrated and liberally inclined Moscow *Gazette of A. Gattzuk* was suspended for eight months on the authority of the Minister of the Interior. Earlier, in 1884, this paper had received three reprimands, had been suspended for one month, and subjected to preliminary censorship. Its first reprimand resulted from the publication of Nicholas S. Leskov's article "Notes of a Nobody." Leskov's article, the authorities felt, "jeered at the Orthodox clergy, both secular and monastic, and presented their training, life and activities in the most unprepossessing light." A month later the paper received a second warning for continuing publication of "Notes of a Nobody" and "for a pointed reference to the reprimand it had received." Finally, the *Gazette of A. Gattzuk* was given a third reprimand for an article attacking the *Moscow News.* According to Tolstoy's report the paper, in its thirty-second number, "out of hatred for the principles and the institutions that this publication (the *Moscow News*) defends, . . . maintained that only adventurers, various two-faced persons, and outright swindlers could contribute to it." Such a low assessment of M.N. Katkov's journal naturally could not be left unpunished.[34]

In 1889 the censors again grew active and the Supreme Commission banned the *Siberian News.* In his report Durnovo said that this paper's attitude was expressed by "an obvious sympathy for all those very regrettable occurrences that are begetting democratic tendencies among some sections of our public; by attempts to implant the idea that Siberia should take care to weaken its ties with Russia; and on every convenient occasion, by efforts to discredit the government's orders and the provincial administration's activities." The reason, according to Durnovo, was that the paper was controlled by political exiles, but the immediate justification for closing down on the *News* was the founding of the University of Tomsk. Because of this, the Minister of the Interior maintained, "the government is obliged to take especial care to protect the youths studying there from harmful influences."

The *Russian Courier* and the *Russian Cause* also had to stop publication because of censorship. In September, 1889 the *Courier* received its third reprimand and was subjected to preliminary censorship as a result of the article "The Gentry's Howls and Arguments for Begging

Alms." This dealt with the indebtedness of landowners to the Nobles Bank, and according to Durnovo, the article "expressed all the afore-named newspaper's spite against the gentry." Alexander III commented on the report concerning this reprimand: "I completely approve. It would be desirable to put an end to this foul newspaper." And once it was subjected to preliminary censorship, the *Russian Courier* had to terminate publication.

The *Russian Cause,* a weekly published in Moscow, was edited by S.F. Sharapov. In 1888 it was twice reprimanded[35] and in 1889 again rebuked for its "harmful course." In fact this paper took a liberal-Slavophile position, but Tolstoy claimed this resulted in "firstly, an extremely hostile attitude toward our diplomacy, expressed in a very crude manner . . . without regard for Russia's interests; and, secondly, in attempts to demonstrate that Russia has lived a proper life only at the time of the *zemskii sobors* [assemblies of the land] . . . ." The immediate cause of the third reprimand and a six-month suspension of publication was an article-pamphlet purporting to be an outline of the Code of the Nobility. Written from an anti-gentry point of view, "it serves," Tolstoy claimed, "as merely a single example of the clearly democratic tendency of this newspaper." In any case, after its third reprimand and a simultaneous suspension, the *Russian Cause* collapsed. Commenting on Tolstoy's report, Alexander III wrote: "A really rotten newspaper."

Such was the martyrology of the Russian periodical press. The limitations imposed by decree and the various punishments created insufferable conditions for Russian publicists. In these circumstances it was almost impossible for public opinion to find expression, and any criticism of government policy was completely banned. Yet, whatever the persecutions of the censorship, thought could not be confined to the Procrustean bed of official ideas and public opinion sought other outlets. These were partly provided by journals published abroad (such as the *Herald of the Peoples' Will, Social Democrat* and *Common Cause*) and illegally distributed in Russia. Otherwise, the legal press continued to find ways to criticize individual government policies, although with a muffled voice and in Aesopian language.

Further, despite the extremely propitious conditions created for the official press,[36] its representatives were never able to gain that influence of which the government dreamed. On this matter one contemporary, A.A. Kizevetter, recalled: "I can categorically testify that the *Moscow News'* and the *Citizen's* circle of sincere readers was anything but large . . . . If one has to name journals that held a really wide following among readers at large, to be sure one would have to mention the *Notes of the Fatherland*, with the satires of Saltykov-Shchedrin, the *European Herald*, with Arseniev's 'Domestic Review,' and the *Russian News*, which served as the vehicle of the progressive Muscovite professors. *Notes of the Fatherland* was cut out at the roots by the Pobedonostsev-Tolstoy scythe at the very beginning of the period of 'counter-reform' and its voice was silenced. The *Russian News* and the *European Herald* maintained their flame unquenched throughout the gloom of those times. And it must be said that among wide circles of the public the authority of these journals was extraordinarily high." Notwithstanding the persecutions visited by the censorship upon Russian literature, its development could be no more prevented than could the development of human thought. In this area any kind of censorship must remain helpless. As Saltykov-Shchedrin wrote in a letter to N.A. Belogolov, "literature will live forever."

CENSORSHIP OF BOOKS AND PLAYS

The policies of censorship with regard to the publishing of books now require attention. According to data collected in L.M. Dobrovolsky's *The Banning of Books in Russia, 1825-1904*, during the years 1881 to 1894 inclusive, seventy-two books were prohibited.[37] Among these were religious-philosophical works by Leo Tolstoy *(What I Believe, Popular Tales* and *On Life)*; Ernst Renan's *Philosophical Dialogues* (banned for its "extremely materialistic and atheistic inclination"); S.A. Vengerov's *A History of the Most Recent Russian Literature*;[38] the anonymous work, *Alexander Sergeevich Pushkin: His Life and Work*;[39] Vladimir Giliarovsky's *Godforsaken People*;[40] and volume two of V.A. Bilbasov's *History of the Reign of Catherine II*.[41] Volume four of N.S. Leskov's *Collected Works* was banned and according to the reports of the censorship committee "all six volumes of Leskov's works, in spite of the author's indisputable general loyalty, are nonetheless unfortunately impudent pamphlets about the church administration in Russia and the corrupt morals of the lower clergy."

Ibsen's plays and Victor Hugo's *Les Miserables* were also interdicted. Frequently the emperor became directly involved in these decisions. He thought, for example, that it was impossible to allow the printing of Vladimir Soloviev's philosophical works.[42] Similarly, although there were several occasions when he supported Leo Tolstoy (Alexander evidently respected him as the author of *War and Peace*), the tsar could treat this writer with his characteristic coarseness. Further, the emperor might hold different opinions at different times about an individual book. To cite one case, he first forbade the publication of the *Kreutzer Sonata* but, as Feoktistov noted in his diary on February 14, 1890: "The

Minister of the Interior agreed with Pobedonostsev's and my opinion, but when he discovered that the Emperor had read Tolstoy's story, he considered it necessary to learn his (the Emperor's) opinion about it. 'Of course,' said the Emperor, 'we cannot permit it to be published, because it is written on a completely false theme and with great cynicism. Only the *skoptsi* (or eunuchs), if you please, satisfy him.'[43] After a visit from the Countess Sophie Andreevna Tolstoy, however, Alexander III permitted the story's inclusion in the *Collected Works*, declaring that 'he himself would censor the works of her husband.' " Apparently the emperor wanted to emulate his favorite uncle, Nicholas I, who personally had censored the manuscripts of Pushkin.

The report of the Main Directorate for the Press for the ten years 1882 through 1891 stated that in this period a grand total of 65,237 manuscripts were prepared for publication and examined by the censorship committees of Petersburg, Moscow, and Warsaw. Of this number, the publication of 1,561 was prohibited, or a little less than two percent. Manuscripts written in Ukrainian comprised the largest percentage of banned manuscripts. Here the proportion was 32.7 percent. The censorship of foreign publications was equally active. According to the above-mentioned report, during this decade 93,565,260 books and issues of foreign periodicals entered the country. These works provoked some 117,527 rulings by the censors, of which 9,386 favored proscription of the publication in question. "Consequently," the report concluded, "for every twenty-five books or journals examined, two were prohibited."[44]

A fuller understanding of the censorship in the suppression of particular books may be gained from the main directorate's circulars. A number of these documents barred the importation of certain books and journals. These included Ukrainian periodicals printed in Lvov and the works of Russian writers printed abroad. These latter included in particular Leo Tolstoy's brochure *The Kingdom of God Within Us*.[45] The reprinting of many works already previously published was also banned, including Karl Marx's *Das Kapital* and Taras G. Shevchenko's privately published nationalist poem *Haidamaki*. Nonetheless the censorship policies for books were not as merciless as those affecting journalism. Although numerous works were banned, the satires of Saltykov-Shchedrin, the stories of V.G. Korolenko, and the works of other progressive writers were, in fact, published.

In the matter of theatrical censorship, during 1882 to 1891 inclusive, the censors examined 3,947 Russian, 869 German, and 339 French plays. Many of these were banned, the statistics being: 1,314 Russian (33%), 38 German (4.5%), and 16 French (.5%). "These figures are a result," Feoktistov wrote, "of an extremely dangerous tendentiousness, the absence of literary merit and, frequently, indecent content." In fact, the prohibition of such a large percentage of plays was more a result of their tendentious tone than of their low level of literary merit; it is well known that the definition of this latter quality is not within the competence of a censorship department.

It must be stressed that general permission to stage a particular play did not mean it could be performed on the stage of a low-priced public theater. Such theatres had their own special censor, whose powers were based on a circular of February 14, 1888. According to this document the "Sovereign Emperor," acting on the basis of a report of the Minister of the Interior, "is pleased to establish, in the form of a provisional measure, the following regulation: for performances in a 'popular' theatre, or in theatres attended, due to the low price of seats, predominantly by the common people, only those plays can be selected that are permitted by the theatrical censor and have the approval of the Main Directorate of the Press, obtained by a special petition from the theatre owners or the authors and translators." This measure was necessary, the main directorate maintained, as "the common people, because of the level of their intellectual development, their own opinions and their ideas, are frequently capable of completely misinterpreting that which would present no similar danger for any educated person; therefore, plays that contain nothing reprehensible from the general point of view may prove for them (the common people) unnatural and even harmful."

OTHER FORMS OF CENSORSHIP

The Main Directorate of the Press paid special attention to the supervising of libraries, which it considered breeding grounds for "seditious ideas." During the 1880s and early 1890s, the number of libraries and bookshops grew rapidly. According to the main directorate's figures, on January 1, 1882 the Ministry of the Interior had 640 libraries and reading rooms under observation, and by January 1, 1892 the number had risen to 850 (an increase of 32.8%). Meanwhile the number of book shops increased by almost forty percent (from 1,204 in 1882 to 1,684 in 1892).

On January 5, 1884 special regulations were issued on the organization of libraries.[46] These gave the Minister of the Interior the right to grant permission for the opening of libraries and to approve their operating staff, while governors were allowed to dismiss individuals working in libraries. The Ministry of the Interior was further permitted, on its own authority, to close a library when this seemed necessary, and the minister held the power to control book holdings in the libraries.

The Main Directorate of the Press and the Department of Police then composed a list of books which must be removed from library shelves.

The year 1884 witnessed the first purge of libraries. In accordance with the "Alphabetical List of Printed Works by His Majesty's Order of January 5, 1884 Not to be Circulated by Public Libraries and Public Reading Rooms," 133 books, editions of collected works, and periodicals (originally permitted by the censorship) were removed from libraries and reading rooms. Among these were eight journals: The *Russian Word* for 1857 to 1866; the *Contemporary* for 1856 to 1866; *Notes of the Fatherland* for 1867 to 1884; *The Cause* for 1867 to 1884; *Foundations* for 1881 and 1882; all issues of the *Banner; Word* for 1878 to 1881; and *Russian Thought,* from its founding to 1884.[47] The works of Nicholas A. Dobroliubov, Nicholas K. Mikhailovsky, Dmitry I. Pisarev, Fedor M. Reshetnikov, the second volume of Nicholas G. Pomialovsky's *Works*, and Karl Marx's *Das Kapital* were among the banned books.

This imperial regulation marked the beginning of a systematic purging of libraries. On January 1, 1894 a new list of prohibited books was published ("The Alphabetical List of Printed Works by Point Three of the Note to Article 175 of the Censorship and Press Statutes Prohibited by the Minister of the Interior from Circulation in Public Libraries and Public Reading Rooms"). The 1894 list included titles of 165 books and collected works, as well as the eight journals. Among the banned works were the sketches and tales of V.G. Korolenko ("Makar's Dream," "The Ice Rumbles," "On Easter Night," "In the Last Compartment," and others) which had been published in Moscow in 1892. Other prohibited volumes were Vsevolod M. Garshin's tales (*Four Days*) and Gregory A. Dzhanshiev's *The Epoch of the Great Reforms*. (A well-known liberal publicist, Dzhanshiev had written a panegyric about Alexander II and other reform statesmen of the 1860s.) Also banished from the shelves were volumes twelve and thirteen of Leo Tolstoy's *Works* (containing his popular tales and legends as well as the *Kreutzer Sonata* and the *Fruits of Enlightenment*).

The regulations of January 5, 1884 were accompanied by a special, confidential circular of the Department of Police. This circular stressed the need of special attention to ensure the implementation of each point of the regulations, and emphasised that applications for permission to open libraries should be approved "only in cases where there is complete conviction of the absolute political reliability of the persons applying and, in cases of the slightest doubt, such applications are to be turned down." Another circular, issued on July 1, 1884, instructed that a manager of a public library or popular reading room must give a written guarantee not to circulate books prohibited by the Main Directorate of the Press and the Department of Police.[48]

The Department of Police maintained constant surveillance of libraries. On March 10, 1883 a special circular gave instructions covering the free reading rooms that had just opened in St. Petersburg and Moscow, mainly for workers and students from the lower and secondary educational institutions. This document pointed out the importance of establishing a "careful supervision over the choice of printed works" in these reading rooms and of permitting only the books and periodical publications approved . . . for the lower educational institutions and for popular reading." Later, on May 15, 1890, special regulations were issued to govern working procedures to be followed by free reading rooms.[49] Then, at the beginning of 1894, the Main Directorate of the Press again reminded censors (by means of a special circular) of the need "for the strictest selection of books for popular reading. Such publications are to be treated with special attention and strictness above and beyond a mere application of the general censorship regulations." This opened the way for the most arbitrary decisions.

In these ways the censor kept a careful eye on public libraries and reading rooms. A confidential letter of Minister of the Interior Durnovo to Minister of Education Delianov, written in February 1894, observed: "Among the prominent social phenomena of the last year is the sudden development among the various elements of the intelligentsia of efforts to foster a rise in the level of the people's education by organizing popular lectures, opening libraries and reading rooms for the factory and village population and, finally, by distributing without charge among the people cheap publications in the form of books and brochures of a scientific, moral, and literary nature." Yet, he complained, the controls over these libraries and reading rooms were clearly inadequate, and private societies were distributing various kinds of books without supervision. The same was true of village libraries: if not attached to a school they were beyond any control whatsoever. "From the information we have in the Ministry of the Interior," continued Durnovo, "it may be concluded that this movement, which has taken hold of young people, is developing consistently, and that it does not have the characteristics of a fortuitous and temporary phenomenon. On the contrary, it seems that some program is being systematically implemented and that this represents one of the means anti-government groups are using to fight the government at the legal level."

According to Durnovo, this movement had stirred both publishing houses and various educational organizations to increased activity. But "the censorship, which operates within defined legal limits," he observed sadly, "is not always able to combat the skilfully disguised propagation of certain ideas. Because of the lack of a formal basis on which to prohibit books, works are allowed to enter popular circulation that are not always suitable from the point of view of the people's comprehension and view of the world, and that are incompatible with the spirit of Orthodoxy and the life of the Russian state."

For these reasons Durnovo asked Delianov to raise the question of subordinating the Petersburg Committee for Literacy and all its branches to the Ministry of Education. Further, he argued, this ministry should establish control over the various private societies "that are engaged in the task of popular education." Above all else, Durnovo's letter shows clearly the great difficulties created for the censors by the public awakening of the early 1890s.

Two other forms of censorship remain to be mentioned. These were the ecclesiastical and the postal censors. But since these questions are not properly a part of this study, here their existence will merely be noted.

During the years 1881 to 1894 the ecclesiastical censors were very active. Of the seventy-two items prohibited from the lists of the publisher L.M. Dobrovolsky, fifteen were banned by the ecclesiastical censorship. Among these books were Leo Tolstoy's *Popular Tales* and his pamphlet *What I Believe,* books on the history of the Old Believers, and so on. Meanwhile the censorship of mail was also carried out on a fairly extensive scale. Unfortunately it has been impossible to uncover any kind of summarized statistics on this subject as the files of the Department of Police contain only extracts of letters intercepted in 1883 and 1884. Nonetheless, these alone comprise sixteen extensive volumes,[50] which indicate the volume of work in the "Black Office."

Otherwise, this survey of the censorship policies and their operation during the reign of Alexander III best can be concluded by the comments of the *Satirical Dictionary of Contemporaries.* "Mr. Feoktistov's administration," it noted, "was marked by important and resolute measures, taken in a protective spirit. A certain element among the journalists —those with so-called 'liberal tendencies'—suffered greatly. The contraband, *between-the-lines* literature that previously had been successfully smuggled past the customs officers of the censorship, was now subjected to careful examination and suppression; the Aesopean language that only recently had flourished now completely disappeared from the printed page. In conclusion, in all fairness it must be said that never before had censorship achieved so much in accomplishing its purpose, and never had it been so piercing, so vigilant and so strict as under the guidance of Mr. Feoktistov." Indeed, during the 1880s and early 1890s the censorship was surprisingly effective.

CHAPTER VII

EDUCATIONAL POLICIES

DELIANOV'S FIRST STEPS

Of all areas of government policy, reactionary principles were most consistently applied in that of education. The government clearly outlined its aims in this field as early as the manifesto of April 29, 1881, and these were inspired by Uvarov's tripartite formula of "Autocracy, Orthodoxy, and Nationality."[1]

Baron A.P. Nikolai headed the Ministry of Education, but he could not be trusted to pursue these aims. In the spring of 1882 he was replaced by I.D. Delianov, whose appointment was advocated by Pobedonostsev and Katkov. "I saw Delianov," the Director-General of the Holy Synod wrote Alexander III three days before the new appointment, "and found him completely ready to fulfill Your Majesty's will. I don't think it is possible at present to look elsewhere for another candidate for this post. Besides, his name will immediately make clear the goals the government seeks."

Delianov's political views fully accorded with the task before him. Referring to the preservation of autocracy, he wrote: "At present this is of the utmost importance and only in it, regardless of the blunders of the government of the moment, lies Russia's salvation." Otherwise Delianov was not distinguished by great intelligence and did not even enjoy the respect of his own colleagues and partners within the government. Most of them held him in the lowest esteem. Feoktistov called him "a buffoon" and said that Tolstoy, when talking of his former assistant, used "language that was almost censorious." Again, according to Polovtsov, A.D. Dmitriev, superintendent of the St. Petersburg Education District, referred to his minister as "the Armenian zero." Another colleague, B.N. Chicherin, described Delianov as "servile and a nonentity" and as one of "the rabble of the human race."

"It is almost the same as if Katkov had been appointed," noted D.A. Miliutin in his diary when he heard of Delianov's new position. "It is the restoration of Count Tolstoy's ministry, which won the hatred of all Russia. Between this former régime and the future one the only difference will be in the lining: with Tolstoy the lining was bile, and with Delianov it will be idiocy. Poor Russia." Everyone shared this low opinion of the new minister and, in fact, he lacked initiative, depending completely on Pobedonostsev and Katkov. These gentlemen continually advised Delianov, and the majority of the ministry's projects were sent to Moscow for Katkov's review and approval.[2] Further, Delianov, like Tolstoy before him, had A.I. Georgievsky, Katkov's minion, at his elbow throughout his term as minister. Georgievsky was a member of the ministerial council (as representative of the Committee of Studies). He kept Katkov informed of Delianov's every step.[3] Tolstoy once told Georgievsky: "You have sold your soul to Katkov"[4] and, indeed, this was the case.

Shortly after taking office Delianov made a number of changes within his ministry. Paul A. Markov, who had become assistant minister in 1880, during the liberal era, was replaced by Prince Michael S. Volkonsky (who had been superintendent of the St. Petersburg Education District under Tolstoy). Although he was the son of the Decembrist Sergei Volkonsky, personally he was a reactionary and had been nicknamed "the grimy one."[5]

Delianov's plans for education suited perfectly the government's general political intentions and coincided with the views of Tolstoy. In higher education, the new minister sought to destroy university autonomy and to "improve" the composition of the student body by diminishing the number of new students from the "intelligent proletariat." Delianov further wanted to abolish higher education for women. Meanwhile, in the secondary schools he sought to introduce "order and discipline" and to preserve the classical system of education. Gymnasiums were to be the sole secondary schools from which one might obtain entry into a higher educational institution and, to improve the composition of gymnasium student bodies, students from the less prosperous sections of the population were to be excluded. Otherwise, the new minister foresaw no major changes in the lower and elementary school systems. Their teaching should, he believed, be conducted in the spirit of "autocracy, orthodoxy, and nationality." He did, however, propose to improve industrial and trade schools in order to meet the demands created by economic development. But in Delianov's opinion the creation of such schools would have another positive aspect: as he observed in his official report for 1884, this would make "the entry of children from the lower strata into the male and female gymnasiums more difficult."

Such was the substance of Delianov's program. In practice the new minister turned his attention first to the secondary schools. On November 20, 1882 he issued a circular which observed that "recently individual students in thirteen gymnasiums, one progymnasium, and ten modern schools have displayed the more or less noticeable effects of the pernicious influence of criminal propaganda. Furthermore, large collective

disorders and unheard of—in fact, almost unbelievable—outrages by
particular students have occurred in the Fourteenth Gymnasium and
the Fourth Modern School." Apart from this Delianov complained that
"students of the secondary educational establishments have been insufficiently careful in their compliance with established regulations regarding uniforms, and with respect to proper decency and decorum." Students, he wrote, were smoking, using walking sticks and riding crops,
attending clubs, masquerades, taverns, cafes, and so on. "From all these
reports and examples," the circular argued, "it can only be concluded
that the supervision of students has become very lax and that the heads
of the secondary educational establishments, as well as the other mentors
of youth, have not taken the necessary measures to maintain discipline.
Consequently it has suffered a grievous decline."

The Minister of Education therefore introduced a series of measures
"for maintaining order and discipline" in the secondary educational
establishments. These consisted of "precise" adherence to the regulations of May 4, 1874 (defining the conduct of students), to the regulations on punishments, and to those on the disciplinary powers allotted
school authorities (that is, compliance with all the regulations worked
out during Tolstoy's ministry and discarded in the early 1880s).[6] This
circular stressed that directors of secondary schools "held full responsibility for the proper organization of all aspects (of school life) and that
development of character and the maintenance of discipline must be
recognized as being at least as important as scholarly pursuits." Delianov
further instructed superintendents of education districts that heads of
institutions who could not carry out this program were to be dismissed.

In 1882 the minister revealed his "anxiety" about students who had
finished public elementary schools. A circular of December 28, 1882
noted that pupils in these institutions came chiefly from the peasantry
and, as they would have no chance "to retain the knowledge acquired in
school, the public schools have great difficulty in fulfilling their task."
Furthermore, "among other circumstances exerting an unfavorable influence on the further development of the younger generation finishing
the public schools," Delianov observed, "an extremely important consideration is that once boys and girls have left the school system they
have, for the most part, no books to help them retain the knowledge
acquired earlier in school." Therefore, "actively seeking measures that
might promote greater success in achieving the aims of the public school
system, and bearing in mind that this task consists of confirming religious and moral ideas among the people," he proposed that graduating
pupils be supplied with a small library.

A "model collection" for such a library would comprise five books:
a prayer book with commentaries; a psalter; the sacred histories (Old

and New Testaments); the Gospels; and a book explaining the divine service. "Such a present," the circular concluded, "would be the best possible farewell gift the school could give the graduating boys and girls; at the same time it will afford them a chance to retain the knowledge from their education most important for their lives—the knowledge of the law of God and an ability to read it." This statement clearly revealed the Minister of Education's views on the task of elementary schools: he perceived them as having mainly a clerical purpose.

At the other end of the education spectrum, Delianov's initial steps were measures "for the elimination of disorders in the higher educational institutions." At the end of 1882 a Special Commission had been created under the chairmanship of Prince Volkonsky, the Assistant Minister of Education. This body concluded that recalcitrant students should be drafted as soldiers and recommended: "(1) that in exceptional cases of insolent conduct and gross insubordination to the authorities, when the offense follows upon a number of similar occurrences, those named are to be expelled from the higher educational establishment and drafted into a disciplinary battalion; (2) that other young persons who have been expelled from these same institutions for various offenses are to be drafted for compulsory military service in the ranks."

Alexander III ordered that the commission's decision be discussed by a committee that included a number of ministers (Tolstoy, Delianov, Nabokov, Posiet, Ostrovsky, and General Peter S. Vannovsky), the director of the Naval Ministry, Shestakov, and the Director-General of the Holy Synod. This committee, with the exception of the Minister of War, Vannovsky, and Shestakov, supported the commission's proposals. The objections of these two led to a compromise: the students expelled from the higher institutions were only to lose their exemptions and be taken into military service by means of a lottery (that is, in the usual way).

On receiving this decision, Alexander III made the following comment: "I agree to this measure *as an experiment,* but I suspect it will be insufficient and will not give the expected results." Hence the emperor ordered the committee to reconsider its conclusions. This was done in June, 1883. Again the committee, with the exception of Vannovsky and Shestakov, agreed with the proposals of Volkonsky's commission (apart from making a few minor changes).[7] For their part, Vannovsky and Shestakov insisted that this decision would contradict the Statute on Military Service, for it "proposes a *punitive measure* and transforms service in the army's ranks into a *punishment.*" A most "awkward" aspect of this measure was, they argued, that it would increase the spread of revolutionary ideas among the troops. "For the army to accept the committee's proposed measure," they said, "would mean acting directly in the interests of revolutionary propaganda, which seeks every effort to penetrate the army with its ideas."

When the emperor learned the results of the committee's renewed deliberations, he had this question raised in the Committee of Ministers. After discussions on February 7 and 14, 1884, a majority of fourteen ministers rejected the committee's decision.[8] According to the minutes of the Committee of Ministers, "it is the deep conviction of fourteen members that this would be an insult to every soldier . . . who has become accustomed to considering military service as a supreme honour." The majority of the ministers maintained that "the adoption of the projected measure would also directly contradict that principle of justice which does not allow two punishments for one and the same offense." (By this they meant expulsion from the educational institutions *and* forcible service in the army). Finally, they warned, the measures recommended by the committee could only increase dissatisfaction with the government and help spread revolutionary propaganda among the troops.

Nonetheless the chairman of the Committee of Ministers and a minority of five members (Reutern, Tolstoy, Ostrovsky, Nabokov, Delianov, and Posiet) favored the committee's proposals. They wanted "to permit, as an experiment for approximately three years, the drafting of some students expelled from the higher educational institutions into a corrective and disciplinary form of compulsory military service." In this manner the minority not only approved the drafting of expelled students, but also wished that this be carried out "as an experiment" on a fairly wide scale.

These opinions were sent to Alexander III, who commented: "Although I do not share the fears and opinions of the 14 members, I suggest that a final decision on this matter be postponed until the approval of the new university statute." Whereas it was not mentioned in the statute itself, the minority decision of the Committee of Minister's or, more accurately, of the earlier committee, apparently was approved and implemented, although during this period in a very restricted form only.[9]

On July 7, 1884 Delianov issued a secret circular concerning the political reliability of students. The gymnasium authorities, he noted, were ignoring the ministry's instructions of January 12, 1880. These had ordered them to forward reports to the universities about students admitted, which would cover "their course of gymnasium study and the moral quality of their lives outside the classroom." The minister pointed out that "from judicial investigations and reports the ministry has received from district authorities on the results of their enquiries concerning the diffusion of anti-government propaganda among the students, it is evident that . . . young persons frequently have been accepted as (university) students who have already, while attending the secondary educational establishments, revealed themselves to be maliciously inclined and even members of secret circles . . . . From this, among other things, it follows that the authorities of the various educational institutions, either due to imprudence or stupidity and possibly through criminal leniency, in their certifications sometimes have pointed out the excellence of conduct of those undeserving (of this recommendation)." Therefore Delianov again instructed the directors of the gymnasiums to provide to higher educational institutions detailed and "thorough" reports on the graduates of their schools. This, together with his other measures, made the new minister's intentions sufficiently clear.

THE UNIVERSITY STATUTE OF 1884

Delianov's first serious undertaking was his reform of the higher educational system. As early as April, 1875 a commission headed by Delianov had been formed to prepare a new university statute. In February of 1880 its draft statute was presented to the State Council but, because of the changing political circumstances and the attendent sudden retirement of Tolstoy, was returned to the commission. In May of 1881, again under Delianov's chairmanship, another commission was established to prepare regulations for supervising students. In a memorandum on this body's work, the new Minister of Education openly attacked the existing university statute and argued the necessity of immediately replacing it with a new law.[10]

Although the draft for a new university statute was introduced into the State Council at the end of 1882, discussion did not begin until the end of 1883. Consideration of this issue was postponed because of Alexander III's coronation in May. "Following conversations with members of the Council and the Grand Duke," Polovtsov recorded in his diary, "I went to Pobedonostsev to get his agreement to dropping discussion of the university statute during the present session. He shared my opinion that the students should not be stirred up before the coronation . . . ."[11] Delianov's intended measures to limit, if not entirely liquidate higher education for women were also shelved because of fears of public discontent. "As for news," wrote Georgievsky to Katkov on June 10, 1882, "I can tell you that at the insistence of M.N. Ost(rovsky), supported by K.P. Pobed(onostsev) and Count D(mitry) A(lexandrovich), (A.D.) Dmitriev's plan to curtail entry into the higher women's courses this year . . . will not be carried out. This is because they do not want to create still greater dissatisfaction than that which supposedly already has been aroused by the appointment of Count D.A. . . . . So the evil we have suffered for so many years must now be borne for one year more." It is clear that in 1882, and especially prior to the coronation, the government remained cautious about announcing reactionary changes that might stir up the public.

The draft of the new university statute presented to the State Council in 1882 was the same draft, with a few changes, that the despised Tolstoy had drawn up at the end of the 1870s. The basic difference between it and the existing statute of 1863 was that the proposed law would destroy university autonomy. To this end it insisted on the need "to strengthen the government's influence on the university administrations" and, although the university academic council was named the "highest instance in academic affairs," in practice this body's rights were considerably diminished. According to the 1863 statute, for example, a professor's chair was filled by an election in this academic council and the successful candidate then was confirmed by the minister. The latter might appoint a candidate only when a chair remained unfilled. The proposed statute, however, accorded the university council's choice merely "the weight of a recommendation." At his discretion the minister might approve the person elected by the council, appoint a professor from among other candidates suggested by the university community, "or choose an outside individual." This meant that the most important question of university life—the filling of professional vacancies—no longer would be decided by the university's academic council. Similarly, a host of other questions resolved within the academic council now were to be settled ultimately only by the superintendent or the minister (Articles 21 and 24 of the draft statute).

The proposed statute granted wide powers to a superintendent of an educational district. "When he recognized the necessity," he might attend sessions of both the council and the faculty assemblies. In both places he would enjoy precedence but would not preside (although he might assume this function in cases of special importance). The draft also lent superintendents the right of depriving certain categories of academics (such as assistant professors) of the right to lecture. Again the proposed statute clearly encroached upon the universities' autonomy.

A second aspect of this draft concerned the question of state examinations. It proposed that these be given by special commissions appointed by the Minister of Education. This was Katkov's cherished dream: it would give the ministry a chance to establish very broad control over the whole system of university lecturing and, better still, allow the ministry to influence even the content of the courses taught. As early as 1879 he had written Alexander III about the new statute and stressed: "The most important section of the projected reforms concerns the proposals on examinations. According to the draft, these will not be conducted by the professors giving the lectures but by a special commission, and will cover a broad general program so that the examinations will serve not only to test the students but also be a means of regulating the lectures of the professors. The state examinations will determine the content and limits of the university courses." In other words, the introduction of a state examination system was to destroy independence in university lecturing. Finally, a third innovation was a suggested increase in the supervision of students. This would be entrusted to inspectors and the university administration, whose roles were to be considerably increased.

Describing this plan to Miliutin, A.V. Golovnin wrote: "In essence the whole sense and main aim of the reforms is to subordinate completely all activities of students and teachers to an arbitrary admin(istrative) authority: it makes autocrats out of the superintendents and the minister . . . . Is it possible the present chiefs, among whom there are intelligent, sophisticated and educated men, really think that slavish teachers and slavish students (as in the Jesuit schools) can be beneficial for the state and for the government? Do they not understand that this kind of system leads to moral disintegration and the collapse of a state?" The draft, meanwhile, provoked diverse opinions within the State Council. It was decided, therefore, to hold preliminary discussions prior to any general meeting. On October 10 a conference took place in Tolstoy's office but its participants failed to reach an agreement. All those present would have allowed the universities (or, to be precise, the academic councils) to be deprived of their independence for, according to Polovtsov, "Count Tolstoy produced a great deal of information to show how misguided in their expectations were those men who, in 1863, had placed the responsibility of carrying out administrative duties on collegiate bodies of university professors. The academics are, according to him, no better than children and are incapable of administrative activities that differ so much from academic labors." But the proposed state examinations aroused hot debate and Stoianovsky, Bunge, and Pobedonostsev particularly opposed establishing state examinations outside of the universities.

On October 11 another conference took place, this time in the State Council under Grand Duke Michael Nikolaevich's chairmanship. Again disputes broke out on the subject of the examinations. "After a meeting of more than three hours," sighed Polovtsov, "Delianov agreed that the examining commissions should sit within the walls of the university, but he maintained that the minister must retain the right of removing professors giving courses from these commissions. The disagreement between Delianov and all the rest of those present centered on this (point)." The preliminary meetings achieved no unanimity within the council on the issue of examinations. Further, during the ensuing detailed discussions of the draft statute in the Combined Departments and the council's General Sessions, disagreement grew rather than diminished, and spread to still other questions. Meanwhile Delianov apparently made additions to various points during the draft's discussion in the Combined Departments.

On October 22 the Combined Departments of Laws and State Economy began their discussions of the proposed statute. While there was still general agreement on the measures increasing the powers of the administrative authorities, the debates on the examinations became hotter than ever. Polovtsov described the scene as follows: "All those present opposed this measure. Nikolai pointed out that it was a humiliating expression of distrust in the universities. (Nicholas V.) Isakov maintained that it aimed at restricting the rights the universities had been given regarding admissions and at making it more difficult for the young people whom the government hitherto had attracted to them (the universities) to gain entrance. These young people would now be justly dissatisfied and there was certainly no need to increase the number of dissatisfied. Before doing this, one should open to them some alternative means of education and work by developing the modern (schools) and technical education. (Michael E.) Kovalevsky pointed out the impossibility of finding sufficient personnel for examinations outside of the universities. Bunge insisted that the professors who gave the courses take part in the examinations. Pobedonostsev very subtly, sometimes ironically, but in a speech with a generally conciliatory tone, insisted that punitive measures had their dangers, but so did the rejection—which had been the case far too frequently of late—of preventive measures." Following long hours of argument Delianov finally agreed that these examinations should be held in the universities rather than in the superintendents' offices, a concession that he had made earlier in the preliminary and unofficial meeting of October 11.

In the next session, held on October 29, Delianov was again forced to give in. This time the question was that of appointing rectors. On a motion by Kovalevsky and Pobedonostsev, the departments resolved to appoint as rector one of two candidates elected by the professors. It should be noted that Pobedonostsev opposed the draft statute and attempted to influence Delianov directly. On November 14 Polovtsov recorded in his diary that Pobedonostsev told him that "he had visited

Delianov and asked him, when he had continued his protests, if the Emperor had agreed with this project, as it would likely result in such ruin in the field of education that Delianov, the man guilty of the reforms, would never survive them."

Katkov was greatly irritated by Pobedonostsev's opposition to the draft statute. On November 27 he attempted in a long letter to gain the director-general's support. Katkov said nothing concrete about the proposals themselves, but argued that their main virtue was the fact that they had been drafted by Tolstoy and Delianov. "Is it possible," he asked rather maliciously, "that Count Tolstoy—who had been entrusted with the security of the state—is so feather-brained that having administered personally the Ministry of Education and spent a decade dealing with the university question, he has abandoned himself to the blowing winds of fanaticism? Can it be that the State Council is being presented with a draft law that is so filled with monstrous absurdities that you find it necessary to enter a coalition even with the sworn opponents of your own ideas as the only way to save Russia from the disaster dreamed up by Count Tolstoy?"

Besides, he pointed out, Delianov had been Tolstoy's chairman on all the commissions dealing with university problems, and he concluded by underlining the political significance of university reform. "The efforts of the party of disintegration (that is, the supporters of a moderately liberal course)" wrote Katkov, "follow the slogan: *the worse things are, the better they are*. Then they try to ensure that not a single measure or law is approved that would evidence our government's competence or the possibility of good legislation being produced by our form of administration. A reform of the universities would be the first restrictive measure of the present reign. After it a number of other reforms must absolutely follow in the judicial department, in the provincial administration, and in other areas . . . . The failure of this legislative measure will thus not only affect the universities alone, but will influence all other affairs of state."

The Combined Departments' discussion of the proposed statute continued from the end of 1883 until the beginning of May of 1884. The question of examinations—discussed in detail at the end of November, 1883—remained especially contentious. At that time Delianov, under Katkov's influence, attempted to take the offensive. Katkov saw the statute's chief merit as the separation of examinations from teaching and, in the summer of 1884, he warned Alexander III: "Nothing will be essentially changed unless the examinations are separated from the lecturing."[12] This proviso, naturally, would give the government the means to keep professors as well as students in line. As for Delianov, he outlined his opinions on this issue in a special memorandum, written in early 1884 and entitled "Supplementary Information on the Question of University Examinations." He now argued that one of the virtues of the proposed statute was that it would free the minister in his choice of members for the examination commissions and suggested that such members need not themselves necessarily have a university degree. Consequently an examination commission might be composed of servile civil servants who would readily carry out the wishes of their superiors.

The Combined Departments reached no agreement on this problem, but almost unanimously rejected this section of the draft. Only State Controller T.I. Filippov and Tolstoy's assistant, Durnovo, supported Delianov.[13] Meanwhile the majority within the Combined Departments found several of the draft's articles unacceptable and made a number of changes in the original document. For this reason the reactionary minority of the State Council strove desperately to prepare for the council's General Session and mobilised all their forces. Georgievsky, in a letter of April 11, 1884, told Katkov: "I asked Iv(an) D(avidovich) to obtain one copy (evidently of the draft as drawn up after the Combined Departments' amendments) and immediately send it to you. Still, it would be even better if you were able to come to Petersburg at this time, in order to save what can be saved. I am thinking in particular about the secretaries, and the preservation of the fee payments.[14] Without these everything will be turned topsy-turvy, with confusion and nonsense as the result. Iv(an) Dav(idovich) has raised no objections (to the departments' amendments) in spite of all my persuasion and requests."

Then, on May 25, four days before the General Session, the Minister of the Interior called a meeting of his allies at his home. There they worked out their plan of action. The next day N.A. Liubimov gave Katkov a detailed account of the proceedings: "Yesterday Count Tolstoy held a meeting at his place. Apart from Iv(an) Dav(idovich), Ostrovsky, Filippov, Count Shuvalov, and (Samuel A.) Greig, Georgievsky and myself were invited. Count Shuvalov will speak at the (council) meeting about rectors and deans, Ostrovsky about program matters, Filippov on the examinations, and Count Tolstoy about the fees." Thus the various roles were handed out.

In the General Sessions arguments broke out about the manner of appointing rectors, deans, and the secretaries of faculties and the academic councils. In the end, nineteen members of the State Council favored the ending of elections to these posts, while twenty-five opposed this measure. Otherwise the debate centered on the membership of the examination commissions, the payment of fees, and some other questions. Describing the course of discussion in the council's General

Session, Polovtsov wrote: "Count Shuvalov spoke in favor of govern-ment-appointed rectors. He was opposed by Nikolai and Golovnin, but supported by Count Tolstoy. Ostrovsky spoke on the issue of the pro-gram and lecture system . . . . Filippov gave a long, feeble and dull speech on the topic of the examination commissions, Tolstoy supported him, but Nikolai answered in what one may call an unexpectedly bril-liant manner. Delianov put forth a few more shallow remarks, simply, dully and stupidly repeating all that Katkov and Georgievsky have shoved into him. In summary, then, the session went well enough—that is, it passed without creating a scandal for the State Council."

In the end the results of the General Session's discussion duplicated those of the Combined Departments. The followers of Katkov, Tolstoy, and Delianov were again a minority. In general, the points of disagree-ment can be listed as follows: the system of examinations; the teaching programs; the method of appointment of rectors, deans, and secretaries of the faculties and role of the academic councils; the filling of vacant professorial chairs; the conditions set down for giving lecture courses; the distribution of lectures on certain subjects by courses and by semes-ter; and the payment of lecture fees.

In June the State Council's "memorial" or report was presented to Alexander III for his approval. Although the emperor was undecided, representatives of the minority, led by Katkov, successfully attempted to influence the tsar. On July 8, for example, Katkov wrote a long letter to the emperor. He insisted that the minority's opinion be approved and stressed the need for separating the state examinations from the instruc-tion. As Katkov saw it, it would be better to postpone issuing the statute "than to issue a law that is insufficient and useless."

On August 12 Alexander III called a conference on the university question at Ropsha, near St. Petersburg. All those attending, apart from Pobedonostsev, belonged to the minority of the State Council. Even the chairman of the State Council, Grand Duke Michael Nikolaevich, was not present. Polovtsov reported, according to the account of Pobedo-nostsev, the only majority representative in attendance, that "Delianov, Tolstoy and Ostrovsky fervently defended the minority's opinion, and demanded that the Emperor either accept their views or replace them, which would have been very difficult for him to do." On August 13 Liubimov wrote Katkov and, evidently on the basis of information from Delianov, gave him a detailed account of the meeting. This letter makes it clear that Pobedonostsev originally defended the majority opinion but, in the end, announced "that if two ministers (of Education)—a former as well as the present one—give us such firm assurances of suc-cess, then one must, in the end, give one's approval." "Thank God! It seems that this matter will end happily and without any strings attached," wrote Liubimov when assessing the results of the conference. But everyone was not so confident of final victory. The participants of the August 12 meeting therefore resolved not to spread the news and to tell only those most intimately involved the results of the discussion. Nonetheless, their doubts soon proved groundless: on August 15, 1884 Alexander III approved the minority's decision in its entirety.

The aspect of the final law that distinguished it from the original bill was in Katkov's mind the section dealing with state examinations, but it is useful to review the final statute in comparison with that of 1863. To begin with, the new statute considerably increased the authority and rights of superintendents of education districts. Article 8 stated firmly "that the responsibility for higher guidance in all instructions for maintaining order and discipline within the university belongs to the superintendents." Further, the rectors and deans, who earlier were elected by academic councils and confirmed by the administrative authorities, by the statute of 1884 were selected first by the minister and secondly by the superintendents of the districts. The minister could also fill vacant professorial chairs. According to article 100 of the new statute, "on the opening of a vacant professorship, the Minister of Education can either fill it at his own discretion . . ., or allow the university to elect a candidate, who is then subject to his approval, for the vacant post."

The independence of the academic councils was considerably restricted and now embraced only three categories of competency. Firstly, the council decided annually on "the total number of medals to be awarded to regular and external students for their work on required subjects." In the second place, the council approved the conferral of academic degrees upon the persons receiving them and, thirdly, it confirmed the petitions of the faculty for award of the doctoral degree. Any other decision by an academic council was subject to confirmation by the superintendent or the minister. Whereas under the statute of 1863 the "expenditure of sums allotted for purchase of educational supplies by faculty" had been fixed by independent decisions of the council, now even these must be approved by the minister. Other matters previously discussed by a council were similarly transferred to the competence of the university administration and the inspector of students became a member—with full rights—of this latter body.[15] Otherwise, university courts were completely abolished and the inspector's powers substantially enlarged: he now combined both judicial and administrative authority. Indeed, since the inspector awarded stipends to students, his powers over them increased still further.

By the terms of the statutes of 1863 these inspectors were elected by a university council from among its members[16] or from state officials who had completed the university, and this election was approved by the minister. Further, the inspectors had been subordinated to the council and the rector. The 1884 statute, however, granted to the minister the power to appoint inspectors who were now no longer subordinate to university authority. "Being placed under the authority of the superintendent," the new law stated, "the inspector is subordinated in his activities to his rector and carries out his legal orders."[17] In this way university autonomy was destroyed, the authority of the superintendents and inspectors of students extended, and the latter officials established as essentially independent of the universities.

The statute of 1884 introduced two forms of examinations—faculty and the university (state). The members of a university commission were to be appointed by the Minister of Education.[18] At the same time, tests replaced the previous practice of semester examinations.[19] The aim of these tests was to check on a student's formal fulfillment of course requirements (that is, his attendance at lectures, completion of assigned work, and so on) rather than his mastery of knowledge. The new statute further required students to pay lecture and laboratory fees to a maximum of fifty rubles per academic year. Otherwise, the university collected up to five rubles per half-year for its own use, and up to one ruble for each weekly teaching hour for the lecturers.

The rights of assistant professors were broadened to allow them to offer courses that paralleled those taught by professors.[20] This was undoubtedly a positive step that helped train future professors and, at the same time, its influence was reflected by a rise in quality of the lectures given by the professors.

An analysis of the statute as a whole makes clear that the discussions in the State Council had forced Tolstoy and Delianov to retreat a good way from their original positions. This is best demonstrated by noting the newly-established state examinations. Their nature had been considerably altered in comparison with the original proposals but, although the reactionaries had not gained everything they wanted, Katkov and his friends considered the new statute a great victory. They viewed this law as the first step on the road toward a full affirmation of the principle of autocracy. "The new university statute," Katkov wrote in the *Moscow News*, "has an importance beyond the sphere of education. It is important because it marks the beginning of a new movement in our legislative activity. Just as the statute of 1863 was the beginning of the systematic destruction of state authority, the statute of 1884 heralds a renewal of government and the restoration of responsibility to the authorities . . . . Thus, gentlemen, government goes, and government returns . . . ."

IMPLEMENTATION OF THE UNIVERSITY STATUTE

The new statute determined the Ministry of Education's further policies in university matters and, in implementing it, the authorities adopted a whole series of other rigid disciplinary and police measures. None of these succeeded in pacifying the students. Disorders had broken out at the University of Kiev as early as the autumn of 1884. As a result, the university remained closed, on Delianov's orders, until January 1, 1885. The events in Kiev had an impact on the other universities, but the most striking incidents occurred in Moscow. On October 20 a group of Moscow University students demonstrated on Strastny Boulevard, in front of the offices of Katkov's paper, as a protest against the closure of the University of Kiev. The result was the arrest of over one hundred persons, including seventy-five students.[21]

In May, 1885 Delianov reinstituted student uniforms (which had been abolished in 1861). On May 6 "Regulations for Students" appeared that defined the proper conduct for students both on university premises and in their private lives. These regulations, in particular, rejected any notion of "corporateness" among the students. Stating that "students are recognized as individual guests of the university," the creation of all social organizations, apart from those of an educational character, was prohibited.

Also in 1885 the "Regulations for Examination Requirements for Selecting Graduates in the State Examinations" were issued. These set out "to give a clear indication of the pursuits required of the students" and in this way to determine the general content of instruction—that is, the faculty programs of study. The regulations ordered, for instance, that "the basic philological education in both practical and methodological aspects comprises classical languages and their literatures, and includes the disciplines and practical knowledge relative to them." Hence the basic obligatory subjects for a Historical-Philological Faculty were classical philology and ancient philosophy, which were to be studied throughout the entire eight semesters.[22] Similarly, for a Law Faculty the basic subject was to be Roman Law, for this was "the universal subject, so vital for any educated jurist, regardless of his country or the state he serves." Moreover, the ministry's direct tutelage of the universities went further than the definition of general course outlines: the ministry needed to approve faculty semester plans for weekly lecture and laboratory hours.[23]

In March of 1886 Delianov distributed to the superintendents of education districts a circular dealing with the situation in the universities and stressing the powers the new statute lent to administrative authorities. The minister began by directing the superintendent's attention to the extensive authority that they and the university administrations now enjoyed. "With such power . . . you are, of course, not to delay in calling the university rectors' special attention to the need for making every effort to unify the activities of the administration, the faculty meetings, inspectors, and of all persons in these bodies, so as to guarantee order and tranquillity within the universities, where presently sedition once more has dared to raise its head."

Delianov then outlined a detailed program for the work of the inspectors. They were to "keep a vigilant watch inside the university and, where possible, outside it, for any appearance or indication of agitation among the students." The minister ordered that "those students discovered to be in any way engaged in the above-mentioned activity, or inclined to give way to its influence, are to be placed under special surveillance." Meanwhile he demanded a "redoubled watch" over student attendance at lectures and their "fulfilling of all obligations laid upon them by the regulations concerning the semi-annual tests." To the same end Delianov hoped that lecturers would not refuse to lend the authorities their full assistance "in the task of guaranteeing that academic pursuits within the university follow their proper course and that the young people are protected from consequences that would prove disastrous for them." He also recommended that the minor misdemeanors of students should not be allowed to pass unnoticed and concluded that it was necessary "in the appropriate cases to enter into communication with the police, to profit from their assistance, and to give them, on your part, full co-operation . . . . Along with frequent personal contacts with representatives of the civil authorities in the university town, you, for your part, my dear sirs, should not block any attempt to establish a full unity of action between both university inspectors and the police . . . ."

In early 1887 Delianov issued another circular on the problem of "preventing light-minded youths from being excited by political agitators." This ordered the higher educational institutions to arrange the "collection" of signed statements from all students and free auditors specifying "their non-participation in any association such as, for instance, nationality societies, and so forth, as well as their non-membership in even legal associations, unless they have specific permission from their immediate superiors. Each student is to be warned that in the event of his membership in any association being discovered, he will be dismissed immediately from the institution." At the same time Delianov attempted to militarize the formalities at institutions of higher learning. In May, 1887 a circular ordered students, "for the purpose of maintaining accepted courtesy," to stand rather than sit while replying to examiners. This procedure was justified on the ground that "such an examination procedure exists for officers in the military academies and for students in the Military Medical Academy."

After the events of March 1, 1887, when St. Petersburg University students were discovered organizing a terrorist plot, further action seemed imperative. In June the Committee of Ministers examined Delianov's proposal "On Measures for the Regulation of Students in Upper and Secondary Educational Institutions of the Ministry of Education." The ministers approved Delianov's plans and raised the student fee for lectures from ten to fifty rubles, quite apart from the separate fees paid to the professors. On June 26 a secret circular to the rectors of universities and other institutions of higher learning insisted that only those persons were to be accepted as students "about whom the necessary information has been furnished by the directors of the educational institutions in which they had studied and taken qualifying or final examinations."

All these measures proved useless in the face of growing student discontent. The largest outbreak occurred at the University of Moscow at the end of 1887, and is known as the "Bryzgalov affair." Alexander A. Bryzgalov was inspector of students and had established within the university a system of provocation and harsh repression that earned him the immense respect of Katkov. "I saw Bryzgalov, dear Ivan Davidovich," Katkov wrote Delianov on January 24, 1885, "and after our conversation I value all the more the treasure you have found in him."

The Moscow disorders began on November 22 when A. Siniavsky, one of the students in the Law Faculty, publicly slapped Bryzgalov. The unrest waxed massive in character as hundreds of students were involved in the excitement that followed. As a result, the university closed on November 30 and, although Delianov was forced to dismiss Bryzgalov, ninety-seven students were expelled. The immediate consequences were new student disorders at the universities of Kazan, Petersburg, Kharkov and Odessa. By the end of the year four more universities had been closed (Petersburg, Kazan, Kharkov, and Novorossiisk), as well as the Kharkov Technological Institute and the Kazan Veterinary Institute. The government, notwithstanding the new university statute and the accompanying measures, obviously had failed to suppress the student movement.

At the beginning of the 1890s the Ministry of Education therefore contemplated new measures to restore order within the universities. Katkov's minion, A.I. Georgievsky, chaired the Ministry's Committee of Studies and he prepared an interesting report entitled "Measures for Establishing of Order in the Universities and thereby in the Other Educational Institutions, and for Prevention of Future Student Disorders or the Greatest Possible Reduction of Such Events and their Harmful Consequences." In this Georgievsky argued for still another increase in the authority of the administration. This might be achieved by appointing rectors, deans, and faculty secretaries for an unlimited period rather than a term of four years. He wanted, moreover, "special instructions" issued "to the superintendents to explain all their extensive and many-sided powers and responsibilities with regard to governing the universities . . . ." Indeed, Georgievsky maintained, the powers of these officials should be considerably extended and stricter measures applied to the professors and general teaching staffs of institutions of higher learning. Point 6 of his report referred to the need "of taking every measure to change the dominant spirit of the personnel in the professorial bodies."

Georgievsky outlined the proper sequence for such measures. The first steps should be taken in the University of St. Petersburg, then in Moscow, and finally in Novorossiisk. "All efforts," he wrote, "must aim at ensuring that professorial posts are filled by people who are talented, who stand at the top of their disciplines, and who at the same time are sincerely devoted to the throne, the fatherland, and all the precepts of its history, and thus are fully patriotic in their outlook. This should be a *conditio sine qua non*. A professor should be appointed when the course is created, along with the stipend." Henceforth the indispensible condition for a professorial appointment would be the scholar's devotion to crown and nation, interpreted in the most reactionary and chauvinistic sense of those words.

Accordingly, Georgievsky insisted it was necessary, "starting with the appointing of assistant professors, and then with every promotion in either grade or rank or any honor or reward and, in general, on any opportune occasion, to impress on the lecturers and professors that they must be the mentors of youth as well as men of learning, and that the course of their official careers is strictly dependent upon their honestly fulfilling a mentor's obligations in the proper patriotic spirit." Lecturers shown to be "openly unreliable" or having "a bad influence" on students, Georgievsky recommended, either should be dismissed or transferred to a provincial university. Such reprisals might be implemented when a university was closed "because of disorders." Then the government should dismiss all professors so as to "make all the necessary changes at the same time."

The report's next section concerned students. In the first place, Georgievsky thought that the numbers of university students should be cut in half (that is, from 9,252 to 4,100 students) over a period of five years. "The number of students is to be reduced to match the available facilities and resources both with regard to proper conditions of study and the maintenance of strict supervision over them." To this end, he recommended that the universities accept only those whose examination marks in Russian composition, Latin, Greek and mathematics made up no less than 3.75 points (out of five). To obtain a "proper"—that is, a reactionary—student body, Georgievsky insisted on retaining in force the rule obliging the directors of gymnasiums to send references concerning the applicants' "truthfulness and reliability." He wanted tuition fees to be kept "at their present level" which, he believed, would help keep students from the poorer strata of the population out of universities.

Meanwhile Georgievsky proposed a strengthening of controls over student work and recommended the adoption of the following measures: "To re-establish in all their strength the 1885 regulations on semi-annual tests (on the basis of a proper attendance at lectures, an active participation in seminar-laboratory work under the guidance of the lecturers, the prescribed amount of home work, and examinations) . . . . At the same time, the yearly course examinations, which were re-established in 1889 in spite of the fact that they contravened the statute of 1884 and which had proved completely useless earlier during the operation of the statute of 1863, should be completely abolished." Obviously Georgievsky was more interested in the punctilious observance by students of existing university regulations than he was in the knowledge they displayed in examinations.[24]

In order to control the students further, he recommended that the number of resident inspectors be increased to ensure a ratio of no more than seventy-five students for each such official. In addition Georgievsky wanted "to establish harmony between the activities of the police and the inspectors with regard to the students, through an exchange of information between them on student misdemeanors and enterprises." He even outlined measures for combatting breaches of university regulations and the tactics to be used against those participating in unauthorized meetings. For this purpose he suggested a list be made "of all participating in a meeting, with the most active being especially noted." In cases where the arguments and admonishments "of the inspector, and then of the rector, prove unavailing, the superintendent is to be summoned." He was to order the immediate dispersal of the gathering. If the student disobedience continued, he would "call in the police, who are to *waste no time in words* but immediately arrest to a man those who disobeyed the authorities." The arrested students were to be subsequently placed in solitary confinement in the cells of a civil or military prison.

Later the report gave an equally detailed outline of the punishments to be imposed for participation in a strike, depending on the behavior of the participant. The stiffest penalty was "for an insult to one of the academic officials or a member of the police department." A culprit guilty of this was to be liable to solitary confinement for the course of one year or to service in a disciplinary battalion for a period of two years.

Georgievsky maintained that such regulations were necessary because of the great likelihood of further outrageous incidents and student disorders. He wanted other measures to bring "an improvement and strengthening of the disciplinary and deportment aspects of the gymnasiums." These included the guidance of home reading by the class tutors, discussions on literary themes, and so on. He wanted a "special deportment committee" under the chairmanship of the director of the gymnasium to be created for each class. Consisting of the inspector, the "teacher of the Law" (that is, the priest) and the class tutor, this committee would enjoy extensive rights, including that of birching youths under eighteen years "when extraordinary offenses demanded exemplary punishment." With this Georgievsky concluded his report. His suggestions were much harsher than the statute of 1884, but fortunately they were never officially adopted.

Nonetheless, the government continued its attempts to pacify the universities throughout the 1880s and early 1890s. The authorities sought to subordinate the whole system of university education to one goal: the universities should prepare specialists in various areas of knowledge but these specialists should be, first and foremost, devoted to the throne (that is, to the idea of autocracy). This was the overriding consideration, and the educational side of university life was pushed into second place. But, although the government could congratulate itself on some achievements, it was unable to reach major victories in the area of university education. Its efforts to transform the professors into servile officials, to change the composition of the student bodies, and to pacify the students, all failed. The student's unrest did not subside. In spite of the significant increase in the fees, moreover, little change occurred in the social composition of the student body.

Statistics for the universities of Moscow and Kharkov, and incomplete data for the University of St. Petersburg, illustrate this fact. According to the reports of Moscow University, the social composition of the student body in 1884 and 1894 is shown in the first table on the opposite page. Even if the figures are not fully comparable at all points, the conclusion can still be drawn that there was only an insignificant increase in the percentage of children of nobles and officials (1.91). At the same time (although it is impossible to measure precisely) there was a decrease in the number of students from artisan families and families without rank. Yet the number of peasant students increased. If peasants are combined with cossacks (who were undoubtedly placed in this category in the 1884 report), the increase is three percent. Thus the social composition of the student body had changed but little.

Parents' Status	1884	1894
Nobles and Officials	46.27%	48.18%
Ecclesiastical	9.29	6.40
Honorary Citizens and Merchant's Rank	13.05	—
Honorary Citizens and Merchants of the First Guild	—	11.80
Artisans and Persons Without Rank	25.65	—
Artisans, Persons Without Rank, Merchants of the Second Guild	—	24.07
Peasants	4.21	5.33
Cossacks	—	1.97
Foreign Citizens	1.53	2.25

At the University of St. Petersburg the percentage of students from the families of nobles and government officials was 58.64 in 1884 and 65.32 in 1894. But here one should remember that a fair number of students whose families were, in practice, without civil service rank were included in the category of nobles and officials.

The figures for Kharkov University for the years 1885 and 1895 are fuller:

Parents' Status	1885	1895
Nobles and Officials	41.24%	37.02%
Ecclesiastical	8.14	4.39
Cossacks	3.31	3.92
Merchants	12.71	13.33
Artisans and Classless Persons	27.69	35.14
Peasants	3.34	4.16
Foreigners	0.98	2.04
Others	2.59	—

Once more, what changes there were appear to have little significance in the light of the government's cherished objectives.

EDUCATION OF WOMEN

As early as 1881 the Commission on the Question of Strengthening the Supervision of Student Youth, of which Delianov served as chairman, concluded that the Higher Courses for Women should be immediately either terminated or "reorganized on a new basis." Yet the political considerations mentioned earlier prevented action at that time. Nonetheless, in 1882, after D.A. Miliutin's retirement as Minister of War, the Women's Medical Courses offered by the Nikolaevsky Military Hospital in St. Petersburg were discontinued.[25]

During the mid-1880s the question of abolishing the Higher Courses for Women was once again placed on the agenda. This time the initiative evidently came from Prince Meshchersky. On November 16, in one of the diaries forwarded to Alexander III, he penned a note favoring the closing of the women's courses: "I have been at Gresser's (the Petersburg city governor) . . . . During our conversation he made some interesting observations on the Higher Courses for Women. According to him, the present courses are a mask for the anarchist contagion." A few days later, on November 19, Meshchersky returned to this issue. "I had supper with Delianov last evening," he wrote, "and told him of my ideas on the Higher Courses for Women. Delianov completely shares my distrust and dislike of these courses. He intends to raise the question of ending such courses—but gradually—by closing further entry into them. Thank God!"

In 1886 a special commission, under the chairmanship of Delianov, was convened to consider this issue. It included representatives from the Interior and Education ministries. They concluded "that while no statute, order or regulation has been worked out, it is necessary to stop the further congregation in the cities of unmarried girls who are not seeking an education so much as freedom—a word they frequently misinterpret." Delianov presented a report along these lines to Alexander III. He proposed closing entry to the Higher Courses for Women until a law could be prepared to deal with these institutions. And on May 12, 1886 Alexander III approved this request of his Minister of Education.

Delianov's archives contain a signed carbon copy of what was evidently a confidential letter concerning the termination of admission into the Higher Courses for Women. "The data," Delianov wrote, "presented by Generals Orzhevsky and Gresser, the Chief of the Kiev Gendarme Administration (Vasili D.) Novitsky, the Superintendents of the Education Districts, and two professors of the University of Kiev who have investigated the women's courses in Kiev, present a very sorrowful picture . . . . In order to prevent further harm . . . the M(inistry) of Ed(ucation) has given orders that the admission of new students into the existing Higher Courses for Women in Petersburg, Moscow, Kiev and Kazan is to be halted until new regulations are drawn up for the Higher

Courses for Women." Hence this step evidently was based on information provided by the gendarmes.

At the beginning of 1888 the chairwomen of the Petersburg Society for Raising Funds for Higher Courses for Women petitioned Alexander III to reopen admission to the courses, and he agreed. She requested some indication of the form such courses should take and, by this time, the Ministry of Education had readied special regulations on the subject. These permitted the Higher Courses for Women to be set up in a private educational institution so that no special rights would be conferred on their graduates. The size of the student body was set at four hundred, and the courses were to be divided into two sections: historical-philological and physico-mathematical. The students attending the courses had to live either with their parents and relatives, or in a dormitory.

On June 13 and 20, 1889 the Committee of Ministers examined and approved these regulations. Entrance to such courses was to be "provisionally" permitted as of August, 1889, "prior to the issuing through legislative channels of general provisions concerning the question of the organization and content of Higher Courses for Women." In other cities, apart from St. Petersburg, entrance into these courses was finally reopened only in 1890.

SECONDARY EDUCATION

No really major problem confronted the government in the area of secondary education. Tolstoy, as Minister of Education in the 1870s, had already established the classical system. Hated by teachers, students and parents alike, this system was perceived as a deliberate means of dulling the minds of Russian youth. "All (the student's) attention," B.N. Chicherin recalled in his memoirs, "was concentrated on a sterile cramming of grammatical forms that neither animated youthful minds with the living spirit of the classical writers nor gave them a decent knowledge of the language. F.E. Korsh, who as Professor of Classical Literature in the University of Moscow was in the position to be the best judge, was astonished because the students entering the university knew less Latin than previously even though the number of hours (they spent on this subject) had been doubled . . . . And along with this growing stupidity about grammar, the most important subjects taught in the gymnasiums—history, Russian language and Russian literature—were completely neglected. The younger generation even forgot how to write." Since this evaluation aptly describes the reality of the classical system, the comments of other authorities can add but little.

From the government's point of view, the positive side of the classical system was that it stifled Russian youth, distracted them from social questions, and simultaneously created a cultural barrier for the poorer students who wanted to enter the university. In his report to Alexander III for 1890, Delianov made this quite clear: "One should not lose sight of the fact," he wrote, "that because of the present structure of our society, it is impossible to establish regulations forcing the universities to accept only the gentry and, in general, students belonging to the upper estates. Therefore the easier the course in the secondary schools is made, the greater will be the influx of persons of all estates into the universities." Yet even in this regard the classical systems proved a failure, as the pass levels in gymnasiums and progymnasiums, as well as in the technical schools, were greatly lowered. Delianov's report for 1884 showed the gymnasiums had passed 68.2 percent of their students in 1883, and 68.8 percent in 1884. The percentages for the progymnasiums in these years were 65.3 and 65.5, and for the technical schools 66.9 and 69.1 respectively.[26]

There was, meanwhile, an extraordinary growth in the number of "voluntary" drop-outs. "From 1882," Delianov wrote in his 1884 report, "the number of students who have voluntarily left secondary school before completing their course has increased annually. In the Vilna Education District the percentage of such students was 15.2 in 1882, 19.2 in 1883, and 20.6 in 1884." This is evidence of the abnormal state of affairs existing in these schools but to the Minister of Education these figures meant nothing of the kind. He insisted that his basic task was rigidly to preserve the classical education system, even though he admitted that the secondary schools had to "be put in order" (for, he claimed, they had been shaken up by his predecessors—Andrei A. Saburov and Baron Nikolai). As noted above, Delianov began this process with his circular of November 20, 1882. His efforts to strengthen "discipline and order" in the schools, and attempts to change the composition of student enrollment by admitting only children from the prosperous sections of the population, were further steps in the same direction. Nicholas I's gymnasium regulations of 1828 were obviously Delianov's ideal.[27]

During the period under review the Ministry of Education made full use, as did the police, of informers to maintain surveillance of the students. The primary responsibility was placed on the class tutors, whose role was increased by a circular of June 26, 1884. It stated openly that "when the class tutor is visiting a student, he is to attempt, among other things, to ascertain what persons have visited the student's rooms, with whom he has had dealings, and the subject matter of his leisure reading." The same document ordered that when superintendents of the education districts were selecting people for the posts of director and inspector in secondary schools, and making recommendations for rewards, they were "first of all to keep in mind those class tutors who have steadily and with conspicuous success carried out the training and moral development of the students so that every aspect of their lives has been affected . . . ."

The concluding paragraph made clear which "aspects of their lives" should be of greatest interest to the class tutors. It instructed that "class tutors will bear an equal responsibility with the director and inspector if the pernicious influence of false ideas, disseminated by ill-intentioned persons, is discovered in the classes entrusted to them, or if any of the young people themselves are observed participating in any criminal plot and these acts are not discovered in good time by the institution." In this way responsibilities usually allotted to the police were assigned to school administrators and class tutors.

"Training" the students meant, of course, inculcating in them the spirit of autocratic and feudal ideas. Here another of Delianov's special circulars merits examination. This directed that it was inadmissible to omit a student's title from a class list (that is, evidently, from the class records). "An educational institution," read the circular, "does not have the right to neglect to identify a student by the titles belonging to his family. As this could cause the student to forget the honors of his ancestors, which should edify and serve him as the ideal for his own life, I therefore request . . . that orders be given by the education districts to eliminate the aforementioned irregularities."

As early as 1879, during Tolstoy's term of office, the Ministry of Education had instituted the so-called "black list." This meant that a secondary school student who had been implicated "in reprehensible activities" of a political nature, and expelled from his school, lost the right of admission to any other. A circular letter from the minister informed all schools of this fact. Delianov now re-established and expanded the use of this procedure. The Ministry of Education's archives contain numerous circulars stating that a certain student has been expelled "for a stubborn and recurrent unwillingness to submit to the orders of the gymnasium's authorities," or "for his extremely insolent manner with regard to the gymnasium's authorities." True, there is no explicit order that the person named was forbidden admission into another educational institution but the very fact that such information was circulated speaks for itself. Take, to cite one example, a secret circular of December 13, 1883 which reported that "the director of the Kherson Progymnasium and an assistant class tutor of the Second Odessa Progymnasium encountered (two students) on the street. The first was Ratner, a student in the final year of the Elizavetgrad Progymnasium.

He was dressed in peculiar clothing, carrying a walking stick, and had a cigar in his mouth, but he wore the gymnasium student's peaked cap, with its badge, on his head. The second was Alexis Vasilkovsky, a former student of the Odessa St. Paul Realschule, who had been dismissed in accordance with Article 17 of the Regulations. He was wearing a gymnasium topcoat as a cloak." When these youths were stopped by the aforementioned "responsible persons," who demanded to see their student cards, one student replied rudely, while the other "went further and insulted the assistant class tutor." Then the circular concluded with the stereotyped phrase: "We have the honor of imparting the above to your Excellencies for your information, in case you may receive applications . . . for their admittance into one of the educational institutions entrusted to your districts for the continuance of their studies."

This signifies, naturally, that their admission was prohibited; otherwise there would have been no need of a circular. Further, the Ministry of Education insisted that regulations regarding uniforms be observed "to the letter." Indeed, Delianov had to issue a special circular (in response to a petition of one superintendent) that permitted the wearing of an oilskin coat and hood "over the uniform" during rainstorms. Otherwise the students would have had to continue wearing soaking gymnasium uniforms. It was by these methods that the ministry hoped to strengthen "discipline and order" in its secondary school system.

SOCIAL ORIGINS OF SECONDARY STUDENTS

One of Delianov's other objectives was to change the social composition of the gymnasium student bodies and to transform these schools into semi-privileged institutions. Although some efforts were made in the early years of his ministry, it was only in 1887 that the minister began to act in earnest.

The first step towards restricting the admission of children with certain categories of parents was taken early in that year, and behind it lay a definite plan. A circular of February 19, 1887 prohibited the entry into gymnasiums of children whose parents were prostitutes, brothel-owners or tavern-keepers.[28] These pupils might be admitted only "in exceptional cases" with the sanction of the ministry and on condition that the child was found to be "uninfluenced by a vicious environment" (that is, by having lived in the students' dormitory of a boarding school rather than at home).

Contrary to what one might expect, the real reasons behind this and other similar measures were political in nature. On April 11, 1887 Delianov presented to Alexander III a report entitled "On Closing Admission into Preparatory Courses of Gymnasiums and Progymnasiums for the School Year 1887-1888." This began by pointing out that originally the preparatory classes had had a positive influence, for "even more educated and prosperous families had difficulty in providing their children with any proper basic preparation for admission to a gymnasium." Once these preparatory classes were established, however, children "from families of every class and condition" had begun to enroll in them.[29] This had increased the difficulties of children "who had received a better training, due to the condition of their families and a good preparation at home," and who were seeking entry into the first grades of the gymnasiums. "Thus," Delianov argued, "the preparatory classes have facilitated the preparation of everyone for an education in the gymnasiums. This has, of course, served to attract to the gymnasiums and progymnasiums the children of those classes of society who should be satisfied with an education in the lower schools. Now, on the contrary, they (the preparatory classes) are hindering the entry into gymnasiums of children from the more educated families."

For this reason the minister recommended that entry into these classes be closed during the 1887-1888 school year, and that preparatory classes finally be abolished in the following school year. Alexander agreed and the measure was approved.[30]

On June 5 of that year the minister presented the emperor with another report: "On Curtailing the Number of Gymnasium and Progymnasium Students and Changing the Enrollment Composition." Outlining the history of this question, Delianov recalled that a commission of the ministers of Education, Interior, State Domains, Finance, and the Director-General of the Holy Synod had concluded that the admission of children from the less prosperous classes into gymnasiums and progymnasiums should be restricted. This commission also had proposed banning the entry into these schools of children whose parents were lower in rank than merchant of the second guild. At that time Delianov had intended to submit this proposal, once it received the emperor's preliminary approval, for consideration by the Committee of Ministers. His report makes it clear, nonetheless, that Alexander III thought this measure "inopportune and inappropriate." The tsar thought it "better to achieve the goal of averting an influx of those children, considered unsuited for secondary education because of their home conditions, into gymnasiums and progymnasiums by some other means."[31] Even Alexander III recognized the impossibility of discussing such a measure in the Committee of Ministers, let alone the more independent State Council.

In his report of June 5, 1887 Delianov noted that he had consulted the ministerial commission further on this question. This body concluded that, apart from a raise in tuition fees, one ought "at least . . . to make it clear to the authorities of the gymnasiums and progymnasiums that they were to accept into their schools only those children who are found in the care of persons who can be a sufficient guarantee of proper supervision at home and who can provide the financial resources necessary for the completion of their education. A stringent observance of this regulation will free the gymnasiums and progymnasiums of the children of coachmen, servants, cooks, laundresses, petty tradesmen, and other such persons, because their children, with the exception, perhaps, of those endowed with genius, should not properly seek a secondary or higher education."[32]

This time Alexander III approved the proposal of his education minister. On June 18 a circular was issued announcing that the categories of children indicated above were not to be admitted to the gymnasiums. This circular developed in more detail the idea that it would be harmful to lead these children "to an attitude of disrespect toward their parents, to dissatisfaction with their existence, and to a sense of bitterness about the existing and, by the nature of things, inevitable inequality of property relations." Apart from banning the entry of children from the lower strata of the population, the circular ordered that "if there remain among the students already admitted those who owing to the home circumstances of their parents or their relatives are having a harmful influence upon their comrades, they should be expelled from the gymnasium or progymnasium without regard for the two-year term indicated in Article 34 of the Gymnasium and Progymnasium Statute, or for the formal regulations on punishment." In this way the circular suggested an immediate purge of the gymnasium students, regardless of the limits of the existing regulations and laws. The minister concluded by stressing the need of a raise in tuition fees in gymnasiums where they had not yet reached the prescribed level.

This document became known as "the circular on cooks' children" and gained a great deal of notoriety. It stirred the indignation of the democratic segments of the population, of the intelligentsia, and of some members of the ruling classes. General Kireev, adjutant to Grand Duke Konstantin Nikolaevich, wrote in his diary on September 2, 1887, that "Delianov's circular is causing indignation and laughter. He wrote that the dir(ectors) were not to admit the children of hall porters, cooks, doormen, and so on, into the gym(nasiums). How stupid can one be? In the first place, there might well be some Lomonosovs among them and, secondly, one could have achieved exactly the same result without any publicity. This could be done, for ex(ample), by simply demanding more difficult entrance examinations in, say, Fre(nch) and

Ger(man), or by giving orders for better training for the poverty-stricken gentry, whom it is advisable to support. But, worst of all, the circular itself is *illegal*; the law makes no provision for any such restrictions."[33]

Even an obscurantist like Meshchersky was scandalized by Delianov's instructions. "I will not conceal from you," he wrote Alexander III on September 4, 1887, "that daily I am visited by people from the provinces who sadly tell of the very bad impression that Delianov's 'cooks circular' has made on everyone. Their irritation and anger are aroused because, as you know, it is not Delianov who is being censured, but rather it is you yourself who is the subject of all the talk. I have implored Delianov to write an explanatory circular that would mollify people and efface the impression he has made, but what is my voice? . . . ."[34] Meshchersky also made every effort to belittle the circular's significance in the pages of his own paper, the *Citizen*. "For some reason," he wrote hypocritically, "this circular has been regarded by public opinion, as expressed in the press, as an attempt to place limits on some aspiration for higher education among the people, and to block this road for persons of the unprivileged and non-propertied estates. Distorted gossip leads to such absurdities that it is possible for newspapers to say that the government has resolved to prevent all estates, apart from the nobility, from entering the gymnasiums."

The liberal press was naturally indignant about the circular. In its lead article for August 27, 1887, the *Russian News* pointed out that "it still remains uncertain as to how it (the circular) fits in with the existing law. The law permits children of all estates, without regard for rank, to study in the gymnasiums (Article 23 of the statute of July 30, 1871). Yet the Honorable Minister's circular abolishes this law which, as such, can be abolished only by legislative action." The *European Herald* analysed Delianov's circular in greater detail. In his "Domestic Review" for September, 1887, K.K. Arseniev treated the document in a very sharp manner. He argued it was absolutely absurd to assert that the less prosperous children lacked the atmosphere for study, or that they were morally depraved. "From among the impoverished gymnasium students," Arseniev pointed out, "are recruited the numerous class of tutors, and this allows one to maintain that not only does poverty not constitute an absolute obstacle to studying, but that it actually furthers a combination of school work and outside occupations . . . . Persistent and conscientious labor is the best guarantee against moral degeneration and the best substitute for insufficient home supervision. This is why there is no way that one can claim that the gymnasium students with the worst moral attitudes come exclusively from the families of laundresses, coachmen, 'and other such people.' Were this the case, morality would have flourished all the more in educational institutions open solely to the higher estates. And can we really say that this is the case?" After this caustic observation, Arseniev demonstrated that Delianov's willingness to admit children "endowed with genius" was pure demagoguery. "How are they to ascertain the extent of such genius," he wrote, "if a refusal, based on the investigation of 'home circumstances' precedes admission to the entrance examinations?"

Delianov's circular succeeded in outraging all levels of Russian society but, as a result of the measures excluding poorer children (that is, abolishing preparatory classes, raising tuition fees, and openly banning the admission of certain groups of the population), the social composition of gymnasium students changed somewhat. This is apparent from the following statistics on students' social origins:

Social Status of Parents	1884	1892
Hereditary and Personal Nobles, and Officials	49.2%	56.2%
Ecclesiastical	5.0	3.9
Urban Estates	35.9	31.3
Peasants and Others	7.9	5.9
Foreigners	2.0	1.9[35]

That such changes were deliberately created is shown by the fact that during the same period the social composition of the modern school students was altering in the opposite direction.[36] This can be seen from the following statistics:

Social Status of Parents	1884	1892
Hereditary and Personal Nobles, and Officials	42.7%	38.0%
Ecclesiastical	1.8	0.9
Urban Estates	41.8	43.0
Peasantry and Others	10.9	12.7
Foreigners	4.8	5.4

It should also be remembered that the sum total of students in male gymnasiums and progymnasiums had, between 1885 and 1894, diminished from 72,592 to 63,004.[37]

MODERN SCHOOLS

At this point it is worth looking at the measures affecting the secondary schools, and especially the modern schools (Realschulen) that were discussed in the normal legislative process. In November, 1886 Delianov presented the draft "Statute for Modern and Industrial Schools" to the State Council.[38] This legislation envisaged a basic reorganization of the modern schools which would transform them into general educational institutions for training specialists with a secondary-school level of technical education.[39] According to the draft, the preparation of specialists at the secondary level would be divided into two stages. The first, a five-year general educational stage, would be the purpose of the modern schools. "The modern schools," stated the first section of the draft statute, "have as their aim the provision of a general education, accommodated to practical needs and the acquisition of technical knowledge at the secondary level by the youths studying in them."

The second stage was to be a four-year course in special technical schools. These would provide training which, "although elementary, is fundamental and fully practical." Along with this, the modern schools themselves might hold supplementary classes and thereby serve as secondary technical schools for commercial, technical, agricultural, engineering, and other similar subjects. This basic reorganization would make impossible the admission of modern school graduates into the higher technical educational establishments. "The higher specialist schools," commented Delianov, "have no need of special educational institutions, with a course of study easier than that of the gymnasium, to prepare students for them."

The section dealing with the reorganization of the modern schools in Delianov's draft was a logical continuation and completion of the reforms of 1871. Only one type of secondary general educational school would be preserved—the classical gymnasium. Polovtsov, describing Delianov's proposal in his diary, wrote: "The whole draft aims at the destruction of practical education and would make available only an insignificant training in handicrafts. The modern school student will lose even the right of transferring to one of the higher technical schools, which in the future will be filled by students from the classical gymnasiums."

Delianov's plan was discussed in the Combined Departments on February 7, March 7, and April 9, 1887. While the draft's proposals on the development of technical education were generally approved, disagreement arose over the proper purpose of the modern school. Five members (Delianov, Vyshnegradsky, Plehve, Veshniakov, Vannovsky) "took the view that there was no need for modern schools which would prepare their graduates for entry into the higher specialist or technical schools, for a sufficient number of gymnasiums already existed to serve this purpose." These five thought this measure would lead naturally to a reduction in the number of students admitted to the higher educational institutions. Since at that time there were some 700 to 800 admissions a year from the modern schools, this decline in admissions would produce a general reduction of between three to four thousand in the total number of students. Still, "in the opinion of the five members, there is no reason to deplore this (reduction) as, in the field of higher education, quality is much more important than quantity. Here quality has suffered, and continues to suffer greatly, because of, firstly, the overcrowding of the universities and, secondly, the lowering of moral and intellectual standards in the specialist schools which are filled almost exclusively by graduates of the modern schools." But a majority in the Combined Departments took a different stand. Thirteen members, including A.A. Abaza, Kaufmann, Kakhanov, Bunge, and Konstantin K. Grot, believed that the modern schools should be general educational institutions preparing student contingents for entry into the higher specialist educational establishments.

Discussions in the General Session of the State Council also produced no unanimity of opinion. Eight council members (Tolstoy, Delianov, Vyshnegradsky, Vannovsky, and others) supported the view of the Combined Departments' minority that the modern schools should have a five year course "to provide a general education accommodated to practical demands and to the acquisition of technical education at the secondary level." Nonetheless, the majority of the State Council (thirty-four members) supported the views of the Combined Departments' thirteen members,[40] although they argued their case in a rather original manner. "One must not forget," stated their decision, "that the classical gymnasiums, despite all their virtues, do not achieve their goals without victims. Many youths, even talented ones, find the task of studying ancient languages beyond their ability. First they fall behind and then, usually before the sixth year, they drop out completely, without finishing the course. At present such youths can transfer to modern schools, receive an education there, and so become useful to society. With the closure of the modern schools there will be nowhere to place them . . . . Because of this such youths will become failures in the full sense of the word and will merely increase the contingent of the dissatisfied, which is the most dangerous element in the country." It was evident, the council majority concluded, that the closing of the modern schools would be a serious blow to "the upper classes of society." In their opinion, this blow would be "felt especially by that part of the impoverished gentry who have not held their own in the economic struggle with the other classes of the population. The ever-prospering merchants and petty bourgeoisie will have no difficulty in sending their children to gymnasiums and universities. Yet with the closure of the modern schools the poorer gentry will lose the only modest—but still independent of private wealth—avenue of practical education open to them and that allows their children entry into positions of public service." For these reasons the majority of the council maintained that "the children of the gentry, raised by enlightened customs and in a sound understanding of social and governmental responsibilities, will be rapidly pushed out by the children of people who have just risen from a position of serfdom and total ignorance."

The majority had still one other argument to advance. The plan to down-grade educationally the existing one hundred and four modern schools, in which over twenty thousand students were then studying, would cause their parents—for the most part officials or members of the gentry—to wish to withdraw their children from these institutions. "Only extremity," the majority argued, "will compel them (the parents) to submit to the distressing necessity of seeing their sons in the service of some industrial tycoon, merchant or factory owner, and occupying a subordinate position as a hired technician, salesman, or factory foreman." For this reason parents would rush to get their children into gymnasiums and, as the existing gymnasiums would be unable to meet the demand, new gymnasiums would have to be opened.

These arguments could not but influence Alexander III, who considered himself to be the "foremost nobleman" in Russia. On looking through the journal of the council's debates, he concluded: "This bill is to be dropped. I have given the Min(ister) of Edu(cation) orders on this matter." Despite this rebuff Delianov, in October, 1887, placed an amended draft ("On Modern Schools and Industrial Schools") before the State Council. Now the modern schools were, in accordance with the emperor's will, to have a six-year course of study. Otherwise, the draft remained as before. In other words, the modern schools were to be educational institutions providing a general education to persons entering secondary technical schools. Although the modern school course was extended from five years to six, the new draft offered no expansion of the program of studies suggested earlier. Delianov, having received the tsar's orders to retain the six-year modern school course, left the rest of his previous draft untouched.

The Combined Departments discussed this proposal in November, 1887, and January, 1888. Although approving the organization of industrial schools, the departments retained their doubts about a basic reorganization of the existing modern schools and decided "to separate the question of these schools entirely from the other matters discussed." Complying with this demand Delianov, on March 11, 1888, presented a new draft statute for the modern schools alone. This time no serious disagreements arose in the Combined Departments and the proposed statute, which preserved the existing organization of the modern schools, was approved.

The Combined Departments' resolution stated that, apart from the six basic classes, the modern schools were "to establish preparatory classes where these could be maintained by using the available means." The fifth and sixth classes, "depending on local needs," might be divided into two branches: a general section and a commercial (or some other) one. Finally, a fourth point ordered that "in the general section one further, higher and supplementary class may be established to prepare students for entry into the higher educational establishments." Thus, in the final analysis, Tolstoy and Delianov failed in their attempt to destroy the modern schools as secondary educational institutions.

THE CLASSICAL GYMNASIUMS

Whatever admiration existed within the Ministry of Education for the classical system of gymnasium education, it could not remain blind to the particular deficiencies so continuously criticized in the press. "I cannot," wrote Delianov in a presentation to the State Council in 1889, "pass over in silence the several deficiencies revealed during these eighteen years (1871-1889) and the somewhat one-sided manner in which the instructions of the Ministry of Education have been applied in the teaching department. This narrow application is reflected unfavorably in the success of teaching particular subjects. Thus, for example, the teaching of ancient languages has been, generally speaking, more or less dominated by a one-sided grammatical approach. The study of a detailed course of grammar and exercises in the translation of separate sentences and artificially composed fragments from Russian into the ancient language, therefore, has pushed the reading and explanation of writers into second place. Frequently the texts of writers have served mainly as material for oral and written exercises in etymological forms and syntactical changes."

In the spring of 1889 a large commission, under the chairmanship of M.S. Volkonsky, was created to review the existing programs. The work of this commission was guided by four principles. The first of these was, *while preserving the existing classical system of education*, to establish shorter programs that would not damage the substance of that education." The second principle was the continued concentration on the study of ancient grammar in the junior classes, but the allotment of more time in the senior classes to reading texts from ancient authors. The third consideration was a proposed lightening of students' homework and, fourthly, a means was to be found to distribute the weekly lessons more evenly.

As a result of this commission's labors, in March, 1890 Delianov brought before the State Council a proposal "On Changing the Scheduled

Number of Weekly Hours in Male Gymnasiums."[41] This sought a reduction in the number of weekly lessons in ancient languages (from 49 to 46 in Latin, and from 36 to 35 in Greek),[42] but, at the same time it entailed the removal of natural history instruction (introduced in 1877) from the school curriculum. "I recognize it as unconditionally necessary," wrote Delianov, "to exclude natural history from the number of subjects in the gymnasium course . . . . While the study of this subject is recognized as being of some use, inasmuch as it acquaints the students with the products of the three realms that surround us and at the same time develops in the students the valuable ability to observe and compare material objects, nonetheless the contribution of this subject to the formal development of students is probably very limited at best." In addition, Delianov maintained that the study of natural history would only be worthwhile if eight hours a week were devoted to it. That, he said, was impossible. Meanwhile, the number of weekly geography lessons were reduced from ten to eight.

The number of weekly lessons allotted to some other subjects was increased. Those devoted to the "law of God" were expanded by two, and one was added to the study of Russian. It was recommended further that "the teaching of the history of Russian literature be replaced by the reading and analysis of the more remarkable works in the Russian language." (The definition of "remarkable" was, of course, open to various interpretations!) With regard to history, Delianov wanted the episodic junior course replaced by an elementary one, as well as some redistribution of lessons within this subject which would increase the time spent on Russian history. Another increase of two hours was suggested for lessons in penmanship.

In analysing this project one must note first its reactionary character. Apart from the small—or better, minimal—cutback in the number of hours devoted to the ancient languages (more or less forced upon the authorities) and the somewhat decreased attention given to Latin and Greek grammar, the other proposals held retrograde and restrictive purposes. An increase in the number of hours spent studying the "law of God," the exclusion of natural history from the curriculum, and the abolition of a systematic course in the history of Russian literature, offer sufficient evidence of the considerations guiding those who had drawn up the bill.

During April and mid-May, 1890 the Combined Departments of Laws and the State Economy examined both this presentation and an earlier proposal for extending summer vacations to two months. This second proposal aroused no opposition but the first provoked serious arguments that reflected the hostility felt by the majority of the council's members toward the system of classical education. Polovtsov, describing the Combined Departments' first session in his diary, wrote: "A meeting of the Combined Departments on Delianov's proposal for decreasing the number of lessons in gymnasiums. The proposal is essentially misleading because the work is increased rather than decreased. Still, in order to calm the general dissatisfaction, the number of hours allotted to the Latin and Greek languages are somewhat curtailed. The council passed on to the question of curtailing classical studies. (Peter G.) Redkin, Bunge, Filippov and Vyshnegradsky all favored this. In the end, all those present, except for Delianov, considered it necessary to reduce the 14 weekly lessons in Latin and Greek . . . . After a five-hour debate Delianov, finding himself alone, declared that he would consider and think through this question."

Finally, at the end of a three-day discussion, Delianov compromised on the number of hours assigned to Latin. These were cut from 46 to 42 hours per week, but he remained steadfast on all the remaining points. Pobedonostsev, Ostrovsky and Plehve supported him, but the remaining sixteen members of the Combined Departments considered that 42 hours of Latin were still too many. They argued in favor of 36 hours and that the other six should be devoted to natural history.

These members insisted that "an acquaintance with the natural world around us is necessary for a general secondary education . . . . The students' complete ignorance of the basics of natural science would be a painful flaw in their knowledge and make it difficult for them, as once was the case, to pursue courses in the higher applied sciences." In addition, the majority also opposed abolishment of the course in the history of Russian literature. The minority justified this step by the unsatisfactory way in which this subject was taught. "Not infrequently," they claimed, "the teachers do not read the works of literature themselves, but give bad outlines of opinions (themselves frequently very unsatisfactory) concerning these works, and this only leads to arguments." The majority, however, remained unconvinced.

On May 28 the General Session of the council considered this proposal. The Combined Departments' minority opinion was supported by five members of the council, among whom were the three members of the minority themselves (Pobedonostsev, Ostrovsky and Delianov). Now they were supported by Durnovo, the Minister of the Interior, and Peter I. Salomin, another council member. Their views were opposed by the remaining thirty-four members, who supported the departments' sixteen-member majority opinion. "The Council," Polovtsov recorded in his diary, "discussed the matter of the number of Greek and Latin lessons. Abaza caustically ridiculed Delianov, who begged forgiveness for having so capriciously changed his mind three times." Nevertheless, even though a majority in both the Combined Departments and the General Session opposed the minister's bill, the emperor approved the minority opinion. Thus Delianov, by means of an insignificant reduction in the hours of teaching for Greek and Latin, succeeded in abolishing Russian literature and natural history from the teaching curriculum.

ELEMENTARY SCHOOLS

During the reign of Alexander III there were no major changes in the primary school system although the number of schools under ecclesiastical control increased rapidly. In 1879 the Committee of Ministers had examined a measure "On Granting the Orthodox Clergy Proper Influence in National Education." This was discussed in connection with other proposed measures for the suppression of "anti-government propoganda" (in other words, revolutionary ideas). At that time the ministerial committee "expressed its unanimous conviction that the moral and religious development of the people, who are the basic bricks of every state system, cannot be achieved without the clergy playing a predominant role in the work of the public schools."

It was not until 1884 that a practical step was taken in this direction by the law of June 13 on parish schools subordinated to the Holy Synod. This measure concentrated parish and grammar schools in the ecclesiastical system[43] and made a decisive move toward placing primary education in the hands of the clergy—a goal cherished by Pobedonostsev. Nonetheless, the actual problems of organizing these schools, which were to be run by the parish priests, aroused serious misgivings. The clergy had to conduct daily services and prayers, and many people worried that these duties would interfere with the normal operation of the schools. Even such an ardent champion of every reactionary measure as Katkov voiced these fears in the lead articles of the *Moscow News* for December 14 and 15, 1884.

In any case, parish schools began to spring up like mushrooms following the rain. In 1884 there had been some 4,000[44] but, according to the Synod's data, in 1893-1894 there was a grand total of 31,835 such schools with almost one million (981,076) students enrolled. Further, in 1893 these schools cost 3,079,685 rubles.[45]

During the early 1890s secular elementary schools again came under attack. In 1891 Delianov issued a circular ordering that when a new school was opened by the Ministry of Education, the latter's officials were "first to get in touch with the ecclesiastical authorities." At the same time, however, the Senate ruled that officials of the Ministry of Education were not obliged to accept "as absolutely binding the opinions communicated by ecclesiastical representatives or to make the opening of new secular schools dependent on an agreement with the spiritual authorities." Yet all this made the work of the Ministry of Education very difficult and, during the latter half of the 1880s and the early 1890s, the number of parish schools increased substantially, even if the data on this growth remains far from reliable. The absence of proper organization, and the desire of local ecclesiastical authorities to report their own successes, meant that statistics were not very strictly recorded and inaccuracies naturally erred on the side of exaggeration.

On this matter we have direct—and sufficiently authoritative—evidence from General Kireev, whose sources are undoubtedly trustworthy. "Count Tolstoy, Minister of the I(nterior)," he sadly noted in his diary on June 5, 1894, "told Georgievsky that he has completely accurate information that the Church schools exist only on paper. Sasha (Georgievsky) confirms this view. One marshal of the nobility told Georgievsky that in his locality, according to the ecclesiastical department, there are calculated to be 104 (or 94) schools. In fact, there are only four or five. Yes, and with what joy the news that the schools had been assigned to the jurisdiction of the Holy Synod was greeted."[46] Thus, while there was a certain increase in the activities of these schools, it was significantly less than was claimed. One must conclude from this that a number of factors—the absence of proper conditions for the organizing of the parish schools, the opposition of the local zemstvo organizations, and so on—prevented the government from successfully liquidating the secular elementary school system.

CHAPTER VIII

THE LAW ON LAND CAPTAINS

ORIGINS

At the end of 1885 A.D. Pazukhin, now ensconced in the Ministry of the Interior, began working on the draft of a major counter-reform. By the spring of 1886 he had completed his task. Apparently the original drafts have been lost but Pobedonostsev, Pazukhin himself, and Feoktistov, who received his information from Minister of State Domains Ostrovsky, have left accounts about the nature of the project. In his diary Feoktistov claimed that Pazukhin had drawn up this proposal, which envisaged the creation of new officials called land captains and a reform of the zemstvos, without even consulting Tolstoy.

In March of 1886 Pazukhin finished his report and presented it to his minister. Although Tolstoy, in Feoktistov's words, was "completely satisfied with it," he decided to show the report to his closest colleagues before presenting it to Alexander III and the State Council. Pazukhin's draft was therefore sent to Pobedonostsev, Ostrovsky, and Minister of Justice Manasein. Several days later, on April 2, Tolstoy invited them, as well as Pazukhin, to a meeting on the subject. Feoktistov, who evidently had been told of the meeting's proceedings by Ostrovsky, wrote: "Alas! It was immediately apparent that there were some sharp criticisms. It was not that anyone questioned the basic principles of the reforms. Everyone agreed that it was necessary to establish a firm authority in the administration of the peasants and to turn the zemstvos into organs that served, rather than opposed, the government. But everyone also pointed out the flagrant defects and absurdities contained in the draft. Pazukhin's replies were far from convincing and Tolstoy made almost no response at all. He was as depressed as he could be." Feoktistov further said that Tolstoy considered Manasein to be the main critic and that he had made up his mind to complain to the tsar about him.

Manasein was not Tolstoy's only problem. Neither Pobedonostsev nor Ostrovsky solidly supported him and, according to Feoktistov, even Plehve, Tolstoy's own assistant minister, raised objections on becoming acquainted with it. Pazukhin's first efforts therefore resulted in a complete fiasco.

Pobedonostsev, in his letter of April 18 to Alexander III, outlined the contents of the first draft. It proposed that a "county land captain" be established as a county institution. Appointed on the emperor's authority, the new official would unite both judicial and administrative powers. Meanwhile the justice of the peace would be abolished in the countryside and the more complicated judicial cases, Pazukhin suggested, could be forwarded to the city justices of the peace. Otherwise, complaints concerning the decisions of land captains would be examined by a county board of these officials. At the same time Pazukhin proposed changes in the zemstvo electoral system and the replacing of zemstvo boards by new executive organs, to be called the "Office for Zemstvo Affairs." This new office would be composed of the local administration and two members from the zemstvo.

Pobedonostsev reported that all those who discussed the draft supported its spirit "but, when it came down to the details, everyone was bewildered. This immediate response is explained by the immense problems of uniting administrative authority and judicial powers in the single person of the land captain as proposed by Pazukhin." Hence the basic objections evidently concerned the land captain's judicial functions.

Pazukhin himself, in a letter written to Katkov several days before the conference, maintained that Pobedonostsev originally had been favorably impressed by his proposals. Then, under Manasein's influence, the director-general had changed his mind and become convinced: "1) that with regard to peasant affairs the reform should be limited to transferring the supervision of peasant administration to the existing justices of the peace; and 2) that one should retain for the zemstvo assemblies a certain influence in appointment to posts, even if this meant the election of candidates. This is a well-known liberal demand. I tried to bring Pobedonostsev to a sound view of this matter, and I succeeded. But it is impossible to be certain of him. Man(asein) has a strong influence on him."

In another letter, written after the meeting in April, Pazukhin reported: "The results of the recent meeting of ministers was celebrated by Petersburg as a victory of Manasein over Tolstoy and of liberalism over reaction. It is impossible to say with any certainty that Pobedonostsev had freed himself from Manasein's influence. He (Manasein) is an intelligent man, with a strong character and a terrible self-esteem. Once he has come out against the very basis of the reform, he will not deviate from this course and will hold prisoner   Konstan(in) Petr-(ovich)'s intelligence and weak will. In addition, it is impossible to count on Ostrovsky. He also lacks firm principles." Nonetheless Pazukhin had not abandoned all hope of bringing pressure on Pobedonostsev in order "to free him from the influence" of Manasein. When Pobedonostsev travelled south during the summer of 1886 he planned to stop for several days in Moscow and, on June 7, Pazukhin sent a special letter to Katkov requesting the latter to use his influence on the Director-General of the Holy Synod.

During the course of 1886 the draft legislation was revised in the Ministry of the Interior by a Special Commission created by Tolstoy for this purpose. Consisting of ten members, the commission was headed by Assistant Minister of the Interior Prince K.D. Gagarin, but its driving force was Pazukhin. This body included governors (N.P. Dolgovo-Saburov of Simbirsk, I.M. Sudienko of Vladimir, Victor V. Kalachev of Kostroma, and Alexis F. Anisin of Viatka) and provincial marshals of the nobility (Andrei E. Zarin of Pskov, P.A. Krivsky of Saratov, Gregory V. Kondoidi of Tambov, and A.R. Shidlovsky of Kharkov). Their discussions lasted seventeen sessions, held from September to November, 1886. On the basic question at issue—the granting of judicial authority to land captains—the Special Commission supported Pazukhin. Only Shidlovsky firmly rejected this step, declaring that "neither in our own, nor in any foreign legislation can one find an example of such extensive powers being granted to a single official, or even to a whole collegiate body." Nonetheless, in the end only some insignificant amendments were made in the draft and these were mainly reactionary in nature.[1]

On December 18 Tolstoy presented a report outlining his program of projected reforms to Alexander III.[2] It contained six points: "1) For the management of peasant affairs and the maintenance of order in the countryside, an administrative government institution must be created that unites all authority in such a way that the limits of the latter conform with the actual needs of the rural population. The above-mentioned institution should be linked to the central authorities by way of the provincial institutions. 2) The zemstvo and city institutions must be brought into the general structure of national institutions. The principle of public self-administration presently serving as the underlying basis of these institutions must be replaced by the principle of state administration, assisted by representatives of the local population. 3) The power of the Minister of the Interior to supervise the zemstvo, city, and peasant administrations must be so established that the Minister may exert more influence upon the activities of these institutions than at present. 4) The principle of filling positions in local administration by election must be restricted as much as possible and replaced by a system of government appointment. 5) The nobility must be accorded a larger part in the conduct of local affairs than they presently enjoy. 6) Court cases involving offenses of secondary importance must be transferred from the judicial establishment to an institution directly tied to the administrative authorities."

Tolstoy further argued for a reform of the courts that would some-what narrow the area of their competence and relinquish it in part to the administrative authorities. While the minister admitted the impos-sibility of introducing all these reforms into the local administration simultaneously, he proposed to begin by reforming the peasant adminis-tration, and then the zemstvos.

Having outlined the recommended reforms as a whole, Tolstoy turned to the details of the individual points. In his opinion, management of the peasant administration should be concentrated in the hands of the Ministry of the Interior and entrusted to the new land captains, who would perform both administrative and judicial duties. These officials would deal with the following matters: 1) decisions on land questions within the competence of the existing County Offices for Peasant Af-fairs; 2) the supervision of all peasant institutions, including administra-tive bodies and volost courts; and 3) hearings of minor civil and criminal cases that arose in the county. The land captains would be appointed by the Minister of the Interior from among the members of the local gentry. Candidates were to be proposed by the governors and marshals of the nobility, and would have to satisfy certain qualifications with regard to education, property and official status.

Above the land captains he envisaged a collegiate institution—the "County Board of Land Captains," chaired by the county marshal of the nobility. When examining administrative matters, the county police chief would attend its sessions, and when judicial cases were under review, the assistant prosecutor of the district court would join the body. Consequently, Tolstoy's new proposals differed little from Pa-zukhin's original draft. The sole basic ammendment was that Tolstoy did not seek the abolition of the institution of justice of the peace or the extension of the land captains' authority to a significant number of towns and cities.

Further on in his report the Minister of the Interior dealt with the zemstvos and the need for radical reform in this area. Criticizing the Kakhanov Commission's proposals, he observed that the condition of the zemstvos would improve only after elimination of "the basic flaw in these institutions, that is, the fact that they have not been made a part of the general system of state administration and remain unique public institutions, independent of government authority, that pursue their activities with complete independence in the area of competence entrusted to them." Tolstoy therefore proposed that the zemstvos be transformed into administrative institutions subordinate to the Ministry of the Interior. In the future, not a single decision of a zemstvo assembly should be implemented without the approval either of a governor or the minister. Appointment to zemstvo posts were to be made by the administration rather than by election. Finally, the report proposed major changes in the system of zemstvo elections. Electoral classes, based on the amount of property owned, would be replaced by new curias of estates (gentry-nobility, town and city dwellers, and peasants) for the election of deputies to the county zemstvo assembly. Large landowners now were to be granted the automatic privilege of being zemstvo deputies without election.

Tolstoy's report revealed a full program of counter-reform. The feudal "estate" principle was to be upheld against that of bourgeois property. The gentry estate was to be granted the leading role in all aspects of public life and all vestiges of zemstvo independence were to be abolished. Such were the basic principles of the Pazukhin-Tolstoy plan, outlined in the "historical document" so valued by Alexander III.

FIRST LEGISLATIVE PROGRAM

In accord with the procedure outlined in Tolstoy's report, the State Council first received a bill to reform the peasant administration and create the institution of land captain, as prepared by Pazukhin. The draft, dated February 5, 1887, was in the hands of the council by the end of that month. Tolstoy had attempted to ensure a favorable reaction from the more influential members. At the beginning of January (that is, before sending the draft to the council), he discussed it with Pobedonostsev, Ostrovsky and Manasein and, Pobedonostsev told Polovtsov, they all approved Pazukhin's project.

But Tolstoy was attempting to deceive his colleagues and in this he failed. Polovtsov, in his diary entry for February 23, recorded: "In the State Council I had time to chat with Pobedonostsev, Manasein and Ostrovsky about the draft Count Tolstoy has presented for the reform of the local administration. This was supposedly prepared in consultation with them. Pobedonostsev says that they were informed only of the general outlines (12 points), but that he knew nothing about the details of the whole affair and that, in general, he is only of secondary importance in this business. (He said) that the chief role should be played by Manasein in his capacity of Minister of Justice. Manasein told me that he is opposed to the draft from start to finish and that he will write a detailed rebuttal." Hence, when arranging matters with Pobedonostsev, Manasein and Ostrovsky, Tolstoy failed to tell them of the project in detail, but limited himself merely to provisions which would not, he hoped, arouse their opposition.

At this point it is worth examining the bill presented by the Minister of the Interior in the State Council. Tolstoy's report prefaced the draft and repeated—although at greater length—the basic arguments of his report to the emperor of December 18, 1886. Once again he began by criticizing the recommendations of the Kakhanov Commission. The confusion in the countryside, he argued, was due to the absence of strong authority; but his detailed presentation admitted the impossibility of a simultaneous reorganization of the whole local administration.

The minister's report insisted that land captains enjoy both judicial and administrative powers. "Everyone who is conscious of the ruinous consequences for the countryside caused by the lack of authority points out the urgent necessity of a restoration of the administration's supervision of the rural population in general and of peasant public institutions in particular . . . . But no reform seeking this end can be crowned by success . . . if in its implementation the fatal error, which already has cost Russia so dearly, is repeated. This (error) is rooted in the assumption that there are two different categories of authority—one for the conduct of the administrative aspects of peasant administration and the other for settling secondary judicial cases that arise in rural localities."

Tolstoy pointed out that an entire series of factors made it impossible to transfer management of the peasantry's public affairs to the existing justices of the peace. The justices would regard these functions as being of secondary importance, he argued, and they were not sufficiently trained for such activities, and so on. In addition, he noted that with these powers the justices of the peace would fall under a dual authority (that is, they would be responsible to both the Ministries of Justice and the Interior).

Finally, Tolstoy claimed, the fact that justices were elected did not ensure that the government would have the necessary influence. "What guarantee," he wrote, "is given by the balloting of a zemstvo assembly, composed of people of the various estates who are not responsible for their actions?" Nonetheless, although his statute foresaw a combination of administrative and judicial authority in the office of land captain, the existence of the institution of justice of the peace was not directly attacked. At this point the minister merely suggested some reduction in the number of justices. As for the gentry, Tolstoy believed that only this group was capable of showing real concern for the *muzhik*. The minister (or, to be correct, Pazukhin) wrote: "As in the past, the Russian landed gentry remains more than an estate or social group in the general structure of the state. It is, rather, a state institution that upholds lasting traditions of steadfast devotion to the throne and honest service to the people."

The draft legislation gave concrete form to the principles found in the preamble. According to Article 10, land captains were to be appointed from 1) local gentry who had served no less than three years as marshals of the nobility, or 2) persons of military or civil rank not less than twenty-one years of age and who owned—or had wives or parents owning—enough property to allow them to participate personally in the election of deputies to the county zemstvo assembly. A third point permitted a reduction by one half of the property qualification if the person who was seeking the position of land captain had a higher education, or if he had served for three years as a rural arbitrator, justice of the peace, or permanent member of the office for peasant affairs. Another article (12)[3] stated that "if there is an insufficient number of persons with . . . the right of assuming the position of land captain, members of the local gentry who have served not less than three years in one of the positions listed in Article 10, Paragraph 3 and who do not own the amount of land indicated in that paragraph, but who do maintain farmsteads within the county in question, may be appointed to this post." Finally, Article 17 noted that if there was no member of the gentry in the county with the required amount of land, the Minister of the Interior enjoyed the right to appoint a commoner to the vacant post "on the basis of the general regulations for appointment to government positions."

An analysis of the conditions required of candidates for the post reveals that while the land captains' sphere of activities was extensive, the qualifications demanded of them were very few. No educational qualification of any kind was to be required of those holding the post. Apparently every swaggering but impoverished little nobleman who had inherited from his parents a single estate might aspire to this position. Further, service as an elected representative of the gentry (that is, as a marshal of the nobility, and so on) was considered by the draft's authors to be the best school for "honest service to the people."

The suggested functions of the land captain were diverse in nature. According to Article 25 of the draft, this official was to be charged with: "1) the conduct of the peasants' public institutions and the responsibility for their correct administration; 2) the execution of decisions concerning the organization of the land of the various categories of country dwellers; 3) decisions in judicial matters . . . ." The land captain was to find his greatest responsibilities in the area of peasant self-administration. Charged with supervising these institutions and everyone holding posts in the village and volost administrations, it was his job to convoke volost assemblies, approve their agendas, supervise elections for public office, confirm those elected, and to review the decisions of volost courts. This official further would hold the right of dismissing unsatisfactory volost and village clerks, as well as of bringing members

of the volost and village administrations to trial. As for property questions, the responsibilities of the rural arbitrator were to be given the
land captain.

The judicial functions of this new official would include the hearing
of a considerable number of cases previously assigned to the justices of
the peace. Like the justices, the jurisdiction of the land captain was to
be limited to civil suits involving sums not higher than 300 rubles. But
there were some cases involving damages caused by livestock to fields
and "other injuries to land," as well as any civil suit arising from labor
contracts involving agricultural work—that were to be heard by the land
captain "regardless of the sums involved." Otherwise, he would enjoy
extensive rights to punish office-holders in the village administrations.
The land captain might impose penalties on administrators (have them
arrested for up to seven days, or fine them up to five rubles).

According to Article 39, a land captain could impose similar punishments on artisans and peasants and, with respect to the latter, try them
in the court of the volost where the offense had been committed. In
practice this would allow a land captain to sentence peasants to corporal
punishment for the volost courts, which were now to be completely
subordinated to this new official, could impose this sentence. It must
be added that Article 46 of the draft made a number of the land
captain's decisions final and not subject to appeal. These included judgements in civil suits involving sums of thirty rubles or less and criminal
cases involving fines of not over fifteen rubles.

The court of second instance (appeals of the land captain's administrative and judicial actions) was to be composed of the land captains of
a county. The county marshal of the nobility was to chair this body,
which would include all land captains and the chairman of the local
county zemstvo board. The county police chief and the assistant prosecutor of the district court were to attend the sessions with the rights of
members.

Finally, a Provincial Office for Village Affairs was to act as a court of
third instance for appeals against decisions of land captains. This was to
be headed by the governor and composed of the provincial marshal of
the nobility, the vice-governor, the directors of the fiscal board and
the control board for state domains, the prosecutor of the district
court, the chairman of the provincial zemstvo board, and one permanent
member. The office was generally to supervise "the successful fulfillment by the land captains and the conferences of these captains of the
responsibilities charged to them." This office was further to give final
approval to a number of decisions made by land captains, the most important of which were connected with the trials of persons holding posts
in the volost and village administrations.

Despite the fact that this projected office was supposed to exercise general supervision of the land captains' activities, the bill left open the question of their immediate administrative subordination. According to Article 48, land captains were to be subordinated "to the supervision and guidance of the local governors and the Provincial Offices for Village Affairs," while governors held the right of provincial tours in order to inspect the work of the land captains. Nonetheless, the latter were not subordinated to the governors in the strict sense. Further, although county marshals of the nobility were to be accorded the right of reviewing the activities of the land captains, this was merely a "right," not a "duty." Also, according to the draft, a land captain was to receive a salary of 2,500 rubles a year, including his travel funds and office expenses. In brief, such were the contents of Tolstoy's and Pazukhin's draft law which, in effect, sought the complete transfer of power in the countryside to the landed gentry.

The project was distributed for the comments of a number of ministries and departments and, by the beginning of March, 1887, observations began to be made in the State Council concerning the proposed legislation. Minister of Justice Manasein's response contained the most serious objections. Although he agreed with Tolstoy on the impossibility "of a combined and simultaneous legislative reformation of the whole structure of local administration," he still suggested that a "fully independent examination of the proposed reformation . . . is possible only if these reforms do not go beyond making specific corrections in the existing organs . . . ." But, he said, the proposed reforms were of a different order for they would have a very harmful affect on one existing institution—the justice of the peace. Further, the Minister of Justice pointed out, the creation of new institutions to supervise the peasant administration seemed, according to the sense of the draft, only a first step of a general plan of reform. "Meanwhile," he wrote, "the proposal does not contain the data and plans, even in their most general outlines, of the other reforms planned in this area." Consequently he considered it impossible to judge the practical aspects of the proposed reforms "without considering the nature, even if only in broad outline, of the reforms that the ministry contemplates for the zemstvo institutions and the county administration, quite apart from the radical changes affecting the institution of the justice of the peace."

Manasein offered several specific comments about the draft. He first analysed the thesis that all problems in peasant affairs were rooted "only, or at least chiefly, in the feebleness and remoteness of the institutions supervising their administration, and that the removal of this cause will lead to an essential improvement in peasant matters." In

Manasein's opinion, this premise remained far from proven. He then turned to the issue of combining administrative and judicial powers within the peasant administration. Here the Minister of Justice rejected the claim that the county justices of the peace were unsuitable for this role; some of the arguments made in the draft against using justices, "if merely reversed might equally be cited against the Ministry of the Interior's supposed ability to combine administrative and judicial powers in the persons of the land captains."

In analysing the rights the bill conferred on land captains, Manasein concluded that they would enjoy unusually extensive powers over persons holding posts in the peasant administration as well as over the inhabitants of their districts generally. He then demonstrated convincingly that the right assigned a land captain, on occasions when he "finds his own powers of punishment insufficient," to try in volost courts those charged with negligence in their duties, meant that the land captain in practice was being given the right of sentencing people to corporal punishment.[4] This was inevitable because "in such cases the volost court is an executive instance; because it lacks the right of discussing the legality of a land captain's orders it will be obliged to submit to his orders." (It should be remembered that the land captain might also impose disciplinary measures upon the court itself!) In addition, the minister argued that the land captain's powers would be especially awesome inasmuch as "in fact no appeals were permitted regarding the majority of the decisions and orders of the official in question." He therefore maintained that in reality the actions of the land captains would be uncontrolled, as the right of investigating them was conferred solely upon the county marshals of the nobility.

Following these remarks Manasein dealt with the requirements demanded of candidates for the new post. He agreed with the draft provisions for estate and property qualifications but pointed out an essential flaw in the proposed legislation. The distinction between hereditary and personal nobles had been ignored and Manasein believed that a second property qualification should be set for the latter category. Since the presumed aim of the reform was "to create in the persons of the best members of the landed gentry the strong authorities necessary for the ordering of the peasant administration—authorities who would enjoy the respect of both the government and the local population"—Manasein regarded the lack of any educational qualification as another basic error that completely contradicted this goal. Finally, he also criticized the judicial procedures envisaged for land captains. Tolstoy had described the principles of jurisprudence that were to reign in the chambers of these officials as "a specially simplified judicial procedure." In fact, the Minister of Justice charged, this meant the abolition of the controversial method of trial, the elimination of lawyers, and an end to proper weighing of evidence.

Ostrovsky, the Minister of State Domains, returned a short but completely sympathetic reply and promised to make detailed remarks orally during the State Council's meetings. Yet he represented his position somewhat differently in a conversation with Polovtsov. On February 23 the latter wrote in his diary that "Ostrovsky says he informed Tolstoy that it was impossible in the short time allowed him to write a detailed commentary but, while he expressed his general sympathy with its (the draft's) general principles, he reserved his full freedom of discussion in the State Council."

Minister of Finance Vyshnegradsky was also very sympathetically disposed to Tolstoy's draft statute. He maintained that "the proposed reform is an urgent necessity if firm order is to be established in the country districts of the empire. Your proposal, in its main outlines, fulfills this purpose." But although Vyshnegradsky "sincerely hoped for its full success," he still opposed particular parts of the bill. His most essential objection concerned the question of the land captain's judicial functions. These would, the Minister of Finance thought, create a situation in which four separate courts—the volost court, the justices of the peace, the district court, and the land captains—would be operating simultaneously in rural areas. Therefore Vyshnegradsky suggested that either the land captain be given only the judicial competence granted the rural arbitrator, or that the justices of the peace be abolished entirely and their duties transferred to the newly-created official. While he recommended that supervision of the land captains' activities be strengthened, he still wanted the new officials themselves to be allowed to impose the same penalties as the volost courts (that is, to make use of corporal punishment). Finally, the Minister of Finance maintained that it was necessary to raise the age qualification to twenty-five years and to lower the salary to 1500 rubles.

D.M. Solsky, the State Controller, made no general assessment of the project, but concentrated on the land captain's proposed judicial functions. Although he did not oppose transferring some judicial matters to their charge, he entertained doubts about the correct way of dividing jurisdiction between the land captains and the justices of the peace. This transfer of functions, he feared, might endanger the existing institution of justice of the peace. In this way Solsky really expressed very cautious opposition to the draft.

Kakhanov returned a very detailed reply. In characterizing the existing system of local administration, he pointed out that because its institutions had been created at different times without a unified plan, it was now a conglomerate of diverse layers. Because of this, he argued, it was impossible to change the system's separate branches without examining all the others connected with them. As for Tolstoy's proposed legislation, Kakhanov wrote: "The organs proposed . . . are not intended to handle a single area of general administration. We know from practical experience that the areas involved, apart from the task of police security, naturally break down into the following seven branches: 1) public health and veterinary service; 2) public food supplies; 3) public welfare; 4) fire fighting and construction sections; 5) roads; 6) public education; and 7) the development of trade and industry. All the essentials of the work of local administration are to be found in these categories." Yet the draft did not propose to charge the land captains with a single duty from any of these branches. So it was evident, Kakhanov concluded, that even after these new officials had been created, the areas mentioned would continue to be handled "within the borders of the county's territory in precisely the same way as it had been handled up to this time."

On the issue of the land captains' judicial functions, Kakhanov expressed particularly sharp objections. He thought the creation of special courts, subordinated to the Ministry of the Interior and having no relationship whatsoever with the Ministry of Justice and the Senate appeal processes, was completely inadmissable; it would mean that these judicial procedures would be separated from those set forth by the existing judicial statute. Other serious reservations concerned the qualifications proposed for the land captains. Kakhanov pointed out that the draft "not only subordinated, but even sacrificed" every qualification, be it one of education or of property, to that of estate (*soslovie*). He argued that the mere fact that a man belonged to the gentry could not guarantee "a more or less broad mental outlook that is solid enough to enable him to occupy so difficult a position" for the conditions of life, and especially the absence of material prosperity, "frequently destroy both traditions and convictions that have been formed over the course of long years." In concluding, Kakhanov again strongly protested the proposed procedure for appealing the land captains' judicial decisions, which would exclude any appeal being made to the Senate.

An analysis of the replies outlined above makes it clear that in one way or another all were critical of Tolstoy's proposals. The objections included criticisms both of the new institution as a whole and of particular aspects of the draft bill. Among the latter, the major problems were the land captain's proposed judicial functions and the qualifications expected of candidates for this post.

The Minister of the Interior or, more accurately, Pazukhin, wrote a refutation of these criticisms. He defended the draft law in its original form and no concessions were made, even when they would have coincided with Tolstoy's own views. The Minister of the Interior, for instance, insisted on preserving justices of the peace, although Vyshnegradsky's objections offered him a chance to abolish this institution as an alternative proposal. Furthermore, he rejected—although unconvincingly—the finance minister's proposal that land captains be permitted to order corporal punishment. Indeed, Tolstoy's view was typical of Gogol's heroes. "Experience shows," he wrote, "that in matters of peasant administration, corporal punishment is frequently very wholesome and, in some cases, the only expedient means of influencing the people. The local authorities, even though they are not empowered to do so by existing legislation, frequently have recourse to this measure in cases of peasants who, guilty of disobedience and impudence, are brought by the volost authorities for sentencing in a volost court . . . . Because of the extremely low moral and intellectual level of the peasant population, it is impossible to govern them without applying corporal punishment in some cases." This meant that although it was expedient to grant the land captains the right of so punishing peasants, this should only be done indirectly, by means of the volost courts. In this manner the land captain himself would remain on the sidelines while a peasant was sentenced to flogging by other peasants.

In countering Manasein's observations about the lack of control over the land captains, Count Tolstoy pointed out that the land captain was envisaged as "an active influence upon the people, who would be freed from all bureaucratic formalism." It was consequently impossible to subordinate this official in the usual way and the Minister of the Interior wrote: "Inadvertent mistakes and formal omissions by persons holding this post should be regarded leniently, but lapses in the sense of the moral duty required of them should bring a condemnation that is all the more strict even if the person's actions are completely correct in a formal sense." These were the "theoretical" foundations for the allegedly necessary freedom of action to be granted the land captains. As for Manasein's remarks about the pro-gentry character of the proposed reform, Tolstoy answered with an extensive declaration imbued with Pazukhin's spirit. Postulating "the absence of any antagonism between gentry and peasantry," the Minister of the Interior insisted that the proposed reforms would help "strengthen the moral ties between these classes."

TOLSTOY'S AMENDMENTS

Because of Tolstoy's many opponents it was imperative to gain some preliminary agreement, even if only among a few of the most interested ministers and officials. As noted above, the first efforts in this direction, made before the planned reform had been placed before the State Council, had collapsed. In his diary Polovtsov maintained that the council chairman, Grand Duke Michael Nikolaevich, told him as early as November, 1887 that Alexander III had ordered Tolstoy to call a meeting of the ministers concerned before replying in the council to Manasein's comments. This was to produce some preliminary agreement so that those involved would be unanimous in the later discussions.

Tolstoy tried in every way to delay calling this conference of "conciliation." According to Polovtsov, the meeting took place only on January 17, 1888, and even then it proved indecisive. Further meetings of "reconciliation" were held, but without Tolstoy's participation. The Ministry of the Interior was now represented by Plehve, Prince Nicholas D. Golitsyn, and Pazukhin. But these gatherings were no more successful than the first and unaminity remained elusive.

The same was true of a State Council meeting called by its chairman on March 28, 1888. Apart from Grand Duke Michael Nikolaevich, it was attended by Tolstoy, Ostrovsky, Manasein, Pobedonostsev, Vyshnegradsky, the chairman of the Department of Laws, Baron Nikolai, the chairman of the Department of the State Economy, A.A. Abaza, and Polovtsov. "After complimenting Tolstoy," wrote Polovtsov, "the Grand Duke asked the other ministers if they could agree about anything in the draft . . . . Ostrovsky assumed the role of leader and answered that they agreed with the general features but not on the smaller details. On these they reserved the right to speak freely in the Council. Manasein pointed out that up to now they still had not decided the respective competence of county (land captains) and justices of the peace, and Vyshnegradsky insisted that he would never agree to the high salary (2500 rubles) conferred on the new post. This latter subject raised the financial issue in general—about which Tolstoy had not troubled himself. Tolstoy estimated this burden at two and a half million (rubles), but Nikolai put it at four. And this is to be charged to the zemstvos, which are already burdened by the zemstvo taxes." At the conclusion of the meeting Baron Nikolai suggested that discussion of this statute could not possibly be completed before the summer holidays. Abaza proposed that it be introduced in the autumn and all those present accepted this proposal.[5] This decision pleased the bill's opponents as they wanted to postpone debates as long as possible because of the very rapid deterioration of Tolstoy's health.

Despite the uncompromising position of Tolstoy and his associates, the criticisms made by the majority of the State Council's influential members had their effect. The second version of the law, presented by the Minister of the Interior in November, 1887, was substantially identical to the first, but the third differed somewhat from both earlier versions. Dated March 8, 1888, this latter version contained a new formulation of the land captains' judicial functions.[6] The new Article 29, which defined these responsibilities, stated that suits in disputes of not more than 500 rubles relating to land rental matters and hiring of agricultural laborers, remedies in breached ownership cases, and cases concerning damages and other injuries to land, were to be handled by the land captains "in the style of judicial-police hearings." Cases concerning forest offenses also would be examined by the land captains, but only when the sums involved did not exceed 300 rubles. In this way the new draft somewhat curtailed the new judicial functions of the proposed official.

Also revised was Section 1 of Article 39. This dealt with the land captains' rights to impose punishments for offenses "against the administrative order and the public peace and interest." The earlier versions had allowed the land captains to punish artisans, among others. The new version, however, did not mention artisans. Furthermore, the section permitting land captains to try peasants in the volost courts (and so subject them to corporal punishment) was also amended. In the new edition this section stated that in cases where a peasant deserved a more severe penalty than the land captain could impose, the latter held the right to order "the hearing of the case to the established judicial system." But even this version did not preclude the possibility of the case being transferred to a volost court.

FURTHER DEBATE

Throughout 1888 comment on the proposed reforms continued in the State Council. At the beginning of that year Baron Nikolai, chairman of the Department of Laws, presented some very critical observations. He concentrated on two basic questions: the pro-gentry nature of the reforms and the judicial and police functions that Tolstoy proposed to grant land captains. On the first point, Nikolai claimed that the institution of land captain would acquire an openly "gentry" character. "It will be easily suggested to the peasants," he wrote, "that the new institution is nothing but a disguised revival of the landowners' police, and that the peasant population once again is being placed utterly under the thumb of the landlords, who are attempting to restore serfdom." He believed, moreover, that the government should appoint whomever it considered necessary to the post of land captain, regardless of estate origins.

On the second issue, Baron Nikolai thought it inexpedient to re-establish, on a broader basis, the administrative and police courts which had been abolished at the end of the 1860s. "With regard to criminal cases," he wrote, "this court has more the aspect of a reprisal than of a proper court, for the single judge is at the same time the policeman who executes his own decision."

In the autumn of 1888 the State Council received two further replies. Again both were highly critical of Tolstoy's bill. The first was sent by a member of the council, State Secretary B.P. Mansurov, and the other by Count Vorontsov-Dashkov, the Minister of the Imperial Court.

In Mansurov's opinion, local administrative reform should aim at strengthening both the police and judiciary, but not at creating some intermediate institution that united both of these functions. "The separation of administrative authority from judicial authority," he wrote, "is the cornerstone of every well-organized state. This is true not only in theory, but it proves far truer in practice . . . ." He considered that "the unification and strengthening of administrative powers within the county should not be sought by transferring some judicial functions to administrators but, rather, by returning to them all those (powers) that their departments have lost as a result of various accidental or transitory circumstances." Turning to the frankly pro-gentry nature of the reforms, Mansurov wrote: "Even if one fully sympathizes with the ministry's ideas, one may still remark that this proposal belongs to the order of things which may be done, but not enshrined in a legislative act."

Vorontsov-Dashkov's reply differed fundamentally from the rest of those received earlier. He not only made serious criticisms, but concluded with a positive alternative which, although it did not follow the liberal blue-print, could serve as the starting point for drafting a rival plan for the local administrative reforms desired by so many.

Polovtsov's diary contains a number of entries about conversations on the necessity for such a counter-plan. In his note for November 10, for example, he described a talk with Baron Nikolai on the impossibility of limiting oneself only to criticisms of Tolstoy's proposals. "Ba(ron) Nikolai," Polovtsov wrote, "believes that something along the lines of a counterdraft, on which the opposition to Tolstoy could agree, must be prepared." The next day Polovtsov had a similar conversation with Pobedonostsev, and the director-general also argued the need for such a counter-proposal.

For this reason Vorontsov-Dashkov's very long reply is worth examining. In opening he pointed out that it was impossible to examine properly a proposal dealing with particular branches of the local administration but envisaging a transformation of the whole system.

Consequently he considered a separate discussion of the draft law on land captains to be impossible. Furthermore, Vorontsov believed this official would increase, not eliminate, the existing defects of the local administrative system. This was a basic flaw. "The greatest defect in the present system of county administration," wrote the Minister of the Imperial Court, "is the extraordinary abundance of separate county authorities and offices. As a consequence, the county has a multitude of authorities who are, in practice, powerless . . . . *The implementation of this proposed draft will increase still further the multitude of county institutions by replacing a single, collegiate, peasant office with several independent land captains who possess extensive authority and are subordinated to no one, apart from the governors.*" More detailed criticisms followed, including several from the financial standpoint. Vorontsov pointed out that no new burden of expenditure could be placed upon the zemstvos, for many of them already lacked the finances to pay the salaries of medical assistants, teachers and other employees.

The positive aspect of this reply was Vorontsov's alternative plan for reform. He suggested the creation of "county captains"—an official who would concentrate in his hands all administrative functions. "*Uniting in his person all the separate parts of the county's local administration*[7] and directing their activities in accord with the views of the government, he should be responsible for good administration, security, and order within the county." Such county captains, appointed from among the landowning gentry, were to be handed full administrative power, including that of the chairmen of the zemstvo assemblies and the town councils, although judicial authorities would remain independent. Further, the county captains would have as their immediate assistants officials called "section captains," also appointed from among the local gentry. The authority of this official would extend to the entire population of a volost.

Vorontsov's central ideas were very close to those of Tolstoy and Pazukhin, but there were two very essential differences. In the first place, the section captains, as distinguished from the land captains, were to supervise all branches of local administration and, secondly, they would hold administrative and police—but not judicial—authority over all classes or estates within the volost. This counterproposal was very well received. According to Polovtsov even Kakhanov, one of the most radical members of the State Council, favored its adoption and insisted only that the elective principle be retained.

By the autumn of 1888, on the eve of the State Council's discussion of Tolstoy's proposals, the latter was therefore confronted by the almost unanimous opposition of the council's members. During this time both the council's chairman and State Secretary Polovtsov worked very actively to ensure the draft's rejection by replacing it with Vorontsov's proposal during the debate in the Combined Departments. According to Feoktistov's reminiscences, Grand Duke Michael Nikolaevich requested Pobedonostsev and Ostrovsky to undertake the task of explaining the defects of Tolstoy's proposals to Alexander III. "I myself can do nothing," the Grand Duke naively admitted. "Though I have often urged the Emperor to call a meeting in which He could listen to both sides, He will not listen." But neither Ostrovsky nor Pobedonostsev were themselves willing to take on this responsibility.

Polovtsov claimed that in the days before the Combined Departments' meeting he busied himself with securing Tolstoy's defeat. On December 1 he called on Baron Nikolai and urged him "to promote disagreement on the question of whether the draft on land captains should be examined, or whether wider issues should not be raised and the need for the . . . institution of the county captain recognized. This disagreement could then pass through the General Session to the Sovereign. Once he had settled these doubts, the draft would either be returned for discussion, or sent back to Tolstoy for a complete rewriting." That same day Polovtsov visited Mansurov and Pobedonostsev as well. He advised the former on the position to take in the debate and sought Pobedonostsev's promise to oppose Tolstoy's draft. Nonetheless, the Director-General of the Holy Synod was extremely evasive and declared that "because of his first impressions he would oppose Tolstoy, but he could not bind himself to any categorical promises as it was impossible to foresee beforehand the course of debate."

December 2, the last day before the meeting, was an especially busy one for Polovtsov. This is revealed by his diary, which records: "Visits: a) Kakhanov, who immediately agreed with me; Stoianovsky was there, and he also promised his support. b) Peretts, who would only agree to join whichever side had the greater chance, so as to be able to conform . . . . c) (A.A.) Abaza, whom I persuaded not to attend, so that Tolstoy would not have the right to say that he, Abaza, was a captive of the Council."

The Combined Departments (of Law, State Economy, and Spiritual and Civil Affairs) began their discussion of Tolstoy's bill on December 3, 1888. The debates can be reconstructed from the meeting's report, Polovtsov's diary entries, and the account Pobedonostsev gave to Alexander III (in which he gave the details of the disagreements). During the course of the three sessions, held on December 3, 10, and 17, disputes centered on one issue: should the proposed institution of land captain be one dealing exclusively with the peasant administration or should it be an organ of general administration? Or, in essence, which proposal was preferable: Tolstoy's or that of Vorontsov-Dashkov? Baron Nikoali, the chairman for the session, and many of those present (Vorontsov-Dashkov, Kakhanov, Stoianovsky, K.K. Grot, Mansurov and others) favored transforming the institution of land captain into one for general administration. According to Polovtsov, the initial session resolved to create a sort of "conciliation commission" to see if a compromise might be found. This group was headed by Peretts and consisted of Mansurov, Stoianovsky, D.G. Derviz, and E.V. Frisch; Plehve, as Tolstoy's deputy, represented the Ministry of the Interior. They held a number of meetings in Peretts' quarters, but failed to achieve any agreement as Tolstoy, who sensed that he had the tsar's support, refused to make any concessions.

Pobedonostsev, in the special report sent as an appendix to his letter to the emperor of December 29, outlined the bones of the controversy: "Everyone, although from differing points of view, opposes the draft in the form in which it is presented. Essentially all the opposition can be reduced to one issue: Count Tolstoy wants to construct an authority to deal with the peasant commune. But it is impossible to free such an authority and to set it up properly without tying it to all the other authorities. At the very least one must place the land captain in such a position that he will have authority in a whole territorial district and be directly liable to the general provincial authorities. Anything else would lead to confusion."

Nonetheless, Pobedonostsev, with the support of Ostrovsky and Manasein, proposed in the December 17 meeting that discussion of this issue should not be prolonged and that the Combined Departments should turn their attention to the draft itself. In the above-mentioned report the director-general included a detailed account of his speech and defended his view by saying it was necessary not to waste time. "Disorder is growing in the villages," he maintained, "and the question of establishing order there is very urgent. It is impossible to refute the Minister of the Interior on this point, and so one must deal with his proposal and accept it for discussion." Then Pobedonostsev described in some detail the characteristics of peasant institutions which demanded, in his opinion, serious reorganization. In conclusion he suggested that they not dwell on their disagreements, but agree that the institution of land captain was predominantly one for peasant affairs and begin examining the draft article by article.

Anything but general approval greeted this proposal and, as a result, two decisions were adopted. The first resolution—that of a minority of the Combined Departments which included, among others, Tolstoy,

Pobedonostsev, Ostrovsky, and Vyshnegradsky—read as follows: "Seven members recognize the necessity, as the basis for any reform, of establishing the principle that the land captains are officials supervising the peasant administration and are not officials with a general administrative competence." The majority decision, on the other hand, represented the views of the remaining eighteen members. They argued that the institution of land captains must be established "in the form of an institution belonging to the general structure of the administrative institutions within the county." In addition, the majority believed that at the second level, instead of a county conference of land captains, a county office should be established. This office should comprise the responsible officials of the county administration, and include only a single land captain. The eighteen members also warned that "the planting of land captains in the soil of peasant institutions may easily be construed as a measure aiming at the restoration, even if in a changed form, of those powers of the gentry over the peasantry lost when the latter were freed from feudal dependence, and in any case, as a law that is harmful to the legal equality of the peasants and their self-administration."

The stalemate within the State Council clearly made further discussion of the draft law impossible. Consequently the Combined Departments decided to suspend their own debates and forward their two resolutions, through the General Session, to the emperor for his judgement. Yet in fact the question was already settled. According to Polovtsov, Alexander III, in a conversation with Grand Duke Michael Nikolaevich, chairman of the State Council, strongly favored Tolstoy's proposal. "As evidence of the need of creating land captains as quickly as possible, the Sovereign cited Tolstoy's testimony that if this was not done, peasant mutinies undoubtedly would blaze up during the coming summer." As Polovtsov concluded in his diary on December 12, 1888: "With these words, the whole question already has been resolved . . . ."[8]

On January 16, 1889 the General Session of the State Council discussed the resolutions forwarded by the Combined Departments. This debate brought the following results: thirteen council members voted for Tolstoy's proposal and thirty-nine voted against it. Thus the majority of the General Session was solidly behind the majority opinion of the Combined Departments. The opinions were then sent to the emperor and on January 29 he noted the following resolution on the council's report: "As I agree with the opinion of the 13 members, I desire that justices of the peace be abolished in the counties so as to guarantee the necessary number of land captains for the county and to lighten the heavy tax burden in the county. Part of the work of the justices of the peace can be transferred to the land captains and the volost courts, while the smaller and most important part can be given to the district courts. In any case, it is my earnest desire that these changes not prevent the final examination of this project before the summer recess . . . ."

This resolution not only signified approval for the Tolstoy and Pa-zukhin project but gave life to a secret desire they had not ventured to espouse openly—the abolition of justices of the peace. Mentioned only in the first version of the draft, at that time this idea had been rejected by everyone.

Alexander's decision was a direct result of Prince Meshchersky's influence. On January 27, exactly two days before the tsar's comment on the State Council's report, an article entitled "The Voice of a County Marshal" in the newspaper *Citizen* argued that it was inexpedient to preserve the justices of the peace. Nonetheless, the granting of judicial functions to the land captain was a fundamental breach of the principle of separation of judicial and administrative powers as proclaimed by the judicial statute of 1864.

THE FINAL LAW

After Alexander III's instructions concerning the judicial functions of justices of the peace and land captains, the statute's approval was merely a formality. As a result further consideration by the Combined Departments, which continued from March to June, 1889, could not fundamentally change the new law. Still, the articles touching several important questions needed detailed reformulation in the light of the emperor's decision. "A session of the Combined Departments on the issue of Land Captains," Polovtsov noted in his diary on March 4, 1889. "All of the ministers responsible still have nothing prepared; the State Council has had to postpone all essential questions and could only conditionally approve some insignificant details of the draft law introduced by Count Tolstoy."

Only minor changes of detail were made in the law during its final examination by the Combined Departments. Both Tolstoy and I.N. Durnovo defended each point of the draft and the most basic change, made in spite of Tolstoy, concerned the demand for an educational qualification for land captains.[9] Apart from this, some articles concerning the rights of the land captain were rewritten, but their essence remained unchanged. The efforts of Polovtsov, Manasein, Kakhanov, Peretts, and A.A. Abaza to prevent the post of land captain from becoming the exclusive preserve of one estate—the gentry—ended in failure.

Meanwhile discussions proceeded apace because of Alexander III's insistence that they be finished before the summer vacation. The General Session of the State Council then approved the results of the deliberations of the Combined Departments, practically without examination, in a single day. On July 6 Polovtsov recorded: "A l-hour meeting of the General Session of the Council on the matter of land captains. The remarks made were empty and the Departments' report remained without a-mendment . . . . The National Convention decided matters with this same speed when the Fatherland was declared to be in danger."[10] Finally, on July 12, 1889, the new law was approved by Alexander III.[11]

The final law differed slightly from the draft outlined above. In accord with Articles 6 and 7, persons might become land captains who had served not less than three years as marshal of the nobility (and those in this category must meet no property or educational qualifications), who were local hereditary nobles not less than twenty-five years in age and with a higher education, or who had served three years as a rural arbitrator, justice of the peace or permanent member of the Office for Peasant Affairs as long as they or their parents or wife owned one half of the amount of land necessary to qualify for participation in elections of the first curia to the county zemstvo assembly. Should a shortage occur of those listed in the categories set out in Article 7, the law then permitted the filling of this post with personal nobles who had completed a course in a secondary educational institution or had civil or military commissioned rank, on condition that they meet half of the property qualification indicated above. Otherwise, the post of land captain could also be filled by personal nobles with a higher education, or service of not less than three years in one of the positions enumerated in Article 6, even if they lacked the land qualification and owned but a single farmstead.

Despite the inclusion of an educational qualification, the law permitted persons without a secondary education to be appointed land captains. Article 7 allowed the position to be filled by persons with the rank of collegiate registrar, even if they enjoyed, as was said, only "a incomplete home" education.[12] However, even this insignificant educational qualification immediately fell under attack. Polovtsov noted in his diary on November 25, 1889: "I met . . . Plehve, the Assistant Minister of the Interior. He told me, as if it were great news, that in his report to the Sovereign on Thursday, Durnovo sought His Majesty's approval for abolishing an educational qualification for land captains."[13]

Article 15 of the new law stated that should the number of qualified local gentry prove inadequate, the Minister of the Interior might appoint other persons as land captains. They must have an education no lower than the secondary level.[14] In any case, all candidates for the position of land captain were to be appointed by the governor, in consultation with the marshal of the nobility, and then confirmed by the Minister of the Interior.

The range of administrative activities assigned land captains was generally the same as envisaged in the drafts discussed above. There had been some changes in detail, which were mainly reactionary in nature. For instance, the law did not enumerate clearly the penalties that land captains might impose on peasants or on persons holding posts in the peasant administration. True, Article 22 did order that "in the area of managing the administration and the land settlement of the village inhabitants, the land captain is charged with fulfilling those obligations which, according to the laws in force, belong to the rural arbitrators . . . ." This transferred the administrative rights of the latter to the new officials.[15] Yet as far as the peasant public administration was concerned, the land captains' powers were considerably greater than had been those of the rural arbitrators. For, if there was no member of the county police on the spot, a land captain could, according to Article 29, exercise police powers. Article 28 instructed that complaints concerning persons with positions in the volost or village administration were to be handled by the land captain "on his own authority." Article 29 also granted this official the right to discharge volost or village clerks if they were unreliable. Meanwhile, the independence of volost and village assemblies was significantly diminished, for the new official was granted, by Article 30, the right to suspend their decisions and forward them for examination by the county conference of land captains.

The land captain's greater powers as compared with the rural arbitrator were especially evident in regard to the volost courts. The emancipation statute of February 19, 1861 had created volost courts as institutions independent of administrative officials; these courts now fell under the jurisdiction of the land captains. The "Provisional Regulations" for volost courts (included in the Statute on District Land Captains) stated that each village society would elect candidates for the volost courts and from that group the land captain would appoint the judges. The number of candidates had to be twice the number of judges to be chosen. Chairmen of the volost courts were appointed by county conferences of land captains, but on the nomination of the appropriate land captain. The chairman's functions might even be assigned to another representative of the administration—the volost elder.[16] Further, whereas previously the decisions of volost courts had been final, according to the new law verdicts now might be appealed to the land captains. The latter could either rule on such appeals themselves or, in cases of sentences involving more serious punishments, forward them for the decision of the county conference.

At the same time, the new law considerably expanded the role of the volost court, thanks to the abolition of the justices of the peace.

Its competence was extended to include civil cases, disputes and suits as high as 300 rubles in value, as well as cases of inheritances of up to 500 rubles. This court also received the right to impose fines to a limit of thirty rubles and jail terms of up to fifteen days instead, as previously, of only three rubles and seven days.

The land captains' own judicial powers were very extensive.[17] Most of the cases previously tried by justices of the peace were handed over to these officials. In the cities (except St. Petersburg, Moscow and Odessa, where justices of the peace were retained) an institution known as the city justice was created. These officials were appointed by the Minister of Justice. Otherwise, the position of county member of the district court was established within the county and the cases previously heard by justices of the peace not transferred to land captains, city justices, and volost courts were heard by this official.

The new law altered only slightly the composition of the county conference of land captains as compared to the earlier proposal. With the abolition of the justices of the peace, the county conference became the second institution of appeal for reviewing judicial decisions of land captains and city justices, as well as for some verdicts of volost courts. The county conference could therefore sit in both an administrative and a judicial capacity and, in this way, the power of the land captains was extended over both the rural and, indirectly, the urban population (by virtue of its power to reverse the decision of a city justice). The Provincial Office for Peasant Affairs envisaged by the draft law was now named the "Provincial Office". In addition to making administrative decisions, it also "settled protests and appeals for reversal of final sentences and decisions of the county conferences."

Such were the basic provisions of the law of July 12, 1889. The new institution of land captain increased the government's control over the peasants, strengthened the role of the landed gentry in the countryside, and prolonged still further the life of these survivals of feudalism.

CHAPTER IX

COUNTER-REFORMS IN ZEMSTVO AND CITY GOVERNMENT

THE ZEMSTVO STATUTE OF JUNE 12, 1890

Pazukhin's plan for counter-reform, prepared as early as the autumn of 1886 for discussion in the Ministry of the Interior's Special Commission, envisaged an electoral system based on the estate principle. County zemstvo assemblies were to comprise deputies elected by the three estates (the gentry, urban inhabitants and peasants), each voting in its own electoral conventions.

For the gentry the land qualification was more or less left as before, although it was raised for lesser landowners. Earlier, the possession of one-twentieth of the deputy's qualification brought the right to vote; but Pazukhin's draft foresaw raising this figure to one-tenth. For city electors the draft recommended a substantial raising of the qualification. The right of standing for election was to be granted only to those who owned real estate valued, for the purposes of zemstvo taxation, at not less than 15,000 rubles. Even merchants of the first guild, if they were not great homeowners, would now be deprived of the right to be a deputy. Apart from this, it was proposed that small property holders, if they owned real estate of one-tenth of the above qualification, could take part in authorized city electoral congresses. In electoral assemblies of peasants, owners of land or real estate valued at not less than 15,000 rubles were to participate, as were electors chosen by the volost meetings. Otherwise, representatives of the clergy and those renting land were to lose the vote.

To sum up, the draft law sought to increase considerably the role of the gentry, and to prevent elected deputies from resigning their positions. Furthermore, the county zemstvo assemblies were no longer to contain solely deputies elected by the congresses. Following Katkov's lead, Pazukhin proposed to include without election great landowners, representatives of the Ministry of State Domains and Appanages, representatives of the clergy (appointed by the local ecclesiastical authorities), and a deputy for each town within the county. As before, the chairman of the zemstvo assembly would be the marshal of the nobility. The zemstvo board, elected by the county assembly, was to be replaced by an executive institution—a Zemstvo Office. This too would be headed by the marshal of the nobility and include three other deputies—one from each estate—appointed by the governor.

The provincial zemstvo assembly would have as members the county marshals of the nobility, persons elected by the county assemblies as provincial deputies, and the great landowners (as unelected members). In addition, the director of the executive office of the Ministry of State Domains and Appanages, a representative of the clergy, and two members of the municipal council (*duma*) of the provincial capital, were to be included "with the rights of membership." In this way a substantial portion of the membership of the provincial zemstvo assembly would be appointed, not elected. The executive organ—the Provincial Zemstvo Office—was to contain four members. A chairman would be appointed "by His Majesty's authority" and selected on the basis of a recommendation of the Minister of the Interior, while three other members would be chosen "from the number of those persons who satisfy the requirements indicated in Articles 7 and 8 of the statute on land captains" (that is, from among those eligible to hold that post). These members were to be appointed from among the deputies of the provincial zemstvo by the governor, in consultation with the marshal of the nobility, and confirmed by the Minister of the Interior. Thus the executive of the zemstvo institutions would become a body entirely appointed by the authorities. Appointment, rather than election, was a basic theme of the projected counter-reform.

These provisions would almost completely destroy the independence of zemstvo assemblies. "To the zemstvo assemblies . . . ," read Pazukhin's draft, "belongs the general supervision and, *jointly with the governor*,[1] the administrative authority in zemstvo matters; to the Zemstvo Office belongs both the policy and the effective administration of zemstvo business." The independence of the Office itself would be even more restricted. It would lose even the right of implementing the assembly's decisions "as long as these instructions are not approved as proper by the Minister of the Interior or the governor."

By Pazukhin's proposal zemstvo deputies would be fined for failing to attend sessions and, if this occurred frequently, be brought to trial. Otherwise, the governor's powers *vis-à-vis* the zemstvos were to be considerably extended. He would be permitted to interfere in their everyday work, investigate their business and impose administrative penalties on the staff of their county and provincial Offices.[2] In this way Pazukhin sought to end the zemstvos' independence. Indeed, he openly stated this in one article, which read that the zemstvo establishments were to "function under the higher supervision of the Minister of the Interior and under the immediate supervision of the local governor."

The Special Commission discussed and generally approved these measures between October 29, 1886 and January 31, 1887[3], and made only a few amendments. Meanwhile, the Ministry of Interior received numerous comments on these proposals from various provincial marshals of the nobility. These demonstrated convincingly that the draft law aptly reflected the landed gentry's aspirations. In fact, the most reactionary of this group called for a complete abolition of the zemstvos. A certain N. Skariatin, for instance, in his letter to the ministry recommended the complete "eradication of zemstvo institutions and their replacement by the Provincial Offices of Zemstvo Affairs" which, apart from the provincial marshal of the nobility, would be composed of six bureaucrats.

In January, 1888 Tolstoy presented this draft law to the State Council and distributed it for the ministers' consideration. From the latter it evoked a number of comments, an analysis of which reveals three distinctive groups. The first consisted of those who generally approved of the proposals but suggested changes in the details. This group included Delianov, the Minister of Education; Posiet, the Minister of Communications; and Count Vorontsov-Dashkov, the Minister of the Imperial Court. The second group approved the principle of the reform, but wanted serious alterations in the final statute. Pobedonostsev was one of these and his reply contains some basic criticisms.

The Director-General of the Holy Synod agreed completely that the electoral system needed to be transformed into one based on estates and believed in the expediency of restricting the membership of zemstvo assemblies. On various other questions, however, his views were somewhat different. He argued, for instance, that a further increase in the electoral qualifications was necessary. "The smaller the circle of electors," he observed, "the more satisfactory the elections will be." Further, in Pobedonostsev's opinion, it was important that Jews should "*not be allowed to take any part whatsoever* in the elections or be elected as deputies." While he recognized that some deputies should be selected by appointment rather than by election, he strongly objected to the proposition that these persons be great landowners. Instead, Pobedonostsev believed that these deputies should be persons whose reliability was unquestioned and the fact that a man is "a great landowner is, *in itself*, far from a sure guarantee in this regard. Not infrequently it is precisely the great landowners and the wealthy who introduce a spirit of confusion and fantastic wordiness into the zemstvo assemblies." Hence, he proposed, generally it would be more expedient to elect candidates rather than the deputies themselves and then select the latter from the candidates by lottery, subject to confirmation by the governor.

The director-general also opposed a stipulation concerning a deputy's obligatory title, suggesting that his activity itself "could be converted into a *formal obligation.*" He urged the need "to give as great a chance as possible for local figures to take an interest in public affairs, based on moral principles and on moral ties with the locality. For this a certain *amount of freedom* is necessary. This will not endanger anything . . . ," he thought, as the activities of the zemstvos would be well controlled by the authorities.[4] Indeed, Pobedonostsev's most fundamental criticisms concerned the proposed restriction of zemstvo independence. While he firmly believed in tightening the controls over their activity, he nonetheless firmly rejected their transformation into semi-bureaucratic institutions of state. "I do not see," he argued, "either the clear necessity or the utility of radically changing the principle of zemstvo organization, or of integrating them into the general system of institutions clearly governmental in nature and which have a civil service and bureaucratic character. I do not, therefore, anticipate that any benefits will be derived from replacing the board by a Zemstvo Office which, in the form proposed by the draft, will undoubtedly have a bureaucratic character." Apart from the director-general, M.N. Ostrovsky criticized the proposals and disliked the liquidation of the zemstvo's elective components.

A third group of ministers utterly rejected the project. The most important of their replies was that of Manasein. He maintained that unless a great deal more evidence was produced, it was "scarcely possible to be convinced of any urgent necessity for a basic reform in an area which embraces the entire structure of local public life; for the total abolition of that system, the results of which still have not been ascertained; or for the introduction of a new one, the usefulness of which can be proven only by theoretical considerations." He therefore resolutely opposed granting to provincial administrations the right to interfere in the everyday life of the zemstvos, for this would in practice destroy any independence on the part of the zemstvo institutions. He also objected to members of the Zemstvo Office being appointed by the government. "It cannot be doubted," the Minister of Justice wrote, "that full mutual confidence and unity of purpose between the board and the assembly's guiding majority is necessary for success in the joint activities of the zemstvo assemblies and their executive organs—be they boards or offices." For this reason he argued that the elective principle should be preserved.

On several points Manasein supported Tolstoy's bill (for example, he wanted great landowners included as members of the zemstvo assemblies). At the same time, even though he generally disapproved of the estate principle, the Minister of Justice did suggest that if the influence of the gentry in the zemstvos was really diminishing, then elections by estates must be adopted. Finally, he also agreed to a certain increase in the powers of the crown over the zemstvos. Meanwhile Solsky, the State Controller, took a similar stand and suggested that Tolstoy had "presented neither sufficient information nor a firm foundation for legislative measures."

Hence the draft statute failed to win unanimous support and even such pillars of reaction as Pobedonostsev and Ostrovsky subjected it to serious criticism. For this reason the bill was revised and amended. To accord with Pobedonostsev's observations, the article making great land-owners automatic members of the zemstvo assembly was deleted. In its place the Minister of the Interior would have the right, "in some exceptional cases," to include as assembly deputies persons "enjoying the special trust of their localities who are entitled to participate in electoral assemblies;" however, the number of such deputies was not to exceed one third of the total number of assembly members. Further, the elective principle was preserved for the zemstvo executive organs (the boards) and the government was to receive merely the right, in cases when neither a chairman nor members of a board could be approved, to appoint persons with the appropriate qualifications to these positions. Nonetheless, despite these amendments, the essence of the draft did not essentially change.

These revised proposals were reintroduced into the State Council on February 4, 1890 and discussions began in the Combined Departments on March 3. They received a far from friendly reception for "the majority of the members," noted Polovtsov in his diary, "rejected the underlying intention of this draft law. This sought to destroy the present significance of zemstvo institutions, their independence and their elective basis . . . . Durnovo felt himself being driven from a position which, because of His Majesty's protection, he had considered unassailable." But the election procedures were approved as formulated. A system was established by which peasants elected only candidates for deputies and the provincial administration then selected the actual zemstvo assembly members from among those elected. "In this way," the departments maintained, "it remains possible for a governor to exclude all unsuitable persons from the members elected." Furthermore, the property qualifications were somewhat lowered because of an increase in land values during the preceding decade. Naturally, this suited the interests of the impoverished gentry.

The numerical composition of the zemstvo assemblies was approved in the form proposed and the size of these bodies was cut roughly in half. As for the zemstvo boards, the elective principle was retained; however, both the board's chairman and members were now subject to official confirmation. Government appointment of board members was allowed, but only in cases when confirmation of those elected was repeatedly refused. The most serious disagreements broke out over the issue of zemstvo independence. As noted above, the draft would have made all decisions of the zemstvo authority dependent on the approval of the administrative authorities. But the Combined Departments refused to approve this. They concluded that it was scarcely necessary to burden the provincial administrations with zemstvo questions and suggested that "following the enactment of the new law, the zemstvo assemblies shall, as before, make their own independent decisions about the issues placed within their competence, although they must remain within the limits prescribed by law." In this connection the departments stated that only decisions touching the most important questions were to be subject to confirmation.

The Combined Departments also disagreed with the article that envisaged granting governors the unconditional right to suspend any zemstvo assembly resolution and even to implement their own decisions instead. On this matter Polovtsov noted in his diary that, "following a long debate and the attacks of N. Abaza, Frisch, (D.G.) Derviz, B. Mansurov, and Vyshnegradsky, it was decided that governors might suspend zemstvo resolutions when a) they contain a violation of the law; b) they affect state interests; and c) they are clearly injurious to the population. This is, to be sure, a very weak bridle to apply to the dreams of the bureaucrats but, for all that, it changes the draft for the better." In spite of this, the new version of this article considerably expanded the governors' rights in comparison with the statute of 1864. Finally, the Combined Departments somewhat amended the article dealing with the Provincial Office for Zemstvo Affairs and zemstvos were permitted to appeal decisions of these offices to the Senate. Nevertheless, the rights of the administrative authorities with regard to the zemstvos had been considerably expanded and governors now were permitted to investigate zemstvo boards, whereas this previously had been the prerogative of the zemstvo assemblies.

On May 28 the General Session of the State Council approved the decisions of the Combined Departments and, on June 12, the draft law was approved by the emperor. This final statute differed considerably from the original draft, which had tried to destroy completely the zemstvos' independence. In fact, the zemstvo counter-reform did little to change the character of the zemstvos. As a result of the new estate electoral principle, the percentage of gentry deputies in them did increase somewhat. According to one study, the percentage of "nobles" in the county zemstvo assemblies rose from 42.4 in the years 1883-1885 to

55.2 in the 1890s. In provincial assemblies the comparative figures were from 81.6 and 89.5 percent. Yet despite changes in membership, the nature of zemstvo activities did not alter. In fact, rather the opposite proved to be the case as, during the 1890s, the liberal tendency of the zemstvos grew even more pronounced. This illustrates how Russia's economic development had strengthened the democratic tendencies of a certain element of the gentry, which was the most politically active. One authority, B.B. Veselovsky, observed that during the 1890s "anti-estate tendencies began to be dominant" among the gentry in the zemstvos. Thus the reform of 1890 failed to transform the zemstvos into dens of gentry conservatism.

The second important aspect of this counter-reform was the increase of government control over zemstvo activities. The results of this were especially apparent in the years immediately following the enactment of the law of 1890. Earlier the governors had been able to revoke decisions of the zemstvo assemblies only when these were illegal. Under the new law the governor (or the Zemstvo Office) held the right to rescind an assembly's decision if he considered it unsuitable. Yet the increased political consciousness of the early 1890s did not allow the government a chance to make much use of these powers, and the existing conditions clearly tended to impair the usefulness to the government of this new statute.

THE MUNICIPAL STATUTE OF JUNE 11, 1892

The situation in the system of municipal public administration was considered unsatisfactory by both the Ministry of the Interior (under Tolstoy or Durnovo) and Alexander III. In 1887, to cite one example, the report of the governor of Kostroma had mentioned defects in the existing municipal statute. On this report the emperor noted: "As if this were news! The government has long realized how absurd municipal self-administration is for Russian cities." Hence the question of a new municipal statute was naturally placed on the agenda.

On July 2, 1890, when the State Council had completed discussions of the zemstvo statute, the new Minister of the Interior, Durnovo, sent a circular letter to the governors stressing the need to begin work on a new law regulating municipal government. "According to the schedule established for the organization of local administration," he wrote, "the recently completed zemstvo reform should be followed by one for the cities; this must be initiated without delay." Durnovo also pointed out that any statute for the cities must harmonize with "the zemstvos in their new form."[5]

Dwelling in some detail on the flaws of the existing statute, the Minister of the Interior saw the most glaring of these as the overwhelming influence exerted in the electoral assemblies by representatives of the commercial and industrial class, "whose numbers in these assemblies are further increased by electors such as salesmen, whose services are completely at their masters' disposal."[6] Durnovo also mentioned the numerical predominance of Jews in the electoral assemblies within the Pale of Settlement. Their numbers, he felt, gave them the chance "to elect as deputies . . . those persons of the Christian faith who are either firmly connected to them by various economic ties or directly dependent upon them in some material way." As other deficiencies the minister enumerated the large size of the city councils, the government's insufficient powers in the confirmation of mayors and their assistants, and so on.

In confronting these problems Durnovo insisted that the governors "lose no time and get to work compiling the appropriate . . . statistics and suggestions for changes which should, in your opinion, be made in the municipal statute." To this end he requested these officials, at their discretion, to consult "those persons who, by virtue of their experience and knowledge, can be of most assistance in this matter." The governors were directed to present their reports by October of that same year.

By the end of 1890 the ministry had received a multitude of responses from "the provincial authorities." These are of great interest and it is worth examining the most important of them. Forty governors and two city governors wanted to increase government supervision over "both the legality and the propriety of the activities of municipal institutions." Fourteen governors believed that the Provincial Office for Municipal Affairs "should not be a provisional and consultative body attached to the governor, but a permanent institution, and should not be a judicial body of final appeal, but merely an intermediate one."

All the governors and three city governors suggested "that the main and general deficiency in the existing municipal system is the participation in the general city elections of small property owners, petty tradesmen and proprietors of small workshops, as well as of merchants' salesmen." These persons comprised a majority of the electors[7] and, in the opinion of the "provincial authorities," they "not only are of no essential use but, on the contrary, are harmful because of their insufficient general education and illiteracy, as well as because of the complete dependency of salesmen on their masters . . . . In general, these electors, who cast their vote on the orders of others, do real harm to the city administrations. They place their votes at the disposal of the interested persons upon whom they are dependent and are open to promises, intimidation, entertainment, and direct bribery at the most inconsiderable of prices. The well-to-do capitalists influence them and direct them for their own interests, or for the advantage of their own parties in the city elections . . . ." Guided by these considerations, the governors demanded that salesmen,[8] small tradesmen and manufacturers[9] be deprived of their electoral rights. They also thought small property owners should either lose these rights or, at the very least, have them limited.[10] Eighteen governors and three city governors favored the inclusion on the electoral rolls of persons who rented separate apartments "of a certain value."

Thirteen governors and one city governor argued that the three existing electoral divisions (curias) be abolished. At the same time, nine thought that the electors should be transformed into curias of estates. Apart from this, nine governors[11] and the Odessa city governor wanted to place Jews in a special curia, while six governors, headed by Shakhovsky of Estonia, urged that "prior to the revision of legislation concerning the Jews, they must be deprived of all participation in the municipal administration." Otherwise, sixteen governors and two city governors suggested that each electoral assembly elect deputies from its membership alone "in order to remove the possibility of personal election battles, to diminish the force of demoralizing forms of electoral agitation and to paralyse party struggles."

Fifteen governors and one city governor felt that the county or provincial marshals of the nobility, or a special appointee of the Minister of the Interior, should be chairman of the municipal council. The overwhelming majority of "local authorities" (twenty-seven governors and two city governors) insisted on having all members of the city board confirmed by the government, while half of them considered that this condition should be extended to cover "everyone whom the council elects to posts in the municipal public administration." Finally, twenty governors proposed that the city executive, or mayor, and all the members of the city board be granted the rights accorded state officials.

Such were the fundamental recommendations received from the provinces. All were definite in seeking a comprehensive increase in the government's powers over municipal administration and a significant decrease in the number of electors. This latter goal was to be achieved by disenfranchising the petty tradesmen, craftsmen and salesmen. Furthermore, many governors insisted on electoral rights being granted to persons renting apartments (government officials, teachers, doctors, zemstvo employees, and so forth).

On March 1, 1891 Durnovo presented the State Council with a draft for a new municipal statute. In his preface the Minister of the Interior again listed the defects of the existing law found in his circular of July 2, 1890 to the governors and noted the replies of these "local authorities," a summary of which was distributed in the council. At this time

Durnovo categorically rejected the suggestion that individuals renting apartments should be granted the vote. He justified this in a rather original way, writing: "Many of the responses of governors declare . . . that in place of petty tradesmen, who are to be excluded from the electoral lists, persons renting apartments should be added to the electoral colleges, as they are the people who are the most intelligent and interested in the conduct of public services. This would still raise a number of major problems . . . . The municipal statute of 1870 already has been studied and, from the experience of the entire twenty-five years during which it has been in force, naturally no definite conclusions can be drawn, apart from purely theoretical ones, which are without serious significance. In practice it would follow that we should fear that the inclusion of apartment dwellers into the councils would lead their activities energetically down false paths in both economic and political spheres." Apparently the minister was not disturbed by the other comments of the "local authorities," for he made no further reservations.

Durnovo did note that the draft of a new municipal statute had been compiled in the Economics Department (of the Ministry of the Interior). Then, he told the council, in order to test this draft with the help of persons with "practical experience in the organization of the city population—the mayors," he had found it useful to have a "wide-ranging discussion" of it in a Special Commission chaired by his assistant minister, Plehve.

The resulting draft law first of all set out considerably to augment both the governor's actual supervision and his powers of guidance over municipal government institutions. The municipal statute of 1870 stated that "the city's public administration is to act independently within the limits of the authority assigned to it," and that "the supervision of the legality of its conduct (belongs) to the governor." The new draft law, however, said nothing about "independent activities" and considerably expanded the rights of governors. Article 4 of the draft, for instance, stated: "The governor is to supervise the correctness and legality of the public administration's conduct and direct the above-mentioned (administration) so that it is useful to the state and meets the needs of the local population. He is permitted to make proposals to the local administration with regard to its opportune discussion and resolution of the matters entrusted to it." In this way the governor's control of the city council's activities would be enhanced substantially.

The bill proposed major changes in the electoral system. According to the statute of 1870, everyone who owned real estate "subject to taxation for municipal purposes" and without fixed limits to the property's value, enjoyed the right to vote. But the new legislation would grant this right only to persons who owned property of fixed valued (in the capital, 3,000 rubles; in provincial capitals or other cities with a population higher than 100,000, not less than 1,500 rubles; in other provincial towns and large county towns, not less than 1,000 rubles; and in all other towns, not less than 300 rubles). Apart from property owners, those possessing mercantile and industrial concerns who could claim "through their enterprises a voting certificate of the First Guild,"[12] were also to have electoral rights. Otherwise, a two-year residence requirement was to be established for all electors.

Through these provisions most of the mercantile and industrial class, excepting the merchants of the first guild, would be deprived of electoral rights and the number of electors greatly reduced.[13] But it must be admitted that the level of participation by persons qualified to vote under the statute of 1870, according to the data collected by the Ministry of the Interior, had been surprisingly low during the four-year period of 1889 to 1892.[14]

The new law also sought basic revisions in the electoral system. Instead of dividing electors into three groups or curias (according to tax liability), Durnovo proposed a single electoral assembly. Nonetheless, according to one provision, "if the number of electors is more than 300, and if no less than one-fifth of these persons are not members of the urban classes, the latter, together with representatives of teaching, educational and charitable institutions, will form a special electoral assembly." In this event both assemblies were to elect separately the appropriate number of deputies.[15] This meant, of course, that the bill envisaged a special electoral assembly for the gentry. The representatives of the "non-city estate" could be only the gentry and government officials (the latter overwhelmingly also members of the gentry).

According to Article 27, the number of non-Christian deputies should not exceed one-fifth of the total number. As for the Jews, the proposal would deprive them entirely of the right of election to the municipal administration. An exception was made for the nine western provinces. There the governors were granted the right to include "worthies from among the Jews" among the deputies of the city council.

If at the time of election, and then after a second vote, less than two-thirds of the required deputies were elected, Article 39 stipulated that the term of incumbent deputies be extended by order of the Minister of the Interior, and board members simply be appointed. Meanwhile, the proposed statute laid down rigid obligations for deputies. Article 44 stated that "none of the deputies may, without important reasons, absent themselves from council sessions," and Article 45 set forth the penalties for violating this rule. "Should a deputy not appear in the council and not provide legitimate cause, or if the council considers such cause insufficient, the council is permitted to pass a resolution on a vote of two-thirds of the deputies present, that the delinquent (deputy) be subjected to the penalty defined in Article 1440 of the Code of Punishments." No such provisions had been included in the statute of 1870.

The rights of city councils were to be curtailed substantially and their actions circumscribed by several petty regulations. The statute of 1870 had allowed them to petition, on behalf of the city or town, higher governmental authorities "on (matters) of local utility and necessity." The new draft (Article 47, Paragraph 20) stated that the council was to make "representation through the governor to the higher authorities regarding (matters) of local utility and necessity." In addition, while the earlier law had permitted the convocation of council sessions at the discretion of the mayor, on the request of not less than one fifth of the deputies, and also on the governor's demand, the proposed statute read differently: council sessions were now to be limited to four each year (March, May, September, and November). Even the agendas of these sessions were to be determined "on application of the mayor to the governor." Extraordinary sessions of the councils might occur only with the sanction of the Minister of the Interior in St. Petersburg, of the governor-general in Moscow, and of governors in other cities.

Finally, according to the existing law, discussions of questions in a council were initiated on the motion of the mayor or a deputy, on the demand of the administrative authorities, or on the request or appeal of a private individual. Strange as it may seem, the phrase "on the demand and declaration of government officials" was absent from the new draft, its place being taken by a new clause—"on the proposal of the board." This provision thus contradicted the general tenor of Durnovo's proposals. But despite this lapse, a governor's control over a council's decisions was substantially strengthened and the bill made his powers more concrete. Articles 61 and 62 enumerated those decisions which required confirmation by the governor and the Minister of the Interior. Any other council resolution, even if not subject to the governor's confirmation, might become operative only "if the governor had not acted against its implementation within two weeks of the day the resolution was received." When a governor felt it was impossible to approve a council decision, he was to forward it for examination by the Provincial Office for Zemstvo and Municipal Affairs, whose decision was to be considered final (Article 63). In other cases the final decision was left to the Minister of the Interior (Article 69).

According to Durnovo's draft statute, the mayor of a provincial capital was, as previously, to be confirmed in office by the Minister of the Interior, and in a county seat, by the governor. The innovation was that now, according to Article 96, when the person elected was not approved by the minister or the governor, the latter might either order the council to hold new elections or appoint someone else for the term covered by the election. Meanwhile, Article 98 was new in principle and would make mayors, members of the boards, and city elders "part of the State service."[16] This in turn would place municipal officials in a position of great dependency with respect to the government authorities. Then, at the end of the bill there were "Regulations for the Consolidation of the Municipal Public Administration" (as an appendix to Article 40). These stated that "in settlements where the number of persons with the right to vote is less than 100, an assembly of representatives of the local householders will be established instead of a municipal council." Some ten to fifteen representatives would be elected, under the guidance of a person appointed by the governor, from among those owning real estate valued for tax purposes at not less than 100 rubles.

An analysis of Durnovo's draft legislation reveals that its main aim was to reduce as far as possible the independence of the municipal administrations and generally to subordinate them to the authority of the central administration. Otherwise, the draft sought a substantial reduction in the number of voters by depriving the petty, and part of the middle bourgeoisie, as well as salesmen, of the right to vote. This right would now be based mainly on the ownership of property and the wealth demanded of this category of electors was deliberately much lower than that asked of electors from commercial and industrial circles.

Durnovo's draft municipal statute was distributed for the comments of various ministers and departmental heads in the usual manner. Several responded by making extremely fundamental criticisms. State Controller T.I. Filippov expressed serious reservations and commented on two questions: firstly, he opposed the preference shown property owners and, secondly, he spoke as a resolute supporter of giving voting privileges to those renting apartments. "I cannot accept," Filippov wrote on this latter issue, "that the introduction into the city council of representatives from the other classes of city inhabitants raises any essential impossibility. I think it is both just . . . and fully acceptable that those persons renting apartments should participate in municipal elections. In view of the fact that the value of the apartments they rent can serve as an appropriate standard for establishing a property qualification, I do not see how there can be any political danger if their participation is surrounded by restrictive conditions, such as a fairly considerable property qualification based on the value of the apartment, more or less continuous residency in the city, and so on." In replying to Filippov, Durnovo argued:

"If twenty years ago, with the then-prevailing attempts to broaden electoral rights and to build a public administration on a representative basis,[17] it was not acceptable to admit the tenants of apartments to public affairs without further legislative discussion, then now, when the guiding thought on representation is different and more in accord with the political conditions of life today, the broadening of the aforesaid right in this way, to include not a native but an alien and more-or-less haphazard element of the city and suburban population, would hardly be appropriate and, in its consequences, scarcely expedient." In this matter Durnovo obviously was guided by general political considerations rather than by concrete objections.

Finance Minister Vyshnegradsky pointed out that some property owners with the right to vote paid no more, and sometimes even less in city taxes than did the merchants of the second guild who were now to be deprived of this right. "Apart from the injustice to the Second Guild," wrote Vyshnegradsky, "in practice the proposed measure may provoke basic dissatisfaction in localities where there are no Merchants of the First Guild at all, or where their number is very insignificant." For this reason he insisted that merchants of the second guild, except in the capitals, be granted electoral rights. But Durnovo, in his reply to Vyshnegradsky, again held his ground.

Manasein, the Minister of Justice, on the whole favored the draft statute but objected to a number of articles which he thought infringed unnecessarily upon the interests of the municipal governments, such as the limits placed on the council's management of city property. He thought that "in reforming the public administration of the smaller towns, one can scarcely improve the state of town finances by destroying completely any vestige of independence." Like State Controller Filippov, Manasein was also a proponent of including people who rented apartments among the electors "as the persons who are most intelligent and interested in the affairs of the city." Finally, the Minister of Justice criticized the principle of establishing an election qualification based on the ownership of real estate, but not on the degree of material prosperity as a whole. But once more Durnovo stood firm.

The State Council began the examination of Durnovo's draft city statute on May 25, 1891 but then shelved it until the end of January, 1892. According to Polovtsov, Durnovo's presentation completely lacked the necessary statistical data, and time was necessary for its compilation. Hence the Combined Departments began a full discussion of the draft only on January 25, 1892, continued it throughout the course of February, and then finished on April 25.

Again, as in the case of the other counter-reforms, Durnovo's bill met serious opposition. "In opening discussion of such a wide-ranging and important issue," the minutes read, "the Departments recognize it as deserving their full attention. As the idea of organizing the municipal public administration on the principles recently adopted for the organization of the zemstvo institutions is fundamental to this proposed law, it is impossible not to consider it as being essentially correct." Nonetheless, the departments observed that even this consideration could be applied only in so far "as it is not hampered by natural differences between conditions of city as compared to country life."

The Combined Departments were favorably disposed to the draft's attempts to improve the composition of urban public administrations and "to establish more precise and definite regulations for their activities." Those proposals envisaging the subordination of the activities of a municipal public administration "to the more detailed supervision of the government" merited, in the departments' opinion, special attention and approval. They also argued that an absence of effective government control was one of the greatest defects of the municipal statute of 1870. Therefore the departments, according to their minutes, "find no obstacle to accepting those proposals of the draft statute which aim at granting the Minister of the Interior and the provincial authorities the same powers in the affairs of the city public administration as has been given the administration in zemstvo affairs by the statute of June 12, 1890."

After such praise for the draft as a whole, the minutes noted that, "at the same time, however, the Departments find it undesirable to go beyond these limits and to subordinate the activity (of municipal public administration offices) to restrictions that have not been established for the zemstvos. It ought not to be forgotten that in matters of public administration unnecessary governmental tutelage causes just as much harm as does insufficient supervision . . . . Excessive restraint upon the independence of the city organs will hardly be useful. Such measures can only cool interest in public affairs among the best representatives of the local population and be disadvantageously reflected in the quality of persons serving on the city councils and boards. On the other hand, such an arrangement also will be awkward from the standpoint of the government interest. If excessive restrictions are placed on the councils and boards, they will lose their significance as responsible institutions of public administration and their entire administrative center of gravity will be transferred to the provincial administration." In the opinion of the Combined Departments, this would be undesirable for the provincial administration's range of responsibilities was already extensive enough.

If one allows for the characteristic tone of such minutes—which aimed at smoothing over sharp disagreements—it is clear that the proposal of Plehve and Durnovo won little support in the State Council. Referring to the debates, on February 8, 1892 Polovtsov noted in his diary: "The Council's main task is undoubtedly to render harmless the draft with which it has been burdened." According to this same witness, N.S. Abaza was an especially energetic opponent who frequently voiced sharp criticisms of individual articles. Plehve, on the other hand, stood forth as the statute's main champion. The bill was also strictly criticized by Kakhanov, Manasein, B.P. Mansurov and Stoianovsky. Manasein continued to insist that electoral rights be granted to those leasing apartments and pointed out that the participation of this category of the population in the municipal administration "promises great advantages." For their part, N.S. Abaza, Kakhanov, Mansurov, and Frisch insisted that merchants of the second guild also be accorded the right to vote.

As a result of these arguments, a number of basic changes appeared in the final statute. Except for those living in the capitals, merchants of the second guild did receive electoral privileges and the general residence requirement was reduced from two years to one. At the same time, the Combined Departments rejected the proposal that a special electoral assembly be created for persons of "the non-urban classes." Another group of amendments concerned the sections dealing with the government's rights of interference in the business of the city administration. The proposed law's Article 4, for instance, envisaged supervision not only "of the correctness and legality of the actions" of city governments, but also the direction of their activity "so that it is useful to the state and meets the needs of the local population;" this was now abridged and the last condition was deleted. Article 64, which limited the number of council sessions to four a year, was also amended. The new version determined the number of council sessions as not less than four, and not more than twenty-four a year, while the governors were not allowed to regulate the period of a session's duration. Another change affected Article 39, which was revised to state that if the number of deputies elected was insufficient, the Minister of the Interior might fill only the empty seats, but not extend the term of the existing establishment.

Discussion of the Minister of the Interior's proposed right to pass final judgement on council resolutions provoked an especially stormy debate. "In the Combined Departments," noted Polovtsov, "there were hot arguments over Article 69 of the draft municipal statute. According to this, the Minister of the Interior is granted the right to annul any decision of a council and to substitute his own in its place." In the end, the Combined Departments left final judgement in the overwhelming majority of such cases to either the Committee of Ministers or the State Council.

The contents of Article 96 were also revised. According to the draft law, the governor was permitted, when a person elected to a post could not be approved, either to call new elections or to fill this post "by government appointment." The departments approved of a second election, but resolved that these positions might be filled by appointment "only in exceptional cases, when all available means of filling these offices by the generally established methods have been exhausted." Regarding the problem of establishing consolidated municipal public administrations, the departments' decision was again somewhat different from that proposed in the draft. Such consolidations were, in each instance, to be examined first in the Committee of Ministers.

The Combined Departments refused to support the granting of the vote to individuals renting apartments, even though their members were on the whole sympathetic to such a suggestion. "The Departments find," the minutes read, "that the proposed measure merits their full attention. But it is scarcely possible to enter upon an examination of it at present, as an absence of sufficiently firm data does not permit a correct judgement to be made about the means by which this measure could be realized. As a consequence, and bearing in mind that one counts upon the Minister of the Interior to consider the aforesaid question again, when there appears to be a pressing need for this, the Departments consider that it is more prudent not to predetermine this question at the present time."

Then, on February 29, another stormy dispute broke out concerning Jewish participation. "Disagreement occurred on the question of allowing Jews to participate in the city administration," Polovtsov noted. "According to the draft, this is admissible only in the western provinces where the governors will appoint several deputies from among the loyal Jews. Before the session Durnovo whispered into each member's ear that this was the Sovereign's will." Despite this warning, the majority of the departments' members, on the initiative of N.I. Stoianovsky, spoke out for granting those Jews who lived outside the Pale the right of a role in the cities' public administration. Twenty members voted for this proposal, and only four against.[18] But, since Alexander III was categorically opposed to any such suggestion, the Combined Departments stated that "having heard a statement explaining the difficulties of deviating from the general direction of the government's policies at the present juncture, the Departments do not feel it possible to insist on the preservation of the right to participate in municipal administration for those Jews who are permanently residing outside of the Pale of Settlement."[19]

Although discussions in the Combined Departments resulted in a number of significant amendments to the bill, they did not change its essence. The majority of revisions concerned relations between the administrative authorities and the institutions of city self-government. Nonetheless, the control exercised by crown officials over the latter was strengthened, even if some of the extremes were eliminated and it received a more logical form.

On May 13 the General Session of the State Council approved the decisions of the Combined Departments without serious amendment and on June 11, 1892 the emperor finally approved the bill as law. The Municipal Statute of June 11 greatly reduced the independence of the institutions of municipal government, increased the rights of the state administration, and transformed the members of the city boards into civil servants. At the same time, vital changes were made in the electoral system: the law deprived a large element of the lower urban middle class of the right to vote; in essence this increased the importance of the gentry. Here is found the real significance of this law for the reactionaries. But whatever the government's motives, the new electoral system exerted a positive influence on the composition of the municipal councils. The increase in the relative weight of persons of the non-urban classes—that is, of the gentry homeowners and the representatives of various institutions and societies owning property in towns—favored an increase in the number of deputies from the intelligentsia professions. This implied an increase of persons with secondary or higher educations and, in conditions of waxing social and revolutionary crisis in Russia, such an increase naturally led to the growth of a spirit of opposition among the representatives of the urban population.

CONCLUSIONS

Political reaction began immediately after the murder of Alexander II thanks solely to the circumstances then existing. The downfall of the "People's Will" party, the absence of any other revolutionary group, the weakness of the peasant movement, the insignificant opposition of the workers, and the political indifference enveloping large numbers of the intelligentsia in the wake of the events of March 1, 1881—together these given conditions favored the charting of a reactionary course. The concrete forms given the reaction were largely determined by the autocrat "of all the Russias" and his intimate circle of advisers. Here Pobedonostsev, Tolstoy, Katkov and Meshchersky played leading roles.

Politically, the period of reaction may be subdivided into three stages. The first of these—from the end of April, 1881 to the summer of 1882—was a period of transition from the more liberal policies of Alexander II's last years. This transition was hidden behind a screen of demagogic promises and pledges during Ignatiev's term as Minister of the Interior. The second stage, with which this study opens, covers the years 1882 to 1885. It was characterized by the open declaration of reactionary policy, a "restoration of government" as Katkov called it, even though the government possessed no practical program for implementing its reactionary principles.

During these years the autocracy feared to adopt principal measures. In the first place, the coronation hindered action because the government did not wish to nurture the discontent already widespread among the public. Further, the government was still somewhat uncertain about the strength of the opposition it faced. Yet this was a period, first, of struggle within the regime against the "liberal" ministers Bunge and Nabokov and, second, of the first reactionary measures as applied to education, the most important of which was the new university statute, confirmed in 1884. Thirdly, the progressive press was firmly repressed. It was in the area of censorship policies that the reactionaries achieved their greatest success. Feoktistov, who accepted the post of director of the Main Directorate of the Press in 1883, had succeeded by 1886 in silencing almost all progressive press publications.

Finally, the third stage—1886 to 1894—was characterized by a further reactionary offensive. This period was marked by the institution of Pazukhin's program, which envisaged the establishment of the estate, or class principle (favoring the gentry), in the countryside (the law on land captains), and in institutions of zemstvo and municipal public administrations. It was during these years—especially in the early 1890s—that policies of chauvinism grew in strength. Characteristic of such policies were the russification of the borderlands and the massive repression suffered by the Jews. The "Multansky affair," the forced baptism of the Buriats and other similar events took place during these years. Meanwhile, arbitrary administrative activity by central state institutions and officials of provincial administrations—the governors—grew very widespread. The fact that such behavior could occur is explained by two factors: the general conditions in the country and the protective attitude taken by Alexander III and his intimate advisers to those responsible for such conduct.

At the same time this period was characterized by the increasing use of a hypocritical system of deliberate falsehood in both the government's declarations and the practices of the police and bureaucracy. This resulted not so much from the personal qualities of the higher officialdom as from an almost complete absence of public opinion within the country. Indeed, public opinion was completely silenced.

The government's policies carried an obviously pro-gentry bias and sought to preserve these survivals of feudalism. In the sphere of finance and economics, however, a completely contradictory trend was apparent. The abolition of the poll tax, the introduction of new, modern principles of fixing the rates of taxation and a continued rise in import duties (a trend that found full expression in the customs tariff of 1891)—these policies stood absolutely opposed to the general political aims advanced by the Russian autocracy. Such contradictions arose because the economic aspects of government policy were essentially outside the autocracy's control. Necessities of state forced the regime to seek an increase in its revenues and this consideration, in turn, demanded a form of taxation that would guarantee the greater effectiveness of future efforts to fill the state treasury. As feudal principles of taxation could not ensure the necessary results, the transition to new—modern—forms of revenue was vital.

A significant portion of the budgetary income derived from various taxes levied on commercial and industrial enterprises; the increase of these revenues required the development of commerce and industry. Hence protective measures in the form of customs tariffs were implemented to support industry. These, naturally, promoted the development of capitalism. Hence the industrial upsurge of the second half of the 1890s was based largely on the government's economic policies during this period of study. In addition, the success of these economic policies was conditioned by the fact that they accorded to some degree with the natural course of social and economic development. Yet the basic question arising from the latter part of this study concerns the actual success of the government's other policies during the years 1882 to 1894: What did they achieve? Even a period of government reaction lasting a decade and a half could not prevent the social and political development of Russia; therefore the results of the reactionaries' efforts were somewhat varied.

The government scored its greatest successes in the area of strengthening the repressive and arbitrary powers of the administration and the police, and in its policies of militant nationalism, which led to the oppression of non-Russian peoples. The regime also won some victories in its struggle against advanced social thought, wherein the persecution of the censorship grew very far-reaching (although the reactionary unanimity of thought of Katkov's dreams remained beyond the government's grasp). The reactionaries marked similar progress in the area of education: university autonomy was abolished and a militaristic and police regime established in the secondary schools. Further, the classical system of education was retained in its original form (which was hated by everyone) and definite steps were taken toward transforming the primary elementary schools into an ecclesiastical system. Nonetheless, the hopes of Tolstoy, Delianov and Pobedonostsev remained far from actuality, and student discontent continued. Despite all Delianov's measures, moreover, the statistics on the social origins of students marked almost no change whatsoever. Similarly, Pobedonostsev's efforts to transform the elementary schools into institutions dominated by the ecclesiastical authorities were, thanks to the opposition of the zemstvos, unsuccessful.

Thus the government failed in its expectations even in policy areas not directly or indirectly tied to social and economic developments. The causes were many, but various forms of public opposition, the absence of unity within the government, and several other circumstances all played a part. Although Alexander III made changes in the membership of his government, it did not acquire a homogeneous composition. Along with Tolstoy, Pobedonostsev, Delianov and those who were "at one with them," the government also contained Nabokov, and subsequently Manasein, Bunge and Shestakov, whose outlooks were very different. Quite apart from this, on a number of particular and very basic questions disagreement broke out even among the outstanding reactionary statesmen (Pobedonostsev, Tolstoy and Delianov). Such disputes occurred, for example, during discussion of the draft university statute, the law on land captains, and on other occasions. Similar situations arose in the Committee of Ministers (although very rarely) whereupon one minister's proposal failed to win approval. When only isolated disagreements occurred in the Committee, in the State Council—which contained a number of dignitaries from the preceding reign who represented the liberal bureaucracy—opposition to reactionary legislative projects was the usual rule. In any case, these differences of opinion within the upper circles of government could not but influence the practical forms given to the various reactionary principles.

The government had least success—and at times experienced utter failure—in measures that directly touched social and economic developments. The most glaring example here is the agrarian legislation which, aiming at preserving the existing feudal and patriarchal relationships, exerted almost no actual impact on events. The law of 1889 on peasant migration created a number of barriers and made movement more difficult, but in reality it had no influence whatsoever. The same is true of the law dealing with village repartitions and family subdivisions of peasant land. Again the practical gains of this enactment were minimal. Whereas the number of legal land repartitions and family subdivisions did diminish, the number of such actions—undertaken unofficially—showed a considerable increase. Once again it can be said that the counter-reforms proved incapable of achieving the results expected by the government.

The statute on land captains brought the greatest success as compared with the other reforms mentioned. This strengthened the power of the landowning gentry over the peasantry and concentrated both administrative and judicial functions in gentry hands. But even this measure did not produce all the desired effects. Pazukhin's utopian reactionary plan for the rapprochement of peasantry and gentry, who were "tied together by the bonds of the centuries," could not halt the weakening of the gentry's position and influence in the country's political life, let alone the deterioration of their economic situation. The zemstvo counter-reforms had even less impact. The government's attempts to reorganize the zemstvo institutions on an estate or class basis, and to lend them a "gentry character," seemed superficially successful. Yet the process of the "bourgeoisization" of the gentry, and hence a liberalisation of their views as well, meant that within the zemstvos themselves there was an increase in the number of liberals rather than of Pazukhins and their ilk. Therefore the zemstvo counter-reforms did not—in spite of reinforced government control and a certain increase in the gentry element—change the essential liberalism of the zemstvo institutions.

Much the same must be said about the counter-reforms in city government that restricted the independence of the municipal offices of public administration. True, the law of 1892 deprived the petty bourgeoisie (local merchants and salesmen) of their electoral rights. This increased the role in the city councils of property owners and of representatives of institutions owning urban property, but it simultaneously magnified the percentage of oppositional elements by adding to the representation of the liberal intelligentsia.

It was in these ways that the government remained powerless in areas of policy that in one way or other were connected with Russia's social and economic development. Further, the early 1890s were marked by the terrible famine of 1891 and 1892—the "all-Russian disaster," as contemporaries called it. Wide sections of the public (predominantly the democratic element) participated actively in the battle against this disaster, the government standing revealed as totally incapable. This event served as a signal for the beginning of a new upsurge of public political activity. "The famine of 1891 and the cholera epidemics of 1891-92," wrote Minister of Education Delianov, "promoted an increased influx of youth into the countryside and as a result revived the efforts of Russian youth—which had somewhat subsided during the 1880s—to raise by their own initiative the intellectual level of the people." The youthful Russian Social Democratic movement played an important role in this upsurge and even the Department of Police recognized its influence. The *Historical Survey of the Organization and Activities of the Department of Police* states that "its (the Social Democrats' propaganda) particular growth became noticeable in the early 1890s. The criminal organizations, under various names, revealed their existence more boldly after 1894 and 1895 when, under the name "Union for the Struggle for the Liberation of the Working Class," they turned their attention to propaganda about the workers' struggle with the capitalists. In 1896 they organized numerous strikes and work stoppages, first in St. Petersburg and then in the majority of other industrial and factory centers." This same period saw a revival in other areas of public life, expressed in new outbreaks of student unrest.

Under these conditions it was impossible to continue the reign of active political reaction that had prevailed throughout the 1880s and early 1890s. The fact that the plans of Muraviev for new judicial reforms could not be implemented was a direct result of the new social developments. The latter also necessitated a new factory law, which came as a direct consequence of the strike movement of 1896. Meanwhile the government, under new pressure from the public, was forced to retreat somewhat from policies of open reaction (although the general tenor of its activities remained the same as before).

It may be concluded that the political reaction of the 1880s and early 1890s aimed at preserving and strengthening the survivals of feudalism and serfdom. It succeeded in somewhat retarding the country's development and found its expression in reactionary statutes and a massive increase in arbitrary and quasi-illegal behavior by the police and bureaucracy. But it still could not divert the general course of social and economic development, or halt the growth of advanced social thought in Russia, in spite of repression by censorship and other reactionary measures. On the contrary, this prolonged period of reaction, with its suppression of everything progressive and tremendous growth of arbitrary political conduct, built up within the public such hatred for the autocracy that it could be released only in a revolutionary explosion. This same period of reaction laid bare to all the crisis of the autocratic system and the decadence of its leadership, beginning with the imperial family and culminating with individual local authorities. For these reasons the political reaction of the 1880s and early 1890s was one of the factors behind the later revolutionary events of 1905 to 1907.

NOTES *

FOREWORD

1. P.A. Zaionchkovsky, *Krizis samoderzhaviia na rubezhe 1870-1880-kh godov* Moscow, 1964.
2. I.I. Shelymagin, *Fabrichno-trudovoe zakonodatel'stvo v Rossii (vtoraia polovina XIX veka)* Moscow, 1947.
3. K.A. Pazhitnov, *Polozhenie rabochego klassa v Rossii.* 3 vols. Leningrad, 1924-1925; M.S. Balabanov, *Ocherki po istorii rabochego klassa v Rossii* 2 parts, Moscow, 1926.
4. L.G. Mamulova (Zakharova), *Zemskaia kontrreforma 1890 goda,* Diss. Moscow University, 1962; G.I. Shchetinina, *Universitetskii vopros v 70-80-kh godakh XIX veka i universitetskii ustav 1884 g.* Diss. Moscow University, 1965; E.M. Brusnikin, *Politika tsarizma po krest'ianskomu voprosu v period politicheskoi reaktsii v 80-kh–nachale 90-kh godov XIX veka.* Diss. Moscow University, 1965.
5. Joseph Bloch was the editor of the German publication, *Sozialistische Monatshefte.* (Editor)

INTRODUCTION

1. In 1881 anti-semitic agitators charged the Jews with complicity in the assassination of Alexander II and provoked pogroms in Kiev, Odessa and elsewhere. Although not officially sponsored, the authorities did little to prevent these outbreaks. (Editor)
2. The "Kazan demonstration," which resulted in the arrest of thirty-one persons, took place in front of Kazan Cathedral on December 6, 1876. It was the first Russian political demonstration to involve workers. (Editor)
3. For the English text of this manifesto, and of other basic documents and statutes of this period, see George Vernadsky, ed., *A Source Book for Russian History from Early Times to 1917* (New Haven, 1972), III, 671-705. (Editor)
4. After strikes at the Morozov textile plant at Orehovo-Zuevo, near Moscow, and elsewhere in 1885-1886, a new law was issued requiring employers to pay cash wages on a regular basis and to reduce the fines charged for breaches of factory discipline. (Editor)
5. This Marxist organization, which included Lenin, had merged two earlier ones and is considered one of the most important of the early Social Democratic groups. (Editor)
6. On the Kakhanov Commission, established to prepare a plan for reorganizing the local administrative system, see Chapter IV. (Editor)
7. P.A. Zaionchkovsky, ed., *Dnevnik gosudarstvennogo sekretaria A.A. Polovtsova, 1883-1892.* 2 vols. Moscow, 1966.
8. T.N. Granovsky (1813-1855), professor of general history at the University of Moscow, and the novelist I.S. Turgenev (1818-1883) were representatives of Russian liberalism. Here Zaionchkovsky is suggesting that during his life Feoktistov switched from the left to the extreme right in politics. (Editor)

* All notes are from the Russian text unless marked "Editor."

9. E.M. Feoktistov, *Za kulisami politiki i literatury, 1848-1896*. Leningrad, 1929.

10. The Slavophiles emerged as a major Russian intellectual force in the 1840s (in opposition to the "Westerners"). They argued for a peculiarly Slavic form of Russian development rather than a mere imitation of Western European experience. (Editor)

11. A.A. Pushkin (1833-1914), the son of the poet Alexander Pushkin, was at this time a major general in His Imperial Majesty's Suite. (Editor)

12. All these gentlemen were members of old Russian families and high court officials. (Editor)

13. At the end of 1885 a Special Commission investigated the work of the Cherpovets district zemstvo, in Novgorod province. As a result, the provincial administration assumed control of its activities. (Editor)

14. Peter I. Chaikovsky (or Tchaikovsky) (1840-1893), the composer of *Swan Lake* and other famous pieces, died in somewhat mysterious circumstances—either of cholera or by suicide. (Editor)

15. The memoirs of A.V. Bogdanovich (wife of Lt. Gen. E.V. Bogdanovich) were published in edited form as *Tri poslednikh samoderzhtsa* (Moscow-Leningrad, 1924).

16. A.F. Koni, "Triumviry."*Sobranie sochineniia* (Moscow, 1966), II, 253-328.

17. This was the trial of a group of young populist terrorists, among whom was Lenin's older brother, Alexander Ulianov. Condemned to death for plotting the tsar's death, he was hanged on May 8, 1887 at the age of twenty-one. (Editor)

18. A.A. Kizevetter, *Na rubezhe dvukh stoletii: Vospominaniia, 1881-1914.* Prague, 1929.

19. V.P. Meshchersky, *Moi vospominaniia*, 3 vols. St. Petersburg, 1897-1912.

20. P.A. Zaionchkovsky, ed., *Dnevnik D.A. Miliutina*. 4 vols. Moscow, 1950.

21. B.N. Chicherin, *Zemstvo i Moskovskaia gorodskaia duma*. Moscow, 1934.

22. *K.P. Pobedonostsev i ego korrespondenty*. 2 vols. Moscow, 1923; and *Pisma K.P. Pobedonostseva k Aleksandru III*. 2 vols. Moscow, 1925.

23. Russia was at this time encouraging Serbia to attack Bulgaria, as Alexander III was outraged by the latter's unification with Eastern Rumelia. These events led to the collapse of Russia's Balkan policy. "Oreanda" was an imperial estate in the Crimea. (Editor)

CHAPTER I

1. As another example of such mistakes, Zaionchkovsky observes that Alexander III spelled "griby" (toadstools) as "gryby." (Editor)

2. A verst is 3,500 feet, or two thirds of a mile. (Editor)

3. When Alexander's teacher, Professor A.I. Chivilev of Moscow University, learned that his pupil had become heir to the throne, he was utterly horrified. According to E.M. Feoktistov, he remarked to his colleague, Professor K.N. Bestuzhev-Riumin: "What a pity that the Sovereign did not persuade him to give up his claims; I can't reconcile myself with the idea that he will be ruling Russia."

4. Polovtsov remarked about her (in his diary): "What a foolish, untalented woman." In another entry he observed: "Her Majesty spends most of Her time on gossip and dresses." She had one other quality—she loved dancing until exhausted and considered this more important than the rearing of her children. In his diaries Feoktistov also mentions her frivolity.

5. The Military Order of St. George was Imperial Russia's most coveted decoration. Created in 1769 by Catherine II, it had four degrees of crosses for officers, and four more for enlisted men. Zaionchkovsky's own note here points out that it was Russia's highest decoration and so rare that only one first degree cross had been given for the great 1812 campaign (to General M.I. Kutuzov). (Editor)

6. Although Maria Fedorovna's relationship with her husband is not the topic under discussion, it might be noted that she was not particularly faithful. This is eloquently revealed by her correspondence with an aide-de-camp, one Count Vladimir Sheremetev, which is found among her papers. In one letter Sheremetev, addressing the empress, wrote "I kiss your *dainty teeth.*" (Zaionchkovsky's italics). For her part, she signed her letters to him with the affectionate "*Votre* old Mary."

7. The formulation of the triple creed of "Autocracy, Orthodoxy, and Nationality" is usually ascribed to Count S.S. Uvarov, Minister of Education under Nicholas I. (Editor)

8. Feoktistov says that he personally saw this dictum written as "an Imperial comment" on a letter of Baron G.O. Ginsburg, who had petitioned for an amelioration of the Jews' position in Russia. The Gospel reference concerns the "legend" of the trial of Christ. When Pilate condemned Christ to be crucified, he told the Jewish Pharisees: "Be his blood upon you and upon your children."

Polovtsov supports this view of the emperor's attitude. Writing in his diary on April 18, 1890, he noted; "Durnovo told me that the Emperor nourishes a special hatred for the Jews. As proof of this, he points out that the Sovereign wrote on Ginsburg's recent report, which defended the Jews, a number of acid comments to the effect that the Jews deserved everything that happened to them. He wrote that they themselves had wanted the blood of Jesus Christ to remain 'upon us and our children.' " In his entry for November 18, 1891 Polovtsov again noted that the emperor had a "fierce hatred of the Jews."

9. But the emperor added: "Nonetheless, it is not to be permitted." All the same, this was not because he was anxious about the Jews, but rather because he feared any mass movement, even if it had a reactionary inspiration.

10. It was this union that led to Russian attempts to dethrone Prince Alexander of Bulgaria and the loss of Russian influence for over a decade. (Editor)

11. This does not mean that Alexander III was lazy, or that he did not want to get at the meat of matters. On the contrary, he was very industrious, spending many hours daily on affairs of state. An analysis of his daily notebooks shows that he spent several hours each evening on his work and frequently only got to bed at one or two o'clock in the morning. Polovtsov mentions this in his diary.

12. Boleslav Markevich (Boleslaw Markiewicz) (1822-1884) was a popular reactionary novelist. His works—which have little literary merit—described various single-handed struggles of patriotic aristocrats against the forces of Polish "nihilism." (Editor)

13. Bazarov and Lopukhov are the radical protagonists in I.S. Turgenev's novel, *Fathers and Sons* (1862) and N.G. Chernyshevsky's *What is to be Done?* (1863). (Editor)

14. Golovnin, in a letter to Miliutin, wrote: "The other day Giers told me that it is remarkable how successful the Sovereign has been in playing His part in affairs of state. Not only does He attentively listen to reports, but discusses them and is personally aware of the needs of, and events in the empire."

Miliutin also mentioned this in his diary, writing on April 26th, 1884: "Since the moment He mounted the throne, the Emperor really changed for the better. Now there is no trace of that light-minded and presumptuous disdain with which, as heir, He used to regard all established methods of conducting affairs of state. There are no more of those pointed, decisive, and categorical verdicts with which He was wont peremptorily to end a discussion. Last May I had the chance to see this for myself."

But there had been no change. Such beliefs were merely a natural product of human nature: men always want to believe that their own hopes are being fulfilled by those who hold power over them.

15. As in any autocratic regime—in which there is no freedom of thought or public opinion—Alexander III was on the whole incapable of any objective understanding of the significance of his own policies. He sincerely believed that these would guarantee the grandeur of Russia and the happiness of the people. He never realized, for example, that his system of administration differed very little from that of Nicholas I. According to Grand Duke Konstantin Konstantinovich, Alexander, on hearing Professor Ya.K. Grot lecture on Pushkin, was genuinely astonished that the poet could have written anything at all under the censorship of that day.

16. At the same time there were occasions when Alexander III revealed his characteristic hypocrisy. I.A. Shestakov, for instance, noted in his diary: "With regard to the report, the Sovereign remarked very sadly that He had received a very touching letter from the mother of one of the criminals. In it the poor woman expressed her conviction that her son had been arrested by mistake, for he had always displayed tender family feelings and the purest and most innocent of inclinations. The mother pleaded to be allowed to see her son and tried to persuade His Majesty that her boy could not be guilty. The Tsar authorized the visit and later sadly told of how the poor mother had been disillusioned. Her son was a desperate fanatic and, by his own admission, was a member of the terrorists." Yet his sympathy did not prevent Alexander III from sending the son of this poor mother to the gallows.

A second example relates to the judicial system. It is well known that the emperor hated jury trials and could not endure an independent judiciary, and that he did his best throughout his reign to eliminate both these features of the system. Yet in 1894, when the newly appointed Minister of Justice (N.V. Muraviev) asked him "On what basis are reforms to be introduced?", Alexander III replied: "On the basis of the inviolability of the judicial statute" (of 1864).

17. A.N. Mosolov, governor of Novgorod, visited Cherevin in 1894 and wrote: "I purposely arrived at breakfast time, in order to catch him and, hopefully, to find him sober. But although his mind was still clear, I found him already in his cups."

18. Cherevin told these stories to P.N. Lebedev, a well-known physicist and professor at the University of Moscow. Lebedev met the general at his sister's house in Strasbourg; she was married to a professor at the university there. He then evidently passed the story on to the revolutionary journalist V.L. Burtsev, who published it in 1912 in *Future*, a newspaper he edited in Paris.

19. V.N. Lamsdorf recorded in his diary a small but interesting detail that shows the simplicity of Alexander III. N.K. Giers told Lamsdorf that the emperor continually had grown fatter during the last years of his life. One day Giers observed that the tsar's "riding breeches had been expanded by means of a large, wedge-shaped patch."

20. Polovtsov, in a diary entry for January 26, 1892, also remarked on the tsarevich's childishness: "Grand Duke Alexander Michaelovich dropped by and told me he had spent last night at Count Sheremetev's. The Tsarevich and Xenia

were also there. They spent the evening playing, running around the house and hiding." As Polovtsov observed, this was a "peculiar pastime for a twenty-four-year-old heir to the throne."

21. Zaionchkovsky's source for the stories of both the gathering of Hussar "wolves" and Nicholas' supposed alcoholism does not appear to be the most reliable. He bases these on V.P. Obninsky's *The Last Autocrat* (Berlin, 1912). Obninsky, who allegedly had been a Guards officer himself at one time and had, Zaionchkovsky says, "known Nicholas well," does not appear to have been an admirer of the Imperial family. (Editor)

22. Meshchersky's own testimony bears this out. On several of the notebook diaries (preserved in Alexander III's archives), he wrote: "To the Tsarevich—for the perusal of His Imperial Highness."

23. This speech, literally only a few sentences in length, was written for Nicholas II by one of his advisers (several sources identify the author as Grand Duke Sergei Alexandrovich). The tsar had not learned to outline his own thoughts for himself, and he read the speech from notes. According to contemporaries, he read this text as prepared for him, but this is not quite accurate: instead of the word "vain" he read "senseless." V.P. Obninsky says that "Nicholas II held the text of His speech in the bottom of His hat, so that He could frequently glance at it."

24. A.A. Polovtsov's diary gives an interesting evaluation of the grand duke's role in the state. Polovtsov was preparing the draft of the rescript, commissioned by the emperor to be issued on the day of the coronation in the name of the chairman of the State Council, and he noted in his diary (on May 15, 1883): "Here you have the luck of human history. In a hundred years—perhaps in a thousand—some historian, reading through the rescripts of the Grand Dukes, will write that the worthy Michael Alexandrovich was the heart and soul of the reign of Alexander III. And this when actually there is almost no difference, as far as simple-mindedness is concerned, between him and his brother Nicholas. It is, I suppose, necessary on such a day to single out one prince of the Imperial House to go onto the stage and persuade the foolish crowd that he is truly a statesman." (Brother Nicholas is, of course, Grand Duke Nicholas Nikolaevich, the Elder.—Editor)

25. On September 24, 1893 A.S. Suvorin, editor of the conservative paper *New Times,* noted in his diary that "Grand Duke Alexander Alexis played baccarat . . . . He made bets of 500 and a thousand francs."

26. On November 22, 1904 the ex-revolutionary L.A. Tikhomirov recorded in his diary that "there was a scandal at the Mikhailovsky Theatre. The public shouted 'Get out of the theatre' at the dancer-mistress of Grand Duke Alexis and 'You are wearing our cruisers and battleships' in reference to her jewels. They yelled so loudly that she was unable to complete the act."

27. Polovtsov recalls that Grand Duke Nicholas' brother, Michael Nikolaevich—who was also not renowned for his intelligence—was at a complete loss when Nicholas Nikolaevich went mad, "as he was astounded that a man of such excessive stupidity could still lose his mind."

28. A.A. Kireev made a similar comment about Vladimir Alexandrovich. In his diary entry for December 17, 1889 he observed that the grand duke was a "lazy egotist who bulged out of his breeches."

29. Chaikovsky set several of Grand Duke Konstantin's poems to music. Particularly well-known is his "I opened the window and could not bear the sadness."

30. This latter is scarcely true: Stasov had no reason to be heartened by useful social activities undertaken by other members of the imperial family.

31. Feoktistov claims that he was told this by Pobedonostsev himself.

32. The "Zemskii Sobor," or Assembly of the Land, had been a Russian equivalent of the Estates General. During the early seventeenth century it had had some political importance, but then fell into disuse. In the nineteenth century the Slavophiles believed that its revival would be a uniquely Russian answer to the Westerners' demands for a parliament. (Editor)

33. To some extent this process is reflected by the number of letters from Pobedonostsev to Alexander III. In 1881 there were 42; in 1882, 26; in 1883, 24; in 1884, 9; in 1885, 18; in 1886, 18; in 1887, 21; in 1888, 14; in 1889, 6; in 1890, 4; in 1891, 9; in 1892, 8; in 1893, 10; and in 1894, 2.

Naturally it was not merely a matter of the number of letters; there was also a considerable change in the nature of their content. While the earlier ones dealt with various affairs of state, those for the last four or five years were devoted almost entirely to matters concerning the Synod.

34. A.V. Bogdanovich and A.A. Kireev frequently referred in their diaries to the decline of Pobedonostsev's influence.

35. In all fairness to Pobedonostsev, he did have a program on one question—the judicial system. In 1885 he compiled a project for judicial reform. This would have restored the features abolished by Alexander II's judicial statute.

36. Tolstoy had gained his reputation from two monographs: his *History of the Russian Financial Administration from the Founding of the State to the End of Catherine II's Reign* (St. Petersburg, 1848), and *Le catolicisme* (sic!) *romain en Russie* (St. Petersburg, 1864), and from a number of articles.

37. As Iu.G. Oksman, the editor of Feoktistov's reminiscences, noted, this is not quite accurate. Pleshcheev's poems, published in 1840, had no general dedication. The subtitle, "To Count D.A. Tolstoy," is on page 12, in connection with the poem, "She Pities Me." (Pleshcheev was not only a poet, but also had been a member of the Petrashevsky circle—Editor).

38. This refers to the peasants of the village of Vakino and the town of Shushnakov in Zaraisk county of Riazan province. They had belonged to Tolstoy's wife. An agreement had been reached with the liberated peasants by which the count and countess had taken the best land; then the Tolstoys, instead of allowing the peasants to take the useless portion, had contrived—in spite of the law of February 19, 1861—to increase the sum of the peasants' *obrok* payments in return for this land. The dissatisfied peasants lodged a complaint on this matter, which the rural arbitrator decided in their favor.

The case then passed to an arbitration court. Tolstoy himself appeared as representative for his wife, and he won a verdict favorable to their own interests. But in the end the Main Committee for Proper Land Settlements in the Countryside, thanks to the position taken by Grand Duke Konstantin Nikolaevich, its chairman, decided in the peasants' favor. Their case had been defended by A.M. Unkovsky, the well-known Tver liberal and friend of M.E. Saltykov-Shchedrin.

39. On May 8, 1889 A.V. Bogdanovich recorded in her diary a conversation with the metropolitan of St. Petersburg about Tolstoy's illness: "He didn't feel sorry for Tolstoy. Besides, he said, no one could remember when he had last received the eucharist. He had not once been to St. Issac's Cathedral or dropped in at the Synod's chancellery during his time as Director-General. It (the Chancellery) had been only a place to hang his coat."

As director-general Tolstoy had shown his ignorance of even a basic knowledge of the Gospel texts. According to B.N. Chicherin, he revealed this "in the speeches he delivered during his trip through Russia" when he remarked that "the French proverb says that a prophet isn't recognized in his own homeland." Here the director-general interpreted the words of Christ as being a French proverb! "The speech was published," says Chicherin, "and many were greatly amused by it."

40. In April, 1866 Dmitry Karakozov, a student, attempted to kill Alexander II. (Editor)

41. The explosion of a bomb planted in the Winter Palace by the "People's Will" terrorists in 1880 convinced Alexander II to allow Loris-Melikov to establish his "dictatorship of the heart," which attempted simultaneously to conciliate society and repress the revolutionaries. Tolstoy's dismissal was one of the government's conciliatory gestures. (Editor)

42. Tolstoy was dismissed just before Easter, on Good Friday. (The phrase referred to here is a parody on the Orthodox Easter greeting "Christ has risen," to which one replies "He has risen indeed." (Editor)

43. Tolstoy feared he was one of the terrorists' targets. P.V. Orzhevsky, his assistant minister and commander of the Gendarme Corps, played on this terror and intimidated Tolstoy so as to keep him continually under control. I.A. Shestakov says that Tolstoy spent two thousand rubles on his personal protection.

Feoktistov mentions this, as does P.A. Valuev. On September 10, 1882 the latter noted in his diary that "Yesterday I saw Durnovo, the Assistant Minister of the Interior. He said that Count Tolstoy fears for his life and that General Orzhevsky plays on this string. When Durnovo told Count Tolstoy that it was useless to place all the police at Orzhevsky's disposal, Count Tolstoy replied: 'Let him have all the responsibility, and let them shoot at him instead of at me.' "

44. Nicholas Stankevich's "circle" of young intellectuals, formed at Moscow University in the 1830s, was mainly interested in German philosophy and it included many who later achieved diverse prominence, including the critic V.G. Belinsky, the anarchist M.A. Bakunin, and the conservative Slavophile K.S. Aksakov. (Editor)

45. Khlestakov is the young, stupid, yet seemingly candid Petersburg bureaucrat in N.V. Gogol's comedy, *The Inspector General*, performed in Moscow in 1836. (Editor)

46. The Polish rising of 1863 against Russian rule caused many nationalistic Russians to fear that their zeal for reform had gone too far. The implication is that Katkov shared such fears. (Editor)

47. In 1077 Emperor Henry IV of Germany had waited barefoot in the snow for three days to receive conditional absolution from Pope Gregory VII at Canossa. (Editor)

48. B.N. Chicherin confirms this story. He recalled that Katkov's "naive wife, after his death, asked the Moscow Land Bank for the coupons for ten thousand shares that her husband had deposited there. She could not believe it when they said there were no shares to be found. The ten thousand had been an annual present from Lazar Solomonovich Poliakov." Hence the only difference between this evidence and Abaza's concerns the sum of the graft Katkov was receiving.

Chicherin recounts another story that is typical of Katkov's greed. In his memoirs the former wrote that "I know very well that the Morshansko-Syzransky (railroad) line management handed over some 5,000 rubles directly to him."

49. "Kuzma (also Kozma) Prutkov" was a collective pseudonym under which Count A.K. Tolstoy and his cousins, A.M., A.M. and V.M. Zhemchuzhnikov, published satirical writings and nonsense verses (between 1853 and 1863). "Prutkov" was allegedly a self-centered, arrogant, complacent and naive clerk in the Ministry of Finance, and his "writings" satirized conservative and reactionary attitudes. (Editor)

50. Meshchersky had been commissioned to organize a school for artisans named after the late heir to the throne. According to Feoktistov, he had embezzled from the funds allotted for this purpose.

51. The paper's aim was defined as being "to unite and consolidate those of us who make up the poor, wandering flock of adherents of a serious monarchical principle in Russia, and to give us strength in the battle against nihilism on one hand and Prussian constitutionalism on the other." Publication was to begin in 1882.

52. Meshchersky spent three pages in begging for this money, writing that it "is everything to me but, frankly speaking, it is 'nothing' to you."

53. This letter was written in 1876 and refers to Meshchersky's journey to Vienna and Belgrade. On September 16, 1876 Pobedonostsev informed Alexander that Meshchersky had sent a packet of letters from abroad "with a request that it be given to Your Highness."

54. In one of Meshchersky's letters to the tsar in 1883, he wrote: "This year makes it, alas, a decade during which I have been prevented from seeing and listening to You."

55. On July 14, 1883 Meshchersky, thanking Alexander III for an appointment, wrote: "You are the Sovereign of two houses; in both of them You are master. One house is Your court and there You see everyone. To give me access there is almost unthinkable (though possible on rare occasions, when authorized). Nonetheless it seems to me that I must not hope for a place as a guest there . . . .

"But You have, Majesty, a second house. This is Your Soul . . . . No one but God sees You there.

"As always I will entrust my letters to the post box and You, my Sovereign, if You will sometimes grant me the favor and joy of a reply could send me a little letter *via* K(onstantin) Petrov(ich). Yet I must promise not to indulge myself in these impudent dreams of happiness. Indeed I do not have the right to do so when I remember everything I should remember."

In this way their relationship was maintained in secret.

56. These diaries were also sent in secret. In one of his letters Meshchersky mentions the methods used: "The departure of (A.S.) Vasilkovsky (a Court administrative official) places me in a difficult position, and I am uncertain about how I may call Your revered attention from time to time to my diaries. I have an *instinctive fear* of sending them by mail—a fear that they may be intercepted and read. I have something ready, but don't know how to send it. Perhaps You will permit me to send it *via* the Bureau of the Most August Children—by means of Vasilkovsky—or perhaps through S.I. Witte. He is a man who can keep a secret and say not a word to anyone."

This letter is also interesting for the light it casts on the degree of intimacy existing between Witte and Meshchersky.

57. The second "unfortunate circumstance" was the influence of Pobedonostsev.

58. Meshchersky not only spoke about the benefits that the Russian people would derive from the birch in his confidential diaries, destined for Alexander III, but openly in his newspaper. On December 16, 1888 he hypocritically wrote in the *Citizen*: "Stop flogging, and authority will disappear. Just as the Russian needs his salt and the Russian *muzhik* needs his black bread, so he needs the birch. If man will die without salt, so the people will perish without the birch . . . . Love of mankind demands the birch."

59. To understand Zaionchkovsky's thrust here, it should be recalled that the word *prosveshchenie*, usually translated here as "education," also means "enlightenment" in the broader sense. Hence the Ministry of Education could be called the "Ministry of National Enlightenment." (Editor)

1. Polovtsov's diary contains an even more damning portrait: "Ostrovsky, the Minister of State Domains, . . . represents the type of most despicable and dangerous bureaucrat; he is an envious and servile toady. One by one he betrayed (A.A.) Abaza with Loris, and then Ignatiev, and he will take the first chance he gets to harm Tolstoy, Bunge, or even Pobedonostsev, just as long as it is to his— Ostrovsky's—advantage."

2. This is Feoktistov's term. He also notes that Tolstoy often used censorious terms when speaking of Delianov.

3. The term *Pugachevshchina* (referring to the peasant and cossack rising led by E.I. Pugachev from 1773 to 1775) became used generally to denote the wide-spread peasant rising that many feared was imminent. (Editor)

4. Here Tolstoy is referring to two high officials in the Ministry of Finance: A.A. Richter and M.E. Kovalevsky. Feoktistov observed that "the first had at one time worked with (N.A.) Serno-Solovievich, who was later exiled to Siberia, while the second had hidden the famous (S.G.) Nechaev for several days after he had committed a murder at the Petrovsky Academy."

5. Plehve's archives contain a letter from him to Tolstoy (dated December 28, 1886) that deals with Reutern's retirement from his post as chairman of the Committee of Ministers. On this letter Tolstoy wrote: "Does no one know who is to be appointed to this post?" Thus, only three days before the event, Tolstoy did not know about Bunge's appointment.

6. Polovtsov is presumably referring to the emperor's, not Reutern's initiative. (Editor)

7. The fact that these ideas about the supremacy of the Russian nationality were elaborated by a man who was German in nationality and Lutheran in faith is not remarkable: as a rule proselytes become the most extreme among the orthodox.

8. Nonetheless, Bunge finally did admit "that the union of the plenitude of administrative powers and judicial authority in one person . . . . proved in practice to be a fortunate thought."

9. Bunge believed the principle of communal landownership to be a cause of the spread of socialist thought. Many Russian statesmen, quite apart from the liberals, were critical of the commune. P.A. Valuev and A.E. Timashev both expressed sharp criticisms of this institution.

10. The title uses the word *soslovenie,* or estate, in the sense of the French *"état."* On some occasions this term will be translated as "class," which is more meaningful to the Anglo-American reader. (Editor)

11. The "rural arbitrator" was a local official established to supervise the division of land between the former serfs and the landed gentry in accord with the provisions of the emancipation of 1861. (Editor)

12. Pazukhin did not envisage the gentry as a closed caste and he believed that "the entry of new and healthy elements will awaken the landed gentry as an estate."

13. On October 10, 1886 Muraviev wrote to Plehve: "I have placed in your friendly hands all my official and, therefore, all my personal destinies." He frequently reminded Plehve of this fact.

14. V.D. Gadzhello was charged with having illegally ordered the flogging of Alexander Korolev, an assistant barrister and nobleman, who had been brought to the police station when drunk, and of Fedor Nikolaevsky, a Moscow University student, who had tried to rescue Korolev. But despite Muraviev's efforts, Gadzhello was given a stiff sentence: he was permanently exiled to Siberia.

15. One of the police witnesses, for example, freely admitted that the "blank warrants of arrest were signed beforehand; the text could be filled in later and not even shown to the person arrested."

16. In May, 1894 General Kireev, who was close to the court, recorded in his diary a story that reveals Alexander III's attitude to legality. Prince A.K. Imeretinsky, the chief military prosecutor, told Kireev that "not long ago the Sovereign pardoned Zherebkov, who had coldly and foully pumped two bullets into a comrade. Earlier He had pardoned the scoundrel Bartenev, the murderer of Vysinskaia, but had an artillery officer (in the Caucasus) arrested for trapping some civilian and killing him (though it is true that the civilian did not want to fight a duel). Imeretinsky proposed that he be reduced to the ranks."

17. Perhaps Alexander III's greatest deficiency as a statesman resulted from his own limited abilities: this was his intoxication with his own power. He had difficulty in distinguishing between his "rights" and the "laws." V.N. Lamsdorf's diary contains the following description of the emperor: "He is not wicked, but He is drunk with power and too narrow to see things as they really are. He can't understand that there are limits placed on arbitrary power. They say that General Vannovsky privately compares Him with Peter the Great. 'He is Peter, with his cudgel,' the War Minister remarks. 'But no,' he continues, 'if we are to be accurate, here is only the cudgel, without the great Peter.' "

18. One example of this was the exiling of a peasant of Kovrovsky county (in Vladimir province) to Eastern Siberia for his systematic refusal to make redemption payments.

19. This occurred, to cite one instance, with regard to charges against the governors Prince A.D. Nakashidze of Elizavetpol, and P.V. Nekliudov of Orel.

20. In all fairness it should be mentioned that the Committee of Ministers sometimes did reject illegal propositions. Thus the Minister of the Interior's request that the peasants in Ufa province be made collectively responsible for forest offenses was twice refused. But this was apparently the exception, for no similar cases have been discovered.

21. Valuev was dismissed when a Senate investigation in 1881-1882 revealed that the Bashkirs in Ufa province had been plundered of their lands. As Minister of State Domains, Valuev bore the final responsibility (even though he was personally not implicated), but the real reason for his dismissal was Alexander III's personal dislike of him.

22. During Alexander III's reign those holding other posts were also given seats in the State Council.

23. Nikolai was chairman of the Department of Laws, and Abaza of that for State Economy.

24. This river runs through St. Petersburg, now Leningrad. (Editor)

25. In the Russian edition Vyshnegradsky is incorrectly identified as Minister of Education. (Editor)

26. This was written after one of Anastasiev's letters (addressed to an acquaintance named Stechkin) was intercepted by the police. In it Anastasiev complained: "I am up to my neck in work, with three sessions a week in the Department as well as a General Session and the time spent in the Committee of Ministers. I hardly have time to read the reports; I dare say that this haste is reflected in bad legislation."

27. Polovtsov, in his diary entry for January 15, 1891, also mentioned this business: "Martynov had managed the affairs of the (Court) stables very badly; lately the rumors about his misuse of funds have become increasingly persistent.

So it was decided that Martynov should be dismissed, but he had the insolence to demand that he be appointed Senator. The Emperor's first reaction was to collapse in laughter and refuse point-blank, but later He bacame less adamant about this request, and . . . Martynov has become a Senator."

28. One such example is the Senate's decision concerning Governor Nekliudov of Orel, who had been charged with the mass torture of the peasants of Oboleshevo village in Orel province.

29. This occurred in the case of the Lutheran pastor, Grimm, who was exiled to Siberia by the Riga district court.

30. The law of May 3, 1883 was to regulate the rights of the Old Believers, but the Synod used it to repress them. Attempts at suppressing them increased substantially and in 1887 and 1891 conventions of missionaries working among the schismatics were held in Moscow to plan further measures.

31. At this time the First Section was the most significant. In 1882 the Second Section was liquidated, and its business passed over to the State Council where a Codification Section was set up in the State Chancellery. In 1880 the Third Section had been closed down and taken over by the Ministry of the Interior as the Department of Police. The Fourth Section (known as the Department of the Empress Maria Fedorovna) managed charitable institutions for women and continued its existence, but under the new title of "H.I.M. Own Chancellery for the Department of the Empress Maria."

32. Next to this sentence Alexander III wrote: "This remark is more than just strange."

33. The "Table of Ranks" (or, more correctly, the parallel tables of civil and military ranks) had been established in 1722 by Peter the Great. Each civil or military rank entitled its holder to certain class or "estate" rights, so that a commoner who took up state service and reached the specified rank could become either a personal, or even a hereditary "noble." (Editor)

34. This does not include ownership of city real estate, a town residence, or a summer house.

35. Zaionchkovsky's figures here are inaccurate and apparently leave out one landowning official. (Editor)

36. All forms of landownership (hereditary estates, those purchased, or owned by wives) are included here. If the estate was jointly owned with others in the family, the official was considered to own only half of the land. A desiatina equals 2.7 acres. (Editor)

37. As before, all forms of landownership are computed.

38. Another representative of the Russian great landed gentry was Minister of Education Delianov, who was an Armenian in nationality.

39. Feoktistov says that the philosopher V.S. Soloviev once scornfully asked F.P. Elenev, a member of the Main Directorate of the Press, "if it was true that there were administrative instructions that brothels might only employ women of the Orthodox faith." But Feoktistov did not appreciate the question's sarcastic barb, and remarked: "Poor Soloviev—to have come to this."

40. In a front page article on these events in an 1883 issue of the *Moscow News*, Katkov attacked the Polish press for "refusing to accept the fact that it was a Russian and not a Polish university that had been founded in Warsaw."

41. In an effort to weaken Polish nationalist sentiment after the anti-Russian uprising of 1863, the territory of the Kingdom of Poland became known as merely the Trans-Vistula district of the empire. (Editor)

42. The Russian text—which reads "not only lovingly, but with outright hostility"—evidently contains a misprint. (Editor)

43. Feoktistov's instructions (issued as head of the Main Press Directorate on March 31, 1883 to the St. Petersburg Censorship Committee) after a Polish-language paper had used the phrase "Polish colony in St. Petersburg" and this had been repeated in the Russian press, are of interest. "May I call to your attention," wrote Feoktistov, "to the fact that the word 'colony' by definition must refer to an acknowledged colony abroad, and may in no way be applied to Russian subjects of Polish origin living in St. Petersburg, the capital of our state. The Main Directorate of the Press suggests that the St. Petersburg Censorship Committee take steps to see that the Polish public of St. Petersburg is not, in censored publications, referred to as the Polish colony."

44. The autonomous Grand Duchy of Finland had its own Senate—an executive council under the crown—and a Diet (or House of Representatives of the Lands), composed of representatives elected by the four social estates (nobility, clergy, burgers, and farmers). After 1869 by law it had to meet every five years, but in practice met every three. (Editor)

45. As for Ukrainian literature, the Ministry of the Interior strictly enforced the restrictions of a law of May 18, 1876 and took further steps: the importation of Ukrainian-language periodicals and literary works from abroad, as well as their printing at home, became increasingly difficult. The Ukrainian-language theatre was also persecuted. In 1884 Ukrainian companies were banned from performing in Volynsk, Podolsk, Kiev, Poltava, and Chernigov provinces (that is, in the basic territories of the Ukraine).

The Jewish theatre was similarly persecuted. In a confidential circular to the governors, dated February 19, 1891, the Minister of the Interior stated that it was inadmissible to allow the performance of Jewish plays in slang (that is, in Yiddish). These had been banned earlier by a circular of the Assistant Minister of Interior, dated August 17, 1883.

46. This article argued as follows: "As long as you have the same faith as your oppressors, no one can help you. You are kept, body and soul, in bridle to your tormentors, trapped by the laws and your faith as oakum is in tar. Your spiritual pastors and those who rob you eat and drink from the same trough; they are laughing at you . . . . They rob you of your last kopek for the church and fleece you until you are stripped naked, so that hunger and the burden of taxes force you to remain in the slave's yoke . . . . Destroy the religious chains which bind you to your enemies and those who swindle you!"

47. These were his daughters Louisa (18 years old) and Amalia (12 years old), and his son, Egon (15 years old).

48. The report maintains that Louisa, the eldest daughter, and Magnus Krasmus, a peasant who was present, gave written testimony that the Toropil parents themselves supposedly "desired that their children be accepted into the Orthodox faith, but as they could not—for some reason—themselves be present in person at the ceremony, they had deputised Magnus Krasmus to serve as witness before the priest."

49. Pobedonostsev considered it inexpedient to make this letter public knowledge. "It would have been wise," he wrote Tolstoy, "not to have called attention to the punishments decreed by our criminal code for defaulters from the faith and not to have directly confronted the Lutherans on matters in which solutions are—and especially in the present circumstances—so directly attended with difficulties and reciprocal misunderstandings."

50. According to data compiled by the General Consistory of the Evangelical Lutheran Church, the number of such persons was over 35,000. Meiendorf put the

figure at 30,000, while the bishop of Riga maintained that there were 18,000 persons who had "deviated from Orthodoxy."

51. The figure 178 is taken from an 1895 report of Meiendorf. According to A.F. Koni, the number of pastors tried in Latvia "reached 56."

52. The St. Petersburg Judicial Bench revised this sentence and applied Article 193 to Grimm. But A.A. Kuzminsky, the prosecutor (and husband of D.A. Tolstoy's sister), appealed this decision. He transferred the case to the Senate and, A.F. Koni says, tried to pressure this body. But Kuzminsky's appeal was rejected. In this incident both Koni and Minister of Justice Manasein showed a great deal of courage, because the emperor himself favored the decision reached in the Grimm case by the Riga district court.

53. Along with the All-Russian Orthodox Missionary Society there existed a number of Orthodox fraternities that were engaged in spreading the faith. The largest of these—the Baltic Orthodox Brotherhood—had been founded in 1822.

54. This appeared in the *Citizen* on February 12, 1892, but it did not necessarily mean that this paper's editor was indignant about the methods used in Christianizing the Buriats. His attitude was rather the result of his embittered relations with the Director-General of the Holy Synod. On this occasion he was criticizing Pobedonostsev (Meshchersky frequently used his paper for this purpose).

55. These verdicts were reached at the sessions of May 14, 1891, November 24 and December 22, 1892. On June 16, 1892 the Council of Ministers completely quashed a sentence of the Menzelinsk criminal and civil court. In this case the person convicted had repented and expressed his wish to return to the bosom of Orthodoxy. He was therefore pardoned.

56. The draft for the "Provisional Regulations for the Jews" was prepared by Count Ignatiev but met with serious opposition within the Council of Ministers. Thus the regulations were finally adopted in a considerably revised form.

57. The italics are Zaionchkovsky's. (Editor)

58. This report was signed by eight members: Pahlen, Georgievsky, Mitskevich, Martens, Lozino-Lozinsky, Prince K.M. Golitsyn, Gerard, and Koloshin. The latter declared: "I do not share the guiding principles outlined in this report," but said he would keep his opinion to himself. So he was, in fact, virtually against the proposals.

59. On June 16, 1887 the Committee of Ministers discussed Delianov's proposal and, on June 18 the Minister of Education issued a circular restricting the entry of children from the poorer strata of the population into progymnasiums and gymnasiums. This, naturally, also affected the Jews.

60. According to data from the superintendents of educational districts, in gymnasiums and progymnasiums the percentage of Jews was considerably diminishing from year to year. Thus, in the Moscow district, it dropped from 5.6 per cent in 1886 to 3.5 per cent in 1891, and to 2.5 per cent in 1893; in the Vilna district the percentage fell from 23.1 in 1885 to 12.1 in 1895; in the Odessa district modern schools the percentages were 20.3 in 1885 and 13.0 in 1894.

61. During the years 1882-1894 the restrictions for institutions of higher learning were never observed. Thus, in 1894 the percentage of persons who were Jewish by religion was 26.3. Yet in St. Petersburg University the number of Jewish students was considerably curtailed, falling from 246 in 1884 to 71 in 1894.

62. As indicated previously, the documents of the Pahlen Commission have been preserved in none of the archival collections and none of the governors replies have been discovered.

63. This remark was made in connection with the appointment of Grand Duke Sergei as governor-general of Moscow. Prince V.M. Golitsyn remarked on this

attitude in his diary. On March 17, 1891 he wrote: "The Jewish question is first and foremost; it is evident that no one is going to stand on ceremony in this regard."

64. In a report to the emperor, Durnovo referred to this as a "beneficial" measure.

65. On June 21, 1882 the Minister of the Interior issued instructions confirming the application of this circular.

66. A later circular of June 25, 1894 extended the expulsion date until June 1, 1895.

67. An author's footnote states that no copies of these instructions were uncovered, but that they are indirectly referred to in documents in Department of Police archives. (Editor)

68. In 1893 the members of the administration of the seaside resort of Dubbelin telegraphed the Minister of the Interior and requested "an immediate order allowing Jewish residence for the length of the Dubbelin bathing season; otherwise the town is threatened with a terrible famine, so have pity and save the poor people."

69. In the end the poll tax was abolished—except for Siberia—as of January 1, 1887.

70. At the end of 1884 the finance minister put forward a new proposal ("On Additional Taxes on Revenues from Commercial and Industrial Enterprises, their Rates and Assessments"). The State Council accepted this and the emperor approved it. This law established a three percent tax on the net profits of joint stock companies and associations. An assessment on revenues of commercial-industrial enterprises was introduced and a rate set of 0.1 percent of the value of the production of plants and factories, and fifteen percent of the guild duty value for commercial firms. Hence Bunge was only partially successful in obtaining his original goals.

71. This law also applied to deposits in credit and loan associations.

72. The revenues from such duties did not compensate for the sums lost by abolishing the poll tax. To increase revenues, in 1886 state peasants were burdened by redemption payments (to make up for the quit-rents and poll taxes previously collected from them).

73. In his draft "On Raising the Import Duties on European Goods," presented to the State Council on March 21, 1885, Bunge wrote: "The measures Germany and France have adopted recognize the absolute necessity of protecting the farmers of these countries from the great slump in grain prices created by the appearance in European markets of the large grain supplies of America, Australia and India. This imposes on the Ministry of Finance the obligation of accommodating to the new situation confronting the Russian export trade."

Because of this, Bunge said, Russia's grain exports had diminished and some of the goods Russia had acquired abroad (and paid for with payments received for grain) would now have to be obtained domestically or be imported in lesser quantities. Otherwise the situation would be reflected in the value of the ruble. To create the proper conditions for the production of these goods in Russia, the finance minister proposed that the tariff on the majority of imported goods be raised to twenty percent. This proposal was accepted.

74. *Obrok* was the money payment made by serfs to landowners in place of actual service as laborers on their lands, in some regions of Russia before 1861. (Editor)

75. According to T.I. Fillipov, Vyshnegradsky had a fortune of a million rubles when he became minister, but by 1892 this had risen to two million.

76. By "three" measures Vyshnegradsky meant *two* monopolies and the re-organized railway duties.

77. A *pud* equals 36 pounds in weight. (Editor)

78. Alexander III approved this decision on October 12, 1889. This was not an isolated incident. In January, 1888 the State Council examined the Minister of Finance's project "On Facilitating the Procedure for Paying Loans to 'The Land Credit Loan Society' before Expiration of the Term." This aimed at making it easier for the landowners to redeem their estates. The State Council approved the draft, and the emperor confirmed it.

79. As Polovtsov put it, Witte was "Vyshnegradsky's dearest accomplice on the the railroad question."

CHAPTER III

1. The idea of removing the police department and gendarme corps from the Ministry of the Interior possibly originated in court circles: P.A. Cherevin had made a similar proposal at the end of 1881.

2. Pobedonostsev wrote to Alexander III and described his conversation as being the fulfillment of "His Highness' " instructions, although he said nothing of the exact nature of the latter. Still, Pobedonostsev frequently made suggestions to the emperor and then, once they were accepted, claimed he had merely been obeying instructions. This had happened in the matter of the manifesto of April 29, 1881.

Katkov referred to Pobedonostsev's role in Tolstoy's appointment. In a letter to the director-general dated November 27, 1883 Katkov, discussing the proposed university statute, wrote: " . . . is it possible that you have returned to your previous views of Count Tolstoy, who holds the leading post in the government *with your help*?" (Authors italics–Editor)

3. The special post of third assistant minister was created on June 25, 1882, and was to be filled by the commander of the Detached Corps of Gendarmes. The Department of State Police, along with the police chiefs of Warsaw and Moscow, were to be subordinated directly to him. The city governor of St. Petersburg, how-ever, was directly responsible to the Minister of the Interior.

4. It would seem that if General Orzhevsky's department did not simply fabri-cate these rumors, it did at least greatly exaggerate them.

5. Sergei P. Degaev was one of the first prominent revolutionaries to serve as a police agent; the system of agent-provocateurs practiced at this time was named for him. When his comrades discovered Degaev's double game they, in turn, persuaded him to kill Sudeikin, the policeman who had recruited him. (Editor)

6. Zaionchkovsky does not date this ambiguous diary note of Shestakov's but, as Orzhevsky served as gendarme commander only from 1882 to 1887, it may refer to his retirement in the latter year. (Editor)

7. This article dealt solely with administrative exile in its general form. It did not indicate the category of persons subject to exile, although the sense of the law was that it was applicable only to those who were politically suspect.

8. Evidently the proposed legal change would merely grant judicial approval to an already existing practice. In Tolstoy's proposal it was not solely the politi-cally suspect who were to be exiled administratively. According to his data, from October, 1881 to May 1, 1883, 104 persons were administratively exiled. Of these, 32 were considered to be politically suspect. Of the remainder, 25 were

exiled for inciting peasants to disorders, 43 for embezzling public funds, keeping dives and for slander. Four others were exiled for inciting former Uniats to abandon Orthodoxy.

9. These envisaged the implementation of a number of administrative measures: the right to subject to search and preliminary arrest persons suspected of political crimes; the right to refuse approval of persons selected to serve in zemstvo or municipal institutions of public administration, and so forth.

10. Two cases of rejection of such requests have been discovered. In 1885 General Roop, serving as provisional governor-general of Odessa, requested that a "state of strengthened vigilance" be introduced into the whole of his area of administration; in 1892 the governor-general of Kiev made a similar request with regard to particular localities in Chernigov province. The Council of Ministers rejected both petitions.

11. Such allowances were disbursed from the so-called "patron's funds," which were not subjected to accounting or control. The allowances were given to various categories of persons, including widows of officials and aged and crippled workers. These payments were demagogic in character; the Department of Police had inherited this function from the Third Section, which was supposed to "support orphans and widows" as well as carry out police work. According to the data for 1891, the general sums of such allowances varied from 720 to 1,200 rubles a month. Disbursed as single payments or on a continuing basis, the average sums varied from five to twenty-five rubles and, in individual cases, reached fifty rubles.

12. In 1887 the "reference table" compiled by the Fifth Office was abolished, and a newly formed Special Registration Section assumed this function.

13. In 1889 there was a redistribution of functions among the various offices. Issuing passports for travel abroad became the job of the Second, rather than the Third, while the latter took over undercover surveillance from the Fifth.

14. It also seems that the number of permanent officials grew somewhat. The budget expenditure on salaries in 1894 showed an increase of 23,800 rubles over that of 1880 (rising from 96,200 rubles in 1880 to 120,000 in 1894).

15. In 1880 the railway police and gendarmes numbered 126 officers and 2,432 other ranks; on January 1, 1895 these figures had risen to 217 and 4,170, respectively.

16. Before 1900 the Warsaw section was known as the Special Chancellery of the Deputy for Police Units to the Governor-General of Warsaw.

17. The functions of the Moscow section and Warsaw special chancellery were identical.

18. The personnel consisted of a chief, his deputy, five officers for missions, a clerk, an assistant clerk, a manager of accounts, an archivist, and a keeper of the journal. In 1881 the St. Petersburg branch organized a special subsection or "desk" to deal with factories and industrial plants. This special section expended 2,560 rubles in that year.

19. The staff comprised the chief of the section, the deputy chief, the clerk, his assistant, and two officers for special assignments.

20. After 1886 the Moscow Okhrana section received up to 7,500 rubles a year for "an increase of its means." Sums spent on secret agents and undercover surveillance made up about seventy percent of its expenditures.

21. By the end of the 1870s the Third Section's estimates for its secret expenditures showed a constant increase (from 186,877 rubles in 1877 to 558,957 in 1880). A comparison of these estimates suggests that this increase was spent mainly on the work of secret agents. The governor-general of Moscow spent some

7,500 rubles for this purpose in 1880, but by 1883 the Moscow Okhrana section was receiving, for the same purposes, 30,000 rubles, and after 1886, 37,500 rubles.

22. In 1883 the expenses of the Department of Police (including those of the Provincial Gendarme Administrations) for such purposes were 343,340 rubles and 66 kopeks, for a third of the year, and 1,030,021 rubles, 98 kopeks for the whole year. In 1895 this sum was 1,026,952 rubles.

23. This is taken from the *Historical Survey of the Organization and Activities of the Department of Police.*

24. In the latter half of the 1890s there must have been some increase in the number of administrative exiles both because of growth of the strike movement and the membership of the "Union for the Struggle for the Liberation of the Working Class."

25. It must be concluded that these figures are incomplete. Several members of the "People's Will," imprisoned in Schliisselburg fortress, are not included, for they do not figure in any of the categories mentioned.

26. According to the circular, Tolstoy's proposal to the Committee of Ministers was based on petitions received from several governors. The circular attempted to prove that floggings were the mildest form of punishment. "It cannot be doubted," it maintained, "that in the particular circumstances of time, place, the nature of the local population, and of the disorder itself, corporal punishment may be the only appropriate and expedient measure and, as it affects only a few malefactors, it is incomparably less harsh than the dispatch of a military (punitive) expedition. This latter brings ruin to the whole population, even when no recourse to arms is necessary.

27. In 1885 there was a mass flogging of the peasants in the village of Gogolev, in Otersk county of Chernigov province, who had tried to prevent a survey being made of land boundaries. Governor Anastasiev, in his yearly report to the emperor, described his handling of these events as follows: "After two decades without firm measures to repress peasant disorders, and in the wake of a whole number of unsuccessful efforts to put down such disorders, . . . this approach (flogging) on the part of the administration stunned the enraged crowd by its very novelty and made a strong impression. A few months later . . . . some volost elders declared to me that it was now easier for them to carry out their duties as the peasants, hearing of the events in the village of Gogolev, had become more passive and regarded authority with much more respect."

28. Meshchersky, when recounting the governor's merits to Alexander III, wrote: "He certainly is an intelligent man. One notes from his stories that he ordered a flogging in order to put down a peasant mutiny. After the company drummer had birched the young loudmouth, he and the rest of the peasant oafs quieted down. Now there has been almost no rebelliousness for two years."

29. Actually, since this forest suffered no blight whatsoever, it proved "necessary" to cut it down because, as the forest was situated on the shore of the Desna river, "a danger of quicksand was revealed."

30. He had evidently promised Durnovo to sell the forest for this figure.

31. Khizhniakov told another story that illustrated Anastasiev's "courtesy" to the provincial ladies. "One day," he wrote, "he entered his sitting room. Several ladies who had come to visit his sick wife were sitting there and talking about the low quality of servants nowadays. Prosecutor Z.'s wife was indignant over the rudeness and other offenses of her cook." Then, when this lady returned home, she found her cook in hysterics. It turned out that Anastasiev, "having listened to the complaints of the prosecutor's wife, had sought to do her a favor. He had

immediately telephoned instructions that her cook was to be flogged so that she would learn to do her work more diligently."

32. The land captain's decision to arrest the women was illegal in the extreme.

33. This very modest account of these events is based on the journal of the Committee of Ministers. Actually, according to Feoktistov's diary, action took place on a considerably greater scale. "The brutal floggings were carried out over the course of several days," he noted. "Many unfortunates received up to 150 strokes, and one old man, unable to withstand the torture, died." As an afterthought, Feoktistov sarcastically observed: "This is evidently just as it should be in a well-organized state . . . ."

It was these events that Leo Tolstoy described in his article "*Le Salut en vous.*"

34. Alexander III was not always so protective of arbitrary governors, especially during the first years of his reign. Events similar to those described, and involving a governor's illegal behavior, occurred in Minsk province at the end of the 1870s. Governor V.N. Tokarev had illegally seized land in the province, treating it as crown property when it actually belonged to the peasants of Lagishino village in Pinsk county. The owners were unwilling to surrender the hay grown on this land to Tokarev and the local officials organized the massive birching and torturing of the peasants. For a long time the case was heard in various appeal courts and finally, at the end of 1884 and in 1885, by the State Council. As a result, Tokarev was dismissed and his further promotion within the service was prohibited.

Grand Duke Michael Nikolaevich, the State Council's chairman, suggested that Tokarev should be treated leniently in the interests of "maintaining authority." Alexander III replied "that in this case there were great abuses and they deserved to be punished."

35. N.M. Klingenberg was governor of Kovno, and Prince N.N. Trubetskoy was governor of Minsk.

36. According to Tolstoy's proposal, the peasants "in spite of every attempt to exact the arrears from them (that is, to entail the defaulters' earnings, to sell their property, and to seize the leases to the hay fields), continued to be stubborn; being prevented from working their own fields, they rented land from one of their fellow villagers. The peasants explained their evasion of redemption payments by their desire to obtain the lime furnaces and forest that belonged to the former landlord, as well as their expectations of a new statute." Presumably the peasants' persistent demands for the lime furnaces and woodland was based on the fact that these had been their property, acquired by them before the emancipation, but in their landlord's name.

37. On November 7, 1889 the Committee of Ministers again examined this question. The new discussion took place because the date of exile had to be postponed until spring of 1890, as the last steamer for prisoners already had departed. This time 17, rather than 20 families, were mentioned, so three families had evidently paid their arrears.

38. The governors made similar attempts in their weekly reports. The history of these reports begins in 1864, when the Minister of the Interior ordered the governors to send weekly secret reports on the conditions in their provinces. But in time this practice had died out. Then, on November 4, 1883, Tolstoy sent the governors "an absolutely confidential circular." This ordered them to forward to him certain information on a weekly basis. "In the weekly reports," the circular read, "you should inform me of all public events and of all information gathered from the reports of the various administrative authorities concerning the nature of

the work of people holding positions in every department . . . ; of their social positions and inter-relationships; of decisions made by public and estate institutions that are deserving of attention; of the various pronouncements and judgements expressed in discussions; of the opinions of every public figure, and of everyone who has generally any influence on the present state of affairs in a particular sphere or region, or on a particular governmental measure, whether proposed or realized; on the existing parties and their attitudes toward each other and toward the authorities of the government; on any significant event; and so on."

All this was highly secret. "It goes without saying," said the circular, "that no one is to be told or informed of my present instructions; they are to be kept to yourself, and no record is to be kept anywhere . . . . The information requested . . . must be collected with the greatest care by you personally, on your own initiative and without issuing any instructions concerning the reports received."

In spite of this categorical order the governors only reported that "nothing worthy of attention had occurred" in the province, included other and ordinary bits of information, or usually made simply no report at all. This seems to suggest that, firstly, the governors were attempting to conceal the real state of affairs, so as "not to disturb the authorities," and, secondly, that "the provincial bosses" had definite "separatist" aspirations and did not want the central government interfering in their "own" activities.

39. Vishniakov's tour of the provinces suffering from crop failures moved Senator F.L. Barykov to write the following verses:

Arriving amidst great hunger
Vishniakov, the Privy Councillor,
Talked and investigated.
And with words of exhortation
He calmed the fears,
Limited the bounds of the misfortune.
Speaking with authority,
He called forth unlimited bread
And so raised the demand everywhere.

About all of this he joyously
Wrote long reports
In servile words.
Durnovo was light of heart
And enjoyed his carefree life,
Convincing everyone how exaggerated
Were the misfortunes of the famine
By the enemies of the state
Who only sought to create turmoil . . .

40. A circular to the governors, dated October 20, 1889, pointed out that "recently there have appeared in a number of provincial newspapers misleading and even false reports about the situation of those living in localities suffering from crop failure and about the absence of measures for guaranteeing food supplies." Further on, it said that the Minister of the Interior, "without wishing to hamper the newspapers' discussion of these events, and recognizing the undoubted utility of the appearance of accurate and appropriate information in the press," nonetheless ordered the governors, "in the censoring of such reports, to conduct themselves with particular care and discretion."

One and a half months later, on December 2, another circular repeated these instructions to the governors. All this is obvious evidence of the ministry's efforts to downplay as much as possible the extent of the disaster.

41. At this time, on December 29, Durnovo proposed in the State Council the allocation of sixty million rubles for famine relief, and announced that the ministry had already spent 83,851,500 rubles for this purpose.

42. According to the statute of February 19, 1861, the agreement of one half of the meeting was required.

43. One author claims the writer was A.S. Ermolov, the director of the Department of Tax Collection, Ministry of Finance.

44. Alexander III approved the State Council's decision on June 8, 1893.

45. At this time Witte was an ardent supporter of the commune. He thought the communal form of landholding was "the one most suitable from the point of view of protecting the peasantry from poverty and homelessness. The commune," he wrote, "shows incomparably greater vitality than one could have imagined." It was only at a later date that Witte became a firm proponent of private land ownership for the peasantry.

46. V.M. Khizhniakov, who in 1887 was chairman of the provincial zemstvo board, says that in that year Anastasiev ordered a search of the board's premises. This did not, of course, produce any results.

47. Alexander III made the following comment on this issue: "What measures has the government taken to deal with this disgrace?"

48. N.F. Rumiantsev, one Popov, the board's chairmen, and two of its members (Yarunich and Belov) were exiled.

49. The commission noted in its report that the zemstvo had acted independently, without the superintendent's permission, in appointing teachers for public schools. In Mosolov's opinion the Cherepovets zemstvo "was made up of socialists who, having got power into their hands, are abusing it recklessly for their own absolutely outrageous ends."

50. In 1883 these had amounted to 2,737,044 rubles and in 1884 to 2,776,597; in 1885 the estimate of proposed expenditures was for a sum of 2,867,581 rubles.

51. The emperor agreed fully with the governor and noted in the margin: "All this is improper; but what can one do to regulate such allocations?"

CHAPTER IV

1. The Special Commission was originally composed of fourteen members: M.S. Kakhanov, M.E. Kovalevsky, S.A. Mordvinov, A.A. Polovtsov, I.I. Shamshin, D.V. Gotovtsev, E.V. Frisch, and others.

2. These were M.S. Kakhanov, M.E. Kovalevsky, S.A. Mordvinov, A.A. Polovtsov, I.N. Durnovo, P.P. Semenov, F.L. Barykov, I.E. Andreevsky, G.P. Galagin, and N.A. Baganov.

3. In all there were 34 members. Of these, nineteen were specially appointed (with the agreement of the appropriate department) and fifteen were invited figures. Among the experts were A.K. Anastasiev, governor of Perm; A.V. Bogdanovich, governor of Voronezh; S.N. Gudim-Levkovich, governor of Kovno; the provincial and county marshals of the nobility G.V. Kondoidi, A.E. Zarin, A.D. Pazukhin, S.S. Bekhteev, and others.

4. Two points of view developed within the conference with regard to the make-up of the village commune. These were expressed in the two versions of recommendations. Nonetheless, both proposed the creation of a village society that would include all classes (or estates).

5. At the time of the first elections a *volostel* was to be elected for a three-year term.

6. Two members of the conference believed the *volostel* should meet certain property qualifications.

7. People with a special business or merchant's certificate were also to be included in the third curia.

8. In Moscow the first two curias (who elected two thirds of the deputies) composed only thirteen percent of the grand total of electors.

9. The conference suggested that marshals of the nobility might also hold this post.

10. Although the head of the financial administration was to be an Office member, the other positions were to have been filled by deputies from the county zemstvo board.

11. Apart from redistributing the number of deputies among the curias and lowering the property qualifications, the peasants' "direct election" also can be considered a "democratic innovation." (Editor)

12. At the same time, congresses of zemstvo specialists would be permitted.

13. Governors were to be appointed "by His Majesty's authority," on the basis of the Committee of Ministers' recommendation of one candidate chosen from a list of three candidates proposed by the Minister of the Interior.

14. The conference's minority thought the head of the provincial police administration should be included among the members.

15. The italics are Tolstoy's. (Editor)

16. The commission's majority opposed "taxing outsiders who do not belong to the society and granting non-peasant members of the village society any rights of participating in its public business."

17. Seven members also maintained it was necessary to create a classless "volost as an independent zemstvo unit," but the remaining 23, headed by Kakhanov, opposed this.

18. Nine members still favored this opinion.

19. In this report Tolstoy deliberately stressed the issues—particularly those touching on the zemstvos—which would irritate Alexander III. "The commission was convinced," wrote Tolstoy, "that these institutions (the zemstvos) should be accepted, alongside of those of the government, as responsible for carrying out within the limits of the law the duties entrusted to them by Imperial authority in the various branches of the administration." This view of the zemstvos' role hardly conformed to that held by Alexander III.

CHAPTER V

1. It was not so much that Alexander III attempted to violate the existing laws (though he not infrequently did do this); rather, he sought to introduce reactionary changes into them. He nonetheless seems to have believed that there was a difference between a despot and an autocrat, and preferred to be the latter. According to Count D.N. Bludov, a statesman of the reigns of both Nicholas I and Alexander II, the distinction was "that an autocrat can by his own arbitrary will change the law, but prior to its change or abolition he must himself obey it." A despot, on the other hand, would not even consider the laws. And there is recorded one case when Alexander III was compelled to revoke a decision (in the case of Pastor Grimm) because it directly contradicted the existing laws.

2. This report contained eleven sections. It should be underlined that this was the only definite program ever drafted by Pobedonostsev, and his memorandum-report was distributed to certain persons.

3. Pobedonostsev himself once had been a strong supporter of public court proceedings.

4. In his letter of March 10, 1884 to A.N. Shakhov, the president of the Moscow Judicial Bench, Pobedonostsev expressed his general views on the judicial statute. "I have not changed my own thoughts on the statute," he wrote. "When I sat on the commission (that drew up the statute), I objected to borrowing recklessly forms from the French Code that were unsuitable in Russia. In the end I fled in disgust from St. Petersburg to Moscow, as I saw that I could not make people listen to reason. Since that time I have become increasingly convinced of the reality of this danger and it is now absolutely clear to me that our foreign clothes hamper us completely. Rapid justice has become possible only for the rich, thanks to the power wielded by the lawyers, while every civil servant is mercilessly stripped of everything. Now we again have judicial red tape, such as I once saw in the Cas (sation) Department (of the Senate) and against the creation of which I protested with all my strength when on the commission."

5. The italics are apparently Zaionchkovsky's. (Editor)

6. There were fifty senators in the Final Appeals Department.

7. The Combined Departments approved the part of Nabokov's proposal dealing with the composition of the higher disciplinary organ, calling it the Higher Disciplinary Office (not "court"—Editor).

8. Meanwhile new rules were established to provide a uniform format for the sessions' minutes, so that those used here are very different from those for the sessions of May 12 and May 15, 1884. In the new style journals, one no longer finds arguments between Council members on the necessity of preserving the principle of judges' security of tenure. On the hand-written version of the minutes for the sessions of May 12 and May 15, 1884 is the word "draft." So the journal obviously was falsified. Polovtsov unfortunately makes no mention of this in his diary, even though such alterations in the journal could only have taken place in his department.

9. Polovtsov claims he was forced to change the journal of the General Session. "Because of Ostrovsky's slanders," he wrote in his diary on May 10, 1885, "I included (in the journal) a statement that persons appointed on His Majesty's authority naturally could not be dismissed by any other authority."

10. The original form of these articles as they appeared in the judicial statute, was as follows:

Article 620: Criminal cases are to be tried in public. The only cases among these that properly can be considered exceptions are: 1) those dealing with blasphemy, insults against the Saints, or attacks on the Faith; 2) crimes against family rights; 3) crimes committed against a woman's honor or chastity; and 4) those involving lewd conduct, unnatural vice, and procuring.

Article 621: As an exceptional measure, court sessions may be closed to the public in the cases ennumerated in the previous article only when the clear necessity for the banning of the public from the proceedings of a particular trial—and the reasons for that action—can be precisely demonstrated.

Article 622: When a particular trial has been declared to be closed, all outsiders are to be immediately removed; if a defendant or plaintiff so requests, relatives or friends may remain in the courtroom, but the number of these must not exceed three for each side.

Article 624: In every case, once the Court President has declared the legal debates complete, the doors of the courtroom are to be reopened. All further judicial proceedings, including the President's comments to those judging the case in question, are to continue publicly.

11. All crimes listed in the previous edition of Article 620 (blasphemy, crimes against a woman's honor, and so on) were now to be consolidated into one of the three main subsections of the new version. (Editor)

12. Giers also endeavored to get the tsar's support for the majority decision. On January 20 Polovtsov noted that "when the journal of last Monday's arguments was read in the State Council, Giers rose and requested permission to read a note he had been given at the last moment by Councillor-Ambassador Martens while he, Giers, was seated in his coach and still undecided. Martens' note claimed that many foreign powers had concluded conventions for the extradition of criminals with Russia only because they had the assurance that the felon being extradited would receive a public trial. Now that it was proposed to give the Minister of Justice the right of abolishing public proceedings, the consequence could only be demands for annulling these conventions." Yet this consideration had no effect: Alexander III became furious, and Giers was startled by his own courage!

13. These "Provisional Regulations" of June 12, 1884 were apparently issued because of the Special Conference's conclusions.

14. The judicial statute of 1864 set the following qualifications for jurors: they must be 1) Russian citizens; 2) not less than twenty-five years and not more than seventy-five years in age; and 3) must have lived no less than two years in the locality where they were to serve as jurors.

In order to qualify, a knowledge of Russian was also required. Section 5, Article 84 established the requirements with regard to wealth. The property qualification was established at the level of 100 desiatinas or "of other real estate valued in the capitals at not less than 2,000 rubles, in the provincial cities and the cities with governors at not less than 1,000 rubles, and at not less than 500 rubles in other places." Otherwise the juror must annually receive as a salary or income from investments, a profession, trade, or business, not less than 500 rubles in the capitals and not less than 200 rubles in other localities.

Section 4, Article 84 permitted the inclusion of peasants on juror rolls if they had served no less than three years in an elective position or as a church elder.

15. This category did not exist in the statute of 1864.

16. According to the data in the Combined Departments' journal, the total number of cases that these proposals would exclude from jury trials could amount to 2,500 annually.

17. The cities of St. Petersburg, Moscow and Odessa were excluded.

18. Yet Manasein did not resign, but remained on as minister for more than four years. Polovtsov, in his diary entry of September 18, 1895, explained Manasein's desire to remain on in the following manner: ". . . when I tried to persuade him not to do this, he replied: 'And can you guarantee that I then will be appointed to the State Council and so keep receiving a salary of not less than 15,000 rubles?' "

19. The jurisdiction of a "district justice" was to be a designated portion of a county or town; that of a member of a county section of the provincial court was to be the whole county; and that of the provincial court, an entire province. The competence of a judicial bench was to have extended over several provinces or regions, and that of the Senate's Justice Departments over the whole empire.

20. A note to the fourth paragraph indicated that in the capitals and large towns "special investigating magistrates" could be assigned to investigate particular cases.

CHAPTER VI

1. "Kozma Prutkov" already had suggested a well-known proposal "For the Introduction of Uniformity of Thought in Russia." He maintained that it was necessary "to establish conformity of opinion about all public needs and government measures." To this end he recommended "establishing an official newspaper that would set the guidelines for opinion on each subject." This government institution, receiving sufficient support from the police and administrative authorities, would thus become the necessary, reliable guiding star "lighting the way" for public opinion.

The journal editor, "Prutkov" maintained, should be a man "worthy in all respects, recognized for his zeal and devotion, famous as an author (in spite of his having entered government service) and ready, in the government's interests, to disregard public opinion and so win respect for his firm belief in its (public opinion's) bankruptcy." Katkov shared these views completely and the portrait of the suggested editor might well be applied to him.

2. Ignatiev, under Pobedonostsev's influence, generally displayed an extraordinarily aggressive attitude toward the press.

3. The "Provisional Regulations" also contained a fourth point specifying that the law was to apply to all periodical publications, including those of government and educational institutions.

4. According to the Main Directorate's reports, in 1882 it employed 26 officials. With another 76 in the Provincial Censorship Committees, this meant a total of 101. By 1892 this figure had risen to 114. In addition, the law of September 30, 1881 provided that in those cities which had no censorship committees, the local press was to be supervised by the vice-governor.

The Directorate itself contained three bureaus. The first handled any matter concerning the periodical press. The second bureau handled all matters concerning the accounts and supervisory sections, the censorship of foreign material and nonperiodical publications, as well as the supervision of printers, bookstores, libraries, and reading rooms. The third dealt with theatrical censorship.

5. Feoktistov's wife, Sophia Alexandrovna ("Feoktistikha" as I.S. Turgenev disrespectfully called her), was a great social success, thereby guaranteeing her husband a successful career.

6. The poet Dmitry D. Minaev, in an impromptu comment on this appointment, suggested that Feoktistov's success was founded on more than his own friendly relations with M.N. Ostrovsky, the Minister of State Domains. He wrote:

Ostrovsky gave Feoktistov
Those horns
With which he would
Furiously batter authors.

7. The fact that Pobedonostsev sent instructions to Feoktistov on the latter's very first day as head of the Press Directorate is evidence that the director-general had had a hand in getting Feoktistov appointed. T.I. Filippov indirectly told him as much. In a letter dated December 11, 1883 he wrote Feoktistov that, "K(onstantin) P(etrovich) told me that before Prince Viazemsky departed . . . . he had already spoken with Count T(olstoy) about you. The latter replied: 'Imagine that! He was the one I had in mind.'"

8. The editor of Pobedonostsev's letters to Feoktistov identified this as Leo Tolstoy's article "What I Believe."

9. This refers to setting up warehouses, with grain elevators, by the Russian American Company. The State Council's discussion of this issue led to serious

differences in opinion. In the end, Alexander III turned the proposal down on the grounds that "it is dangerous for Russia."

10. "I tried to get the documents you need," wrote Feoktistov to Katkov. "I asked Michael Nikolaevich (Ostrovsky), but he had sent all the documents on to (V.I.) Veshniakov. The latter sent the very documents you need to the State Council, where it is awkward to lay one's hands on them. Then I asked Tertii Ivanovich (Filippov) but without success . . . ." It is obvious that Feoktistov did indeed exert himself.

11. On January 2, 1883—his first day as head of the Directorate—Feoktistov ordered the editors of periodicals "to publish no report or account of zemstvo business without having obtained permission from the appropriate governor."

12. G.P. Sudeikin was the police official murdered by the revolutionary and police agent S.P. Degaev; public discussion of the details of this event would have proved extremely embarrassing to the Department of Police. (Editor)

13. A confidential circular from the Minister of the Interior to the governors prohibited any celebrations on the twenty-fifth anniversary of the liberation of the serfs. This noted: "The tremendous importance of the statute of February 19, 1861, the correlation of this law with the vital interests of the two estates (gentry and peasantry), and the significance of the following period of time for the developing and consolidating of beneficial ties between the two estates—all this makes it necessary that special care be taken with regard to any displays recalling the past. And such caution is very difficult to maintain in the general excitement that inevitably surrounds the celebration of festivities."

14. According to the Directorate's report for the ten years 1882 to 1891, in its chancellery "the number of documents received, as well as of those dispatched, continually increased from year to year. For the first half of this decade (1882 to 1886) 27,819 documents were received, and 26,050 sent out. Then, from 1886 to 1891 the total in the first category was 30,596, and in the second, 30,101." Various circular letters of instructions accounted for a large proportion of this volume.

15. These were the assassins of Alexander II. (Editor)

16. Saltykov-Shchedrin, in another letter (written to N.A. Belegolov and dated August 31, 1884) described the *Russian News* in the following words: "This is the only decent and sensible paper that is being published. It is very moderate, but it is honest."

17. Feoktistov made this remark to a representative of the paper in 1887. He was referring to the fact that the *Russian News* had made no comment whatsoever on Katkov's death, apart from briefly noting the event.

18. During this period of study the *Moscow News* received a total of three reprimands, but only after Katkov's death. The *Citizen*, on the other hand, received seven.

19. A.A. Kizevetter recorded a typical example of this man's work. During the 1880s Pastukhov once visited the circus at Vozdvizhenko, but found that all the seats were sold. He had to leave and was furious. Then, although he had not seen the show, he wrote a review of it. In fact, a laconic report appeared in the *Moscow Leaflet* that "the roof of the Vozdvizhenko circus is damaged and in danger of caving in." The next day the circus did not sell a single ticket. This situation continued until the circus owner contributed a large sum to the funds of the *Moscow Leaflet*. Then another small report announced that the roof had been repaired and "all is safe."

20. These were the papers *Droeba* (Times), *Health, Moscow Telegraph, Dawn, Siberian News, Light,* and the journal *Notes of the Fatherland.*

21. These were the newspapers *Gazette of A. Gattzuk, Voice, East, Russian Courier, Russian Cause, Order, Country* and *Echo.*

22. During the previous period of 1865 to 1880 inclusive, eight publications were closed.

23. Only one newspaper—*Order*—closed down in 1882 when it failed to reappear after a temporary suspension of publication. It had been suspended for printing a report on a Moscow City Duma session without having obtained the necessary permission.

24. On January 5, 1883 the *Moscow Telegraph*'s lead article argued that it was necessary "to develop education and modify the system so as to facilitate entry into secondary and higher educational institutions; to have a free press; and, finally, to have guarantees of personal civil liberties." For this article the *Telegraph* was reprimanded once more.

25. During the early 1880s the *Voice* organized a special subscription fund to help Count Tolstoy's former serfs, whom Tolstoy was then persecuting.

26. It would seem that Tolstoy was simply using this excuse to disguise his own fears that resolute action against the *Voice* would endanger him personally.

27. This evidently refers to Sergei A. Yuriev, editor of the magazine *Russian Thought.*

28. The letter is signed "Dobr(ovolsky)" and addressed to one Uspensky, a student in Kharkov.

29. Feoktistov's wife allegedly declared that "her Evgesha accepted the post of head of the Main Directorate of the Press with the single aim of crushing snakes like *Notes of the Fatherland.*" Although it can scarcely have been this simple, her statement is evidence of Feoktistov's attitude toward this journal.

30. Feoktistov later recalled that one of the reasons Tolstoy was so indecisive about *Notes of the Fatherland* was his dislike of attacking Saltykov, an old Lycée classmate. This cannot really have been a major consideration although, according to Saltykov's letter of March 9, 1884 to A.A. Kraevsky, Feoktistov apparently even had mentioned this to the magazine's editor himself.

31. Kraevsky was the journal's publisher.

32. Feoktistov claimed that the initiative for such an unusual measure as an official report came from Tolstoy himself: "Count Dmitry Andreevich considered it necessary to make a detailed declaration of the motives that had guided the government in resorting to this measure. This had not been done in previous cases of this kind and there was not the slightest need of it."

33. V. Yarmonkin published *Light* in St. Petersburg for only a few months in 1883; it quickly died for lack of subscribers. In 1884 Yarmonkin transferred the paper to Moscow, but he remained its editor only in name.

34. In October, 1888 publication of this paper was resumed and continued until 1890.

35. An article entitled "Simple and Extensive Literacy" occasioned the first reprimand, and one entitled "Industry or a Festival of Agriculture," the second.

36. Apart from large subsidies to the *Citizen*, a great deal of money was spent in "buying" the press. Feoktistov's memoirs maintain that, according to Tolstoy, "the government intended to win the support of the newspapers by giving subsidies to one or the other of them; that is, to put it bluntly, by buying them. Tolstoy already had made a report on this matter to the Sovereign, and His Majesty had given the plan his full approval. A sum of up to 20,000 rubles was available for this purpose."

Tolstoy told Feoktistov this before the latter took charge of censorship. The Minister of the Interior wanted Feoktistov himself to handle this delicate operation. "Dumbfounded, I listened to this nonsense . . . ," the latter wrote. "All I could do was explain to Count Tolstoy that there would be hardly a single news-paper publisher who would sell himself for 20,000 rubles, and that even if one were found with such a small appetite, I was still completely in the dark as to how I—standing on the side-lines—could play a part in such a sale."

Feoktistov's story about buying the press is partially and indirectly sup-ported by Tolstoy. In his report to the emperor of February 5, 1883 he mentioned his need to "have at his disposal the sum of 6,000 rubles a year to be spent, in complete secrecy, on the periodical press."

37. Dobrovolsky says that eighty-six books had been banned in the previous fourteen years (1867-1880).

38. I.N. Durnovo, on behalf of the Ministry of the Interior, wrote in his sub-mission to the Council of Ministers: "The author spares no effort in his attempt to portray the government's internal policy in the most detestable light . . . . In writ-ing a history of Russian literature, (the author) tends to extol exclusively those writers . . . . whom he calls 'the bearers of democratic ideals.' "

39. According to the censor, this book showed that Pushkin was intimate with the Decembrists and that, after their suppression, he had become a propagandist of their ideas by peaceful means (despite the censor, the measures of the chief of the Gendarmes, and the reactionary press).

40. The Committee of Ministers observed that "the author does not conceal his sympathy for the victims of vice and corruption and tries to show that it was not their fault that they fell."

41. In his report to the Committee of Ministers, I.N. Durnovo wrote that the author tried "to debunk Catherine II and to show her in an unfavorable light." Feoktistov said that when Alexander III learned the nature of Bilbasov's second volume, the tsar decided "to have the police seize his (research) materials or, at least, that part of them that had been borrowed from the St(ate) Archives. That was all we needed!" Feoktistov exclaimed. "Fortunately I. Durnovo opposed such measures."

42. Feoktistov said that Alexander III, on reading a letter in which V.S. Solo-viev spoke of the persecution and ban on the publication of his works, comment-ed: "His scandalous works are offensive and humiliating."

43. Yet Feoktistov further recounted that according to A.M. Kulminsky, the husband of Countess Tolstoy's sister, Alexander III had once remarked that he had read the book with great interest and that, though it was somewhat obscene, on the whole it remained a very talented piece.

44. The only books and periodicals exempted from censorship were those re-ceived from abroad by libraries of higher educational and some scholarly institu-tions. A circular of May 3, 1888, for instance, freed the Russian Historical Museum from the censor's supervision, while another, of February 16, 1893, allowed Ec-clesiastical Academies the right of free access to foreign books.

45. Some of the more excessively zealous censors petitioned the supervising district prosecutors to bring persons to trial "for the secret possession of banned foreign publications." In this regard Feoktistov issued a circular noting that "the existing law did not make one liable to court proceedings for the mere possession of a book, the circulation of which was illegal, if it was kept for personal use with-out any intention of circulation."

46. These were included in the new, 1886 edition of the censorship statute as a note to Article 175.

47. By the list of 1894 this journal was completely removed, up to and includ-ing the year 1891.

48. When such pledges were violated the censors were recommended not "to initiate prosecution of the accused before a justice of the peace" (due to the illegality of demanding such pledges in the first place), but "to remove the persons involved from library work and, in the event of a second offense, to close down the library."

49. This was included as a note to Article 175 of the censorship statute.

50. An extensive (and, it is evident, insufficiently defined) number of individuals had their letters intercepted: according to Durnovo, in 1891 the mail of A.K. Anastasiev (then a member of the State Council) was being examined.

CHAPTER VII

1. Count S.S. Uvarov (1786-1855) was Nicholas I's reactionary Minister of Education. (Editor)

2. "I commissioned N.A. Liubimov," Delianov wrote Katkov on February 3, 1886, "to draw up a circular in accord with your ideas." In another letter (dated February 21, 1886) he wrote: "I humbly ask you, most deeply-esteemed Michael Nikiforovich, to examine the proposed submission, correct it, and return it to me." Many more similar examples could be cited.

3. Georgievsky kept Katkov *au courant* of every detail of the educational policies discussed with Delianov. Thus he wrote Katkov on March 29, 1885 about his disagreements with Delianov on the examination requirements demanded in the historical-philological faculties. "I had a very long conversation with Iv(an) Dav(idovich)," Georgievsky reported, "but was unsuccessful in my attempts to convince him. He would not budge even though I pointed out that you intended to declare war upon us. 'In that case,' he replied, 'I would have 100 million allies, but Mich(ael) Nik(iforovich) would find no one on his side.' " Nonetheless, this independence subsequently proved to be pure bravado.

4. "*Vous êtes une ame damnée de Kathow.*" Georgievsky reported this comment in a letter to Katkov dated April 19, 1885.

5. Polovtsov wrote that "he was nicknamed 'the grimy one' because he was not exactly 'clean' of having made money out of the Graz-Tsaritsyn railroad, while the zemstvo which had commissioned him to obtain the concession was cheated."

6. In particular, he proposed that in accordance with Tolstoy's circular of July 14, 1879, all students be provided with "exit passes." These would have to be presented " 'on demand' both to police officers as well as to any person to whom the head of the school had given special credentials for supervising students."

7. In the first point (on the drafting of students into the disciplinary battalions), it was pointed out that this measure could not possibly be applied to those younger than eighteen. As for point two (on drafting students into general military service), a six-year period of service was established (but might be shortened "in cases of meritorious service").

Apart from these modifications, the final version observed that the compulsory draft should affect only students who previously, either because of their family status or the results of the lottery, had been exempted from active military service.

8. Among these were Grand Dukes Michael and Nicholas Nikolaevich; Vladimir and Alexis Alexandrovich; and Bunge, Nikolai, Vannovsky, and Shestakov.

9. In 1887 A. Siniavsky, a student at Moscow University, was drafted into a disciplinary battalion for slapping A.A. Bryzgalov, the Inspector of Students.

10. Katkov was also insistent. On April 2, 1882 he wrote Delianov that "the university question ought not to be postponed. By delaying in this matter you are only making trouble for yourself. It would be better to strike at once."

11. But delay in this matter was achieved only with great difficulty, as both Tolstoy and Delianov strongly opposed this course. Polovtsov, on March 14, 1883, noted: "Following the session (of the State Council) Grand Duke Michael Nikolaevich held a meeting. Reutern, Staritsky and Pobedonostsev argued the necessity of shelving the examination of the university statute. But Tolstoy and Delianov insisted that both students and professors were especially obedient at this time of year." This apparently referred to the approach of examinations and the ending of the school year.

12. Delianov also argued in this vein. Polovtsov says that on January 23, 1884 he told a meeting of the Combined Departments that the setting of "examination requirements independently of the university lectures was the alpha and omega of the proposed university statute."

13. Early in January, 1884 Filippov suggested a compromise in his memorandum, "The Newly-Amended Sections on University Examinations."

14. This refers to the fees students paid lecturers for attending each course of lectures, and to the selection of secretaries for faculties.

15. According to the statute of 1863 the inspector participated in the administration's meetings at only those universities where he was "prorector," and then voted "only in student matters."

16. In these cases he had the rank of "prorector."

17. In the same way the statute of 1835 had placed the inspector of students under the superintendent's authority.

18. But those were not the examination commissions of Delianov's and Katkov's dreams. They were composed of professors of a faculty, with a professor from another university serving as chairman. According to the University of Moscow's report for 1894, all seven members of the historical-philological faculty's commission were professors of this faculty. The same was true of the medical faculty's commission. Only one member of the commission of the physics-mathematics faculty does not appear on the list of university professors and so was apparently an outsider.

19. In 1889 the semester register system for semester tests was abolished and course examinations restored.

20. At the same time "authorized readers" were abolished. In the decade following the approval of the new statute the number of assistant professors grew considerably. Thus, on January 1, 1884 Moscow university had 31 associate and assistant professors; by the same date in 1895 there were 120. During the same period the number of professors had not quite doubled.

21. Student unrest in Kiev broke out in connection with the university's fiftieth-anniversary celebrations because of the tactlessness of the rector, Professor K.K. Rennenkampf.

22. This absurdly restricted area of studies did not last long in the historical-philological faculties. In 1889 it was abolished and the previous plan of study restored.

23. As one writer (S.V. Rozhdestvensky) has pointed out, the statute of 1885 did have one positive result inasmuch as it promoted the development of practical study seminars, and so on (that is, of independent student work).

24. A student's laboratory work and seminars were naturally of tremendous significance for training in his specialty. Yet Georgievsky was not interested in

this aspect of the matter; he really wanted the daily student schedule to be so full that they would have no time for extracurricular activities.

25. After abolishing medical courses in early 1883, a committee under the chairmanship of Prince Volkonsky was formed in the Ministry of Education to draw up a legislative proposal on "The Institute for Training Midwives." The resulting draft statute drew sharp criticism from the Ministry of the Interior. One assistant minister (apparently Plehve) declared "that all arguments adduced for the importance of and need for this proposed Institute are not based on any real need of the state for such an institution, but solely on theories of particular individuals who are seeking the so-called 'emancipation' of women." It was only in 1897 that a Higher Institute for the Medical Training of Women was opened.

26. Delianov observed that this "was because of a greater cutback in the number of students from poorer and badly educated parents who, because of their poverty and backwardness, have not been able to raise their children in conditions that guarantee their passing the gymnasium course."

27. In 1828 a commission chaired by A.S. Shishkov published a new set of "Regulations for Gymnasiums and Schools under the Jurisdiction of the Universities" which demanded blind obedience from the students and gave monitors police-like powers over them. (Editor)

28. This circular was preceded by one of July 19, 1886 which recommended that this question be considered in the superintendent's council.

29. According to the data of this report, 3,122 of the 9,386 preparatory class students were "from the lower categories of the taxable estates."

30. On June 11 Delianov issued a special circular on this matter. Preparatory classes were retained in localities where Russian was not the native language of the majority of the population, as well as in the Vitebsk, Chita, Yakutsk, Piatigorsk, and Vladivostok gymnasiums.

31. The text of this report makes clear that the previous report, rejected by the tsar, was dated May 23, 1887.

32. This same report suggested that a number of other questions be considered by the Committee of Ministers. These were: setting the average percentage of Jewish children permitted entry into progymnasiums and gymnasiums; a raise in the lecture attendance fees in the universities; and changes in the modern schools and the opening of industrial schools, in connection with the proposed cut-back in the numbers of gymnasiums and pro-gymnasiums.

33. On September 5, Kireev again remarked on this matter. "The unfortunate circular excluding the children of cooks, and so on," he wrote, "continues to rouse indignation and hilarity. Who is the author of this stupidity? It is obvious what lack of thought lies behind this indecent reversal (of policy). It is supposed to give preference to the nobility, but above all else the most necessary thing is to open modern schools and only then to limit entry into the classical ones."

34. Delianov's circular was supposedly secret and not intended for publication. It became widely known thanks to Kh. P. Solsky, superintendent of the Odessa Educational District. He published in the *Odessa Herald* a circular to gymnasium and progymnasium directors which gave the school administrations instructions concerning the "cooks' children" circular. In this way, as befitted a zealous administrator, he told all.

35. There is obviously an error in the 1892 figures: their total is 99.2 not 100.0 percent.

36. It should be noted that the percentage of "drop-outs" increased rather than diminished during our period. Some 17.8 percent of gymnasium and progymnasium

students dropped out before completion of the course in 1884, and 3.9 percent at the end of the course (evidently those who did not sit for the examination for their certificate); in 1891 those figures were 13.5 and 9.3 respectively. Thus, in 1891, 22.8 percent of gymnasium students left without graduating. The similar figures for the modern schools were 19.0 and 6.8 percent in 1884, and 17.9 and 7.3 percent in 1891.

37. On the other hand, there was a growth in student numbers in the modern schools and female gymnasiums during the same period: in the first category, from 20,517 to 23,555 and in the second, from 35,205 to 45, 544.

38. The draft proposed the creation of the following system of lower secondary and technical education: a) vocational schools for preparation of qualified workers and apprentice artisans (for admission to such schools one needed a general preparatory education in an ordinary church school or a single-class village or town school); b) lower technical schools to prepare master craftsmen for industrial enterprises (the general qualification proposed for these was an education in a county town or a two-year village school); and, c) secondary technical schools to train technicians (for these the usual qualification was to be a modern school education).

39. In the original "Draft for a General Plan for Industrial Education in Russia" as prepared by the Ministry of Education, modern schools were to be retained as eight-year institutions. Later, mainly due to Tolstoy's influence, this question was again subjected to review.

40. Among these were the chairman of the State Council, Grand Duke Michael Nikolaevich, as well as Grand Duke Vladimir Alexandrovich and Pobedonostsev.

41. In October, 1889 Delianov had brought another proposal before the State Council. Entitled "On an Increase in the Term of Summer Vacations for Both the Secondary and Lower Educational Institutions," it was examined with his first proposal.

42. For the study of ancient languages "the chief object of the course should be the reading, interpretation and translation into correct literary Russian of the ancient authors."

43. To this end, in 1883 the Ministry of Education had begun granting the Synod an annual sum of 55,500 rubles for parish schools and the support of schools maintained by the clergy.

44. In the 1870s the number of such schools reached 18,000.

45. According to the report of the Director-General of the Holy Synod to the emperor, by 1893-1894 the treasury had spent 3,279,645 rubles on the organization and building of parish and grammar schools. This was apart from any extraordinary expenditures or the allocation of other sums, particularly by the zemstvos. In 1885, 51 out of 228 zemstvos were subsidizing parish schools; in 1890 the number of such zemstvos had risen to 96, and in 1895, to 144.

46. Katkov also indirectly supported this view in his lead article on church schools mentioned above.

CHAPTER VIII

1. The most important was an amendment to Article 3 which would remove county capitals from the cities under the control of land captains. Hence Pazukhin's proposal had foreseen the new official's powers extending at least as far as these towns and cities.

2. On the first page is the note in I.N. Durnovo's handwriting: "In accord with His Majesty's command this report of the late Count Tolstoy is to be preserved in the Min(istry) of the Int(erior's) archives as an interesting historical document."

3. In the Russian text this reads "Article 2," but this is obviously a misprint. (Editor)

4. Volost courts held the right of sentencing malefactors to up to twenty-three strokes of the birch.

5. Polovtsov drew up a special report on this meeting which he presented to the tsar on March 30. On the whole it agrees with the account given in his diary.

6. This resulted from an agreement reached between Tolstoy and Manasein.

7. All these italics are apparently Vorontsov's. (Editor)

8. Tolstoy's declaration on the possibilities of a peasant uprising in the summer of 1889 was devoid of any factual basis. Evidently even Tolstoy himself did not believe it, but he used the declaration as a spectre with which to frighten the tsar.

9. Tolstoy did not even believe that a man needed a secondary education in order to be a land captain. In the Combined Departments' session of February 11, 1889, for instance, he asked: "Why should we insist on a secondary school education when people who have passed through only a county school can be shown suitable for this work?"

10. This refers to the revolutionary French National Convention of 1793. (Editor)

11. The operation of the statute on land captains did not effect the Kingdom of Poland, the "right bank" Ukraine, Belorussia, Lithuania, the Baltic provinces, the Caucasus, or Siberia (in other words, it did not operate in areas where large landed estates were almost completely absent or where the landlords belonged to a non-Russian national nobility).

12. A parody of the law of July 12, 1889 entitled the "Law on District Land Canaille . . ." wittily pointed out that a "member of the local gentry, who has not finished a county school or institution of similar status, but who can count to three hundred, can be appointed as land captain . . . as long as he has previously served as a chancellery official, first class, in the office staff of a marshal of the nobility, and has been honored with a promotion, even if only on retirement, to the rank of Collegiate Registrar."

13. The Combined Departments examined this question on December 16, 1889. Many land captains did not even hold a secondary education. According to data of the Ministry of the Interior's zemstvo section—drawn up in 1903 on the basis of ten provinces (Vitebsk, Vladimir, Vologda, Voronezh, Kostroma, Novgorod, Poltava, Samara, Tula, and Kherson)—124 of 584 land captains fitted this category. Included here are those who had finished "Junker" schools in which, unlike regular military schools, completion of a secondary school was not required for those admitted.

14. Actually, according to the data on the ten provinces mentioned above, the land captains included not only gentry from other provinces, but also persons who were not of the gentry class. There was, for instance, one non-noble land captain in Novgorod, seven in Kostroma, two in Vitebsk, twelve in Vologda, three in Voronezh, and seven in Samara.

15. According to the Statute on Provincial and County Offices for Peasant Affairs, the rural arbitrator was to confirm volost elders in their posts, could discharge village elders, and also could relieve a volost elder of responsibilities until the issue was settled by a higher authority. Further, he could impose fines of up to five

rubles on those holding posts in the village administration, as well as imprison them for a term of up to seven days.

16. Article 104 of the "General Statute Concerning Peasants Previously in Feudal Bondage" clearly stated that "the volost elder and headman must not be involved in the volost court's proceedings and must not be present at the discussion of cases."

17. These provisions are found in the section on "Regulations for the Organization of Judicial Divisions in Localities where the 'Statute on District Land Captains' is Effective" in the law itself, and in the "Regulations for the Conduct of Judicial Cases Subject to Land Captains and City Justices," issued on December 29, 1889.

CHAPTER IX

1 1. The italics are Zaionchkovsky's. The treatment of the zemstvo statute is relatively brief as it is the subject of L.G. Zakharova's monograph, *Zemskaia Kontrreforma 1890 g.* (Moscow, 1968). (Editor)

2. The Minister of the Interior, "with His Majesty's assent," might impose a disciplinary penalty on a chairman of a Provincial Zemstvo Office. A similar penalty could be imposed on a chairman of a county office on the minister's own authority.

3. Prince K.D. Gagarin, Assistant Minister of the Interior, chaired the Special Conference. It was composed of A.D. Pazukhin, director of the interior ministry's chancellery; Governors N.P. Dolgovo-Saburov of Simbirsk, V.V. Kalachev of Kostroma, I.M. Sudienko of Vladimir, and A.F. Anisin of Viatka; the provincial marshals of the nobility P.A. Krivsky of Saratov, G.V. Kondoidi of Tambov, A.E. Zarin of Pskov, and A.R. Shidlovsky of Kharkov.

4. All italics are Pobedonostsev's. (Editor)

5. At the same time he noted that the extension of the estate (or class) principle to municipal public administrations, as had been done with the zemstvos, would be extremely difficult.

6. On October 1, 1890, of 772 deputies in the seventeen interior provinces, 385 belonged to the gentry or clergy, 175 to the merchants, and only 212 to the artisans and other estates.

7. According to the data provided here, petty-bourgeois property owners, merchants, and salesmen made up 80 percent of the electors in Pskov province, 1,200 out of 3,400 in Vilna, 900 out of 2,950 in Reval, 2,400 out of 3,400 in Minsk, and over 50 percent in St. Petersburg.

8. Four governors disagreed. Three of these (of Tambov, Tobolsk and Tver) thought the number of electors should be increased by including members of the gentry, bureaucrats, and persons with a secondary education.

9. Five governors disagreed.

10. Nine governors disagreed.

11. These were from provinces within the Pale of Jewish Settlement.

12. The statute of 1870 had granted the vote to various agencies, scientific, educational, and charitable institutions, establishments, and societies, companies and other organizations owning real estate within the city.

13. In Moscow the draft would allow only 7,221 instead of 23,671 voters. In Kazan the reduction would be from 6,025 to 905; in Vilna, from 2,085 to 503; in Serpukhov, from 1,012 to 387; in Podolsk, from 338 to 267; in Dmitrov (Moscow

province), from 900 to 170; in Zvenigorod, from 538 to 165. The numbers were particularly cut back in cities within the Pale: thus, in Kharkov, the reductions were from 6,996 to 1,485; in Zhitomir, from 2,990 to 350; in Minsk, from 3,539 to 223, in Kovno, from 1,955 to 97; in Vitebsk, 3,278 to 267.

14. In St. Petersburg only 5,824 of the 21,170 voters took part in the elections; in Moscow, 1,807 of 23,671; in Kazan 568 of 6,025; in Serpukhov, 95 of 1,012, and in Yamburg, only 33 out of 121.

15. This would occur if electors from the non-urban classes, along with representatives of education and teaching institutions and so on, were sufficiently numerous. In Kiev they would have been 30 percent of the electors, in Tiflis, 41 percent, but in Kharkov, no more than fifty persons.

16. According to the 1870 statute, mayors and members of the boards were not to be considered as "included in the state service" except for secretaries of city boards in provincial capitals who reported to the Provincial Offices for City Affairs and so were considered to be in the crown's employ.

17. It is interesting to note that during the reaction of the late 1860s and 1870s, while the 1870 statute was being discussed and drafted, Durnovo supported the democratic proposals.

18. Apart from Stoiansky, Kakhanov, N.S. Abaza, F.A. Terner, and P.A. Markov, all spoke in favor of allowing Jews living outside the Pale to join municipal administrations.

19. In the end, the question of Jewish participation in the municipal electoral meetings was resolved as follows: "prior to a review of laws affecting the Jews," the latter were not to be admitted to participation in the meetings. Within the Pale of Jewish Settlement itself, apart from Kiev, the Provincial Offices for City and Zemstvo Affairs would appoint individual Jews as deputies. But the number of Jews was not to exceed one tenth of the total number of deputies.

INDEX

308   INDEX

Trubetskoy, S.N. 9
Truth 173
Tula 107
Turgenev, I.S. 7, 155
Turkey 15, 16, 17
Tver 21, 124

Udmurts 26
Ufa 3, 102-3, 106, 124
Ukraine 176
Ulianov, A.I. 40, 56-7
Uniate Church 58
Union of Struggle for the Liberation of
the Working Class XII, 2, 265
University statute and universities 4, 28,
34-5, 42, 44, 184-5, 186-201
Uspensky, G.I. 161
Uvarov, S.S. 16, 181

Val, V.V. 101
Valk, A.S. 66
Valuev, P.A. 52, 83, 111, 112
Vannovsky, P.S. 96, 184-5, 211-2
Vasilkovsky, A. 206
Vengerov, S.A. 175
Veselovsky, A.N. 75
Veselovsky, B.B. 249
Veshniakov, V.I. 211
Viatka 222
Vilna 73, 204
Vishniakov, A.G. 104
Vladimir 101
Vladimir Alexandrovich, Grand Duke
22-3, 38, 39, 147
Voice 156, 162, 165, 167-8, 169
Volkonsky, S.G. 182
Volkonsky, M.S. 182, 184, 214
Vologda 118
Volynia 87
Voronezh 118
Vorontsov, V.P. 161
Vorontsov-Dashkov, I.I. 9, 104-5, 112,
155, 234-7, 245
Vyshnegradsky, I.A. 36, 47, 54, 63, 73,
75, 79-81, 101, 107, 147, 211-2, 229,
231, 232, 238, 248, 256

War, Ministry of 155, 202, 184-5
Warsaw 16, 58, 65, 67, 92, 149, 176
William I (of Prussia) 15
Winter Palace 30, 104
Witte, S.Yu. 19, 81, 116

women, education of 40, 182, 201-3
Word 178

Yankovsky, E.O. 97
Yaroslav 114
Yuriev 124
Yuriev, S.A. 168

Zaichnevsky, P.G. 161
Zemskii Sobor 28, 174
zemstvos 3, 4, 5, 9, 21, 49, 98, 117-
24, 127-30, 132-3, 134, 135, 147,
151, 157, 218, 219-23, 226-7, 232,
235, 240, 243-9, 257, 264
Zheliabov, A.I. 160
Zhuikevich 65
Zinoviev, M.A. 68, 70
Zinoviev, N.V. 14

Academic International Press